LEGAL RESEARCH SKILLS FOR SCOTS I

AUSTRALIA
Law Book Co.
Sydney

CANADA and USA
Carswell
Toronto

HONG KONG
Sweet & Maxwell Asia

NEW ZEALAND
Brookers
Wellington

SINGAPORE and MALAYSIA
Sweet & Maxwell Asia
Singapore and Kuala Lumpur

LEGAL RESEARCH SKILLS FOR SCOTS LAWYERS

By Karen Lanya Fullerton, Ph.D. M.A. (Hons),
LL.B., Dip.L.P., Solicitor
Lecturer in Law, The Robert Gordon University

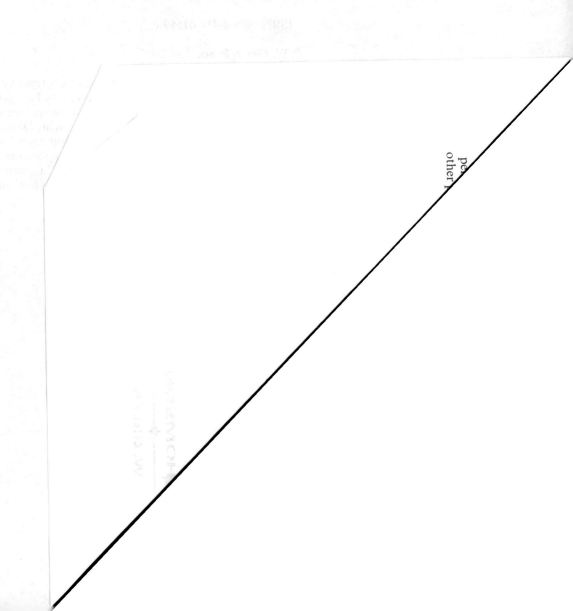

Published in 2007 by
W. Green & Son Ltd
21 Alva Street
Edinburgh EH2 4PS

www.wgreen.thomson.com

Typeset by YHT Ltd, London
Printed and bound in Great Britain by Ashford Colour Printers

No natural forests were destroyed to make this product;
only farmed timber was used and replanted.

A CIP catalogue record for this book is available from
the British Library.

ISBN 978-0-414-01589-0

Acknowledgements

I would like to express thanks to Megan Macgregor for her contribution to the first edition of this book. With regard to this edition, I would like to thank Jill Hyslop and Bronwyn Spicer for their help in the production and format of the text. A large debt of gratitude is owed to Harris Cooper for his unfailing encouragement. I would also like to thank my parents, Lanya Scott and David Fullerton, for their support.

Contents

8. **Information Sources of Relevance to the Scots Lawyer**

11. **International Law**

Part II – Research Skills

12. **Topic Based Research and the Legal Investigation Process**

13. **Making Effective Use of Information**

14. **How to Use your Research to Produce High Quality Work**

Contents

Table of Abbreviations

A

A.C.	Appeal Cases (Law Reports)
A.J.I.L.	American Journal of International Law
All E.R.	All England Law Reports
A.P.S.	Acts of the Parliament of Scotland 1124–1707 (Record Edition)
asp	Act of the Scottish Parliament

B

B.C.C.	British Company Cases
B.D.I.L.	British Digest of International Law
B.J.Crim	British Journal of Criminology
B.Y.I.L.	British Yearbook of International Law

C

C.F.I.	Court of First Instance
C.L.	Current Law
C.L.J.	Cambridge Law Journal
C.L.Y.	Current Law Yearbook
C.M.L.R.	Common Market Law Reports
C.M.L.Rev.	Common Market Law Review
Ch.	Chancery Division (Law Reports)
Crim.L.R.	Criminal Law Review

E

E.A.T.	Employment Appeal Tribunal
E.B.L.R.	European Business Law Review
EC	European Community
ECHR	European Court of Human Rights
ECJ	European Court of Justice
E.C.L.R.	European Competition Law Review
E.C.R.	European Court Reports
ECSC	European Coal & Steel Community
Edin.L.R.	Edinburgh Law Review
EEC	European Economic Community
E.E.L.R.	European Environmental Law Review
EFTA	European Free Trade Association
E.H.R.L.R.	European Human Rights Law Review
E.H.R.R.	European Human Rights Reports
E.I.P.R.	European Intellectual Property Review
E.J.I.L.	European Journal of International Law
E.L.J.	European Law Journal
E.L.Rev.	European Law Review
E.P.L.	European Public Law

E.T.S.   European Treaty Series
EU   European Union
Env.L.R.   Environmental Law Reports
Euratom   European Atomic Energy Community

F
F.L.R.   Family Law Reports
Fam.   Family Division (Law Reports)
Fam. L.R.   Greens Family Law Reports

G
G.W.D.   Greens Weekly Digest

H
Hous. L.R.   Greens House Law Reports

I
I.C.C.   International Criminal Court
I.C.J.   International Court of Justice
I.C.J. Reports   International Court of Justice Reports
I.C.J. Yearbook   Yearbook of the International Court of Justice
I.C.L.Q.   International and Comparative Law Quarterly
I.C.R.   Industrial Cases Reports
I.L.M.   International Legal Materials
I.L.R.   International Law Reports
I.R.L.R.   Industrial Relations Law Reports

J
J.C.   Justiciary Cases
J.C.M.S.   Journal of Common Market Studies
J.I.L.T.   Journal of Information Law & Technology
J.L.S.   Journal of Law and Society
J.L.S.S.   Journal of the Law Society of Scotland
J.R.   Juridical Review

L
L.Q.R.   Law Quarterly Review

M
M. or Mor.   Morison's Dictionary of Decisions
M.L.R.   Modern Law Review
Med.L.R.   Medical Law Reports

O
O.J.   Official Journal of the European Union
O.J.L.S.   Oxford Journal of Legal Studies
OQPS   Office of the Queen's Printer for Scotland
OSCOLA   Oxford Standard for Citation of Legal Authorities

P
P.C.I.J.   Permanent Court of International Justice

Q

Q.B.	Queen's Bench (Law Reports)

R

Rep. B	Reparation Bulletin
Rep.L.R.	Reparation Law Reports

S

S.C.	Session Cases
S.C.(H.L.)	Session Cases, appeals to House of Lords
S.C.C.R.	Scottish Criminal Case Reports
S.C.L.R.	Scottish Civil Law Reports
S.I.	Statutory Instrument
S.J. or Sc. Jur.	Scottish Jurist
S.L.C.R.	Scottish Land Court Reports
S.L.G.	Scottish Law Gazette
S.L.R. or Sc. L.R.	Scottish Law Reporter
S.L.R. or S.L. Rev. or Sc.L.R.	Scottish Law Review and Sheriff Court Reporter
S.L.T.	Scots Law Times
S.L.T. (Land Ct.)	Scots Law Times, Land Court Reports
S.L.T. (Lands Tr.)	Scots Law Times, Lands Tribunal Reports
S.L.T. (Lyon Ct.)	Scots Law Times, Lyon Court Reports
S.L.T. (Notes.)	Scots Law Times, Notes of Recent Decisions
S.L.T. (Sh. Ct.)	Scots Law Times, Sheriff Court Reports
S.N.	Session Notes
S.P.E.L.	Scottish Planning and Environmental Law
SCOLAG	Bulletin of the Scotish Legal Action Group
SPICe	Scottish Parliament Information Centre
Sh. Ct. Rep.	Sheriff Court Reports

T

T.C.	Reports of Tax Cases
T.S.O.	The Stationery Office

U

U.K.T.S.	United Kingdom Treaty Service
U.N.T.S.	United Nations Treaty Series

W

W.L.R.	Weekly Law Reports

Y

Y.E.L.	Yearbook of European Law
Yearbook ECHR	Yearbook of the European Convention of Human Rights

Table of Regnal Years*

Sovereigns	Commencement of Reign	Length of Reign
		Years
William I	October 14, 1066	21
William II	September 26, 1087	13
Henry I	August 5, 1100	36
Stephen	December 26, 1135	19
Henry II	December 19, 1154	35
Richard I	September 23, 1189	10
John	May 27, 1199	18
Henry III	October 28, 1216	57
Edward I	November 20, 1272	35
Edward II	July 8, 1307	20
Edward III	January 25, 1326	51
Richard II	June 22, 1377	23
Henry IV	September 30, 1399	14
Henry V	March 21, 1413	10
Henry VI	September 1, 1422	39
Edward IV	March 4, 1461	23
Edward V	April 9, 1483	–
Richard III	June 26, 1483	3
Henry VII	August 22, 1485	24
Henry VIII	April 22, 1509	38
Edward VI	January 28, 1547	7
Mary	July 6, 1553	6
Elizabeth I	November 17, 1558	45
James I	March 24, 1603	23
Charles I	March 27, 1625	24
Commonwealth	January 30, 1649	11
Charles II†	May 29, 1660	37
James II	February 6, 1685	4
William and Mary	February 13, 1689	14
Anne	March 8, 1702	13
George I	August 1, 1714	13
George II	June 11, 1727	34
George III	October 25, 1760	60
George IV	January 29, 1820	11
William IV	June 26, 1830	7
Victoria	June 20, 1837	64
Edward VII	January 22, 1901	9
George V	May 6, 1910	26
Edward VIII	January 20, 1936	1
George VI	December 11, 1936	15
Elizabeth II	February 6, 1952	–

* The Scottish Kings are not given, inasmuch as the Scots Acts are cited by year and chapter not by regal name, year and chapter.

† Charles II did not ascend the throne until May 29, 1660, but his regnal years were computed from the death of Charles I, January 30, 1649, so that the year of his restoration is styled the twelfth of his reign.

Chapter 1
Introduction

PURPOSE OF THE BOOK

This book is designed to be a user-friendly guide to researching Scots law. It will help the reader **1–1** identify relevant information sources and assess which is the most appropriate for the task in hand. It explains search strategies and techniques that will assist locating material efficiently. The book provides guidance on reading and understanding the materials that an information retrieval exercise locates. It also shows the reader how to use their research to produce high quality work.

The book is primarily intended for the Scottish law student but it will also be of interest to trainees and practitioners who want to update their knowledge about legal research. It includes worked examples, exercises and diagrams to aid explanation. Different search strategies are provided for accessing information from different standpoints. This includes searching by name, searching with incomplete details and searching by subject. To provide you with an appreciation of all the different sources, both electronic and paper, various alternative ways of finding information are described. You may not always have access to the most comprehensive or most current sources. It is therefore important to understand the properties of a range of sources so that you are in a position to evaluate their accuracy and currency and therefore their usefulness to you. Summaries of search strategies are contained in Appendix I for quick reference.

Since the first edition was published in 1999, electronic information sources have improved and **1–2** their use and importance has increased. However, electronic sources are not the sole (and not necessarily the best) way to access all types of legal information. There is a widespread mis-conception held by students new to legal research that electronic sources hold all the answers. This is far from the truth; the reality is that electronic sources create their own problems. If not used properly, electronic sources can end up retrieving large amounts of irrelevant or inaccurate information and wasting a considerable amount of time (and money). It can be quicker and more efficient to find some information using paper sources. Therefore, while electronic sources do have an important role to play, the researcher needs to think about why they are using a particular source. It is important not to use an electronic source just because you are used to finding information online. You should assess which is the most appropriate source and which will locate material most efficiently. This book is designed to help you make these choices.

The early part of the book concentrates on Scots law but Scottish lawyers cannot focus solely on **1–3** Scottish law. United Kingdom and EC law (and indeed some aspects of public international law) are all integral to our system of law. There are therefore chapters dealing with these areas of law. Details of English, Welsh and Northern Irish law are not covered. The book is intended for the Scottish lawyer and there are already many texts covering other areas of the UK. This book will be complemented by on-line updates accessible via the student section of W. Green's website (www.wgreen.co.uk).

STRUCTURE OF THE BOOK

The book is in two parts: Part I deals with the different types of legal information and retrieval strategies and Part II concentrates on research skills.

Part I

1–4 Chapter 2 introduces you to the use of electronic sources for legal research. It is important to appreciate that there is a big difference between recreational use of the internet and using it for legal research. Using the web for legal research presents new challenges and can be both exciting and intimidating. The chapter identifies which type of electronic sources are the most relevant for different types of research queries and looks at strategies for searching the internet and how to find your way through the vast amount of online information available quickly and effectively using search engines. It then identifies the key legal information gateways for Scots lawyers and how they can help you to research more efficiently. Following this, it then identifies the online legal databases most relevant to Scots lawyers and provides you with advice on how to search them effectively and efficiently. Specific search activities are covered in the relevant chapters later on the book. The chapter concludes by helping you to make effective use of the materials you find during your exploration of electronic resources. It sets out criteria by which you should evaluate information found on the internet and the citation and referencing styles for electronic information sources.

1–5 The two leading sources of Scots law, cases and legislation, have been covered in 2 and 3 chapters respectively. The intention is not only to describe and explain the main information sources but to include information on how to understand cases and legislation and to make effective use of them in your research. Case law is discussed in Chapters 3 and 4. Chapter 3 is intended as an introduction to case law and covers law reporting, the principal series of law reports (both modern and older series) and the skills of reading and analysing cases. It also includes a section on taking efficient notes from a case report. Chapter 4 concentrates on the aids to tracing cases and different search strategies that can be adopted.

1–6 Legislation is discussed in Chapters 5–7. Chapter 5 provides an introduction to the various types of legislation and the legislative process. It starts by briefly discussing legislation from the pre-1707 Scottish Parliaments and then looks at the UK Parliament and the Scottish Parliament. There is discussion of the legislative process in both parliaments in order to help explain the various documents that are produced. The layout and structure of the following legislation is discussed: an Act of Parliament and a statutory instrument from the UK Parliament; and an Act of the Scottish Parliament and Scottish statutory instrument. Advice is given on reading, understanding and interpreting legislation. Chapter 6 concentrates on aids to tracing legislation from the UK Parliament and the different search strategies that can be adopted. Chapter 7 adopts the same approach to legislation emerging from the Scottish Parliament.

1–7 Chapter 8 contains short sections on a range of information sources of relevance to the Scots lawyer. They range from the Institutional Writers of the seventeenth to nineteenth centuries to current awareness websites. The main intention is to provide details of information sources for students but some practitioner-orientated materials are also included.

1–8 Chapter 9 looks at some legal information sources which are relevant for UK-wide legal information but which exclude Scots law (either wholly or partially). The sources covered have been limited to those which are widely available in Scotland.

Chapter 10 concerns the European dimension to our legal system. It is intended to highlight **1–9** features of the European system which are of relevance to the Scottish legal researcher, to introduce the principal sources and the key documents of European law and to suggest search strategies for finding information about European law. Chapter 11 discusses public international law and human rights law and includes search strategies for locating key materials.

Part II

This section of the book deals with research skills in the broader sense, as opposed to infor- **1–10** mation-retrieval skills. The chapters follow the stages of the research process. Chapter 12 concentrates on the investigation process. Chapter 13 looks at how to read, evaluate and reference the material you research. Chapter 14 discusses how to make use of your findings to produce high quality pieces of work.

Chapter 12 examines topic based research and the legal investigation process. It provides **1–11** strategies for finding out about a given topic and research strategies for essays and problem questions. Legal research can involve focusing on the substantive rules—such as examining the legal rules for controlling pollution or analysing how the courts have interpreted the wording of the principal pollution offence. However, legal research is not restricted to looking at legal rules in isolation. Socio-legal research examines how law operates in a variety of social spheres, e.g. whether the pollution legislation has changed attitudes and behaviour towards polluting activity. In recognition of this fact Chapter 12 includes a brief discussion of the social science methods of data collection relevant to legal research—questionnaires, interviews and observation studies.

Chapter 13 discusses what to do with the information once you have found it. It looks at how to **1–12** get the most out of lectures and tutorials. It includes reading techniques, the evaluation of documentary material and record keeping. It concludes by discussion of referencing conventions and the construction of a bibliography.

Chapter 14 deals with how to use your research to produce work of a high standard. This **1–13** includes essay writing, problem solving techniques and guidance on how to prepare an oral presentation. The presentation of research and the evaluation of your own work are also covered. Finally, revision strategies and exam technique are discussed.

STYLE OF THE BOOK

This book is not intended to be read from cover to cover. It is envisaged that it will be referred **1–14** to when appropriate. It is intended to be used as a manual not read as a novel. It has been designed so that it is easy to find information. It does not hide information in paragraphs of prose and instead adopts a checklist approach. Diagrams have been included to help explain the use of some of the more confusing sources. Extensive cross-referencing has been used to enable the reader to move easily around the text. However, there is, by necessity, a small amount of repetition. This has been included in an attempt to make the book as user-friendly as possible and to prevent the constant turning of pages.

It is envisaged that the reader will check the contents list to identify the section of the text on a **1–15** particular area. When in the library, or in front of a PC, trying to use the various sources, the reader may find it helpful to read through the worked examples. Use the information source to locate the material in the worked example. You should then find it easier to use the source to find your own material. Bear in mind that the worked examples are correct at the time of printing but that the nature of law is such that the position could have changed by the time you are working through the example.

1–16 Part II (Chapters 12, 13 and 14) covers general research skills. It is suggested that these should be read at the start of your university career and then referred to later as the need arises, i.e. when an essay is set or as the exams loom.

1–17 The book concentrates on sources which are widely available to students in Scotland, official sources of information and information sources which allow free access. This book does not claim to cover all information sources. It is not intended as a reference work for law librarians. This book is not intended to provide an introduction to the Scottish legal system. There are many excellent works which already do this. References are provided to point the reader to texts which deal with specific aspects of Scots law in greater depth.

ELECTRONIC SOURCES

1–18 All websites mentioned are correct at the time of publication but they will quickly become out of date. It is, therefore, recommended that you visit the online updates for this book at Green's website. These will contain up-to-date information. Please note that the author is not responsible for the content of any website referred to in the text.

WHAT IS LEGAL RESEARCH?

1–19 " 'Legal research' is not merely a search for information; it is primarily a struggle for understanding." (M.J. Lynch, "An Impossible Task but Everybody has to do it—Teaching Legal Research in Law Schools" *L. Libr. J.* 1997, Vol. 89, Pt 3, p.415). Legal research skills do not just consist of learning how to use a law library. It is not enough just to locate information—you have to be able to understand and use the information once it has been located.

1–20 Legal research starts even before you get to the law library or log on. It involves deciding what is relevant to your research. This may require the use of problem solving techniques to identify the relevant legal issue. After you have located the information, you have to be able to read, understand and evaluate it. You will then be in a position to make effective use of that material by drawing on it to construct your arguments and to provide authority. Finding the information is a very important, but small, part in the research process.

Finding the leading case on the definition of causation in pollution law is not the same thing as finding the law which will help you advise whether X has "caused" pollution. It is only the first step. Other steps might include:

> ➢ Reading and analysing the case.
> ➢ Reading the authorities it refers to.
> ➢ Reading cases which have referred to it.
> ➢ Reading articles which have commented on the case.
> ➢ Thinking about the arguments in the case.
> ➢ Applying the rules laid down to X's set of circumstances.

Legal research skills

At the time of writing there is an ongoing debate about the future of legal education. However, **1–21** it is widely agreed that:

> "What a student ought to be able to do at the end of any law degree is find the law by proper research and apply it to a given set of facts. A lawyer who simply regurgitates notes, lengthy passages from which may have little or no application to the problem in question and which may in any event be three or four years out of date, is of little value to a modern firm of solicitors." (R. Rennie "What sort of lawyers do we want?" 2007 S.L.T. (News) 1).

It is obviously important that a law student leaves university with an awareness of the basic **1–22** principles in the important substantive areas of law. The author firmly believes that the next most important piece of knowledge that a graduate should have developed is the ability to carry out legal research. When you leave university and gain employment, the substantive law that you have learnt will soon be out of date. You will be expected to be able to find out what the law is **now**—not to dig out your old notes and find out what it was in the past.

Lawyers need to be able to carry out research in a way that is: precise, accurate, current, and **1–23** comprehensive. All university level students need to make good use of their research, be it in essays, presentations, assessments or exams. This book hopes to help students develop these skills.

THE NATURE OF LAW AND LEGAL MATERIALS

The very nature of law poses problems for the law student. When you go to university to study **1–24** law, do not expect the lecturers to tell you what the law is. There is often no single, definitive answer. Instead there are shades of opinion of differing weight. "Psychiatrists have suggested that a student who enters upon the study of law is in search of the security provided by certainty. He expects to find a fixed unchanging body of unambiguous rules which, once absorbed, will furnish a clear solution to any legal problem which arises in a professional lifetime. It is not like that at all." (W.A. Wilson, *Introductory Essays on Scots Law* (2nd ed., 1984), p.1).

The law student has to face the unpalatable fact that there is no single source that will answer a **1–25** legal problem. There is no one place where you can find all of the law. There is no "right" way of finding information; instead there are lots of different methods, with different coverage, different searching facilities, different formats, etc. In order to evaluate the material retrieved, the researcher must be aware of the strengths and limitations of the various information sources. This book offers comments about different information sources and highlights particular strengths and weaknesses.

There are some introductory concepts that you need to become familiar with in relation to legal research:

Primary and secondary materials

Legal literature can be divided into primary and secondary materials. Primary materials **1–26** represent the law and include statutes and cases. They are not someone's view about the law. Secondary materials are those which have been collected and interpreted by someone else. Secondary sources contain commentaries on the law. Examples of secondary sources are encyclopaedias, books, journals and indexes. As a student you will become familiar with both primary and secondary materials. You will need to read statutes and cases to find out what the law is but equally you will want to read commentaries on the law to get the benefit of others' interpretations and views on the primary materials. It is important not to rely solely on secondary sources. They are dependent on the expertise of the author and may be out of date. You may even find that nothing has been written on a topic and that primary materials are your only source.

Authority of legal materials

1–27 Some legal materials are regarded as more authoritative than others. You should be aware of the level of authority attached to the sources which you are using. Cases can be reported in several different series of law reports. There will usually be one series which is regarded as more authoritative. In Scotland the *Session Cases* series is regarded as the most authoritative. If a case is reported there and in other law reports, you should refer to the report in *Session Cases*.

Official and unofficial materials

1–28 Some sources of legal information are official and some are unofficial. This is an important distinction because of the fact that you can rely on the accuracy of official information. It is authoritative. For example, the official publication of EC legislation is in the *Official Journal of the European Union*. There are many other versions of EC legislation which have been produced commercially. They may be easier to access but the content is not authoritative because it has not come from an official source. You should not be discouraged from using unofficial sources (they do after all reprint the official text) but it is important to be aware of their status.

Pace of change

1–29 One feature of the law that causes difficulties for law students is that it changes all the time. However, not all of it changes at the same pace. Some law may remain unchanged for decades or even centuries, while other areas of law change on an annual basis. This means that awareness of the most up-to-date sources of information is necessary, but equally you need to be able to find older works. It cannot automatically be assumed that, just because something is old, it can be ignored.

Importance of currency

1–30 The importance of finding up-to-date information is stressed repeatedly throughout this book. Basing advice to a client on outdated authorities could make your advice completely wrong. In doing so as a solicitor, you would have acted negligently.

Need for precision

1–31 Law students have to come to terms with the fact that the study of law is a precise discipline. Language is used in a precise way. Lawyers use words such as "aforesaid", not to be particularly obscure, but in order to make the meaning beyond doubt. Documents drafted by lawyers (such as contracts and wills) may give rise to significant consequences and may be read some years after they are written. It is therefore vital that the document accurately reflects the original intention.

1–32 Precision is also required in the way documents are read. The study of law involves paying attention to detail. The difference between "may" and "shall" can be crucial to advising a client on a course of action. Researching the law also has to be carried out in a precise way. It is not sufficient to have a vague or hazy knowledge of the law. You need to be able to find the relevant rule and to ensure the currency of your research. A reflection of the need for precision can be found in the nature of law books. Law books differ from other books. You will find that law books contain more precise indexing systems than other books. They contain extra information such as tables of cases and statutes. The fact that the law is constantly changing means that new editions of law books are frequently produced. You must always take care to consult the most recent edition.

The distinctive nature of a law library

Not only are law books different from other books but law libraries are different from other **1–33** libraries. They will tend to contain many more periodicals and reference materials. The law library is a vital component in your studies at university. If you learn how to use it effectively you will enhance your studies and you will find that it will bring benefits to you long into your professional career.

Within a law library the sources of law are not always easy to access: **1–34**

> "there is an enormous and constantly changing mass of decisions, legislative enactments, and administrative rules from which the lawyer must speedily and accurately extract the law applicable to a specific problem ... The task is immeasurably increased because these decisions, as made, and these rules, as enacted, are not published in a subject or classified arrangement but, instead, by jurisdiction and date of decision or enactment." (M.O. Price, H. Bitner and S.R. Bysiewicz, *Effective Legal Research* 4th edn (1979), p.2).

Collections of statutes and cases are published in chronological order due to (a) the vast number **1–35** being produced, (b) the need for prompt publication and (c) tradition. In order to facilitate searching these materials various aids have been developed. They attempt to help access legal information in more meaningful ways. These aids include citators, tables, digests and indexes. However, some of the facilitating aids can themselves prove difficult for the inexperienced user. A library exercise has been included in Appendix II. This should enable you to test your knowledge and ensure that you know your way around the primary materials in a law library.

A law library is not merely the books on the shelves. One important element of a law library is **1–36** the librarian. Librarians have a fund of knowledge and will be able to provide assistance for you. Do make use of them.

Libraries are also far more than their physical appearance. Libraries have online catalogues **1–37** which allow access to resources from both inside and outside the library. It is presumed that you will be given information about your own university library and so subjects such as searching library catalogues have not been covered. Most law libraries' web pages provide online guides to resources which their users are able to access. These have been produced by experts and should be full of useful information for you.

Not only are law libraries different but the electronic sources relevant for legal research are also **1–38** very different from the sources you will be familiar with from recreational use of the internet. Google may be an excellent search engine for general information but it is not an advisable way to search for primary legal materials. Likewise, *Wikipedia* is an interesting experiment in online information distribution but it is totally inappropriate for legal research. As stated above legal research requires information to be current, accurate and authoritative. Do not be foolish enough to end up in the position of the trainee solicitor who was asked to investigate a legal problem and used *Wikipedia* only to be promptly told to go and do the research "properly". Specialist legal information gateways and online legal databases have been constructed to allow access to a huge amount of electronic legal materials. Searching these databases requires an understanding of how they work and the use of appropriate search techniques. An exercise using some of the main electronic sources has been included in Appendix III. This should enable you to test your ability to use the sources appropriately.

1–39   Scottish law students are faced with particular challenges in researching the law. Legislation emanates from three different sources: European institutions, the UK Parliament and the Scottish Parliament. This means that you need to develop an awareness of different types of legislation and different information systems. In addition, legislation emanating from the Westminster Parliament applying exclusively to Scotland can be difficult to find. Historically lack of parliamentary time or interest in the intricacies of our legal system resulted in a piece-meal approach to Scottish legislation with the increased use of Miscellaneous Provisions Acts (as opposed to clearly titled Acts) to amend the law on a range of subjects. This has contributed to the difficulty in finding Scots law.

1–40   United Kingdom texts tend to concentrate on the larger jurisdiction of England and Wales. There may be a short chapter or perhaps just a paragraph pointing out that Scottish law is different. Worse still, some texts exclude mention of Scotland altogether. Scots law has been poorly served by providers of legal information and unfortunately this has continued into the provision of electronic databases. Some of the main electronic databases have failed to include exclusively Scottish material. A final, but not unimportant point, is that dedicated Scottish law books are more expensive than their UK counterparts. The reason claimed is the small size of the potential market.

Despite these difficulties, it is an exciting time to be studying Scots law. When the author was at university in the eighties, doubt was expressed as to whether Scots law would exist as a distinct system by the end of the century. Now, with the advent of the Scottish Parliament, its future is assured and we can look forward to researching Scots law well into the future.

Symbols used in the text

Please note that the following symbols have been used to denote:

📖 paper information source.
🖰 electronic information source.

The law in this book is correct as at May 31, 2007.

Chapter 2
Using Electronic Resources for Legal Research

The last 10 years have seen a huge growth in the availability and sophistication of electronic **2–1** resources and they are now indispensable tools for the legal researcher. Before discussing this further, there is a need to clarify what exactly is meant by electronic resources. They include the internet, however it is important to appreciate that there is a big difference between recreational use of the internet and using it for legal research. Using the web for legal research presents new challenges and can be both exciting and intimidating. A different type of electronic resource is an online legal database which uses a web interface. Major online legal databases now allow access to far more information than could traditionally have been held in a paper library. Some of these databases were initially available on CD Rom but now the majority of CD Rom materials are replications of, or supplementary to, online resources. The CD Rom format allows sophisticated flexible search facilities but has been overtaken by users' preference for more frequently updated materials. Online databases can be updated several times a day whereas most CD Roms are updated on a monthly basis. Further electronic resources used for research purposes are online updates for textbooks, alerting services which can email the user with up-to-date information about developments in a chosen area and podcasts which have been used to accompany student revision guides. This chapter will concentrate on the internet and online legal databases as these are the most important electronic forms for the student legal researcher.

ELECTRONIC RESOURCES AND LEGAL RESEARCH

There is currently a large array of legal materials available electronically: **2–2**

> ➤ Primary legal materials such as legislation and case law. These are available in full text or in digest form. They are also available in their original form and, far more usefully, in revised form which takes account of any changes to their status such as an Act being amended or repealed or a case being overruled.
> ➤ Secondary sources of legal information such as journals and encyclopaedias.
> ➤ Official information from Government departments.
> ➤ Information from bodies such as the Scottish Law Commission and the Scottish Criminal Cases Review Commission.
> ➤ Research material is made available from organisations which sponsor the work, e.g. the Scottish Executive.
> ➤ In addition to legal information, various tools designed to facilitate searching the main online legal sources have been developed such as Justcite. This online citator does not contain any legal materials but provides a way of locating full text materials. Another example is the *Cardiff Index to Legal Abbreviations* site which decodes legal abbreviations.
> ➤ University law libraries have online catalogues that can be searched. They also provide useful guides to legal resources.

> ➢ Information both for and about the legal profession is communicated including details of firms, legal practitioners and advocates. This also includes information disseminated by relevant professional bodies such as the Law Society of Scotland. Information about court administration and the daily business of the courts is also available. Legal aid information is available from the Scottish Legal Aid Board.
> ➢ Material for students includes information on: careers in the law; legal training, student law journals; mooting details; and information designed to help with legal studies such as online tutorials.
> ➢ Universities provide information about their law courses. In addition, most universities also now have intranets to communicate with students and many student materials are provided electronically.
> ➢ Information on the law from a huge array of sources seeking to influence readers' views such as lobby groups/special interest groups.
> ➢ News reports and current awareness materials are also available with an immediacy that it is not possible for paper sources to emulate.
> ➢ Legal publishers and booksellers promote their latest legal publications.

2–3 With this huge amount of electronic material it would be easy to make the mistaken conclusion that you need only consult electronic sources in order to study law and carry out legal research. However, this is not yet the case and will probably not be the situation for some time to come. The reason is that many essential materials are not available electronically. These include:

> ➢ Books. There are few books which are available electronically although this may change in the near future.
> ➢ Older materials in general such as cases, official publications, research, organisational reports, etc. It is important to remember that research does not just start with the start of the electronic age. An awful lot of important material was generated before the 1990s. Many sites and databases started by including current material and have established systems to cope with future material. However, it can often be more difficult to go backwards in time and put archive material into electronic form. There are increasing instances of this happening but there is an enormous amount of important older material which only exists in paper-based sources.

2–4 This means that the legal researcher has to use both paper and electronic sources. They should not be regarded as opposing ways of presenting information. It is a mistake to regard paper as representing a bygone age and electronic as representing the future. They should be viewed as complementary forms of holding data and the fact that you need to use and appreciate both will enhance your learning/research experience.

2–5 Although the increase in the provision of information in electronic form over the past 10 years has greatly aided its accessibility, the nature of electronic information sources can cause challenges for the legal researcher. One of these challenges is the sheer amount of information which can be accessed. It can cause problems by overwhelming the researcher and making it difficult to identify relevant material. Another challenge is the lack of quality control on the internet and a lack of consistency in electronic sources in general. This means that it is vitally important to be able to search electronic sources efficiently and effectively. In order to do this it is necessary to understand how the sources deal with information and to have an appreciation of the strengths and weaknesses of the particular sources. It is also necessary to become familiar with search strategies and techniques appropriate for that particular source. You may be used to searching for information using a favourite search engine but for legal research you need to appreciate different electronic sources and searching techniques. The legal researcher also needs to be able to evaluate the information retrieved from the internet and to be able to reference it for inclusion in a piece of work. These topics are all covered in this chapter. The appropriateness of sources for particular kinds of information retrieval is covered in the specific sections throughout Chapters 4, 6, 7, 8, 9, 10 and 11.

Availability of electronic resources

Materials on the internet can be free to anyone, free but require registration by the user or require payment of a subscription. Some of the key electronic legal information sources for the legal researcher are freely accessible to anyone surfing the net. However, there are several important online databases that are subscription based. This means that you will only be able to access these sources if your university has subscribed to them. You will be able to find out which services your university has subscriptions to by checking its library's web pages. Access to these subscription services will depend on your university. Some provide access through your university password while others use the Athens Access Management System which requires you to use Athens login details. Both methods allow you to access subscription services from any PC. **2–6**

What is the difference between free and subscription legal services? As you might expect services which require payment have various additional features. Generally these include: **2–7**

> ➢ The current status of primary materials, e.g. if a piece of legislation has been amended or if a case has been overruled. This is a particularly important feature. The exception to this is the *Statute Law Database* (see para.6.45) but at the time of writing this is not fully up-to-date and must therefore be used with caution until it has been completed which is expected to be in 2008.
> ➢ The inclusion of citator information allowing the user to trace legal developments over time.
> ➢ The ability to view legislation as it stood at different points in time.
> ➢ Additional information about primary sources such as identifying journal articles about cases.
> ➢ The ability to link between materials, e.g. if an Act refers to another Act you can link directly between the two Acts.
> ➢ The ability to email material in different formats such as word or pdf files.
> ➢ The ability to download information.
> ➢ The ability to print the information in various forms.

In contrast, free sites tend to allow fast access to a more limited range of primary information with little additional information. Examples of free sites containing useful information for legal researchers are the Scottish Courts (see para.4.21), House of Lords (see para.4.23), *Office of Public Sector Information* (*OPSI*) (see para.6.31) and *BAILII* (see para.4.22). Other sites relevant to the legal researcher are identified throughout the book. Material will appear on these sites more quickly than the databases as they are posting the raw documents. The databases are producing additional features (e.g. case summaries) which means that it takes time for these to be prepared. **2–8**

SEARCH STRATEGY FOR ELECTRONIC RESOURCES

Paragraph 2.2 outlined the range of information available electronically, so how do you go about finding it? First of all—have a strategy. Do not just immediately type words into a search engine such as Google. This is **not** to be recommended for researching a legal topic because: **2–9**

> ➤ The search will be so wide that you will get a large number of irrelevant hits as you cannot restrict it to legal information sources.
> ➤ There is no quality control and therefore you do not know the accuracy of the information or the amount of weight that you should attach to it.
> ➤ The free sources of primary legal information (with the exception of the *Statute Law Database*) do not contain amended legislation or details of whether cases have been overruled. This means that if you search for primary materials using a search engine you will retrieve the original version. This is worse than useless as you then have to carry out the further step of finding out if it has been amended. This means that this method of locating information, which is extremely useful for a multitude of other purposes, is not useful for legal research because of the importance attached to identifying the current version of primary materials.
> ➤ Internet subject searches increasingly retrieve *Wikipedia* as high on the order of relevant hits. This online "encyclopaedia" may be an interesting source of recreational material but it lacks the authority and accuracy to be used for legal research.

Step 1 ⇒ Know what you are searching for

What is the purpose of your search? Are you looking for:

> ➤ Primary legal materials such as a case or an Act of Parliament?
> ➤ Journal articles about a topic?
> ➤ Government reports?
> ➤ Debates in the Scottish Parliament?
> ➤ European cases?
> ➤ International conventions?
> ➤ General information about a legal topic?
> ➤ Recent events in an area of law?

This will determine where you start to look for the material.

Step 2 ⇒ Think of appropriate search terms

Think about the subject of your research and the most appropriate search terms to use. Terms can be words or phrases. Construct a list of the possible search terms before you start searching. If you cannot think of search terms consult other sources for help: your lecture notes, a textbook, a reference work or an encyclopaedia. Dictionaries can help to find synonyms. Take into account possible alternative spellings, especially the American form of words.

Step 3 ⇒ Choose the "right" search method

You need to assess whether it would be more appropriate for you to use a:

> ➤ search engine;
> ➤ what are variously called an internet gateway/specialist search tool/subject directory; or
> ➤ legal database such as *Westlaw* or *LexisNexis Butterworths*.

In order to know which one is the most appropriate, you will need an appreciation of how they work, the information they will retrieve for you and appropriate search techniques. These are discussed in relation to the three search methods below.

SEARCH ENGINES

Search engines make use of programs that trace websites across the web. They automatically **2–10** create enormous databases which you can then search. This process is mechanistic and based on word matching. It does not incorporate any form of quality control but, on the other hand, the processes mean that the search engines are useful ways searching and tracing vast amounts of very current information. Examples of search engines are Google, Yahoo and Altavista. They present their results in order of relevancy to your search terms. Although remember that this can be skewed by businesses eager to appear at the top of search engine lists. Companies now exist to advise companies on how to improve their chances of being identified by the leading search engines.

The downside of search engines is that they will produce large numbers of hits which can take a **2–11** long time to sort through. Their search processes also mean that they will retrieve a lot of irrelevant or inappropriate material. They are more suited to general searching than to legal research.

Online searching techniques: **2–12**

> The more specific the search term, the more accurate the results will be.
> When searching by subject, choose your search terms in such a way that they might form the title of a book or an article. An illustration of this technique used by Tilburg University Library and IT services is that if you are looking for information on shoeing horses, the search term horse care is likely to yield better results than either hooves or shoeing. Similarly, Chinese cooking is better than cooked dough balls. However you have to be careful, if you make your search terms too general, they may also yield too general, and therefore unusable, results.
> Make use of advanced search facilities
> Do not limit yourself to one search engine or subject directory. No single search engine indexes all the sites on the web.
> Search engines and directories change frequently. Choose two or three engines or directories you like working with and get to know their ins and outs.
> Use the help function of the search engine; they do actually contain helpful advice.

LEGAL GATEWAYS/SUBJECT DIRECTORIES/SPECIALIST INTERNET SEARCH TOOLS

These are sites which have been compiled by specialists who have used their expertise to identify **2–13** relevant and useful websites and classified them according to subject. The sites will be listed alongside some description of the site which helps the user to determine whether the site will be of use to them. These sites are variously referred to as legal gateways, subject directories, specialist internet search tools or portals. For simplicity this book will refer to them as legal gateways.

  These sites have the big advantage over search engines in that they have been compiled by experts and therefore some quality control has been exercised over their contents. Searching these sites will tend to produce more relevant search results for academic work. You will probably also be able to browse the site which can be a useful way of identifying materials when you are unsure of a precise search term. However, they will retrieve fewer results than a search engine. They are designed for a target user and if you do not belong to that target group you may not find anything of use or worse, fail to find the most useful site. It is therefore important to select your legal gateway carefully.

2–14 When would you use a legal gateway?

1. To identify relevant online resources in an area of law that is unfamiliar.
2. As a check that you have not missed an important online source.
3. They are useful as a source of key links and are an alternative to bookmarking important sites or when you are using a PC where you can not save or access your favourites.

Gateways to legal information

The main legal gateways are listed below separated into three categories Scotland, general UK and worldwide.

⇒ **Scottish**

2–15 *Scottish Law Online* (*http://www.scottishlaw.org.uk/*) describes itself as web portal for lawyers, solicitors or advocates, academics, students or the public who are interested in Scots Law. It is a long established web resource (1997) and includes: an A to Z of Scots law; a resources section which has links to key Scottish sites; Scots Law Student Zone which provides career advice, academic links and an opportunity to share views; an archive for the Scots Law Student Journal; Corporate Zone which contains business related links; and a news section.

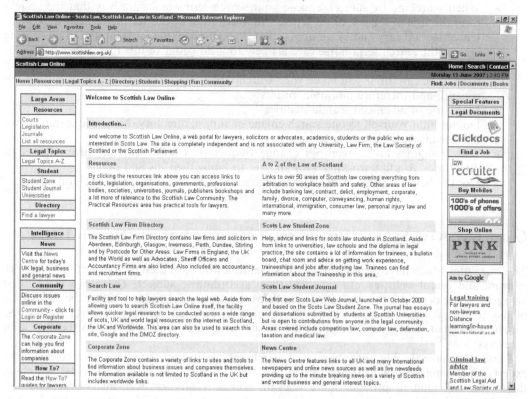

Diagram 2.1: Scottish Law Online

Scottish Legal Resources section on *Delia Venables' Portal to Legal Resources in the UK and Ireland* (*http://www.venables.co.uk/scotland.htm*) contains an up-to-date list of Scottish legal sites and resources with information explaining their content, links to firms of solicitors and Scottish legal publishers.

Scottish Council of Law Reporting (*http://www.scottishlawreports.org.uk/resources/links/ links.html*) contains a set of links, edited by Derek O'Carroll, Advocate, which gathers together links relevant to the Scots lawyer. They are grouped under subject headings and include brief descriptions of the sites.

Intute Social Sciences Scottish section (*http://www.intute.ac.uk/socialsciences/cgi-bin/browse. pl?id= 120877*) contains links with detailed annotations to Scottish legal sites.

Access to Law (*http://www.accesstolaw.com/*) is an excellent site which contains links to legal resources which have been selected and annotated by the Inner Temple Library. Click on the link to Scotland to access its Scottish section.

⇒ **General UK**

Lawlinks (*http://www.kent.ac.uk/lawlinks/*) is hosted by the Templeman Library, University of **2–16** Kent. It is a very useful site to have bookmarked. It contains annotated lists of websites which have been categorised by subject which makes it easy to use. It covers UK and worldwide resources.

Access to Law (*http://www.accesstolaw.com/*) is an excellent site which contains links to legal resources which have been selected and annotated by the Inner Temple Library.

Legal Resources in the UK and Ireland, Delia Venables (*http://www.venables.co.uk/lawyers.htm*) is kept very up-to-date and contains links to the UK and the world. It is very comprehensive and provides a useful narrative about each resource listed. Delia Venables is a computer consultant for lawyers.

Intute Social Sciences (*http://www.intute.ac.uk/socialsciences/law/*) identifies and evaluates legal resource sites with well constructed annotations. It covers the UK and world resources.

⇒ **Worldwide gateways to legal resources**

WorldII (*www.worldlii.org*) was launched in 2002 by the World Legal Institute. It contains 860 **2–17** databases of legal information from 123 countries. In addition to the databases available there is a particularly useful subject category of links under each country which gives an indication of which materials are available in English.

Findlaw.com (*http://www.findlaw.com/*) is a US based site which allows access to a range of legal resources.

Guide to foreign and international legal databases (*http://www.law.nyu.edu/library/foreign_intl/*) is hosted by New York University School of Law and contains access to a large range of infor- mation via useful subject headings.

Guide to Law Online: Law Library of Congress (*http://www.loc.gov/law/public/law-guide.html*) is prepared by the Law Library of Congress Public Services Division. It is an annotated guide to sources of information on government and law available online. It is part of the *Global Legal Information Network* (*GLIN*). *GLIN* is a public database of official texts of laws, regulations, judicial decisions, and other legal sources contributed by governmental agencies and interna- tional organisations. Each document is accompanied by a summary in English.

Legal Information Institute—Cornell Law School (*http://www.law.cornell.edu/world/*). This section of the site gathers a collection of world legal materials country by country. It includes the online sources of constitutions, statutes, judicial opinions, and related legal material from around the world.

LEGAL DATABASES

2–18 Legal databases, or more accurately, legal database services are specialist databases which contain a large range and amount of legal materials. They usually comprise many different databases which can be searched using sophisticated facilities. There are several different legal databases and, although some content is common to several of the databases, they all have different content and functions. This means that ideally you should be aware of the contents of the database before embarking on a search or you may be wasting your time. This is not as easy as it sounds as the databases are continually expanding their content. Legal databases require different search techniques from search engines and retrieve results in a different way. Results appear in chronological order as opposed to relevance. Online legal databases tend to be subscription services, i.e. they are not freely available to everyone. Universities pay subscriptions to these databases which allow all their students to have access during their time at university.

2–19 Why would you use a database?

1. To find primary legal materials. They contain the **revised** form of legislation and provide up-to-date information about the status of cases.
2. Because of the comprehensive range of materials they contain and which can be searched from a single point.
3. The ease with which you can link between different documents.
4. The sophisticated search facilities available.
5. Ease of use.

Westlaw and *LexisNexis Butterworths*

2–20 The two most widely used databases in Scotland are *Westlaw* and *LexisNexis Butterworths*. Both are part of large global publishing organisations. They both provide full text access to primary legal materials: revised versions of legislation, law reports, journal articles as well as European materials and materials from around the world. Both offer alerting services and the ability to print and email materials.

2–21 *LexisNexis Butterworths* does not include exclusively Scottish legislation from the UK Parliament. This means that it does not have a compete set of legislation and therefore reduces its usefulness for the Scottish legal researcher. However, a strength of *LexisNexis Butterworths* is that it includes the *Stair Memorial Encyclopaedia* which is an important information source for Scottish students.

2–22 A strength of *Westlaw* is that it includes the Legal Journals Index which allows the user to search all the law journals in the UK back to 1986. However, a much more limited number are available in full text. *Westlaw* also includes *Renton & Brown's Criminal Procedure* which contains up-to-date commentary on the practice and procedure in the Scottish criminal courts.

2–23 The two databases hold different law reports and journals. From the Scottish point of view *Westlaw* allows access to the *Session Cases* and the *Scots Law Times* whereas *LexisNexis*

Butterworths holds the *Session Cases*, Scottish Civil Law Reports and Scottish Criminal Case Reports. Thus *Westlaw* has the greater coverage with both of the principal Scottish series of law reports. With regard to other law report series you need to be aware of which reports are held by the different databases. Your choice of which to use would depend on the subject of your research, e.g. *LexisNexis Butterworths* is particularly useful for tax.

The reason behind the different content lies in the different publishing links. *Westlaw* is pub- **2–24** lished by W.Green and Sweet & Maxwell which are part of the Thomson Corporation. This means that the publications from these publishers are accessible via *Westlaw* and do not appear on *LexisNexis Butterworths* and equally *LexisNexis Butterworths* publications do not appear on Westlaw.

The user friendliness of a database can depend on the subjective view of the user, however **2–25** results of a survey on the use of legal information sources throughout Scotland recently carried out by W. Green showed that 90% of students preferred *Westlaw*. The highest proportion of responses given for this preference was ease of use.

Both *LexisNexis Butterworths* and *Westlaw* have recently upgraded their services. This book **2–26** contains details of the new services. With respect to *Westlaw* major changes have been made to *Westlaw* UK.

The Scots Law and Scots Crime sections of *Westlaw* will be upgraded in the future and searching in these sections of *Westlaw* currently still uses the system of *case* and *legislation locators* which is not covered in this book.

Other major legal databases

The newest database is the free *Statute Law Database* which was launched in December 2006. Its **2–27** launch means that for the first time in the UK an official, authoritative online database of revised UK primary legislation is available free of charge to the public. Unfortunately it has been launched before all the information on it has been brought completely up-to-date which means that caution must be exercised when using this database until the updating process is complete which is due to be in 2008.

Current Legal Information is a subscription legal research service which is available on both CD **2–28** Rom and online. It contains six datasets designed to facilitate tracing legal developments but it does not contain full text material. *Lawtel* is an online subscription legal current awareness digest service which is a useful service for tracing legislative developments but its case law only includes Scottish cases which are followed in England. *Justis* is another provider of legal databases which do not appear to be widely used in Scottish universities however you may encounter *Justcite* which is a subscription online legal citator (a legal reference search engine). It allows users to identify materials across both free and subscription databases by searching through one interface.

These, and other more specialised databases, are described in more detail in relation to the subject specific content in the appropriate chapters later in the book.

How legal databases work

Legal databases do not work by "thinking" about the data they contain and being able to **2–29** retrieve results by concept or legal significance. Instead they basically work by matching the words and phrases that you enter with words and phrases in their database. Why is this important? It is important that you take this into consideration when constructing your searches. It means that if you are interested in pollution and you enter this term. The system will retrieve all mentions of the word "pollution". It will not automatically know that you are looking for materials concerning the law of pollution and will find materials which contain the word but which may actually be about the law of contract etc.

2–30 This feature of legal databases means that you have to construct your searches carefully in order to retrieve meaningful results. Fortunately legal databases make it easy for you to edit your search or to narrow a search after seeing the results of your original search. While this means that you do not have to get your search terms correct the first time, it can be frustrating and waste time. It is far more efficient to construct appropriate search terms in the first place.

Search techniques for legal databases

At this point it is presumed that you have already undertaken the three steps in para.2.9. You therefore know what you are searching for, have identified the most appropriate search terms and have chosen to use a database.

2–31 Before you start searching you must be aware that no one legal database is totally comprehensive. This means that you cannot use one database to retrieve all legal information. Instead you need to develop an awareness of the content of each of the databases and use them accordingly. If there are certain materials that you need to use on a regular basis you will become familiar with which database has the relevant content. It is useful to check the contents of databases at regular intervals as they are all increasing their holdings and sometimes drop lesser used materials.

2–32 The next step is to appreciate that the database will merely match the terms you use with words in its database and so you need to think about how best to achieve the results you want. In the example used above if you were actually trying to identify recent pollution regulations then you would search under both pollution and regulations by entering both terms.

You might also want to consider whether the term pollution is too general—what type of pollution are you interested in? If you are only interested in water pollution then you should include this term as it will restrict the number of results retrieved to a more manageable level and to ones which are more relevant to your research.

However, you should not be too specific or you will restrict your search too much, e.g. oil pollution in River Tay 2007. If you use too many terms the database will struggle to find exact matches for your search.

Boolean search techniques

2–33 You should consider using Boolean search techniques as all the databases use these although they may use different terminology. Boolean searching means that some words have special roles and they are called Boolean operators or connectors. As the names suggest they affect the way that search terms "connect" to each other. The main connectors are:

⇒ **AND** This searches for material which contains all the search terms entered which are linked by the term AND, e.g. if you enter X AND Y the results retrieved will all be materials which contain **both** the term X and the term Y.

LexisNexis Butterworths' form for the AND connector is "and". If you enter multiple terms *LexisNexis Butterworths* presumes it is a phrase i.e. it will find where the terms are found together but not materials which mention the terms separately.

Westlaw's form for the AND connector is "&" or a space. If you enter multiple terms with no

connectors, *Westlaw UK* will automatically insert the AND connector in between them: "sewage & water & pollution" will retrieve the same as "sewage water pollution".
It is important to appreciate this difference between the two databases.

⇒ **OR** This searches for all the documents which contain either or both of your search terms, e.g. if you search for X OR Y the results retrieved will be materials which contain either X,Y, or both X or Y. This will therefore retrieve more results than using the AND connector as it does not limit the results to material where both terms occur. This can be useful where there are alternative names or spellings for a particular subject.
In both *LexisNexis Butterworths* and *Westlaw*, the OR connector (which in both cases is "or") searches for either or both search terms within the same materials.

⇒ **NOT** This searches for material where one search term occurs and the other search term does not occur, e.g. if you search for X NOT Y you will only retrieve materials which contain the term X and do not contain the term Y. You have to remember that if you exclude materials containing Y you also exclude materials which contain both X and Y which can mean that you can miss some relevant material.
In *LexisNexis Butterworths* the form for NOT is "and not". In *Westlaw* the form is "%".

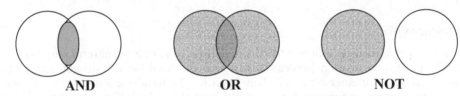

AND   OR   NOT

Diagram 2.2: Boolean Search Connectors

In addition to the above, both *LexisNexis Butterworths* and *Westlaw* have a form of proximity **2–34** searching with grammatical and numerical connectors. The forms used by the databases are similar:

LexisNexis Butterworths	Westlaw	Effect
w/s	*/s*	Search terms in the same sentence
w/*p*	/*p*	Search terms in the same paragraph
w/*n*	/*n*	Search terms within "n" terms of each other (where "n" is a number) e.g. in *Westlaw* sewage /3 pollution will retrieve only materials where sewage occurs within three or fewer words of pollution.
Pre/n	+*n*	The first term preceding the second by "n" terms (where "n" is a number)

Phrases. *LexisNexis Butterworths* presumes that multiple terms entered constitute a phrase. **2–35** *Westlaw* does not make this presumption and therefore in *Westlaw* if you want to search for a phrase you need to put your search terms in the appropriate order and in quotation marks, e.g. "fiduciary duty". Without the quotation marks *Westlaw* would automatically insert the AND connector and therefore look for materials containing both words but not necessarily appearing together.

2–36 **Truncation.** Different databases use different terms to describe this concept and its variants. This is used because if you only enter one form of a word the database will only retrieve results that match that particular form, e.g. if you enter pollution the database will only look for matches with pollution. However, you might want to include pollutant, pollutants, pollute and polluted in your search. Truncation allows you to do this. It means using a short form of a word with a symbol which allows the database to match words with various endings attached to the short form of the word. Examples include: single and plural forms, adjectives and different tenses of verb.

LexisNexis Butterworths and *Westlaw* both use the root expander "!" to allow you to search for terms with multiple endings, e.g. object! will retrieve object, objected, objection, objecting, objectionable. The *Statute Law Database* uses "*" as a root expander.

LexisNexis Butterworths and *Westlaw* both use the "*" symbol to search for words with variable characters. *LexisNexis Butterworths* refers to this as a wildcard and *Westlaw* calls it the universal character. In both systems if you enter e.g. withdr*w, this will retrieve withdraw and withdrew. The *Statute Law Database* uses "?" for this function.

2–37 **Plurals.** Generally the databases will retrieve the plural form of a singular term. However, there are differences regarding irregular plurals. *Westlaw* automatically retrieves irregular plurals, e.g. child will retrieve children whereas *LexisNexis Butterworths* does not: child would *not* retrieve children.

Natural language/free text

2–38 Both *LexisNexis Butterworths* and *Westlaw* have options to search via natural language or "free text" searching. This means that Boolean searching is not used (so you do not need to use the connectors) and you can enter terms in plain English. The database will effectively turn your terms into a Boolean search for you. However, although this sounds like an easier option for the user according to Holland and Webb "the selection mechanism tends to be relatively crude, so a natural language search can actually throw up more irrelevant material than a well-constructed Boolean search" (*Learning Legal Rules* 6th edn (Oxford: OUP, 2006)).

Basic and advanced search options

2–39 Legal databases have different levels of searching. The basic search option tends to be a free text search option. The advanced option tends to allow searching by different fields. Fields might be legislation title, legislation provision, citation, party name, jurisdiction, author, or title, etc. Field searching is possible because part of the publishing process has involved words being "tagged" according to their function within a document. Thus when details of a case are being entered into a database by a publisher legislation titles, party names, etc. are treated in a different way from the normal text of a document. This ensures that they will be recognised as being a member of a certain class of data, e.g. legislation title data. Field searching allows you to search more efficiently as it means that you can narrow your search to a much greater extent.

Keyword/subject categories

2–40 In addition to parts of the document being identified as fields, publishers also classify documents into categories by assigning appropriate keywords or subject categories to them. An illustration of this is the case *Bett v Hamilton* 1998 JC 1 (which appears in Chapter 3). In *Westlaw* this has been given the subject classification of "criminal law" and two keywords have been assigned to it: "offences against property" and "Scotland". This means that if you go into *Westlaw* and use the advanced search option and enter "*offences against property*" and *Scotland* into the *subject/keyword* field you will retrieve this case as one of your search results. Keyword search can be extremely useful however it can depend on whether the publisher has classified material in the same way that the user would classify it. There can sometimes be a mismatch.

Expanding or reducing results retrieved

Databases allow you to narrow your search by searching within your original search results. **2–41** However, this may not be helpful if you have searched using an inappropriate term.

If you retrieve a large number of results you should modify your search to reduce the number of results and ensure that they are relevant to your query. You can do this by:

> ➤ Thinking about your search terms and perhaps substituting more appropriate terms.
> ➤ Using the advanced search option as opposed to the basic search and making use of the field options offered by the database. This will limit your search and make it more specific.
> ➤ Making use of the Boolean techniques by using the AND connector to add additional search terms.

If you retrieve no or few results and you want to increase your results:

> ➤ Look at the way you have spelt your search terms—is it correct? It is amazing how many times you can mistype and a search fails as a result.
> ➤ Think of alternative words for your search terms.
> ➤ Use the OR connector to combine your search terms.
> ➤ Use the truncation techniques noted in para.2.36.

Snowballing

This is a technique which means that you move from the specific to open up a more general **2–42** search. If your search retrieves useful references look at the way the database has classified them. You can do this by locating the subject heading or keywords which have been used to describe them. You can then use these terms to search for more useful results.

   You should also explore any references that are contained in your results and any relevant links from them. You should also look and see if the same author or organisation has published other relevant material.

Summary of when should you use the different types of electronic sources for legal research

It is not terribly useful to lay down general guidelines as this can be very specific to the exact **2–43** type of information that you are looking for and this detailed information is provided in the specific sections throughout the book. However, some general guidance can be provided:

⇒ **When use a database?**
> ➤ When researching primary legal materials as they have the revised full text form of legislation, up-to-date information on the status of a case and information on, and a selection of, full text journal articles about the primary sources. They also contain materials which help you appreciate the significance of the primary materials such as summaries and links to relevant materials which have discussed the case or statute.

⇒ **When use a free source of primary information such as Scottish Courts or *OPSI***
> ➤ When you want fast access to a very recent case or Act.
> ➤ When you are looking for a case which has not been reported.
> ➤ When you want access to the original as opposed to the revised version of legislation.

⇒ **When use a gateway?**
> ➤ To identify relevant online resources in an area of law that is unfamiliar to you.

> ➢ As a check that you have not missed an important online source.
> ➢ They are useful as a source of key links and save you bookmarking important sites or can be useful if you are using a PC where you can not save your favourites.

⇒ **When use a search engine?**
> ➢ Rarely.
> ➢ To conduct an initial survey if unfamiliar with the topic.

EVALUATION OF ONLINE RESOURCES

2–44 Evaluation of resources is not confined to online materials. When carrying out research you should not accept materials at face value. This is because it is important that the material is accurate otherwise your own work will be undermined if you use it. This is discussed in para.13.24 in relation to research materials generally, however there are particular issues relevant to internet materials.

1. Lack of quality control on the internet. Anyone can post material on the internet. It is not like a library where the contents are carefully chosen by information professionals. Books and journal articles are subject to earlier stages of quality control as they have to be accepted for publication by publishers or an editorial board and they are edited before publication.
2. Lack of obvious quality indicators on the internet. Important quality indicators may not be obvious on internet resources, e.g. the source of the material, the date, even the country where it originated. In a library you can clearly see who wrote a book and the legal jurisdiction to which it relates.
3. Lack of separation of different types of materials. One of the advantages of carrying out an internet search using a search engine such as Google is that you can identify a large range of different materials from a range of different sources. However, the downside of this broad sweep approach is that your search results are presented in a list ranked by relevancy to your search terms. This means that authoritative sources such as official sites, e.g. the *Statute Law Database*, can appear next to an advert, a site sponsored by a lobby group, a blog or a chatroom.
4. The amount of materials retrieved by an internet search. A search using a search engine can retrieve hundreds or even thousands of hits. This is very different from a library which may have a small selection of books on a topic which you can take time to compare or browse. You need to be able to evaluate internet materials quickly and efficiently.

Criteria for the evaluation of online resources

Authority

2–45 Who has written the material? Who has published it? Is it an individual or an organisation? Is it an official site? Official sites carry far more authority. Is the author an expert or someone standing on a virtual soapbox?

Ways of locating answers include looking for the author's name or the name of whoever has published the site. This may not be obvious from the homepage. Information may be contained in an *about us* section which can sometimes be on a menu bar. If there is a *contact* option, that may give an email or physical address. You should also look at the URL (Uniform Resource Locator): this is the web address for the page and will be located at the top of your browser, e.g.

http://www.wgreen.co.uk/students. The URL can provide you with more identifying information about the source of the site.

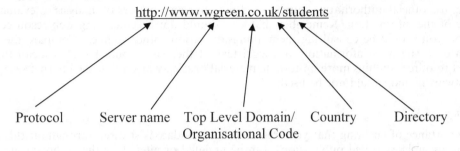

Diagram 2.3: URL Breakdown

➤ The server name is the host computer or server for the web page. Sometimes, but not always, it identifies the name of the organisation concerned. Here the organisation is W.Green.

➤ The Top Level Domain (TLD) can be very useful as it provides an indication of the type of organisation that is hosting the site. Here the TLD is .co. which (like .com) means that the organisation is a company or commercial organisation. You therefore know that it is trying to sell you something. Other TLDs include:

    ⇒ .ac means the organisation is a university, college or school. The US equivalent is .edu

    ⇒ .gov is used by government servers

    ⇒ .org is used by non-profit making organisations or charities

➤ The Country part of the URL identifies the country where the site is hosted. Here the country is the UK. Other examples would be .au Australia, .nz New Zealand, .za South Africa, .ca Canada, .ie Ireland, .in India, .cn China. In the US many sites do not use their TLD which is .us.

However, these are only indications and, as ever there are exceptions to the rules, so you should not always rely on them.

Once you have located the author you should ask the various questions in para.13.25. This may **2–46** involve following links to the homepage of the organisation and assessing its worth as a research source—is it a government body or an unknown entity with a poor out of date homepage? If the author is a person, find out what else they have published. If they are based in the UK and write about UK legal issues check this by entering their name as an author in the Legal Journals Index (which is available as part of the *journals* section of *Westlaw*—see para.8.48). Enter their name into a search engine such as Google and follow up on the results. Are they a member of staff at an academic institution, if so which one? Most university websites list the publications of staff members.

If a website has been mentioned in one of the legal information gateways (see para.2.15) some comment on its content may be included. In addition, the very fact that information professionals have chosen to include it in their listing indicates that it includes reliable and useful information.

Accuracy

2–47   In order to evaluate the accuracy of a web resource: find out about the source of the information; use official authoritative sources; and use your own powers of analysis to evaluate the quality of the information. Remember that you should not be consulting web resources in a vacuum, you should be consulting them alongside various other sources. Compare the information on a site with information in a legal text. If there is a conflict it may mean that the internet resource contains more up-to-date material or it may mean that the internet resource is untrustworthy and should not be used.

Currency

2–48   The importance of ensuring that your research is up-to-date is stressed throughout this book. Web pages, unlike printed publications, can be updated or altered by the author at any time, even on a daily basis. In fast-moving areas of law, web resources may be the only way that you can find the most recent cases. However, it is a mistake to presume that just because something is published electronically that it will be up-to-date. There are many websites which have not been updated for years. It is therefore important to check for currency. The site may contain a publication date or the date of the last update may be displayed—usually at the foot of a page. The *about us* section may contain details of how frequently the site is updated. However, frequently there is no obvious information. How can you find out? Try following some of the links. If the links are out of date then it strongly suggests that the site has not been updated recently.

   If the site has been in existence for at least three years and is regularly updated it is more likely to be a reliable source. A good website will also provide dates for when the website was created and last modified.

   You should also be aware that material on the internet can change very quickly or disappear altogether. This means that it is important to note down the date you accessed a site if you wish to use it as a bibliographic reference in your research. See further para.2.52 on the citation of electronic references.

Content

2–49   Is it updated or in original form? This is very important with relation to primary sources of law and in particular legislation. The text of an Act can be amended many times or be repealed. It is therefore vital that you are aware of whether you are reading the original (and therefore useless version unless you are conducting a historical study) or the revised version.

   Is it relevant to the jurisdiction you are studying? Scotland is a small jurisdiction on the world stage and you need to ensure that the material you retrieve is relevant. The internet has a strong US bias and many of the materials you will retrieve from a search engine will be geared to their legal system. Many UK sites fail to take account of the fact that Scottish law is different and so you need to be aware of this when reading material.

2–50   Is the material appropriate for academic research? The internet contains material for many different audiences and the treatment of a topic will be influenced by the target audience. Before reading the information contained within the website, refer to any notes, prefaces or summaries posted on the site which provide information about the purpose of the website and the range of material covered. Selection criteria used for inclusion of information on the site may be outlined. Try to ascertain whether the publications are aimed at a specialist or general audience. If there are no stated selection criteria you will have to browse through the information available to find out whether or not it is relevant to your research. If the author has included bibliographies and references conforming to academic conventions this would suggest that the target audience are academics and researchers.

The presentation of material on the internet can be an indicator of the quality of the content. The clear and logical arrangement of a website can suggest that the content was also carefully complied. However, beware—good presentation can also mask poor content.

Objectively presented information supported by valid authority is indicative of trustworthy content.

Obvious grammatical and spelling errors tend to imply that the text has not been carefully reviewed or edited prior to publication.

Bias

Is the resource trying to sell something? Is it trying to persuade you to join an organisation? Is it informing or misinforming? **2–51**

By determining the intended audience of a particular web-based resource you will be able to gain an insight into possible bias. Many lobby groups, political parties and individuals have websites whose primary purpose is to persuade others to believe in the same convictions that they do. The objectivity of the resource will therefore help you to determine the accuracy and reliability of the information provided.

A proportion of websites have been created for the purpose of advertising and marketing. Information on law firm sites in particular may have been used for a presentation or may be a brief summary of the law in newsletter form for existing clients. Try to find out the reason for information being published on a website to detect any intrinsic bias which may not be obvious at first glance.

There should be a link at the foot of the home page of a website to the organisation that sponsors or hosts the site. Investigate the host organisation's website by following any such links. If the website is hosted by an academic institution, find out whether the content has been produced by an academic department or a researcher.

The fact that material contains bias does not automatically render it useless. Postings on news-groups can, for example, be a useful source of information about public reactions to the effect of legislation.

If you were researching water quality in Scotland which site would be free from bias: Scottish Environment Protection Agency, Friends of the Earth Scotland, a site which produces bottled water, the Green Party site? The answer is none of the above, however the site of the Government regulator is the most authoritative.

CITATION OF ELECTRONIC RESOURCES

Where legal material is available in both electronic and paper formats you should cite the paper source. This means that if you have used a case, e.g. from *Westlaw*, or an article from *HeinOnline* you should not state that you have accessed via the particular database instead you should reference it in the same way as if you had looked at the paper version. See paras 13.27–13.57 for the appropriate details. **2–52**

You should never include databases such as *LexisNexis Butterworths* or *Westlaw* in your bibliography. This would be the equivalent of noting down your university law library which is also inappropriate.

When referring to URLs you should enclose them with < > symbols as this helps to differentiate them from other punctuation, e.g. < http://www.wgreen.co.uk/students >. This system has not been used in this book because of the requirement to conform to the publisher's house style.

The URL should be split at the end of a line only after the forward slashes in the address.

Hyphens or other punctuation should not be added. The case of the characters in the address should not be altered.

Cases obtained from electronic sources (e.g. Scottish Courts website) and not otherwise reported should use the neutral citation from its date of introduction. This was introduced into the supreme courts in Scotland from January 2005 (see para.3.25) and into the Privy Council, House of Lords, Court of Appeal and High Court in England from January 11, 2001 (see para.9.16). This means that judgments from these courts have been issued with unique judgment numbers and case references and are completely independent of published reports. The reason it was adopted was to make it easier to cite and trace unreported judgments.

Journals that are only published on the internet should be cited with the usual reference details for articles along with the URL for the website and details of the date accessed, e.g. R. Ong 'Regulating Spam in Hong Kong and Malaysia: Lessons from Other Jurisdictions' [2005] 1 JILT < http://www2.warwick.ac.uk/fac/soc/law/elj/jilt/2005_1/ong/ > accessed 29 May 2007.

Web pages should be cited as follows: author or institution, *title*, [type of document—if relevant], date of issue [if available], < URL > and date accessed.

!Examples

2–53 The Network of Heads of European Environment Protection Agencies *The Contribution of Good Environmental Regulation to Competitiveness* 2005 < http://org.eea.europa.eu/documents/prague_statement/prague_statement-en.pdf > accessed 6/01/06.

Department of the Environment, Transport and the Regions, *The Government's Response to the Environment, Transport and Regional Affairs Committee's Report,* October 2000 < http://www.odpm.gov.uk/index.asp?id = 1143711 > accessed 14/12/05.

SEPA 'Mock Trial for Pollution Regulator' Press Release, 10 February 2005 < http://www.sepa.org.uk/news/releases/view.asp?id = 184&y = 2005 > accessed 28/09/05

W Tinning 'Hotel smoking area has legal Lord fuming' *The Herald* (Glasgow 6 April 2007) < http://www.theherald.co.uk/news/news/display.var.1313196.0.0.php > accessed 6 April 2007.

CD Rom material

2–54 As with the internet, if the CD Rom is replicating an existing paper source (e.g. CD Rom version of the SLT) you should reference the paper source. Otherwise, you should include the following details: author/editor, 'title' publisher CD Rom, edition or date.

e.g. A. Smith 'A Load of Rubbish' Awful Publishing Ltd CD Rom Autumn 2006

Emails

2–55 Email communications should be cited in the following manner: author (type of statement and date).

!Example

Statement by Anne Smith (Personal email correspondence 10 May 2007).

Further resources

2–56 Internet for lawyers tutorial

http://www.vts.intute.ac.uk/he/tutorial/lawyers
This is a free tutorial which is an excellent introduction to using the internet for legal research.

Chapter 3
An Introduction to Cases

THE IMPORTANCE OF CASES AND THE DOCTRINE OF JUDICIAL PRECEDENT

You will come across cases throughout your study of law at university and beyond. It is essential **3–1** that you become familiar with the different series of law reports, the various ways of locating cases and the layout and content of a reported case. This chapter will cover law reporting, the principal series of law reports and the skills of reading and analysing cases. Chapter 4 will concentrate on aids to tracing cases and different search strategies that can be adopted. European Community cases are discussed in Chapter 10 and cases concerning international law are covered in Chapter 11.

Case law is important as it is one of the primary sources of Scots law, second only to legislation. The doctrine of judicial precedent allows judgments in previous cases to influence decisions in later cases. The strict version of this doctrine, *stare decisis*, means that: "A single decision from a qualifying court will bind all future courts dealing with the same point of law." (M.C. Meston *et al, The Scottish Legal Tradition* (new enl. edn, 1991), p.11.). Greater discussion of the doctrine of judicial precedent will be found in: *The Laws of Scotland: Stair Memorial Encyclopaedia*, Vol. 22, D.M. Walker, *The Scottish Legal System* 8th edn (Edinburgh: W. Green, 2001) pp.433–456 and R.M. White and I.D. Willock, *The Scottish Legal System* 3rd edn (Haywards Heath: Tottel, 2003) pp.279–313.

This definition encompasses two important concepts surrounding the earlier decision: (a) it has to be binding, that is from a qualifying court, and (b) it has to be "in point". This means that it concerns the same point of law. If both of these elements are in place the later court must follow the earlier decision. This is the theory but, in practice, there are techniques which the judiciary can employ to avoid following a binding precedent—see A.A. Paterson, T.St.J.N. Bates and M.R. Poustie, *The Legal System of Scotland* 4th edn (Edinburgh: W. Green, 1999), Ch.15, Pt. II.

The status of the court

Previous cases can be binding or persuasive on a current case. The status of the previous case **3–2** will depend on the position in the court hierarchy of the court which heard it. In general, decisions from a court higher in the hierarchy will bind a lower court. Courts can be bound in the following circumstances:

Civil Courts

Sheriff Court	**bound** by decisions of	Inner House, House of Lords and European Court of Justice/Court of First Instance*
	usually follows	decisions of own Sheriff Principal
	not bound by decisions of	other sheriffs, Sheriffs Principal or Lords Ordinary

Sheriff Principal	**bound** by decisions of	Inner House, House of Lords and European Court of Justice/Court of First Instance*
	not bound by decisions of	sheriffs, other Sheriffs Principal or Lords Ordinary
Lord Ordinary	**bound** by decisions of	Inner House, House of Lords and European Court of Justice/Court of First Instance*
	not bound by decisions of	sheriffs, Sheriffs Principal or other Lords Ordinary
Inner House	**bound** by decisions of	either of its Divisions, House of Lords and European Court of Justice/Court of First Instance*
	has power to overrule a previous Inner House decision by convening a larger court	
	not bound by decisions of	sheriffs, Sheriffs Principal or Lords Ordinary
House of Lords**	**bound by** decisions of	European Court of Justice/Court of First Instance*
	has power to overrule its own previous decision (Practice Statement [1966] 3 All E.R. 77, [1966] 1 W.L.R. 1234, HL)	

* Decisions concerning meaning or effect of any EC law/treaty (European Communities Act 1972, s.3).
** The Constitutional Reform Act 2005 makes provision for the creation of a new Supreme Court for the United Kingdom which will replace the House of Lords within the next few years.

Note that the decision of the Judicial Committee of the Privy Council on a "devolution issue" is binding in **all** legal proceedings (Scotland Act 1998, s.103).

3–3 The effect of the House of Lords decisions on Scots law:

> ➢ Decisions in Scottish appeals are binding.
> ➢ Decisions in non-Scottish cases on statutory provisions which are applicable in both jurisdictions are probably binding.
> ➢ Decisions in non-Scottish cases on areas of law which are different are not binding but can be persuasive if they concern matters of general jurisprudence.

This is discussed in greater depth in *The Laws of Scotland: Stair Memorial Encyclopaedia*, Vol. 22, paras 270–285.

3–4 *Criminal Courts*

| District Court is soon to become the Justice of the Peace Court* | **bound** by decisions of | "A magistrate sitting in the district court is probably bound by rulings of any superior criminal court or of a single judge or sheriff" D.M. Walker, *The Scottish Legal System* 8th edn (Edinburgh: W. Green, 2001) p.447 |

Sheriff Court	**bound** by decisions of	A single judge in the High Court of Justiciary (Trial) and High Court of Justiciary (Appeal)
	not bound by decisions of	sheriffs
High Court of Justiciary (Trial)	**bound by** decisions of	High Court of Justiciary (Appeal) Single
	not bound by decisions of	judges in the High Court of Justiciary (Trial)
High Court of Justiciary (Appeal)	has power to overrule	A previous High Court decision by convening a larger court
	not bound by decisions of	House of Lords

* Criminal Proceedings etc. (Reform) (Scotland) Act 2007.

Note that the decision of the Judicial Committee of the Privy Council on a "devolution issue" is binding in **all** legal proceedings (Scotland Act 1998, s.103).

Which parts of the previous decision are binding?

Not all of the previous case (precedent) is binding, only the part which deals with the reasoning **3–5** on the same point of law. This is referred to as the *ratio decidendi*. This is discussed in more detail in *The Laws of Scotland: Stair Memorial Encyclopaedia*, Vol. 22, paras 334–345. The *ratio decidendi* will be explored later in the chapter (para.3.31).

Importance of current status of a case

It is not only important to know the details of a case, it is also essential to be aware of the **3–6** current status of that case. The law changes all the time. The status of a case does not remain static. A decision may be appealed to a higher court, which may overturn the original decision. Even when a final decision is reached in a case it may be overruled by a later case and thereafter play no part as a precedent.

There are various things that can happen to a case during its lifetime. These are referred to in the following terms:

➢ Affirmed: The present court agrees with the decision of a lower court concerning the same case.

➢ Applied: The present court accepts that is bound by the ratio decidendi of a previous case and applies the same reasoning in the present case.

➢ Approved: The present court agrees that a decision made by a previous lower court was correctly decided.

➢ Considered/Discussed/Commented on: These all mean that the present court has discussed the earlier case.

➢ Distinguished: The present court decides that an apparently binding precedent is not in point. It has found material differences between the two cases. It, therefore, does not have to follow the previous case. However, the previous case still remains as authority for future cases which are in point.

➢ Overruled: The present court rejects a previous decision of a lower court. The earlier decision is struck out and can no longer be used as authority.

➢ Reversed: The present court disagrees with the decision of a lower court concerning the same case.

THE REPORTING OF CASES

Reported cases

3–7 A huge number of cases are heard by the courts every year but only a small number of cases are reported in law reports. Reporting in the law reports is very different to being reported in a newspaper. Cases are reported by newspapers to entertain/inform the newspaper's readership. Cases which are reported in the law reports are cases which carry some legal significance, i.e. cases which introduce a new principle into the law or which interpret a piece of legislation for the first time. Cases which are reported tend to be appellate decisions which in reality represent a tiny minority of cases litigated in court.

The editors of the various law reports decide which cases are reported and this can mean that the same case appears in several different series of law reports.

How do the editors decide which cases to report? They would all tend to answer that they report cases which are legally significant but what exactly does this mean? The criteria used by the editor of the SLT (supplied courtesy of W. Green) are as follows:

Cases which make new law, either because they deal with novel situations or extend the application of existing rules.
Cases where the judges restate old principles of law in modern terms or which are examples of modern applications of old principles.
Cases where the law is clarified by an appellate court when inferior courts have reached conflicting decisions; also non-appellate decisions discussing issues regularly litigated, e.g. subsistence of missives.
Cases which interpret legislation, unless the matter is peculiar to the parties involved.
Cases which interpret clauses in, for example, contracts and wills, which are likely to be of wider application.
Cases where the courts clarify points of practice or procedure.
Cases which, while turning on their facts, may be of guidance in comparable cases, e.g. decisions of quantum and certain instances of interim interdict.
Cases which turn purely on questions of fact, trite law, bad pleading or which generally contain nothing which has not already been laid down in reported cases are not reported.

Unreported cases

3–8 Unreported cases can be cited in court and the fact that a case has not been reported has no effect whatsoever on its weight as a precedent.

In the past it was very difficult to obtain transcripts of unreported cases. This has become much easier with the advent of courts publishing cases on their own websites and electronic databases which include selected unreported cases, e.g. *LexisNexis Butterworths* and *Westlaw*. Transcripts of unreported cases can also be obtained for research purposes by contacting the Operations and Policy Unit at the Scottish Court Service, Hayweight House, 23 Lauriston Street, Edinburgh EH3 9DQ, email: enquiries@scotcourts.gov.uk. The increased availability and use of unreported cases has resulted in a new citation system for cases see para.3.25.

A permanent record of proceedings is not automatically kept for all cases heard in court. In criminal cases no transcript is kept of summary trials. The same is true for small claims and summary cause cases in the sheriff court.

What is a law report?

A law report is not a verbatim account of the whole court proceedings. It is the judicial decision **3–9**
on a point of law. A law report is concerned with the legal issues and not the factual evidence. A
law report will not contain an account of the evidence, examination-in-chief, cross-examination
etc. The only facts to be included in a law report are those relevant to the legal reasoning in the
case.

How Cases are Published

The development of law reporting in Scotland

Early Scottish law reports were known as "Practicks". These date from the fifteenth century to **3–10**
the early seventeenth century. They are hardly recognisable as a law report as we understand
them today. They have been described as "embryo law reports" (*Stair Society, An Introductory
Survey of the Sources and Literature of Scots Law* (Edinburgh, 1936), p.27). They tended to be
notes compiled by judges for their own use. Publication was not envisaged. They were brief and
consisted of details of legal principle and the parties' names.

Examples of published collections of Practicks are:

> ➢ Balfour's Practicks (1469–1579).
> ➢ Spotiswoode's Practicks (1541–1637).
> ➢ Hope's Minor Practicks (1608–1633) and Hope's Major Practicks (1608–1633).

More details about the Practicks can be found in the Stair Society publication, *An Introductory
Survey of the Sources and Literature of Scots Law* (Edinburgh, 1936), Ch.3.

In the seventeenth century many different individuals published private collections of case
reports. Lists can be found in paras 3.17 and 3.18 below. Gradually law reporting became more
formalised. A large step forward occurred at the beginning of the nineteenth century with the
restructuring of the Court of Session. From 1821, cases from the Court of Session were reported
in the *Session Cases* and the modern system of law reporting was born.

Modern law reporting

Some introductory points: **3–11**

> ➢ Some cases appear in many different series of law reports. If this is the case, the most
> authoritative law report for that jurisdiction should be cited. In Scotland, the most
> authoritative series of law reports is the *Session Cases*, followed by the *Scots Law
> Times*.
> ➢ Some series of law reports are full text and others are digests/summaries, e.g. *Session
> Cases* is a full text series; *Green's Weekly Digest* contains short summaries of cases.
> ➢ Some series are general and others are specific to one area of law. The main series of
> law reports are general (they cover cases on every different subject) and law reports are
> published in chronological order. Specialist series publish according to subject matter,
> e.g. Environmental Law Reports. They will only include cases concerning environ-
> mental issues.
> ➢ Most series of law reports are bound in annual volumes. The current year's issues
> appear as slim paper booklets prior to being bound into annual volumes. They will
> usually be located beside the annual volumes in a law library.

> Many, but not all, series of law reports are now available electronically and can be found in several of the major electronic legal databases.

3–12 The principal modern series of law reports

Title	**Session Cases**
Abbreviation	S.C.
Citation	Since 1907 (apart from the addition of Privy Council decisions from 2001) the citation has been as follows.

Each annual volume consists of four parts which are paginated separately:

(a) Scottish cases decided by the Judicial Committee of the Privy Council referred to as S.C. (P.C.), e.g. *Robertson v Higson*, 2006 S.C. (P.C.) 22;

(b) Scottish cases decided by the House of Lords, referred to as S.C. (H.L.), e.g. *Davidson v Scottish Ministers*, 2006 S.C. (H.L.) 41;

(c) cases decided by the High Court of Justiciary, referred to as J.C., e.g. *Smart v HM Advocate*, 2006 J.C. 119;

(d) cases decided by the Court of Session, referred to as S.C., e.g. *Wright v Paton Farrell*, 2006 S.C. 404.

The series of *Session Cases* which appeared between 1821 and 1906 are referred to by the names of the five respective editors:

First Series	Shaw S.	16 vols. 1821–1838
Second Series	Dunlop D.	24 vols. 1838–1862
Third Series	MacPherson M.	11 vols. 1862–1873
Fourth Series	Rettie R.	25 vols. 1873–1898
Fifth Series	Fraser F.	8 vols. 1898–1906

These are cited by the volume number, the initial of the editor and the page number, e.g. *M'Calman v M'Arthur* (1864) 2 M. 678. This indicates that you will find the report in *Session Cases*, third series, Vol.2, edited by MacPherson, at p.678.

The series began by covering decisions in the Court of Session. The House of Lords (Scottish appeals) was covered from 1850 and was separately paginated, e.g. (year) 3 M. (H.L.) page no. The High Court of Justiciary was included from 1874 and was paginated separately, e.g. (year) 2 F. (J.) page no.

Period covered	1821 to present
Publisher and Editor	W. Green for The Scottish Council of Law Reporting, A.F. Stewart.
Comments	In Scotland the *Session Cases* series of law reports is the most authoritative.

The judgments are revised by the judge prior to publication.

Be wary of separate pagination.

Available in	📖 and 🖱 subscription (currently from 1930) via *Justis*, *LexisNexis Butterworths* and *Westlaw*.

Courts covered	Court of Session, High Court of Justiciary, Lands Valuation Appeal Court and all decisions on Scottish appeals to the House of Lords and the Judicial Committee of the Privy Council.
Format	These reports are arranged as follows:

• list of judges in the courts covered;

• index of case names—accessible by either party's name. These are arranged in four sections under the relevant court: Court of Session (includes Lands Valuation Appeal Court), Court of Justiciary, Judicial Committee of the Privy Council and House of Lords;

• case reports are arranged in separate sections and paginated separately. They appear as follows:

Judicial Committee of the Privy Council

House of Lords

Court of Justiciary

Lands Valuation Appeal Court

Court of Session

At the back of each volume is the following information:

• Index of Matters—a subject index. It includes "Words and Phrases" as a heading.

• Cases referred to judicially in that volume in alphabetical order of the first party.

• Cases affirmed, reversed, commented on, etc. in that volume, in alphabetical order of first party's names.

Updated	six times a year.
Consolidated indexes	No consolidated index but information from *Session Cases* is included in the Faculty Digest. See para.4.29.
Title	**Scots Law Times**
Abbreviation	S.L.T.
Citation	
Full report from superior court	*Standard Commercial Property Securities Ltd v Glasgow City Council*, 2006 S.L.T. 1152
Notes of a report	*F. MacGregor v MacNeill*, 1975 S.L.T. (Notes) 54
Sheriff Court report	*Gardner v Edinburgh City Council* 2006 S.L.T. (Sh Ct) 166
Land Court report	*Crofters Commission v Mackay*, 1997 S.L.T. (Land Ct) 2
Lands Tribunal of Scotland report	*Tennant v East Kilbride District Council*, 1997 S.L.T. (Lands Tr) 14
Lyon Court report	*Douglas-Hamilton, Petitioner*, 1996 S.L.T. (Lyon Ct) 8
Previous citation convention between 1893–1908	Citation was by volume, e.g. *Thomson v Landale*, (1897) 5 S.L.T. 204
Period covered	1893 to present
Publisher and Editor	W. Green, J. Barclay, H.B. Loy.

Comments	Be wary of the separate pagination.
	Not just law reports but also contains articles and professional information.
	Historically published with less time delay than *Session Cases*. Recently the difference has been greatly reduced.
Available in	📖 updated weekly and 💻 via *Westlaw* from 1893 (updated weekly) and CD Rom from 1893 (updated monthly).
Courts covered	Privy Council, House of Lords, Court of Session, High Court of Justiciary, sheriff courts, Scottish Land Court, Lands Valuation Appeal Court, Lands Tribunal for Scotland and Court of the Lord Lyon.
Format	The annual volumes consist of the following information:
	• List of judges in the Court of Session.
	• The law reports are arranged in sections relating to the court which heard the case. The sections are separately paginated and contain separate indexes of cases, case reports and indexes of cases according to subject matter. The sections are:
	Superior courts, sheriff courts, Scottish Land Court, Lands Tribunal for Scotland, Lyon Court.
	• News section. This includes:
	Articles, Acts of Adjournal/Sederunt, appointments, book reviews, business changes, case commentaries, coming events, general information, letters to the editor, parliamentary news, obituaries/appreciations, subject index and taxation.
	Since 1989 two annual volumes have been produced.
	Volume one contains:
	List of judges in Court of Session
	Superior court cases and indexes
	Volume two contains:
	Index of all cases in the two volumes in one index, but organised in separate sections
	News section
	Cases and indexes for cases in sheriff court, Scottish Land Court, the Lands Tribunal of Scotland and the Lyon Court
Details of updates	Published weekly. Cumulative indexes are published after every ten issues.
Consolidated indexes	1961–90 and 1991–2002 cover cases reported in the SLT during these years.
Title	**Scottish Civil Law Reports**
Abbreviation	S.C.L.R.
Citation	e.g. *Taylor v Scottish Ministers* (OH) 2005 S.C.L.R. 577
	Johnstone v Finneran (Sh Ct) 2003 S.C.L.R. 157 (Notes)
Period covered	1987 to present
Publisher and Editor	The Law Society of Scotland, Sheriff M.J. Fletcher.

Comments	Commentaries are included for selected cases.
Available in	📖 and ⏚ via *LexisNexis Butterworths*
Courts covered	Privy Council, House of Lords, Court of Session, sheriff court.
Format	Annual volumes contain the following information:

• Index of cases reported by name—accessible by both parties' name.

• Digest of cases—arranged by subject matter. "Words" is included as a heading.

• Statutes, Statutory Instruments and Court Rules judicially considered.

• Cases judicially considered.

• Case reports. The cases are arranged in two sections: full reports and notes which are paginated as one. Some of the cases are accompanied by commentaries by experts in the area of law concerned.

Updated	Paper and online six times a year.
Consolidated indexes	Index 1987–1996. This consolidates the information contained in the first four tables above for the period.
Title	**Scottish Criminal Case Reports**
Abbreviation	S.C.C.R.
Citation	e.g. *Bennett v HM Advocate*, 2006 S.C.C.R. 62
Period covered	1981 to present
Publisher and Editor	The Law Society of Scotland, Sheriff G.H. Gordon, Q.C.
Comments	Commentaries are by the editor
Available in	📖 and ⏚ via *LexisNexis Butterworths*
Courts covered	Privy Council, High Court of Justiciary, sheriff court
Format	The annual volumes contain the following information:

• List of judges in the High Court of Justiciary

• Index of reported cases—accessible by both parties' names

• Digest of cases according to the subject matter which includes "Words" as a heading

• Statutes and Statutory Instruments judicially considered

• Cases judicially considered

• Case reports. Selected cases are followed by commentaries.

Updated	Paper and online six times a year.
Consolidated indexes	Indexes covering 1981–1990 and 1991–2000 contain the following tables relating to the period covered:

Cases reported

Digest of cases

Statutes and Statutory Instruments judicially considered

Cases judicially considered

The Indexes include cases reported in Justiciary Cases, S.L.T. and the 1981–1990 index includes cases reported in the S.C.C.R. Supplement 1950–80.

The Scottish Criminal Case Reports Supplement (1950–1980). This addition to the series contains a selection of cases decided by the High Court between 1950–80 which had not been previously reported.

It contains the following information:

- Index of cases reported—accessible by both parties' names
- Digest of cases according to subject matter
- Statutes and Statutory Instruments judicially considered between 1950–80
- Cases judicially considered between 1950–80
- Case reports

Title	**Green's Weekly Digest**
Abbreviation	G.W.D.
Citation	Within G.W.D. the cases are referred to by issue number and paragraph number, e.g. 1990 *Fry's Metals v Durastic* G.W.D. 5–272
	This case will be found in the 1990 folder in issue 5 at para.272.
Period covered	1986 to present
Publisher and Editor	W. Green, J. Barclay, H.B. Loy
Comments	It reports all decisions of the Scottish courts received by W. Green. Reports of significance are subsequently reported more fully elsewhere.
	Arranged by subject
Available in	📖 and email
Courts covered	Privy Council, House of Lords, Court of Session, High Court of Justiciary, sheriff court, Scottish Land Court.
Format	Annual Service Files contain:

- Index of cases digested (alphabetical by first party's name)
- Index of subject matter
- Table of statutes considered
- Table of quantum of damages
- Case digests

Updated	40 times a year. Cumulative indexes are published three times a year.
Consolidated indexes	Index 1986–1995—consolidates all four indexes for that period.

3–13 Specialist series of Scottish law reports

Title	**Greens Reparation Law Reports**
Abbreviation	RepLR
Citation	*Forbes v City of Dundee District Council*, 1997 RepLR 48
Period covered	1996 to present
Publisher and Editor	W. Green, D. Kinloch
Comments	Includes commentaries
Available in	📖
Courts covered	House of Lords, Court of Session, sheriff court

Format	Editorial and case reports with a separate quantum cases section. Some cases are in note form.
Updated	six times a year.
Consolidated indexes	Annual consolidated index containing an alphabetical list of first named parties and an index of subject matter.
Title	**Greens Housing Law Reports**
Abbreviation	HousLR
Citation	*Johnston v Dundee City Council*, 2006 HousLR 68
Period covered	1996 to present
Publisher and Editor	W. Green, M. Dailly
Comments	Includes commentaries on the cases.
Available in	📖
Courts covered	House of Lords, Court of Session, sheriff court, Lands Tribunal for Scotland, Decisions of Local Government Ombudsmen, Housing Association Ombudsmen.
Format	Editorial
	Case reports
Update	four issues a year.
Consolidated indexes	Annual consolidated index containing an alphabetical list of first named parties and an index of subject matter
Title	**Greens Family Law Reports**
Abbreviation	FamLR
Citation	*Treasure v McGrath*, 2006 FamLR 100
Period covered	1997 to present
Publisher and Editor	W. Green, R.P. Macfarlane and J.M.L. Scott
Comments	Commentaries are provided
Available in	📖
Courts covered	European Court of Human Rights, House of Lords, Court of Session, sheriff court
Format	Editorial
	Subject index
	Case reports
Update	six issues a year.
Consolidated indexes	Annual consolidated index with an alphabetical list of first named parties and an index of subject matter.
Title	**Scottish Land Court Reports**
Abbreviation	SLCR
Citation	e.g. *Cawdor Trustees v Mackay*, 2005 SLCR 76
Period covered	1913 to present

Available in	📖 and ✐ free digests of cases since 1982 are available online (*http://www.scottish-land-court.org.uk/digest.html*) as are recent unreported decisions (*http://www.scottish-land-court.org.uk/recent.html*)
Courts covered	Scottish Land Court
Format	Index of cases (alphabetical order of first party)
	Case reports
	Digest of cases via subject headings
Title	**Scottish Planning Appeal Decisions**
Abbreviation	SPADS
Period covered	1985 to present
Publisher	IDOX in association with the Scottish Office Enquiry Reporters Unit
Coverage	Planning appeal decisions by the Secretary of State
Updates	Monthly

Reporting of Scottish cases in England

3–14 Some Scottish cases appear in the following English series of law reports:

> ➢ Appeal Cases
> ➢ Weekly Law Reports
> ➢ All England Law Reports

The English law reports are covered in Chapter 9.

Specialist series of law reports covering the UK

3–15 There is an increasing range and number of specialist series of law reports. Examples include: British Company Cases (B.C.C.), Environmental Law Reports (Env.L.R.), Family Law Reports (F.L.R.), Industrial Cases Reports (I.C.R.), Industrial Relations Law Reports (I.R.L.R.), Medical Law Reports (Med.L.R.) and Reports of Tax Cases (T.C.).

3–16 **Older series of Scottish Law Reports**

Title	**The Scottish Law Reporter** 📖
Abbreviation	S.L.R. or Sc. L.R.
Period covered	1865–1924 (vols 1–61)
Courts covered	House of Lords, Court of Session, Court of Justiciary, Court of Teinds
Format	Index of cases (either party's surname)
	Index of statutes
	Index of subjects
	Case reports
	(all paginated together)
Title	**Sheriff Court Reports** (Sh. Ct. Rep.) (usually to be found bound as Scottish Law Review and Sheriff Court Reporter) 📖
Abbreviation	S.L.R. or S.L.Rev. or Sc.L.R.
Period covered	1885–1963 (vols 1–79)
Courts covered	Sheriff Court

Format
First part contains collections of the Scottish Law Review. These contain articles and professional news/information.

Second part (all in the one volume) is Sheriff Court Reports:

Contents

Index of cases (either party)

Digest of cases accessible via subject headings

Scottish Land Court Reports

Index of cases

Case reports

Digest of cases accessible via subject headings

Title	**Scottish Jurist** 📖
Abbreviation	S.J. or Sc. Jur.
Period covered	1829–1873
Courts covered	House of Lords, Court of Session, Court of Justiciary, Court of Teinds
Format	Index of Matters (subject index)

Index of case names

Court of Session (pursuer and defender)

Court of Session (defender and pursuer)

House of Lords

High Court of Justiciary

English decisions generally applicable to Scots law

Scottish cases

Title	**Morison's Dictionary of Decisions** 📖
Abbreviation	M. or Mor.
Period covered	1540–1808
Format	This collection of cases consists of 22 volumes. There are 19 volumes of cases. Volumes 20 and 21 contain a digest of cases from the main volumes. Volume 22 contains supplementary material. There is an Appendix which includes cases which were reported while the Dictionary was being published.

The work is paginated continuously throughout all the volumes. It is not referred to by volume number but by year and page number, e.g. *Johnston v Napier* (1708) M. 16511.

Other works are frequently kept with *Morison's Dictionary*:

Morison's Synopsis (1808–1816)

Tait's Index. This contains an index of the cases in *Morison's Dictionary* in alphabetical order of pursuer.

Brown's Supplement (1628–1794) (B.S.). This covers cases which were not included in *Morison's Dictionary*.

Old reports which covered House of Lords decisions in Scottish appeals   **3–17**

Brown's Synopsis of Decisions (1540–1827)
Robertson (1707–27)
Craigie, Stewart and Paton (1726–1821)

Dow (1813–1818)
Bligh (1819–1821)
Shaw (1821–1824)
Wilson & Shaw (1825–1835)
Shaw & Maclean (1835–1838)
Maclean & Robinson (1839)
Robinson (1840–41)
Bell (1842–1850)
MacQueen (1851–1865)
Paterson (1851–73)

From 1850 Scottish appeals to the House of Lords were reported in *Session Cases*, see para.3.12 above.

3–18 Old reports which covered Court of Session decisions

Morison's Dictionary of Decisions (1540–1808)
Brown's Synopsis of Decisions (1540–1827)
Durie (1621–1642)
Brown's Supplement (1622–1794)
English Judges (1655–1661)
Stair (1661–1681)
Gilmour and Falconer (1665–1677)
Dirleton (1665–1677)
Fountainhall (1678–1712)
Harcarse (1681–1691)
Dalrymple (1698–1718)
Forbes (1705–1713)
Bruce (1714–1715)
Kames (Remarkable Decisions) (1716–1752)
Edgar (1724–1725)
Elchies (1733–1754)
Clerk Home (1735–1744)
Kilkerran (1738–1752)
Falconer (1744–1751)
Kames (Select Decisions) (1752–1768)
Hailes (1766–1791)
Bell (1790–1792)
Bell (1794–1795)
Hume (1781–1822)
Deas and Anderson (1829–1833)
Scottish Jurist (1829–1873) see para.3.16 above
Scottish Law Reporter (1865–1924) see para.3.16 above
Faculty Collection/Faculty Decisions (Old Series) (1752–1808)
Faculty Collection/Faculty Decisions (New Series) (1808–1825)
Faculty Collection/Faculty Decisions (Octavo Series) (1825–1841)
Bell's Dictionary of Decisions (1808–1832)

From 1821 Court of Session cases were reported in *Session Cases*, see para.3.12 above.

Old reports which covered High Court of Justiciary decisions **3–19**

Shaw (1819–1831)
Syme (1826–1830)
Swinton (1835–1841)
Broun (1842–1845)
Arkley (1846–1848)
Shaw (1848–1851)
Irvine (1851–1868)
Couper (1868–1885)
White (1885–1893)
Adam (1893–1916)

From 1874 decisions of the High Court of Justiciary were reported in *Session Cases*, see para.3.12 above.

Old reports covering decisions of other courts **3–20**

Fergusson (1811–1817) — Consistorial Court
Murray (1815–1830) — Jury Court
McFarlane (1838–1839) — Jury Court
Shaw (1821–1831) — Teind Court

Old reports of Sheriff Court decisions **3–21**

Guthrie's Select Sheriff Court Decisions (1854–1892)
Scottish Law Review (1885–1963), see para.3.16 above.

Sheriff court decisions have been reported in *Scots Law Times* since 1893. More detailed information on old sheriff court records can be found in the Stair Society publication, *An Introductory Survey of the Sources and Literature of Scots Law* (Edinburgh, 1936) Ch.10.

Many of the old collections of reports were reprinted at the beginning of this century in a series called *Scots Revised Reports*, which contains selected cases from *Morison's Dictionary*, part of the Faculty Collection/Faculty Decisions, House of Lords Appeals, Shaw, Dunlop, Macpherson and cases reported only in the Scottish Jurist between 1829–65.

More detailed information on the old series of law reports can be found in *Stair Society, An Introductory Survey of the Sources and Literature of Scots Law* (1936), Ch.4.

Citation conventions

In order to find cases in the various law reports it is necessary to become familiar with the **3–22** referencing system for cases. The reference for a case is called its "citation". The citation of a case is made up of five elements:

> ➢ Name of the case—this will usually be the names of the parties involved.
> ➢ Year in which the decision was reported.
> ➢ Volume number of the relevant report, if applicable.
> ➢ Abbreviation for the name of the law report—a table of abbreviations appears at the start of the book.
> ➢ Page number of the volume at which the case report begins.

In order to trace a case, follow the citation, e.g.

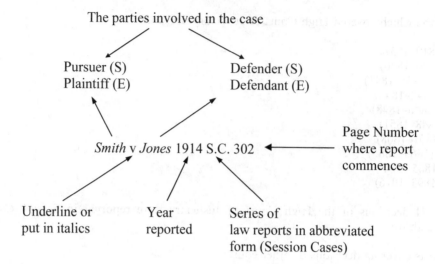

Diagram 3.1: Case Citation

The parties are usually referred to by the pursuer's name followed by defender's name. If the case is appealed the order is reversed.

Note: if a case is published in a printed format and also available electronically, you should reference the printed source for the case.

Criminal cases

3–23   In cases where solemn procedure is used, the Crown is referred to as Her Majesty's Advocate (HM Advocate). If the case is prosecuted under summary procedure, the surname of the Procurator Fiscal is used to represent the Crown.

In certain cases where anonymity is to be preserved the parties are referred to by initials, e.g. *A v B*.

In England, criminal cases are cited, e.g. *R v Smith*. The R stands for Rex or Regina depending on whether there is a king or queen on the throne at the time.

Others

3–24   In shipping cases the name of the ship involved is often used.

Since 2001 law reports published by Sweet & Maxwell (e.g. Criminal Appeal Reports, etc.) have used a case number as opposed to a page number as their citation, e.g. *Dyson Ltd v Registrar of Trade Marks* [2007] 2 C.M.L.R. 14 refers to case number 14 of the second volume of the 2007 Common Market Law Reports.

Media neutral citations

3–25   A system of media neutral citation was introduced into some Scottish courts from January 1, 2005. This means that opinions from the Court of Session, High Court of Justiciary and High Court of Justiciary sitting as an appeal court have been issued with unique judgment numbers. This system means that case references are completely independent of published reports. The reason it has been adopted is to make it easier to cite and trace unreported judgments.

Opinions are numbered as follows:

Court of Session, Outer House: [2005] CSOH 1 (2, 3, etc.), e.g. *McCall v Scottish Ministers* [2005] CSOH 163
Court of Session, Inner House: [2005] CSIH 1 (2, 3, etc.), e.g. *Sutherland v Advocate General* [2006] CSIH 38
High Court of Justiciary: [2005] HCJ 1 (2, 3, etc.), e.g. *HM Advocate v Voudouri* [2006] HCJ 4
High Court of Justiciary sitting as an appeal court: [2005] HCJAC 1 (2, 3, etc.), e.g. *Early v HM Advocate* [2006] HCJAC 65

Also with effect from January 1, 2005, all opinions were issued with paragraph numbering but no page numbers. Any particular paragraph of the case to be referred to is cited in square brackets at the end of the neutral citation, e.g. *Red v Blue* [2005] HCJ 1 [12]. This means that the reference is to para.12 of *Red v Blue* which was the first opinion of the High Court of Justiciary issued in 2005. Media neutral citations were introduced into the judgments of the House of Lords and the Judicial Committee of the Privy Council from 2001:

House of Lords [2001] UKHL 6, e.g. *Davidson v Scottish Ministers* [2005] UKHL 74
Privy Council (for devolution cases) [2001] UKPC D3, e.g. *Robertson v Higson* [2006] UKPC D2

Media neutral citations for English courts are discussed in para.9.16.

Unreported cases with no neutral citation are cited as follows: party names (court and the date of judgement in brackets).

Use of brackets in Scottish case reports

The convention is that where the date is an essential part of the reference to the volume, the year **3–26** is not put in brackets. If the date is not essential, it is put in round brackets or it may not be given at all.

The five series of *Session Cases* between 1821 and 1906 are referred to by citing the first letter of the surname of the editor or chief reporter, e.g. *Goldston v Young* (1868) 7 M.188. This indicates that it was the 7th year of Macpherson's editorship.

After 1906 the year was essential in citations and brackets are not used, e.g. *Errol v Walker*, 1966 S.C. 93.

The earliest volumes of *Scots Law Times* (1893–1908) are cited by volume number using brackets, e.g. *Peden v Graham* (1907) 15 S.L.T. 143.

After 1908, the year alone is used and is therefore essential. No brackets are used, e.g. *Dunfermline D.C. v Blyth & Blyth Associates* 1985 S.L.T. 345.

In summary, no brackets are used by the modern Scottish law reports. Prior to the introduction of neutral citation square brackets were never used in Scottish case citations. Now they are only used in neutral citations. In contrast square brackets are used by most modern English law reports, e.g. The Law Reports, the All England Law Reports and the Weekly Law Reports.

3–27 *Summary—using the citation details to locate the report of the case*

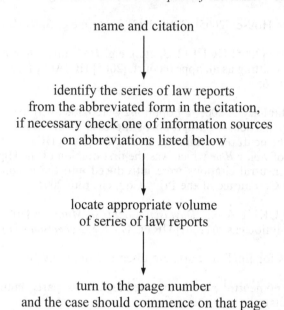

name and citation

identify the series of law reports
from the abbreviated form in the citation,
if necessary check one of information sources
on abbreviations listed below

locate appropriate volume
of series of law reports

turn to the page number
and the case should commence on that page

Diagram 3.2: Using Citation Details to Locate a Case Report

N.B.: Take extra care when consulting law reports which have separate paginations.

Abbreviations—how to find their meaning

3–28 The list of law reports in para.3.12 has included the appropriate abbreviated forms. If you come across an unfamiliar abbreviation, the best source for identifying it is the *Cardiff Index to Legal Abbreviations* (*http://www.legalabbrevs.cardiff.ac.uk*). This web-based service is an excellent resource and can be searched either from abbreviation to title or from title to abbreviation. It contains abbreviations from over 295 jurisdictions.

3–29 The following are also ways of finding the meaning of abbreviated forms of case reports:

> ➢ D. Raistrick, *Index to Legal Citations and Abbreviations* 2nd edn (London: Bowker-Saur, 1993). 📖
> ➢ *The Laws of Scotland: Stair Memorial Encyclopaedia*. There is a table of abbreviations at the beginning of each volume in the series. 📖 and ⌁ subscription.
> ➢ *Current Law*–Monthly Digest, Yearbook and Case Citators all have lists of abbreviations. 📖
> ➢ *Lawtel* provides a list of abbreviations in its case law section. ⌁ subscription.
> ➢ *Osborn's Concise Law Dictionary* 10th edn, (London: Sweet & Maxwell, 2005). 📖

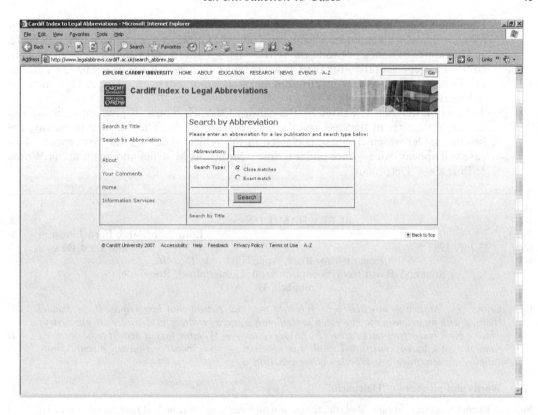

Diagram 3.3: Cardiff Index to Legal Abbreviations

READING CASES

Anatomy of a case

Reading cases is a skill that you will develop through practice. The anatomy of a case has been **3–30** included to introduce you to the layout of cases. Do not expect to fully understand the first case that you read. It will take time to get used to the format and language used by the judiciary.

The case below appeared in the *Session Cases*. Case reports in other series of law reports will be similar but not identical. Different features of the law report are marked with numbers which correspond to the following list:

[1] The names of the parties.

[2] The date when the case was heard in court. The opinion of the court is usually delivered some time after the actual hearing. There is then a further lapse of time before the case will appear in the law reports. In this instance, the case was heard in July 1997 and appeared in the first issue of *Session Cases* for 1998.

[3] The judges who heard the case.

[4] In criminal cases the first named party is usually the Crown and the accused (the pannel) would be the second party. However, here the pannel has appealed the original decision and he has become the first named party; he is referred to as the "appellant". The Crown is referred to as the "respondent".

This case has been initiated under summary procedure and the Crown is therefore referred to as the surname of the Procurator Fiscal in whose area the case is being taken.

Here the Crown appears as Robert T. Hamilton who is the Procurator Fiscal in Dunfermline. In cases taken under solemn procedure the Crown is referred to as HM Advocate.

The names in italics opposite the parties' names are those of their representatives in court. The representative for the Crown is referred to as "QC, A-D". The Q.C. stands for Queen's Counsel and means that he is a senior advocate. The A-D stands for Advocate Depute.

[5] The section in italics is written by the editor of the law report. It gives an indication of the subject matter of the case and the legal issue involved. The first words indicate the heading under which this case is classed in the subject index for the law reports. This case will appear twice—once under Crime—Malicious Mischief and again under Words & Phrases—"Detriment".

JC   1
[1]   BETT v HAMILTON   A
No 1   Lord Sutherland, Lord Johnston
[2]   23 July 1997   and Lord Dawson   **[3]**
[4]   ROBERT JOHN BETT, Appellant — *M E Scott*
                  ROBERT T HAMILTON (Procurator fiscal, Dunfermline), Respondent —
                                      Campbell, QC, A-D

[5]   *Crime — Malicious mischief — Whether material patrimonial loss required — Pannel charged with maliciously moving video surveillance camera resulting in detriment to the benefit which a bank had attempted to secure by having camera — Whether loss of benefit to be obtained*   B
from use of camera constituted malicious mischief — Whether "detriment" meant simply "implied disadvantage" — Whether crime constituted

Words and phrases — "Detriment"   C

[6]   A pannel was charged on a libel, the terms of which narrated that he had maliciously moved a video surveillance camera with a pole or similar instrument so as to point the camera in such a direction that it did not show or record activity in an area which it had been set to cover, whereby the running costs associated with the camera were wasted and the building was exposed to increased risk of housebreaking, theft and vandalism. The pannel tabled a plea to the relevancy of the charge in that it did not set forth a competent charge of malicious   D
mischief. The sheriff held that the acts of the pannel had resulted in detriment to the benefit which the bank had attempted to secure by having a surveillance camera. He considered that the bank suffered a financial loss in that the running costs of the camera were incurred without   E
any benefit and also the bank was exposed to the unnecessary risk of vandalism or housebreaking being committed at its premises. The pannel appealed.
Held (1) that what was required for a charge of malicious mischief was that there should be a wilful intent to cause injury to the owner or possessor of the property, which injury might be either in the form of physical damage or in the form of patrimonial loss; (2) that the running costs of the camera would have been incurred in any event even if it had been pointing in the   F
right direction, so that what had been lost to the bank was such benefit as they might have obtained from the fact that the camera was pointing in the correct direction and possibly deterring vandals or thieves; and (3) that to describe such loss of benefit as patrimonial loss extended the latter concept too far and was altogether too speculative; and appeal allowed.

[7]   ROBERT JOHN BETT was charged in the sheriffdom of Tayside Central and Fife at Dunfermline at the instance of Robert T Hamilton, procurator fiscal there, with a contravention of the Criminal Law (Consolidation) (Scotland) Act 1995, sec 52(1) and a charge of malicious mischief. The pannel tabled a plea to the relevancy in respect of the charge of malicious   G
mischief. After hearing parties, the sheriff made certain deletions to the charge and held that the charge set forth a relevant charge of malicious mischief. The terms of the charge are as set forth in the opinion of the court.

The pannel appealed to the High Court of Justiciary.

[8]   *Cases referred to*:
Advocate (HM) v Wilson 1983 SCCR 420
Monro (George), July 17, 1831 (unreported)   H

Textbook referred to:
Alison, *Criminal Law*, ii, 451

[9]   The cause called before the High Court of Justiciary, comprising Lord Sutherland, Lord
Johnston and Lord Dawson for a hearing on 23 July 1997. *Eo die* the opinion of the court was   I
delivered by Lord Sutherland.

2   BETT v HAMILTON   1997

[10]   OPINION OF THE COURT — The appellant was charged on summary complaint with a con-   A
travention of the Criminal Law (Consolidation) (Scotland) Act 1995, sec 52(1), the relevancy
of which is not challenged, and a further charge purporting to set out an offence of malicious
mischief. The appellant tabled a plea to the relevancy of the second charge. The sheriff made
certain deletions to the charge (which the Crown did not argue before this court should be
restored) and thereafter held that the remainder constituted a relevant offence of malicious
mischief. The terms of the charge, as they now remain, are as follows: "The Royal Bank of
Scotland, having at their own expense, placed and operated a surveillance camera so as to
show and record activity at the front of the building occupied by them in East Port, Dun-   B
fermline, for the purpose of enhancing the security of said building by deterring persons from
acts of housebreaking, theft and vandalism at said building and making it possible to identify
those who carry out such acts, you did on 7 December 1996 in said East Port, Dunfermline,
maliciously move said camera with a pole or similar instrument so as to point said camera in
such a direction that it did not show or record activity in the area which it had been set to
cover whereby the running costs associated with said camera were wasted and said building
was exposed to increased risk of housebreaking, theft and vandalism." The view taken by the
sheriff was that the acts of the appellant resulted in detriment to the benefit which the bank   C
had attempted to secure by having a surveillance camera. He considered that the bank suffered
a financial loss in that the running costs of the camera were incurred without any benefit and
also the bank was exposed to the unnecessary risk of vandalism or housebreaking being
committed at its premises.
    Counsel for the appellant before this court submitted that actual injury or harm, damage or   D
patrimonial loss had to occur before mischief could be established. Neither wasted running
costs nor the increased risk of housebreaking or theft or vandalism could constitute mischief.
In *HM Advocate v Wilson* it was held that physical injury or damage was not necessary
provided that there was an element of patrimonial loss. The accused in that case had activated
an emergency stop button wilfully, recklessly and maliciously and brought a power station
generator to a halt, causing a loss of production of electricity which had to be replaced at a
cost of £147,000. Lord Justice-Clerk Wheatley, having set out Hume's definition of malicious
mischief, said that the basic constituents involved in the crime of malicious mischief were that   E
it had to be a deliberate and malicious act to damage another's property or to interfere with it
to the detriment of the owner or lawful possessor. He went on to say: "It is clear from the
words used in the libel that the Crown seek to establish that the act of the respondent founded
upon was deliberate and malicious. The Crown further seek to prove that this act resulted in a
generating turbine being brought to a halt for an extended period of time with a consequential
loss of generated electricity. In terms of Hume's second ground *supra* this would be an
interference with the employer's property and the wording of the libel is such as to be habile to
carry the inference that the initial positive wilful, reckless and malicious act was intended to   F
harm the employer by causing patrimonial injury ... To interfere deliberately with the plant so
as to sterilise its functioning with resultant financial loss such as is libelled here is in my view a
clear case of interference with another's property which falls within Hume's classification of
malicious mischief, and consists with the words in the phrase." Counsel therefore accepted
that it is not necessary to prove physical damage but argued that there must at least be some
material patrimonial loss before the crime of malicious mischief can be established. In the

present case, as far as the running costs of the camera were concerned, these costs would have   **G**
been expended anyway and there was no additional cost. What was lost, if anything, was the
benefit to be obtained from the use of the camera. The same argument applied to the other
part of the complaint which narrated that the bank lost the benefit of the security of the
surveillance camera. That was not something which constituted patrimonial loss. It is clear   **H**
from what the Lord Justice-Clerk said in *Wilson* that when he used the word detriment he was
referring to patrimonial loss. The only other case involving detriment to an owner which was
held to constitute malicious mischief, apart from *Wilson*, was an unreported case referred to in
Alison, *Criminal Law*, ii, 451 (*George Monro*, July 17, 1831) where an accused was convicted of
opening a barrel, thus allowing the contents to escape, causing loss to the owner of the
contents. Accordingly it was submitted that loss of benefit was not the same as patrimonial
loss and was insufficient to warrant the charge of malicious mischief.   **I**

JC   BETT v HAMILTON   3

In reply the Advocate-depute founded on the words of Lord Justice-Clerk Wheatley that to   **A**
interfere with the property of another to the detriment of the owner would be sufficient. The
word "detriment" in his submission simply implied disadvantage. The bank in the present case   **B**
had installed this camera for a particular purpose and incurred costs in the running of that
security device. If the purpose was destroyed or interfered with then the running costs were
wasted and thus became a patrimonial loss. He submitted that where outlay is incurred to   **C**
maintain a benefit, if the benefit is destroyed then the continuing costs constitute patrimonial
loss. Furthermore loss of protection from vandalism or theft is a serious matter. The camera
was installed to protect the bank against the risk of serious crime and this risk could be
quantified in financial terms. For these reasons he submitted that there was an ascertainable
patrimonial loss in this case and that accordingly the charge was relevant.   **D**

   In our opinion the Crown have not averred sufficient in this case to constitute a relevant
charge of malicious mischief. What is required in such a charge is that there should be a wilful
intent to cause injury to the owner or possessor of the property. This injury may be either in   **E**
the form of physical damage or in the form of patrimonial loss. We do not consider that the
matters referred to by the Advocate-depute properly constitute patrimonial loss. The running
costs of the camera would have been incurred in any event, even if it had been pointing in the
right direction, and accordingly what has been lost to the bank is such benefit as they might   **F**
have obtained from the fact that the camera was pointing in the correct direction and possibly
deterring vandals or thieves. The same can be said of the loss of security which they might   **G**
have sustained through the absence of this camera performing its proper function. In our
opinion to describe such loss of benefit as patrimonial loss extends the latter concept too far
and is altogether too speculative. The bank on these averments suffered no financial loss
whatsoever and therefore there is no patrimonial loss. We shall therefore allow the appeal and
sustain the appellant's plea to the relevancy of the second charge on the complaint.   **H**

[11]   The Court allowed the appeal.

[12]   *More & Co — The Crown Agent*   **I**

[6] This is the headnote or rubric. It is a summary of the case and is not part of the law
     report proper. The temptation to read only the headnote of a case should be resisted. It
     should not be relied upon as accurate. It is written by the editor of the law reports and
     not the judge. Another reason not to rely solely on the headnote is that the significance
     and interpretation of a case can change over a period of time. The headnote remains
     frozen at one point in time and is not altered.
     The headnote will give a summary of:

     (a) Material facts
     (b) Legal issues involved
     (c) Decisions of the court

[7] This section outlines the judicial history of the case.

[8] The entries in italics are the authorities referred to in the case. Here, there is a list of cases and a book. You will see that the cases include an unreported case. The fact that a case is not reported has no effect on its status as a precedent. Alison is one of the Institutional Writers (see para.8.1). In the past only books by authors who were dead would be referred to in court. This convention has been relaxed in recent years and modern authorities do now appear.

[9] This section gives details of the court, the judges and the date of the hearing. In Scotland presenting the judgment of the court is referred to as delivering the opinion of the court.

[10] The opinion of the court is the most important part of the case. In this case there is only one opinion/judgment. Cases can have just one judgment or can have multiple judgments. This makes it more difficult to understand the reasoning as they may reach the same decision but adopt different reasoning. A case can have no ratio decidendi as a result. In recent years the courts have tended to provide one judgment, with the other judges stating that they have read it and agree with it. However, if they wish, judges can still present their own reasoning. If they dissent with the majority view, their full judgment will appear.

There is no one style that judges use to write a judgment. Judgments tend to be individualistic. They are sometimes clear and easy to understand but sometimes they are the complete opposite. Gradually judgments are becoming more reader-friendly with headings being used for ease of reference.

The capital letters which appear down the side of the page allow a precise reference to be given to part of the opinion, e.g. Lord Sutherland starts to discuss the case presented for the appellant at 1998 J.C. 2 D.

[11] The outcome of the case.

[12] The agents acting in the case. Here More & Co. is the firm of solicitors representing the pannel. The Crown Agent is the term used for those acting on behalf of the Crown.

Analysis of cases

In the real world, of course, the outcome is the most important part of a case, but to those studying law it is almost irrelevant. The major point of interest is the reasoning which the court adopted in order to reach its conclusion. This is referred to as the *ratio decidendi*. **3–31**

There is no agreed definition of the *ratio decidendi* and little clear guidance exists on how to identify it. Lawyers will often disagree about the content of a particular *ratio decidendi*. The situation is further complicated by the fact that some cases may have no *ratio decidendi* at all, while others may have more than one. The *ratio decidendi* of a case does not always remain the same. Later cases can re-interpret it and it is possible for a rule which emerged from the original case to be expanded or contracted over a period of time.

Traditional texts tend to be unhelpful with comments such as "recognising the ratio will come with practice". Reading such statements can be frustrating but there is no easy way of learning how to identify the *ratio decidendi*. It requires skills of analysis and interpretation. One way of developing these skills is to read as many cases as possible. You will gradually become familiar with the general format of judgments. If you read cases from law reports which contain commentaries you can check whether your understanding of the case is the same as that of the commentator. More detailed discussion of the *ratio decidendi* can be found in W. Twining and D. Miers, *How to Do Things with Rules* 4th edn (London: Butterworths 1999) and J.A. Holland and J.S. Webb, *Learning Legal Rules* 6th edn (Oxford: OUP, 2006), Ch.6.

3–32 Tips for reading cases

> ➤ You do not need to pay the same amount of attention to all the cases. Pay more attention to leading House of Lords judgments.
> ➤ Concentrate on cases which are the first to define a principle or interpret a statute. Cases which are illustrative of a rule are not as important as those which expounded the rule in the first place.
> ➤ Do not waste time on cases that have subsequently been overruled unless you are specifically interested in a historical perspective of an area of law.
> ➤ Do not spend time reading dissenting judgments unless you are particularly interested in the conflicting arguments.
> ➤ Concentrate on the leading judgment. It tends to be the most important.

Preparation of a student case note

3–33 A student case note is essentially a summary of all the important information in a case. It should only be about one or two pages of A4. The length will depend on the importance of the case. You should not copy out great chunks of the case. The information should allow you to:

> ➤ Find the case again.
> ➤ Understand the case.
> ➤ Appreciate why the case is important.
> ➤ Use the case effectively in an essay or an exam.

3–34 A case note should contain the following:

1. Details about the case:

    (a) names of the parties
    (b) citation (and any alternative citations, if known). This is so that you can find the case if one law report is missing from the library or if you have to use a library with fewer facilities.
    (c) court which heard the case (the names of the judges may be relevant). The court is important because of the doctrine of judicial precedent. If you know which court heard the case, you have an idea of how much weight is likely to be attached to the decision.
    (d) the result. This means whether the appeal was allowed or whether the defender was liable, etc. You should note whether the decision was unanimous or whether a judge or judges dissented.

2. Précis of the *material* facts. Material facts means facts that are legally relevant to the judge's decision. This is to help you appreciate the application of the law in the specific circumstances of the case and to help you understand the operation of the law in practice. It will also help you identify the case.
3. Issue(s) of law raised in the case.
4. Decision made by the court. The decision reached on the legal issues raised.
5. Reasons for the decision made by the court. This is the most important part of the case report and should take up the most space.
6. Additional comments:

    (a) A quotation. Judges sometimes say things in a clear succinct way. You may want to put such a quotation in an essay or it may help to clarify something for you. Perhaps a case contains some famous dicta and you may want to take this down word for word. Any quotation should be short.

(b) Your own opinion of the case. Perhaps you doubt the reasoning. Your lecturer or an article has criticised the case.

(c) You would want to note if the court has done something significant, such as overrule another case or interpret a piece of legislation for the first time.

You could make up a file of individual case notes or alternatively you could put your notes on small index cards. Whichever method you use, make sure that you store them alphabetically. This should enable you to find the relevant case note easily. Adopting a card index system has the added benefit of forcing you to make your notes concise as they have to fit onto the card. This could also be done in electronic form.

!Example of a student case note   3–35

Bett v Hamilton, 1998 J.C. 1
High Court of Justiciary sitting as an appellate court
Appeal allowed

A bank installed a surveillance camera situated to record movement at the front of its premises. Bett was accused of moving the camera so that it no longer covered the area at the front of the bank. The bank continued to pay the running costs of operating the camera while it was out of position and thus not protecting their premises.

What constitutes the offence of malicious mischief? Hume defined it as requiring a deliberate and malicious act to damage another's property or to interfere with it to the detriment of the owner or lawful possessor. Particular issue was whether "detriment" required patrimonial loss or whether some disadvantage would be sufficient.

Patrimonial loss required.

Reasons—The offence was defined as requiring "a wilful intent to cause injury to the owner or possessor of the property. This injury may be either in the form of physical damage or in the form of patrimonial loss". The running costs would have been incurred even if the camera had been pointing in the correct direction. There had been no loss merely a loss of benefit. Loss of benefit did not constitute patrimonial loss.

Chapter 4
Search Strategies for Finding Cases

AIDS TO TRACING CASES

4–1 There are six different types of aids to tracing cases:

➢ Major full text electronic databases which are all subscription services (4.2–4.19).
➢ Electronic collections of full text cases (4.20–4.26).
➢ Collections of digests of cases (4.27–4.33).
➢ Citators (4.34–4.40).
➢ Commentaries on case law and indexes of such commentaries (4.41–4.44).
➢ The series of law reports themselves and their various indexes (4.45–4.46).

These will now be discussed in turn.

Major full text electronic subscription databases

4–2 There are three major full text electronic databases relevant for case law. They all allow access to large amounts of case law although older law reports do not tend to be included. The databases do not merely provide copies of the cases they all provide various additional features. These are discussed in para.2.7 but of particular relevance to case law is the ability to: search by party name, citation and free text; provide information about the status of a case, e.g. whether it has been overruled; provide the judicial history of a case; and identify articles and commentary written about cases.

In Scotland, *Westlaw* is the most widely used database, followed by *LexisNexis Butterworths* with *Justis* databases generally less widely available. With regard to case law, *LexisNexis Butterworths* and *Westlaw* have similar search facilities but have different holdings of law reports. From the Scottish perspective, *Westlaw* has *Session Cases* and *Scots Law Times* while *LexisNexis Butterworths* has *Session Cases*, *Scottish Civil Law Reports* and *Scottish Criminal Case Reports*. Thus *Westlaw* has the greater coverage with both of the principal Scottish series of law reports. With regard to other law report series you need to be aware of which reports are held by the different databases. At the moment both are increasing their holdings and so you should check the listings in their databases for the up-to-date position. You can then quickly choose which is most appropriate for your particular research.

Westlaw	This is a full text subscription database (*http://www.westlaw.co.uk*)	**4–3**
Case coverage	The Law Reports from 1865	
	Weekly Law Reports from 1953	
	Industrial Case Reports from 1972	

Specialist series:
Civil Procedure Reports from1999
Common Market Law Reports from 1962
Criminal Appeal Reports from 1967
Criminal Appeal Reports (Sentencing) from1979
Entertainment and Media Law Reports from1993
Environmental Law Reports from1993
European Commercial Cases from1978
European Copyright & Design Reports from 2000
European Human Rights Reports from 1979 (some judgments date back to 1960)
European National Patent Reports from 2000
European Patent Office Reports from 1979
European Trade Mark Reports from 1996
Fleet Street Reports from 1966
Human Rights Law Reports (UK) from 2000
International Litigation Procedure from 1990
Landlord and Tenant Reports from1998
Lloyd's Law Reports from 1919
Personal Injuries and Quantum Reports from 1992
Professional Negligence and Liability Reports from1995
Property, Planning and Compensation Reports from 1949
Reports of Patent Cases from 1977

Scottish material

Session Cases from 1930
Scots Law Times from1893

Notable series NOT covered

All England Law Reports
Scottish Criminal Case Reports
Scottish Civil Law Reports

Updates

Cases will first appear in *Westlaw* in the current awareness section. This is updated three times and day and a case should appear here on the same day that it is issued by the court. The case will appear in full text in the cases section within 24 hours of being issued. The full case analysis entry will be completed at a later date with cases of greater legal importance appearing the most quickly.

Hints on use

See below

Westlaw UK allows you to look for cases using the *basic search*, *advanced search* or *browse* functions. This will be discussed in turn.

Basic Search. From the welcome page, select the *cases* heading from the navigation bar at the **4–4** top of the screen. This will take you to the *cases basic search* page, where you can search for cases by entering:

➢ *Party name*—just enter the names, you do not need to insert "and" or "v".
➢ *Citation*—You do not have to know the exact citation format in terms of brackets and spaces as *Westlaw* will match it to the nearest citation. For example, [2001] 1 A.C. 1 can be simplified to 2001 1 ac 1 for search purposes.
➢ Key subject terms into *free text*—this allows you to look for terms or phrases relating to the subject matter of the case. *Westlaw* searches for these within the text of all case analyses and the judgments. Searching can be improved if you use search techniques which *Westlaw* refer to as "Terms and Connectors", see para.2.33.

Note that the template is not case sensitive.

4–5 *Advanced search.* To access the advanced search, select *advanced search* in the top right of the *cases basic search* page. The advanced cases search allows you to enter a greater amount of information to further refine your search. In addition to the *free text*, *party name* and *citation* search fields available in the basic search you can:

➢ Search for subject headings, keywords or catchphrases. The *list of terms* link will take you to a listing of legal subjects and keywords as derived from Sweet & Maxwell's Legal Taxonomy. Cut and paste the relevant word into the *subject/keyword* field.
➢ Search for any cases interpreting a specific section, regulation, rule or article of legislation by entering the legislation title or statutory instrument name and number, e.g. Succession (Scotland) Act 1964, in the *legislation title* or *legislation provision* field.
➢ Search for any cases citing specific cases. Enter the party name(s) in the *cases cited (party)* field or the citation in the *cases cited (citation)* field.
➢ Search by the court in which the case was heard.
➢ Search by judge.
➢ Restrict your search by date by selecting one of the periods from the *date restriction* drop-down list or specify a date by entering it in DD/MM/YYYY format.

4–6 *Search results for cases.* The default order of documents retrieved is reverse chronological. If you are more interested in relevancy and how often your search terms appear within the documents, click on *sort by relevance* towards the top right of the screen. The cases result list includes:

➢ Party name.
➢ Subject/ keywords used to index the case using the Sweet & Maxwell Legal Taxonomy, e.g. Causation; Prosecutions; Water Pollution.
➢ Where reported—a list of all citations where the case has been reported.
➢ Links to case analysis (see para.4.13) and each of the full text case reports.
➢ Some results might show status icons next to the title of the case indicating that either the case has been judicially considered elsewhere (indicated by **C**) or that the case has been overruled or reversed on appeal (indicated by **▬**).

4–7 You can edit your search or delete it and start a new one by selecting *edit search* or *new search*, both of which appear at the top left of the page. To refine a long list of results even further, you can search for additional terms. Just enter your new search term(s) in the field at the top of the page and click *search within results*. This can be a useful way of increasing the relevancy of your results.

Browsing for cases. From the welcome page, select the *cases* heading from the navigation bar at **4–8** the top of the screen. This will take you to the *cases basic search* page. As an alternative to the basic search, you can browse for cases by choosing one of the *browse* options. You can browse for any case either by accessing all case analysis documents on *Westlaw UK* or the full text reports and transcripts. The former will include more cases than the latter.

When you select *case analysis documents* (see para.4.13), an alphabetical list of all case reports **4–9** monitored by *Westlaw UK* is displayed with the title of the report on the left hand side and the citation format on the right. Once you have selected a report series name, you will be taken to a list of years or volume numbers for that report. A list of cases in alphabetical order will be displayed for that year. If you select a case report for which *Westlaw* do not hold any full text judgments only a link to the case analysis document will be available. If the full text judgment is available in another report series on Westlaw the full text citation will appear. You can then link to the official judgment.

The *law reports and transcripts* link will display all case reports held on *Westlaw UK* in full text. **4–10** The name of the series appears on the left with the corresponding citation format on the right of the screen. Accessing one of the report series will take you to a list of years or volume numbers for that case report series. Within that list of years, an alphabetical list of cases is displayed. If a case is held in full text in more than one report series, links to all full text reports will be available.

The browse feature allows you to limit the scope of your search to individual publications or **4–11** years. For example, if you only want to search *Session Cases*, select this series of law reports and then enter your search terms in the fields at the top of the screen.

Browsing also allows you to quickly locate a case if you know roughly where it is but cannot **4–12** remember sufficient detail to successfully use a party or citation search. For example you might recall that a case was reported in 1972 Appeal Cases but you cannot quite get the spelling of the party's name correct. The browse feature gets round the problem by allowing you to go to the law report for a specific year and browse the contents. You can see exactly what you are searching by reference to the breadcrumb trail in the blue area above the search box.

Case Analysis. The Case Analysis is a useful feature in that it provides a summary of infor- **4–13** mation about a case with links to materials held within *Westlaw*. The various fields used are:

where reported	This lists all case report series that have reported the case. The list runs in order of persuasive authority of a particular law report series (e.g. *Session Cases*, *Scots Law Times*, Scottish Civil Law Reports).
case digest	This consists of:
	➢ *subject*—the legal subject as assigned by *Westlaw*, e.g. Environmental Health.
	➢ *keyword*—terms contained in the *Westlaw UK Legal Taxonomy* describing issues involved in the case, e.g. intention; pollution; rivers; strict liability.
	➢ *summary*—contains key phrases, e.g. pollution; "causing"; absence of intention or negligence.
	➢ *abstract*—the facts of the case and a summary of the decision.
appellate history	The direct, reported progress of the decision through to appeal, in chronological order.

significant cases citing	This provides a list of selected cases cited within the case. Click the case name and citation to access it (if it is available in *Westlaw*).
cases citing this case	Lists the cases that have cited the case currently being viewed.
legislation cited	This provides links to legislation cited in the case. If legislation is not available on *Westlaw UK* or is no longer in force no links will be available.
journal articles	A list of citations to articles about the case which have appeared in legal journals. Links will go to the full text (if available on *Westlaw*).

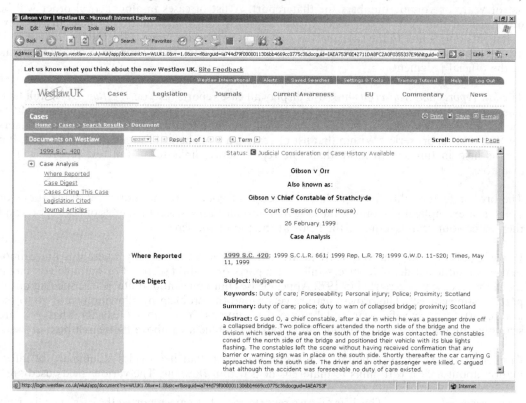

Diagram 4.1: Westlaw Case Analysis

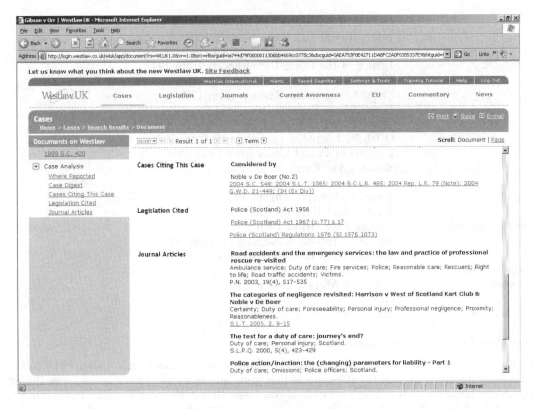

Diagram 4.2: Westlaw Case Analysis

Full text case reports. Westlaw UK uses a system of star paging to indicate the exact pagination **4–14**
of the original printed law report that you are reading. If reference needs to be made from a
case, find the preceding star page number to locate the page number in the hard copy. Citations
to law reports covered by *Westlaw UK* are hyperlinked and take you to the appropriate case
analysis document. In force legislation cited within the case is hyperlinked and takes you to the
full text of the legislation. If any status icons have been applied to the case analysis document,
these will also remain at the top of the screen above the party name.

LexisNexis	This is a full text subscription database (*http://www.lexisnexis.co.uk*) **4–15**
Butterworths	for more details, see para.9.2.
Case coverage	The Law Reports from 1865
includes:	All England Law Reports from 1936
	All England Commercial cases from 1999
	All England European Cases from 1995
	Bankruptcy and Personal Insolvency Reports from 1996
	Butterworths Company Law Cases from 1983
	Butterworths Human Rights Cases from 1996
	Butterworths Medico-Legal Reports from 1986
	Construction Law Reports from 1985
	Education Law Reports from 1995
	Estates Gazette Law Reports from 1985
	Family Court Reports from 1987

	Industrial Relations Law Reports from 1972
	International Tax Reports from 1997
	International Trust and Estate Law Reports from 1998
	Justice of the Peace Law Reports from 1945
	Licensing Law Reports from 2001
	Local Government Reports from 1999
	Lloyd's Law Reports from 1951
	Occupational Pension Law Reports from 1992
	Offshore Financial Law Reports from 1996
	Reports of Patent Cases from 1947–1997
	Simon's Tax Cases from 1973
	Tax Cases from 1875
	Times Law Reports from 1988
	West Indian Reports from 1958
Scottish material	*Session Cases* from 1930
	Scottish Criminal Case Reports from 1981
	Scottish Civil Law Reports from 1987
Notable series NOT	*Scots Law Times*
covered	Common Market Law Reports
Updates	Daily
Hints on use	See below

Searching LexisNexis Butterworths for case law

4–16 Choose the cases tab from the homepage. This opens up the cases search form. The *Select Sources* drop-down list will list the sources that your university subscribes to and you should select whichever series you wish to search. If you know the citation you should enter it into the citation field. Ignore brackets or other punctuation. It is possible to specify a particular page or paragraph if you enter the detail into the box to the right of the citation field.

4–17 If you only know the parties' names you can enter one or both names in the *case name* field. If you use both parties names you should insert "and" between them i.e. Smith and Jones, do not enter Smith v Jones. If you do not know their names, you can enter words or phrases in the *enter search terms* box. You can use Boolean connectors to show the relation of the terms see para.2.33. It is possible to narrow a search to documents published on a particular date or date range. This is most useful if you are searching for recent transcripts of cases as opposed to cases which have been published in the law reports. There is a summary field which allows you to enter terms to search various fields (such as catchwords, headnotes, decisions and facts) within the case summary. The cases search form also allows you to search by court, judges and counsel.

4–18 You can retrieve your results by clicking on *search*. You may look at your search results in several different view formats, available through the View drop-down list on the Results form: List, Expanded List and Full Text. Each view format displays a different level of detail. *List* displays basic information in a numbered list, e.g. name, court, source and date. *Expanded List* is a useful option which displays the same information but also includes your search terms in context. You can click on one of your search terms in the Results list to go directly to that term in the full text document. Once you have accessed the full text there is a *next steps* box which gives you the option of finding related commentary or related cases.

Justis UK and Irish Primary Case Law/ UK and Irish Specialist Case law	This is a full text subscription service. (*http://www.justis.com/*) online and CD Rom	**4–19**
Case coverage	Justis Primary Case Law	

Justis Primary Case Law
The Weekly Law Reports (1953–present)
The Law Reports (1865–present)
Daily Cases (1999–present)
The Times Law Reports (1990–present)
The English Reports (1220–1873)
The Justis Specialist Case Law range comprises the following titles:
CCH Tax Cases (1875–present)
Criminal Appeal Reports (1967–present)
Criminal Appeal Reports (Sentencing) (1979–present)
Family Law Reports (1980–present)
Human Rights (1960–present)
Industrial Cases Reports (1972–present)
Inquest Law Reports (2000–present)
Mental Health Law Reports (1999–present)
Police Law Reports (2000–present,)
Prison Law Reports (1999–present)

Scottish material *Session Cases* (1930–present)

Comments Justis provides a printable pdf of a case report which replicates the pagination of the hard copy exactly.

Updates Most working days

Electronic collections of full text cases

Electronic collections of cases are often free but are restricted to recent cases. These collections **4–20** tend to appear on a website hosted by a specific court and provide the judgments of cases with few of the additional features available from the online databases. Although they provide fast access to cases they have the significant disadvantage that they do not tend to include headnotes or summaries of the cases. This means that you have to read the cases in order to get an idea if they are relevant for your research.

The Scottish Courts website is well structured and it is a useful information source especially for recent Scottish cases. *BAILII* is operated by the British and Irish Legal Information Institute and has the advantage of providing access to much of the free case law available on the web via one search portal. At present it is not widely used by students but it contains superior search facilities to many of the other free web collections.

Scottish Courts Website	This is a free website sponsored by the Scottish Court Service which contains full text opinions (this is the Scottish term for judgment) and a large amount of other information about the Scottish courts (*http://www.scotcourts.gov.uk*).	**4–21**
Case coverage	Court of Session from September 1998 onwards, including opinions in commercial cases from January 1998. High Court of Justiciary, including opinions in some sentence appeals. Sheriff Court cases from September 1998 where there is a significant point of law or particular public interest.	
Scottish material	All Scottish.	
Comments	The site allows you to search opinions by keyword or by structured search. The keyword search searches all opinions on the site whereas the	

structured search allows you to restrict your search to either the supreme courts or the sheriff courts. The structured search allows you to search by: type of opinion, date, judge, pursuer, defender, type of action. The site also lists the 50 more recent opinions (based on date uploaded as opposed to date of opinion).

In addition to opinions, this impressive website contains a huge amount of practical information. It contains details of the Rolls of Court (court business on a daily basis), court fees, Rules of the Court of Session, Sheriff Court Ordinary Cause Rules, all Rules of Court made after 2002, practice notes, various court forms, guidance notes for small claims and summary cause procedure, and a large amount of information for court users.

There is information about the different Scottish courts, details about judges and sheriffs and a virtual tour of the Court of Session. The site also gives details of the bodies involved in the administration of the courts.

There is a useful glossary of more common Scottish legal terms contained in a pdf file accessible by going to the professional section of the site, clicking on *leaflets and guidance materials* on the top left of the page, and then scrolling down to the link to the glossary.

The site includes printable information about the different sheriff courts and locations providing lots of practical information, e.g. photo of the court building, a map and directions.

Updates   Updated at 2pm on the day the opinion is issued.

Hints on use   The site has a public and a professional section. Information about opinions is in the professional section.

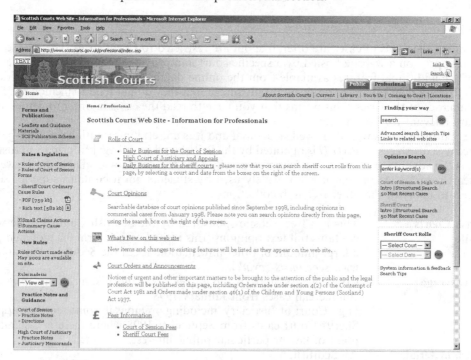

Diagram 4.3: Scottish Courts Website

BAILII
The *BAILII* site is operated by the British and Irish Legal Information **4–22** Institute. (*http://www.bailii.org/*). It is a full text searchable database which includes a large amount of legal information which is freely available on the web.

Case coverage
UK courts.
House of Lords decisions November 14, 1996 onwards.
Privy Council judgments 1996 onwards and selected earlier judgments.
Court of Appeal (Civil Division) and High Court (Administrative Court and Crown Office List), all cases from 1996 to August 1999, all significant handed down decisions September 1999 to December 2002, and all substantive judgments January 2003 onwards.
Court of Appeal (Criminal Division), all decisions from 1996 to August 1999 and some significant handed down decisions August 1999 onwards.
Tribunal
Employment Appeal Tribunal, selected decisions from 1976.
Special Immigrations Appeals Commission decisions from 2003 onwards.
UK Competition Appeals Tribunal decisions from 2002 onwards.
UK Financial Services and Markets Tribunals Decisions 2002–2005.
UK Asylum and Immigration Tribunal (successor to the Immigration Appellate Authority and the Immigration Appeals Tribunal) selected decisions from 1994
UK Information Tribunal including the National Security Appeals Panel selected decisions from 1998.
UK Special Commissioners of Income Tax Decisions from 1999.
UK Social Security and Child Support Commissioners' Decisions selected decision from 1972.
UK VAT and Duties Tribunals Decisions selected decisions from 1989.

Scottish material
Scottish coverage. This merely consists of the contents of the Scottish Courts website, see para.4.21. There are few Scottish cases before 1999.

Comments
All of the data have been converted into a consistent format and a generalised set of search and hypertext facilities added. This means that it is possible to search across all its databases and jurisdictions.

Updates
Daily

Hints on use
Searching cases:
> If you choose a particular database (e.g. Scotland) and then specific court (e.g. Court of Session) you can search its decisions by free text or browse its decisions alphabetically or by year and month within the year.
> A free text basic search on *BAILII's* home page allows a search of the entire database (this could be restricted to Scotland).
> The case law search facility allows you to search the full text judgments by various fields: citation; case name; words and phrases; dates, by court(s) or jurisdiction.
> The advanced field allows searching by terms and connectors, see para.2.33.

> ➢ The results appear in order of relevance. It is possible to resort the results in order of title, jurisdiction or date.
> ➢ Recent decisions can be accessed via the *latest cases* links on the front page.
> ➢ Cases can be browsed in alphabetical order listed by jurisdiction.
> ➢ Significant cases can be browsed by subject category although the current listing is rather out of date.
> ➢ The results appear in order of relevance. It is possible to resort the results in order of title, jurisdiction or date.

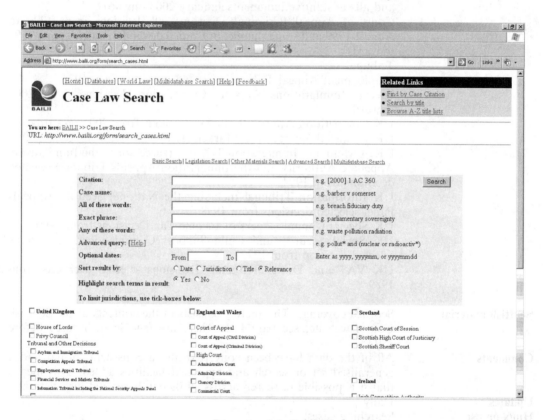

Diagram 4.4: BAILII

4–23 **House of Lords Website**	The House of Lords Judgments appear on a section of the United Kingdom Parliament web pages *http://www.publications.parliament.uk/pa/ld/ldjudgmt.htm* which are freely available on the web.
Case coverage	Html versions of all House of Lords judgments delivered since November 14, 1996. Pdfs of judgments are available since 2005.
Scottish material	Scottish appeals to the House of Lords are included.
Comments	Most recent cases are listed under *what's new* at the top of the site. Underneath you can link to the judgments by year. Within each year the judgments are listed in alphabetical order.
Updates	House of Lords decisions appear on the afternoon of the day judgment is given.

Hints on use	If you use the search box at the top of the page it searches across the Parliament pages which is not particularly useful. The advanced search can be used to restrict search terms to the House of Lords judgments.
Judicial Committee of the Privy Council Website	This is a free website which provides information about the Privy Council (*http://www.privy-council.org.uk/output/page1.asp* click on the link to the *judgments of the Judicial Committee*). **4–24**
Case coverage	All Privy Council cases in full text from 1999 with a small selection of earlier judgments.
Scottish material	The site contains all Privy Council judgments in "devolution cases".
Hints on use	A menu allows you to view the judgments by year. Judgments in "devolution cases" are listed separately at the end of the index for each year.
Scottish Land Court	This is the site of the Scottish Land Court. Click on *court decisions* on the menu bar across the top of the screen. *http://www.scottish-land-court.org.uk/index.html*. **4–25**
Case coverage	The site allows access to digests of cases between 1982 and 2005 (*http://www.scottish-land-court.org.uk/digest.html*) and recent unreported decisions (*http://www.scottish-land-court.org.uk/recent.html*).
Scottish material	All Scottish.
Comments	For recent decisions the site contains a link to a rubric (summary) of the case and a further link to the full text of the decision. The case digests are grouped by subject matter, and within each section the earliest case is detailed first. The digests are very brief and cover from 1982–2005.
Hints on use	See para.3.13 for more details about Scottish Land Court decisions.
Casetrack	This is a subscription service which allows you to trace full text judgments (*http://www.casetrack.com/index.html*). **4–26**
Case coverage	Court of Appeal (Criminal and Civil Divisions) from April 1996 to present. Administrative Court from April 1996 to present. All divisions of the High Court from July 1998 to present. Employment Appeal Tribunal from July 1998 to present. VAT Tribunal from January 2002 to present. Searchable links to House of Lords and Privy Council judgments from November 1996 to present.
Scottish material	Selective coverage of the High Court of Justiciary and Court of Session back to 2000/2001.
Comments	The site is run by Smith Bernal Reporting, the official source of Court of Appeal and Administrative Court transcripts.
Updates	Every day. Casetrack claims its record for making a judgment available is 26 minutes!

Collections of digests of cases

Digests contain brief summaries of cases and can be useful to give you an idea of the contents of a case. However, if you want a full understanding of a case you will need to consult a source which contains the full text.

4–27 Current Law
Yearbooks and   This is a paper service.
Monthly Digests

Case coverage   Digests of all reported cases since 1947 and references to cases (no matter when they were reported) which have been considered, applied, overruled, etc. by the courts since 1947.

Scottish material   Full coverage of Scottish material in *Current Law* since 1991. Prior to that only in the Scottish *Current Law* Series.
                           The Yearbooks have a separate section for Scottish material. The index at the end of each Yearbook does not have a separate Scottish section. Scottish material is indexed under the appropriate subject heading. You are alerted to the fact that it is a Scottish reference if the reference given ends with a capital "S".

Comments   The headings only appear if there is material included under that heading so the headings can vary from Yearbook to Yearbook.
                           The choice of subject category is sometimes not ideal and you may have to check under several different terms, e.g. if you want to check if there have been any cases concerning water pollution, you might have to check under environment, pollution and water.

Updates   Monthly.
Hints on use   Check the relevant subject headings in the Yearbooks and the latest Monthly Digest. These will lead you to a digest of the case and to citations in the law reports. See paras 8.15 and 8.21.

4–28 Current Legal
Information   This is a subscription research tool which comprises six datasets and is available both online and on CD Rom.

Case coverage   It contains the electronic version of the *Current Law* Case Citator (back to 1947) and digests of all reported cases since 1986. The CD Rom version also contains case digests from 1947 to 1985.

Scottish material   Full coverage of Scottish material.
Comments   It allows you to cross-reference to digests of cases which have cited a case, details of the legislation considered and any journal articles or case notes that have been listed in the Legal Journals Index.

Updates   Monthly for CD Rom version, daily for online.

4–29 The Faculty Digest Paper digest of cases.
Case coverage   1868–1922, Vols 1–5.
                           Vol.6—Indexes covering 1868–1922.
                           Faculty Digest Supplements.
                           1922–30, 1930–40, 1940–50, 1951–60, 1961–70, 1971–80, 1981–90.
                           Information is organised in the Supplements as follows:
                           ➢ Cases digested by subject matter.
                           ➢ Cases judicially referred to (including English cases referred to in the Scottish courts but not Scottish cases referred to in English courts).
                           ➢ Statutes, Acts of Sederunt, Statutory Orders, etc. judicially commented on—arranged by year.
                           ➢ Words judicially defined.
                           ➢ Index of cases in the digest—alphabetical order (both parties).

Scottish material   Courts covered: House of Lords, Court of Session, High Court of Justiciary, Lands Tribunal, Land Court. From 1981–90 Supplement it

	also covers sheriff court cases, Scottish Criminal Case Reports and Scottish Civil Law Reports.	
Comments	Useful for tracing older Scottish cases.	
Hints on use	It allows searches to be made by subject, names of both parties, legislation, cases judicially referred to and words judicially defined.	
Lawtel	This is an online subscription legal current awareness digest service.	4–30
Case coverage	It contains summaries of cases from the major English courts. The coverage starts from January 1, 1980.	
Scottish material	The coverage of Scottish material is patchy. It only covers Scottish cases which are followed in England.	
Comments	For UK material it is a very up to date source for recent cases.	
Updates	It is updated daily.	
Hints on use	Choose the case law option from the initial menu. This will take you into a search facility where you type in key words to locate the material which you require or use the focused search to search by various fields.	

The Digest (formerly the English & Empire Digest)	This is a large paper collection of case summaries.	4–31
Case coverage	It covers case law of England and Wales and has a selection of cases from Scotland, Ireland, Canada, Australia, New Zealand and other Commonwealth countries. The current edition consists of 116 volumes.	
Scottish material	Predominantly English, but contains selected Scottish cases in footnotes.	
Comments	The Digest tends to be the most widely available paper source of information about Scottish cases in England.	
Updates	Annual Cumulative Supplement and a Quarterly Survey of recent developments.	
Hints on use	More details can be found in para.9.26.	

Shaw's Digest	Paper digest of cases.	4–32
Case coverage	House of Lords decisions 1726–1868 and Scottish superior courts 1800–1868.	
Comments	The Faculty Digest was a continuation of Shaw's Digest.	
Hints on use	This digest does not always appear in the same format and different editions are bound differently. Cases are arranged by subject. There are indexes of pursuers' and defenders' names at the end of a volume or, if produced in several volumes, in the final volume.	

Scots Digest	Paper digest of cases.	4–33
Case coverage	House of Lords cases 1707–1947 and cases from Scottish superior courts 1800–1947.	
Comments	This was superseded by Scottish *Current Law*.	
Hints on use	This digest also appears in different formats. Cases are arranged by subject. The volumes contain a table of cases and table of cases judicially considered.	

There is a Digest of Sheriff Court Cases reported in the *Scots Law Times* between 1893–1943. Digests of old Scottish cases have been covered in the section starting at para.3.16.

Citators

Citators do not contain the full text or even summaries of a case. They are a method of tracing cases and their judicial history. A citator is a listing of information about a case. They represent a very efficient way of tracking information.

4–34 Current Law Case Citators	A case citator is an alphabetical list of cases which has information listed beside the relevant case. The *Current Law Case Citators* are published in several parts. See below.
Case coverage	All reported cases since 1947 and references to cases (no matter when they were reported) which have been considered, applied, overruled, etc. by the courts since 1947.
	If the case has been reported more than once, each alternative citation is given.
Scottish material	Scottish citators started from 1948 (rather than 1947). Full coverage of Scottish material in *Current Law* since 1991. Prior to that it was only in the Scottish *Current Law* Series.
	Scottish cases are listed separately and follow the listing of English cases.
Comments	This is a useful starting point *unless* the case is very recent (within the last month) or old (pre-1947 and not commented on by the courts since 1947).
	A version of the Case Citator is available in Current Legal Information. See para.4.28 above for details and para.4.39 for searching information.
Updates	Monthly—published in the Monthly Digests which appear in cumulative form each month.
Hints on use	While the Case Citators are an efficient way of tracing cases, they do require the user to have an appreciation of how the citators are organised and it is essential to adopt a systematic approach to searching them. Please see below.

4–35 The *Current Law* Case Citators are in six volumes. Scottish Case Citator volumes are currently:1948–1976, 1977–1997, 1998–2001, 2002–2004, 2005 and 2006. Each volume is divided into three parts:

> ➢ English, Welsh and Northern Irish cases
> ➢ Scottish cases
> ➢ Ship's Names Index (from 1977 onwards)

The English equivalents cover the same periods except that the first citator starts from 1947. The Scottish section of the Case Citator contains the following information:

> ⇒ Details of cases decided or judicially considered in the Scottish courts for the period covered by the volume of the citator.
> ⇒ References to English cases judicially considered in Scotland during the period covered by the volume of the citator.

Scottish cases which have been published in English law reports are included in both the Scottish and English sections of the citator.

The Case Citators contain the following information: **4–36**

⇒ Each volume starts with a list of abbreviations of various series of law reports and journals.
⇒ The full name of any case reported between 1947 and the current year. Cases are listed alphabetically by the first party's name.
⇒ Lists of citations in law reports and journals where the case may have been digested.
⇒ Reference to the *Current Law* Yearbook where the case is digested. Most references have a year before the paragraph number, e.g. 05/5032. This refers you to the 2005 Yearbook, para.5032.
⇒ The history of *any* case (irrespective of date) which has been judicially considered from 1947 to date. The reference given is to the digest of the case which considered the case listed.
⇒ The Monthly Digest contains an updated Case Citator (referred to as the Table of Cases) each month.

Excerpt from Case Citator with features marked **4–37**

---

[2]

[1] Grosvenor Developments (Scotland) v Argyll Stores, 1987 S.L.T. 738 (Ex. Div.): affirming 1987 S.L.T. (Sh.Ct.)
134...**[3]**.....................*Digested*, 87/**4846**: *Followed*, 92/5944, 95/6204: **[4]** *Approved*, 94/5971: *Distinguished*, 94/5970
Grosvenor Metal Co., *Re* [1950] Ch. 63; (1950) 93 S.J. 774; [1949] 2 All E.R. 948; 65 T.L.R. 755; [67 L.Q.R. 25]..*Digested*, 50/**1395**: *Approved and followed*, 93/4826
Group 4 Total Security v Jaymarke Developments, 1995 S.C.L.R.
303..*Digested*, 95/**6365**
Group 4 Total Security v Ferrier, 1985 S.L.T. 287; 1985 S.C.
70...*Digested*, 85/**4092**: *Applied*, 86/4023
Grugen v H.M. Advocate, 1991 S.C.C.R.
526...*Digested*, 91/**4644**
Grummer v H.M. Advocate, 1991 S.C.C.R. 194..*Digested*, 91/**4815**: *Commented on*, 92/5570: *Applied*, 95/5620

Key:

[1] Name.
[2] Citation.
[3] References **in bold** indicate where the case has been digested, e.g. this case is digested in the 1987 Yearbook, para.4846.
[4] References in normal type show where the case has been considered, e.g. this case is approved in a case listed in the 1994 Yearbook, para.5971.

Tips for searching the Case Citators

Make sure that you look in the relevant part. It is very easy to make a mistake and look in the **4–38** English section for a Scottish case.

If you know the approximate year of the case you are looking for, start searching in the appropriate volume and then check all the citators subsequent to the date of the case. This will ensure that you pick up on all subsequent developments.

If you do not know the approximate year of the case, start searching in the first (*i.e.* the earliest) volume and work forward in time. This will make sure that you do not miss any developments.

If the case is not mentioned at all, you may be looking in the wrong section of the citator (England instead of Scotland) or the case may be older than 1947 and have never been considered by the courts since 1947.

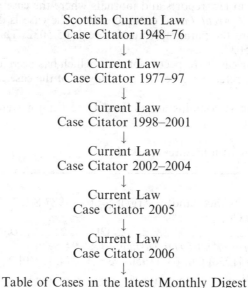

Scottish Current Law
Case Citator 1948–76
↓
Current Law
Case Citator 1977–97
↓
Current Law
Case Citator 1998–2001
↓
Current Law
Case Citator 2002–2004
↓
Current Law
Case Citator 2005
↓
Current Law
Case Citator 2006
↓
Table of Cases in the latest Monthly Digest

Searching the case citators available in Current Legal Information

4–39   Current Legal Information is described at para.4.28. The entry for the case includes the same information which is available in the paper version, with the addition of references to relevant entries in the Legal Journals Index. The key difference between the paper and electronic versions is the ease of cross-referencing. There are hypertext links which allow you to move from one section to another, e.g. the reference to the digest of the case, to the digest itself. This is obviously easier than having to go and retrieve another volume from the shelves. Another advantage is the inclusion of the Legal Journals Index in the system. This allows access to details of articles that have considered the case.

4–40   **JUSTCITE**   *Justcite* is an online legal citator. It is basically a legal reference search engine, providing a cross-referenced index to a collection of legal information. It allows you to identify materials across free databases (such as *BAILII*) and across subscription databases such as *LexisNexis, Justis* and *Westlaw*) by searching through one interface. It provides links to full text material which you can access if available to you (i.e. if the materials are free or the library you are using subscribes to the particular service).

Case coverage	The Law Reports, The Weekly Law Reports, All England Law Reports and many specialist series of law reports such as Lloyd's Law Reports and the Criminal Appeal Reports. It also includes transcripts from the Court of Appeal, Administrative Court and London's High Court.
Scottish material	*Session Cases* is an indexed data source while SCCR and SCLR references are recognised. SLT is not included.
Comments	*Searching Cases*

The home page allows you to search by case name, citation or subject. Alternatively, you can search using the *index* tab. This allows you to browse through a title index of cases listed in alphabetical order nested under various headings (including Scottish cases). It also allows you to browse cases by subject (Scotland is a subject and there are various subcategories), words and phrases, ship's names or by year (Scottish cases can be searched separately). The information retrieved can include:

> ➢ Alternative citations. If you click on any one of the citations a new window will open. This provides you with various sources of the full text of the case which you may be able to access depending on the subscriptions held by your university library,
> ➢ A brief summary of the case,
> ➢ Subject matter categorisation,
> ➢ Cases, statutes and statutory instruments judicially considered,
> ➢ Subsequent cases with details of their effect, if any, on the earlier case,
> ➢ Articles. The numbers of articles are retrieved is very small, e.g. when compared to an identical search using *Westlaw*.

Scottish cases can be searched separately. However, if you search for Scottish cases which have been reported in England you will find that the vast majority of the reference details are included in the UK entry only and that the Scottish entry is very brief. This means that it is better to search under both categories.

Updates	Material is added on a daily basis.
Hints on use	*Justcite* does not support Boolean operators. If you type more than one word in the subject box on the search screen, *Justcite* will look for documents that contain all of those words. You can search for a phrase by putting it into parenthesis, e.g. "reasonably practicable".

Commentaries on case law and indexes of such commentaries

These sources can be particularly useful if you are looking for cases by subject matter.

Legal Journals Index	This is an index which covers over 800 journals from the UK and English language European journals. It contains abstracts of journal articles. It is published in paper but is now more usually encountered in its electronic form which is part of *Westlaw UK*, see para.8.48.	**4–41**
Case coverage	Started in 1986.	
	References to case notes and articles which discuss cases.	

	This index covers all journals published in the UK which are devoted to law or frequently contain articles on legal topics.
Scottish material	Scottish journals currently covered: Edinburgh Law Review, Journal of the Law Society of Scotland, Juridical Review, SCO-LAG, Scots Law Times, Scottish Construction Law, Scottish Human Rights Journal, Scottish Law Gazette, Scottish Licensing Law and Practice.
Comments	In addition to being available as part of *Westlaw*, LJI is also available as part of Current Legal Information on CD Rom and online.
Updates	Paper version and CD Rom versions monthly; online daily.
Hints on use	Paper version: access is via the case index. Cases are cited by either party or by subject headings.
	Current Legal Information version allows you to search by field (case name is one of the fields) and by free text.

4–42 Tables of cases in textbooks

Case coverage	Depends on the text. The table of cases will usually contain the citation and page reference to where it is discussed in the text.
Scottish material	Make sure that you use a Scottish text.
Comments	Make sure that you use the most current text that you can find.
Updates	Depends on the text.
Hints on use	Tables of cases in textbooks are usually found at the beginning of the book after the contents page. The cases are listed in alphabetical order of the first named party.

4–43 The Laws of Scotland: Stair Memorial Encyclopaedia

	This encyclopaedia gives a commentary on Scots law. It is arranged alphabetically in broad areas of the law and contains articles on each area.
Case coverage	Cases are referred to throughout the encyclopaedia.
Scottish material	A Scottish encyclopaedia.
Updates	Paper—Annual Cumulative Supplements and table of cases. In addition the Service Binder is updated twice a year.
	Online (*The Laws of Scotland Online*) is updated bi-monthly.
Hints on use	You can search the paper version by subject or by the first party's name:

> ➤ To search by subject: → Consolidated Index → Relevant volume or reissued title which contains a table of cases → Annual Cumulative Supplement → Service Binder
> ➤ To search by case name: → Consolidated Table of Cases → Service Binder

The online version (*The Laws of Scotland Online*) can be searched by free text.

More details about the encyclopaedia are in the section starting at para.8.2.

4–44 Casebooks

Casebooks (sometimes called Cases and Materials texts) contain excerpts from legal materials on a particular subject accompanied by commentary which discusses the excerpts and puts them in context.

Case coverage	Depends on the text.
Scottish material	Make sure that you use a Scottish text.
Comments	Casebooks can provide a fast and efficient way of getting information about key cases in an area. However, they should not be regarded as a substitute for reading the cases themselves. Casebooks only contain short excerpts from the materials and do not allow the reader to appreciate the complete nature of the legal reasoning in the context of the case.

The series of law reports themselves and the various indexes which they contain

These are fairly cumbersome ways of searching for cases and would only be used if other sources were not available.

Law reports	The series of law reports themselves and the various indexes which they contain	**4–45**
Case coverage	Varies according to the series of law reports. For details of the English series see Chapter 9. The important Law Reports Index is dealt with below.	
Scottish material	For details of the Scottish law reports, see Chapter 3.	
Comments	Not all series contain the same indexes, e.g. some series have separate tables of words and phrases judicially considered. Other series include the information in a subject index under "W" for word.	
	The subject categories adopted are also variable.	
Updates	Varies according to the series of law reports.	
Hints on use	Make sure you look for cumulative versions of the indexes. This will save you having to check the annual volumes. The consolidated indexes are usually published separately but should be located next to the appropriate series of law reports in the library.	

The Law Reports Index	This index provides a continuous indexing system to the principal English law reports from 1951 to date.	**4–46**
	It contains:	
	All cases reported in The Law Reports, the Weekly Law Reports and the Industrial Cases Reports.	
	References to cases reported in:	
	All England Commercial Cases, All England European Cases, All England Law Reports, Criminal Appeal Reports, Lloyd's Law Reports, Local Government Reports, Road Traffic Reports, and Simon's Tax Cases.	
Scottish material	Only important Scottish cases are covered.	
Updates	The index is contained in six volumes referred to as the "Red Indexes": 1951–60, 1961–70, 1971–80, 1981–90, 1991–2000, 2001–2005. There is also a Red Book for 2006.	
	These are updated by Pink Indexes which are published several times a year. More recent updates of the index can be found at the beginning of each issue of the Weekly Law Reports.	
Hints on use	The index contains nine different tables.	

Check table of cases reported and table of cases judicially considered. To ensure that you are up to date, check through: (1) Red Index; (2) Pink Index; (3) Weekly Law Reports. For more details see para.9.19.

SEARCH STRATEGIES FOR FINDING CASES

4–47 This section deals with the different ways which can be used to find cases. This will help you to find cases from different starting points; for instance you may want to explore a new area of law or your knowledge of a case may be incomplete.

There are usually many ways of finding legal information. This section contains lists of various alternative sources along with comments as to their strengths and weaknesses. The most comprehensive sources are listed first, followed by the more limited sources. It is not a simple matter of listing the best and worst sources. A lot may depend on the facilities that you have available to you. You may be fortunate enough to have access to a well-resourced law library. However, you may be faced with finding information with much more limited facilities available to you. Electronic and paper alternatives are clearly marked.

4–48 The following search strategies are considered:

> ➢ Finding cases by name only. This should allow you to find cases when you have lost the citation or where you have an incorrect citation. See para.4.49.
> ➢ Finding cases by subject. This should allow you to search where you may be interested in a specific subject area and have little or no knowledge of the case law. See para.4.69.
> ➢ Finding cases on words or phrases. This allows you to ascertain if a certain word or phrase has been interpreted by the courts. See para.4.84.
> ➢ Finding cases interpreting legislation. This covers the situation where you know of a specific legislative provision and you want to find out if any cases have considered it. See para.4.92.
> ➢ Finding journal articles which discuss a case. Identifying such articles and sourcing them can help you understand the reasoning adopted in a case and help you to appreciate its place in the subject area as a whole. See para.4.104.
> ➢ Current status of a case. You may want to know whether a case is still binding law, whether it has been commented on or overruled. See para.4.113.
> ➢ Finding out about a very recent case. It is very important to be aware of current developments in the law. New cases are reported daily and the sources for very recent cases tend to be different from those for older cases. See para.4.125.
> ➢ Finding cases from other courts, e.g. Lyon Court and the Lands Tribunal. See para.4.135.
> ➢ Finding tribunal decisions. See para.4.136.
> ➢ Putting cases into context—recent cases and older cases. See para.4.144.

There is a summary of the alternative sources for each strategy in Appendix I.

Finding cases by name only—citation unknown

The best method of locating a case when you only know the parties' names is to use one of the online legal databases unless you are looking for an older case in which case see the section starting at para.4.64.

Westlaw ⌁ subscription database

From the welcome page, select the *cases* heading from the navigation bar at the top of the **4–49**
screen. This will take you to the *cases basic search* page, where you can search for cases by
entering either or both parties' names by entering them in the *party names* field. The template is
not case sensitive. You just need to enter the names, e.g. Smith Jones. You do not need to insert
"v" or "and". This will take you to details about the case and the full text if it is available in
Westlaw. See para.4.3 for details of the law reports available on *Westlaw*.

LexisNexis Butterworths ⌁ subscription database

Choose the *cases* tab from the homepage. This opens up the cases search form. If you only know **4–50**
the parties' names you can enter one or both names in the *case name* field. If you use both
parties names you should insert "and" between them, i.e. Smith and Jones, do not enter Smith
v Jones. See para.4.15 for details of the law reports available on *LexisNexis Butterworths*.

Justis UK and Irish Primary Case Law/Specialist Case Law ⌁ subscription and CD Rom
See para.4.19 for details of the law reports available on *Justis*. **4–51**

Current Law Case Citator 📖

This is the best paper resource *unless* the case is very recent (within the last month) or old (pre- **4–52**
1947 and not commented on by the courts since 1947). *Current Law* includes all reported cases
since 1947 and references to cases (no matter when they were reported) which have been considered, applied, overruled, etc., by the courts since 1947. The citators are arranged alphabetically by the name of the first party. The citator will provide you with the citation for the case.
This enables you to locate it in the relevant series of law reports. The *Current Law* system works
well but can be daunting to new users. However, it is worth persevering with this excellent paper
source.

Using *Current Law* to find a citation for a case by name only: **4–53**

> ⇒ **Step 1**: Check through the Case Citators in chronological order. Remember that if it is
> a Scottish case you should check in the Scottish section. If you are not sure if it
> is Scottish, you should check *both* the English and Scottish sections of the
> citators. Cases are listed in alphabetical order of the first named party. If the
> case appears its full citation(s) will be next to it.
> ⇒ **Step 2**: You should then check the table of cases in the most recent Monthly Digest.

!Example

Find the citation for *Galt v Goodsir*. You know that the case is Scottish but nothing else.

> ⇒ **Step 1**: Check the Case Citator volume 1948–1976. Make sure that you check the
> Scottish section. There is no entry.
> ⇒ **Step 2**: Check the Case Citator volume 1977–1997. Again make sure that you check
> the Scottish section. Here there is an entry for the case and three citations are
> given: 1982 J.C. 4; 1982 S.L.T. 94; 1981 S.C.C.R. 225.

Using *Current Law* to find a citation if you remember the name AND the year but *not* the **4–54**
citation:

⇒ Check the appropriate Yearbook and look in the Table of Cases at the beginning of the
Yearbook. All cases included in the Yearbook are listed alphabetically.

If you find the details in the Case Citator as above how can you find more details about the case?

⇒ **To find the full text of the case**:
In the entry in the Case Citator following the name of the case you will find all the citations for the case. For the full text of the case go to the appropriate law report or electronic database.

⇒ **A summary of the case within the paper Current Law system**:
Opposite the entry for the case in the Case Citator the first reference will be for a paragraph number where the case is digested in a *Current Law* Yearbook. The reference is made up of the year/paragraph number. The paragraph number of the digest is always shown in bold. Turn to the appropriate Yearbook and you will find that the entry for the paragraph number will contain a digest of the case.

!Example

In the previous example we established that *Galt v Goodsir* appeared in the Case Citator volume 1977–1997. How can you find out details about it in the *Current Law* system?

⇒ **Step 1**:   Locate the case in the relevant Case Citator. Here we have already established that it is Case Citator volume 1977–1997. Opposite the entry for the case is a reference that says "Digested 82/4292".

⇒ **Step 2**:   Turn to the Yearbook for 1982 and specifically to paragraph number 4292. The entry contains the following information:
"Identification of driver
[Road Traffic Act 1972 (c. 20) ss.6(1) and 168(2)]
Held, that an admission by the owner of a car made under s.168(2) of the Road Traffic Act 1972 that he had been the driver two days before was admissible evidence against him on a charge under s.6(1), although the result of the laboratory test was not known to the police when the request under s.168(2) was made: *Galt v Goodsir* 1982 S.L.T. 94."

Current Legal Information ⌀ subscription legal research service
4–55 This contains an electronic version of the *Current Law Case Citator*. See para.4.39 for search techniques.

Justcite ⌀ subscription legal citator
4–56 See para.4.40.

The Laws of Scotland: Stair Memorial Encyclopaedia 📖
4–57 To search by case name, check the Consolidated Table of Cases and the Service Binder. See para.8.2.

The Laws of Scotland Online (Stair Memorial Encyclopaedia) ⌀ subscription from *LexisNexis Butterworths*
4–58 The online version can be searched by free text. See para.8.50.

4–59 *Tables of cases in relevant textbooks* 📖
Tables of cases in textbooks are usually found at the beginning of the book after the contents page. The cases are listed in alphabetical order of the first named party. This method depends on knowing the area of law involved. Make sure that you find the most current edition of the textbook.

Indexes in the law reports 📖   **4–60**

In order to use the paper volumes of the various series of law reports you need to know both the likely series of law reports and the approximate date.

Most series of law reports include indexes of cases for a specific volume and may have cumulative updates covering many years. The indexes are usually accessible from either party's name. See Chapter 3 for details of the Scottish series and Chapter 9 for the English series.

If the case is recent the following could be used:

> ➤ *Scottish Courts Website* ⌕ free. See para.4.21.
> ➤ *BAILII* ⌕ free. See para.4.22.

Sources useful for UK cases but not for Scottish cases

The Law Reports Index 📖

This index provides a continuous indexing system to the principal English law reports from 1951 **4–61** to date. Remember that only selected Scottish cases are covered. See para.4.46.

Casetrack ⌕ subscription

This mainly covers English cases. See para.4.26.   **4–62**

Lawtel ⌕ subscription legal current awareness digest service

Online digest service. It is updated every 24 hours and contains summaries (not full text) of **4–63** reports from the main English courts. The coverage starts from January 1, 1980. The coverage of Scottish material is patchy. It only covers Scottish cases which are followed in England.

Indexes helpful for locating older cases

The Index to Morison's Dictionary 📖

This covers cases from 1540–1820. See para.3.16.   **4–64**

Scots Digest 📖

House of Lords cases from 1707–1947 and cases from Scottish superior courts from 1800–1947. **4–65** See para.4.33.

The Faculty Digest 📖

This covers cases from 1868–1990. See para.4.29 and worked example in para.4.68 below.   **4–66**

The Digest 📖

This is predominantly an English reference work. Scottish cases are referred to after English **4–67** counterparts.

Check the consolidated table of cases to find the correct volume number. The case table in the appropriate volume refers to the paragraph number. See para.9.26.

!Example of finding an older case

Find the Scottish case of *Branford's Trustees v Powell*   **4–68**

> ➤ This case does not appear in *Westlaw*, *Justcite* or *Current Law*. This would suggest that it is an older case i.e. pre–1947.
> ➤ Check the Faculty Digest.
> ➤ Volume 6 is an indices volume covering 1868–1922. Check in the Cases in Digest Table. There is no entry for this case.

> ➢ The Supplement volumes need to be checked on a volume by volume basis. Volume 1922–1930 does contain a reference to this case and refers you to p.29. The entry there gives a summary of the case and alternative citations: 1924, S.C. 439; 61 S.L.R. 306 and 1924, S.L.T. 334.
> ➢ Reference to this case could also be found by checking the Consolidated Table of Cases in the *Stair Memorial Encyclopaedia*. See para.8.2.

Finding cases by subject

4–69   Encyclopaedias, reference works or textbooks are ideal starting points for research by subject. Unlike an electronic database, they will not just identify a case; they will place it in context. This means that they explain its background and how it fits in to the whole area of law, how it has been interpreted and offer comment on it. Encyclopaedias or reference works can also provide you with the information necessary to refine your search terms which will make searching the full text databases manageable. If you try to conduct a subject search on a database with a broad subject term you will retrieve hundreds or even thousands of hits which it may take a long time to work through. Searching with a more relevant term will produce fewer more relevant hits.

When consulting an encyclopaedia or reference work look at the Table of Cases which will be located at the beginning of the work. This will list cases in alphabetical order.

The Laws of Scotland: Stair Memorial Encyclopaedia 📖
4–70   You can search by subject by checking:

> ➢ Consolidated Index
> ➢ Relevant volume or reissued title which contains a Table of Cases
> ➢ Update by checking the Annual Cumulative Supplement
> ➢ Further update by checking the Service Binder

The Laws of Scotland Online (*Stair Memorial Encyclopaedia*) ⌐ subscription from *LexisNexis Butterworths*
4–71   The online version can be searched by free text. More details are contained in para.8.5.

General reference texts 📖
4–72   These tend to have been updated over the years and run to several editions and you always need to ensure that you use the most up-to-date edition. An example is Gloag and Henderson, *The Law of Scotland* 12th edn (Edinburgh: W. Green, due in 2007). General reference works tend not to provide much detail about cases but should provide you with a citation. If you want a fuller discussion of the case go to a dedicated textbook.

Dedicated textbook 📖
4–73   This will probably be referred to by your lecturer or in a general reference work. If not, check the keyword/subject index in the library catalogue.

Westlaw ⌐ subscription database
4–74   From the welcome page, select the *cases* heading from the navigation bar at the top of the screen. This will take you to the *cases basic search* page, where you can search for cases by entering subject terms into *free text*. *Westlaw* will search for these within the text of all case analyses and judgments. If you want to look for a phrase remember to put it inside quotation marks. Searching can be improved if you use search techniques which *Westlaw* refer to as "Terms and Connectors". See para.2.33.

LexisNexis Butterworths ⟨⟩ subscription database
Choose the cases tab from the homepage. This opens up the cases search form. Enter words or **4–75**
phrases in the *enter search terms* box. You can use Boolean connectors to show the relation of
the terms. See para.2.33.

Justis UK and Irish Primary Case Law/ Specialist Case Law ⟨⟩ subscription and CD Rom
See para.4.19. **4–76**

Justcite ⟨⟩ subscription legal citator
See para.4.40. **4–77**

Current Legal Information ⟨⟩ and CD Rom subscription legal research service
Check the *Current Law* Cases section. The online version covers cases from 1986 while the CD **4–78**
Rom version goes back to 1947. You can search by field (this includes subject or keywords) or
free text. This will lead to a digest of the case and citations in the law reports. See para.4.28.

Current Law Yearbooks 📖
Check the relevant subject headings in the Yearbooks and the latest Monthly Digest. These will **4–79**
lead you to a digest of the case and to citations in the law reports. The Yearbooks have a
separate section for Scottish material. The index at the end of each Yearbook does not have a
separate Scottish section. Scottish material is indexed under the appropriate subject heading.
You are alerted to the fact that it is a Scottish reference if the reference given ends with a capital
"S".
   Check the appropriate subject heading in the index at the back of the Yearbook. The headings
only appear if there is material included under that heading so the headings can vary from
Yearbook to Yearbook. The subject categorisation can sometimes leave a lot to be desired. Be
prepared to search under related terms. For more details see para.8.21.

Subject indexes in various series of law reports

The CD Rom version of the *Scots Law Times* reports 1893 to present allows you to search by **4–80**
keyword.
   Session Cases, the paper version of the *Scots Law Times*, Scottish Criminal Case Reports,
Scottish Civil Law Reports and *Green's Weekly Digest* all have subject indexes. The ease of use
will depend on whether you know the approximate dates and/or the frequency of consolidation
volumes of the subject indexes. If the date is unknown and there are no consolidated indexes,
you would be left searching annually volume by volume. For details of the Scottish series see
Chapter 3. The English series of law reports are covered in Chapter 9.

If the case is recent the following could be used: **4–81**

   ➢ *Scottish Courts Website* ⟨⟩ free, see para.4.21.
   ➢ *BAILII* ⟨⟩ free, see para.4.22.

Sources useful for UK cases but not for Scottish cases

Halsbury's Laws of England 📖 and ⟨⟩ subscription
See para.9.33. **4–82**

Lawtel ⟨⟩ subscription legal current awareness digest service
Lawtel only covers Scottish cases which are followed in England. It can be searched by free text **4–83**
or focused search. See para.4.30.

Finding cases on words or phrases

4–84 It is now possible to search electronic databases for particular words and phrases. However, when searching a database you will retrieve results every time a word or phrase occurs in a case which will be considerably greater than the number of times when they are actually considered by the courts. It is therefore preferable to check sources which have selected relevant cases for you and contain specific indexes of words and phrases judicially considered.

Judicial dictionaries 📖

4–85 These are publications specifically dealing with the interpretation of words and phrases. Scottish publications include: W.J. Stewart, *Scottish Contemporary Judicial Dictionary* (Edinburgh: W. Green, 1995) and A.W. Dalrymple and Gibb, *Dictionary of Words and Phrases* (Edinburgh: W. Green, 1946).

United Kingdom publications include *Stroud's Judicial Dictionary* and *Words and Phrases Legally Defined*. See the section starting with para.8.25 for more details.

Current Law Yearbooks 📖

4–86 Check the Words and Phrases Judicially Considered Tables in the appropriate Yearbooks and the latest Monthly Digest. The table lists words and phrases alphabetically. Beside a particular word or phrase will be the paragraph number for where the case is digested. If you want to look at the actual case report, the digest entry will include a full citation reference. See para.8.21.

Subject indexes of law reports 📖 and ⏻ subscription

4–87 The subject indexes of many law reports include "Words and Phrases" as a subject heading. Law reports which do include this: *Session Cases*, Scottish Civil Law Reports, Scottish Criminal Case Reports, the Faculty Digest and The Law Reports Index.

The *Scots Law Times* CD Rom version of the reports from 1893–1997 allows searching by keyword or phrases.

The Consolidated Indexes to the All England Law Reports contain a "Words and phrases judicially considered" table.

Halsbury's Laws of England 📖 and ⏻ subscription

4–88 The Consolidated Index to *Halsbury's Laws of England* has a Words and Phrases Table (vol. 57). This includes words which are defined or explained in *Halsbury's Laws*. A worked example is contained in para.9.40.

The Law Reports Index 📖

4–89 This index which covers a large number of English law reports contains a table indexing subject matter which includes "Words and Phrases" as a heading. See para.9.19.

Westlaw ⏻ subscription database

4–90 From the welcome page, select the *cases* heading from the navigation bar at the top of the screen. This will take you to the *cases basic search* page, where you can search for cases by entering key subject terms into *free text*. This allows you to look for terms or phrases relating to the subject matter of the cases you want to find. In order to search for a phrase use quotation marks, e.g. if you want to look for cases which have considered fiduciary duty your search should be: "fiduciary duty". Westlaw will search for your search terms within the entire text of all case analyses, official judgments and transcripts.

LexisNexis Butterworths subscription database
Choose the *cases* tab from the homepage. This opens up the cases search form. Enter words or **4–91**
phrases in the *enter search terms* box. You can use Boolean connectors to show the relation of
the terms see para.2.33.

Finding cases interpreting legislation

The easiest method of locating this information is using *Westlaw* or *LexisNexis Butterworths*
with *Current Law Legislation Citators* representing the best paper-based alternative.

Westlaw subscription database
From the welcome page, select the *cases* heading from the navigation bar at the top of the **4–92**
screen. This will take you to the *cases basic search* page, select *advanced search* in the top right of
the screen. Enter the short title in the *legislation title* field and the provision in the *legislation
provision* field. This will retrieve cases which have interpreted the specific provision.

!Example

Find out if any cases have concerned Sch.1 of the Scottish Land Court Act 1993. **4–93**

⇒ Go into the cases section and click on advanced search.
⇒ Enter Scottish Land Court Act 1993 into the *legislation title* field and click on the
schedule option for the *legislative provision* and enter 1 into the box alongside. Click
search.
⇒ View the results which show only one entry and that is for *Maciver v Broadland
Properties Estates*, 1995 S.L.T. (Land Ct.) 9. If you want to see a summary of the case:
click on *case analysis*. If you want to see the full judgment: click on the citation.

Westlaw also offers an alternative method of finding this information. Go into *legislation*, carry **4–94**
out a search for the piece of legislation by entering terms in the search box. When you retrieve
the provision any cases which have cited the provision will appear in the legislation analysis
which can be accessed via the blue left hand navigation bar.

!Example

How many cases have considered s.85 of the Water Resources Act 1991?
If you retrieve s.85 and check the legislation analysis you will see that 35 cases have considered it.

LexisNexis Butterworths subscription database
Choose the cases tab from the homepage. This opens up the cases search form. Enter the short **4–95**
title in the *summary* field. See para.4.15.

Current Law Legislation Citators
The Legislation Citator volumes list cases opposite the entry for the legislation. See para.6.69. **4–96**
How to find out if any cases have taken place concerning a particular statutory provision:

⇒ **Step 1**: Check through the Legislation Citators in chronological order. Look under the
piece of legislation. If a case has taken place, it will appear opposite the statute
or section thereof.
⇒ **Step 2**: You should then check the most recent update for the citator in the Statutes
Service File.

!Example

4–97 Find out if any cases have concerned Sch.1 of the Scottish Land Court Act 1993.

⇒**Step 1**: Check the Statute Citator in the Legislation Citators volume 1989–95. In order to locate the chapter number, check the alphabetical list of Acts at the beginning of the volume. The chapter number is 45. Once armed with the chapter number you can turn to the citator itself. Look under 1993 and within that year at the entry for Ch.45. When you have located the entry for the Act look for the section number. After Sch.1 is a case: *Maciver v Broadland Properties Estates*, 1995 S.L.T. (Land Ct.) 9.

We have so far identified one case which has concerned the relevant section.

⇒**Step 2**: Check the Statute Citator in the Legislation Citators volume 1996–99. There are no entries.

⇒**Step 3**: Check the Statute Citator in the Legislation Citators volume 2000-01. There are no entries.

⇒**Step 4**: Check the Statute Citator in the Legislation Citators volume 2002-04. There are no entries.

⇒**Step 5**: Check the Statute Citator in the Legislation Citators volume 2005. There are no entries.

⇒**Step 6**: Check the Statute Citator in the Legislation Citators volume 2006. There are no entries.

⇒**Step 7**: Check the latest edition of the Statute Citator in the Statutes Service File. Again there are no entries for cases under Sch.1 of the Act.

We can now be certain that (up to the last month) only the one case mentioned above has concerned Sch.1 of the Scottish Land Court Act 1993.

Current Legal Information ✒ and CD Rom subscription legal research service
4–98 The *Current Law* Cases database has a legislation field which allows you to search for summaries of cases which have considered a specific piece of legislation. This will lead you to a digest of the case and citations in the law reports The online version only searches case summaries back to 1986. The CD Rom version searches case summaries back to 1947.

4–99 *Law reports indexes* 📖

➢ *Scots Law Times* has an alphabetical subject index and under the words "statutes and orders" legislation judicially considered is listed in alphabetical order.

➢ Scottish Civil Law Reports has a table in each volume of "Statutes, Statutory Instruments and Court Rules Judicially Considered". This information is consolidated in the 1987–1996 index.

➢ Each volume of Scottish Criminal Case Reports has a "Statutes and Statutory Instruments Judicially Considered" table. These are consolidated in the 1950–1980 supplement and the 1981–1990 and 1991–2000 indexes. The 1950–1980 index contains reference to High Court of Justiciary cases heard before the S.C.C.R. came into existence and previously unreported.

➢ The Faculty Digest contains indexes of "Statutes, Acts of Sederunt, Statutory Orders etc. judicially commented on". Volume 6 contains an index for Vols 1–5; thereafter each volume of the Supplement has its own index.

> ➤ The Consolidated Indexes to the All England Law Reports contain a table of "Statutes Judicially Considered".

Tables of statutes in relevant textbooks 📖
Tables of statutes in textbooks are usually found at the beginning of the book, after the contents **4–100** page and next to the table of cases. The entries will refer to passages in the text that discuss the legislation. Relevant cases may also be discussed at the same point in the text.

Sources useful for UK cases but not for Scottish cases

Halsbury's Statutes of England 📖 and ⌁ subscription
A comprehensive and regularly updated source but which excludes exclusively Scottish material. **4–101**
See para.9.5.

The Law Reports Index 📖
See para.9.19. **4–102**

Lawtel ⌁ subscription legal current awareness digest service
On the *Lawtel UK* homepage click on *browsable legislation*. This option lists legislation cited in **4–103** case law and the list can be viewed alphabetically or chronologically. Click on the name of an Act. This opens up lists which can be expanded. There is a list of cases citing specific sections of an Act and also for a list of cases citing the Act itself. *Lawtel* only lists cases which appear in its database of case summaries and all of the cases cited link to the *Lawtel* case digests. However, Lawtel does not include Scottish cases unless they have been followed in England.

Finding journal articles or case notes about a case

Westlaw ⌁ subscription database
Westlaw is the best way of tracing this information as it contains the Legal Journals Index **4–104** within its journals section. This indexes legal articles and case summaries from over 1,000 journals and dates back to 1986. There are two different ways to obtain this information in *Westlaw*. One is to search the journals section and the alternative is to search the case analysis for the case. To search the journals section access it by selecting *Journals* from the navigation bar at the top of the screen on the welcome page. This will take you to the *journals basic search* page, select *advanced search* in the top right of the screen. Enter either the party names in the *cases cited (party)* field or the citation in the *cases cited (citation)* field. Click search.

Westlaw UK will also identify articles which have discussed cases in the *case analysis* for the case **4–105** concerned. When you search for a case in *Westlaw* (see para.4.4), the results retrieved will offer you a link to the *case analysis* and the full text. If you click on *case analysis* and scroll down to the final section of the *case analysis* it identifies a list of citations to articles about the case which have appeared in legal journals. Links will go to the full text (if available on *Westlaw*) or to an abstract of the article.

LexisNexis Butterworths ⌁ subscription database
This is not as useful for tracing journal articles as it does not have the same coverage as the **4–106** Legal Journals Index on *Westlaw*. Choose the journals tab from the homepage. This opens up the journals search form. Enter the case details separated by "and" in the *enter search terms* box. See para.4.15.

Current Legal Information ⊕ and CD Rom subscription legal research service

4–107 This, like *Westlaw*, also contains the Legal Journals Index. Click on the link to this database and enter the case details in the cases field.

HeinOnline ⊕ subscription database of legal journals

4–108 This increasingly popular database is expanding quickly and is changing its interface at the time of writing. It holds a number of UK law journals in its Law Journal Library. The journals are in full text which can be searched for articles about cases. However, its Scots law holdings are currently limited. See para.8.57.

Current Law Yearbooks 📖

4–109 Check under the appropriate subject headings in the Yearbooks and the latest Monthly Digest. See para.8.21.

Journals 📖

4–110 If you are aware of the date of the case you could check relevant journal indexes. The *Scots Law Times* often contains articles on recent cases. Specialist journals may contain commentaries on recent relevant case law, e.g. Green's Business Law Bulletin, Green's Civil Practice Bulletin, Green's Criminal Law Bulletin, Green's Employment Law Bulletin, Green's Family Law Bulletin and Green's Property Law Bulletin. They are published bi-monthly and contain commentaries about recent cases.

Lawtel ⊕ subscription legal current awareness digest service

4–111 *Lawtel* indexes fewer journals than the Legal Journals Index and the majority of its coverage of journals dates from 1998. To locate articles about a case, select the *articles index* on the home page, then choose the *focused search* option. Use the *case law cited* box to enter the name of the case. However, *Lawtel* has very limited coverage of Scottish cases.

Justcite ⊕ subscription legal citator

4–112 When you search for a case on *Justcite* it will identify articles which have discussed the case at the end of the case information presented. However, most of its coverage of journals is very recent and the numbers of articles retrieved is very small, e.g. when compared to an identical search using *Westlaw*.

Current status of a case (i.e. whether the case has been considered by the court on a subsequent occasion)

Westlaw ⊕ subscription database

4–113 There are two different ways to obtain this information in *Westlaw*.

From the welcome page, select the *cases* heading from the navigation bar at the top of the screen. This will take you to the *cases basic search* page, select *advanced search* in the top right of the screen. Enter the party name(s) in the *cases cited (party)* field or the citation in the *cases cited (citation)* field. This will retrieve details of the cases which have considered the particular case.

An alternative approach is that when you search for a case in *Westlaw* (see para.4.4), the results retrieved will offer you a link to the *case analysis* and the full text. If you click on *case analysis* and then click on *Cases citing this case* in the left hand side of the screen. This will take you to a section of the *case analysis* which identifies a list of citations to cases which have cited the case. Links will go to the full text of the cases if they are available in *Westlaw*.

!Example

Has *Galt v Goodsir* been judicially considered?   **4–114**

   ⇒ Go to the *cases basic search* page.

   ⇒ Select *advanced search* in the top right of the screen.

   ⇒ Enter the party name(s) in the *cases cited (party)* field: *Galt v Goodsir*. This retrieves two results: *Hingston v Pollock* 1990 J.C. 138 and *McMahon v Cardle* 1988 S.C.C.R. 556. You can click through to their case analysis and the full text judgment (here only one of the cases is available in *Westlaw* in full text).

Alternatively:

   ⇒ Go into the *cases basic search* page and enter Galt Goodsir in the *party names* box and click *search*.
Westlaw has retrieved one case.

   ⇒ Click on the *case analysis*. This shows that the case has been judicially considered by two cases. It has been applied by *McMahon v Cardle* 1988 S.C.C.R. 556 and followed by *Hingston v Pollock* 1990 J.C. 138. Clicking on the citations for these cases will take you to their *case analysis* and you can then click through to the full text judgment of the case that is available in *Westlaw*.

Additionally, if you search for a case in *Westlaw* which has been judicially considered, an **4–115** alerting icon will appear in your results list. **C** indicates that the case has been judicially considered elsewhere while ▬ shows that it has been overruled or reversed on appeal.

LexisNexis Butterworths � subscription database
LexisNexis Butterworths will retrieve details of all occasions on which a case has been referred to **4–116** by another case. Go to the *cases* search form. In the *enter search terms* box enter the party names connecting them with w/8. This is called a connector (see para.2.33) and will look for the party names within eight words of each other in any case. See para.4.15.

Justcite ⍤ subscription legal citator
See para.4.40.   **4–117**

Current Law Case Citators 📖
Check through the Case Citators and the latest Monthly Digest, see paras 4.34–4.38. **4–118**

How to find out if a case has been commented on by the courts, distinguished or overruled:

   ⇒ **Step 1**: Check through the *Current Law Case Citators* in chronological order. Remember that if it is a Scottish case you should check in the Scottish section. Cases are listed in alphabetical order of the first named party. Opposite the entry for the case will be details of whether the case has been judicially considered. It will state whether the case was applied, distinguished, followed, referred to, etc.

   ⇒ **Step 2**: You should then check the Table of Cases in the most recent Monthly Digest.

!Example

Has *Galt v Goodsir* 1982 J.C. 4 been judicially considered?   **4–119**

⇒ **Step 1**: In para.4.53 we established that *Galt v Goodsir* appeared in the Case Citator volume 1977–1997. Opposite the entry for the case we also find two references to judicial consideration:
"applied 89/4924
followed 90/5753."

These references are to digests of cases which respectively applied and followed *Galt v Goodsir*.
The digests may be sufficient for your purposes. If not, they will contain the citations for the cases and you can then read the decisions in the relevant law reports.

⇒ **Step 2**: Check the Case Citator volume 1998–2001. There are no entries.
⇒ **Step 3**: Check the Case Citator volume 2002–2004. There are no entries.
⇒ **Step 4**: Check the Case Citator volume 2005. There are no entries.
⇒ **Step 5**: Check the Case Citator volume 2006. There are no entries.
⇒ **Step 6**: Check the Table of Cases in the latest Monthly Digest. Again, there is no entry.

We can conclude that (unless there has been a development in the last month) *Galt v Goodsir* has been judicially considered on two occasions.

Current Legal Information ⌁ and CD Rom subscription legal research service
4–120 Check the *Current Law* Cases section. This covers cases from 1986. You can search by field (this includes cases cited) or free text. Following the example above:

⇒ Enter *Galt v Goodsir* in the cases cited field and click search. This will lead you to references to two cases. By clicking on their names you will be taken to a summary of the case. See para.4.28 for more details.

The Law Reports Index ▭
4–121 Check section on cases judicially considered. See para.9.19.

Checking the status of old Scottish cases

Faculty Digest ▭
4–122 This covers cases from 1868–1990. Check Tables of "Cases Judicially Referred to". See para.4.29 and the worked example in para.4.68.

Scots Digest ▭
4–123 Check tables of "Cases judicially commented on" in relation to the Scottish superior courts from 1800–1947. See para.4.33.
How to find out if an older case has been commented on by the courts, distinguished or overruled

!Example

4–124 Has *Crombie v M'Ewan* 1871 23 D. 333 been judicially considered?

⇒ **Step 1**: Check Faculty Digest. Vol. 6, the indices volume contains a Table of Cases Judicially Referred to. This contains an entry for the above case. It was applied in *Gray v Smart*, 1892 19 R. 692, 29 S.L.R. 589.
⇒ **Step 2**: The Supplement volumes need to be checked one by one:

1922–1930   no entry

1930–1940   no entry
1940–1950   entry—it was followed in *Brady v Napier & Son* 1944 S.C. 18,
1943 S.N. 71, 1944 S.L.T. 187.
1951–1960   no entry
1961–1970   no entry
1971–1980   no entry
1981–1990   no entry

⇒ **Step 3**:   The search has to be completed by checking *Current Law* Case Citators which
do not show any entries.

Finding out about very recent cases

There are now many different sources which make cases available very quickly after judgment   **4–125**
has been given by a court. While it is always important for those studying the law to be as up-to-
date as possible, the widespread availability of recent cases poses some problems. When cases
make their first appearance on websites they are not rated in any way to suggest their legal
importance although the seniority of the court concerned may give an indication of the
importance of the judgment. It can take some time for commentaries which interpret the case to
start to appear and place it into a context. This means that the ability to find very recent cases is
not of particular use to a law student unless a lecturer draws attention to a case or there is a
desire to read the details of a controversial case.

The quickest way of locating very recent judgments is to access the website of the court con-   **4–126**
cerned. The website of the Scottish courts (para.4.21), Scottish Land Court (para.4.25), House
of Lords (para.4.23), and the Judicial Committee of the Privy Council (para.4.24), have been
discussed. If you want to search for very recent cases from several different courts at the same
time BAILLI (para.4.22) is a useful free source. Use the *case law search* function with appropriate dates. Alternatively you can view recent decisions by court in *BAILII's recent decisions list*
which can be reached by a link from the home page.

As mentioned above, these sources do not select the cases by their legal significance. All cases   **4–127**
from the particular courts will tend to appear. However, there are some sources of recent
judgments which do select their content. One example is the *WLR Daily*. This is a free case
summary service from The Incorporated Council of Law Reporting's service (ICLR) and can be
accessed at (*http://www.lawreports.co.uk/WLRD/AboutWLRD.htm*) The courts covered are: the
House of Lords; the Privy Council; the Court of Appeal and all divisions of the High Court; The
Royal Courts of Justice; and the European Court of Justice. The cases reported are cases
deemed to be worthy of inclusion in The Weekly Law Reports, The Law Reports or The
Industrial Cases Reports. You can view daily summaries of *Latest Case*s as they appear or
navigate via the *Monthly Archive*. Alternatively, you can search by subject matter using the
Subject Matter Search. The cases are summarised and appear within 24 hours of judgment being
handed down.

Another free site which is also provided by ICLR is *The Industrial Case Reports Express*. This   **4–128**
can be accessed at (*http://www.lawreports.co.uk/ICRE/icrehome.htm*). It contains summaries of
selected employment law cases which set a precedent, develop a point of law or raise interesting
points from a legal perspective and which will be published in The Industrial Cases Reports.

Cases first appear on *Westlaw UK* in the current awareness section on the day the case is issued   **4–129**
and then appear in full text in the cases section within 24 hours. If you are looking for UK

decisions then Casetrack (para.4.26) and Lawtel (para.4.30) both provide very fast (within 24 hours) access to cases. However, Scottish coverage is patchy on both sites.

4–130 *Daily Cases* is a subscription service provided by Justis. It is a fully searchable web version of the *WLR Daily* (above). It includes judgments of the House of Lords, the Privy Council, the Court of Appeal, all Divisions of the High Court, the Courts-Martial Appeal Court, the Restrictive Practices Court, the Employment Appeal Tribunal and the European Court of Justice. Only cases that develop or clarify a point of law or that set a legal precedent are included. Practice Directions, Practice Notes and Practice Statements are also covered. Its coverage is from 1999 to the present and it is updated most working days.

4–131 Law reports are published in newspapers but these are only short summaries of a case. English daily newspapers which publish law reports are: The Daily Telegraph (*http://www.tele-graph.co.uk* has law reports from Westlaw updated every Thursday), The Financial Times, The Guardian, The Independent and The Times (see para.9.24). The Scotsman used to publish law reports but ceased to do so some time ago.

4–132 Law reports which are published weekly represent the fastest paper source for recent cases. In Scotland the *Scots Law Times* and *Green's Weekly Digest* are both published weekly. In England the All England Law Reports and the Weekly Law Reports are published weekly. The Pink Index to the Law Reports is also updated frequently.

4–133 Note that there is usually a time delay between a judgment being given and the case being reported in the law reports (even the weekly series of law reports). The delay will tend to be a couple of months. The first law report series in Scotland to carry a case will be *Green's Weekly Digest*. This will contain a brief summary of the case.

4–134 The *Current Law* Monthly Digest also provides information on recent cases. See para.8.15.

Finding cases from other courts

4–135 Source of cases from other courts:

> ➤ Court of the Lord Lyon.
> Since 1950 selected cases from the Lyon Court have been reported in the *Scots Law Times*.
> ➤ Scottish Land Court.
> Decisions are published as the Scottish Land Court Reports 1982 to the present. Digests of cases since 1982 are available online (*http://www.scottish-land-court.org.uk/digest.html*) as are recent unreported decisions (*http://www.scottish-land-court.org.uk/recent.html*). From 1964 onwards selected cases have been published in the *Scots Law Times*. Decisions of the Land Court were published as a supplement to the *Scottish Law Review* and *Reports of Sheriff Court Cases*. From 1913 to 1963 the published decisions in each year were bound as the *Scottish Land Court Reports*. You will also find decisions published as an appendix to annual reports by the Scottish Land Court 1912–1981.
> ➤ Lands Valuation Appeal Court.
> Decisions are published in *Session Cases* (since 1907) and the *Scots Law Times* (since 1893).
> ➤ Lands Tribunal for Scotland.
> The website for the Lands Tribunal contains details of decisions made in recent cases that the tribunal considers to be important or significant. There are examples under the

jurisdictions relating to disputed compensation, valuation for rating, tenants' rights to buy, discharge of land obligations, Land Register appeals, and title conditions. There is a free text search facility and the decisions can be browsed by subject. The results retrieved will take you to a summary of the case from where the full text of the decision can be opened. They can be accessed at *http://www.lands-tribunal-scotland.org.uk/ records.html*. Selected cases have been reported in the *Scots Law Times* since 1971.

Finding decisions from Tribunals

Administrative tribunals are not bound by the doctrine of judicial precedent and are generally **4–136** less formal than a court. Some of the cases appear in the law reports but only a small number. They tend to be reports of cases which have been appealed from a tribunal to a court. Many tribunals do, however, publish their decisions.

Decisions of the Social Security Commissioner

All Commissioners' decisions have file numbers beginning with a "C", e.g. CSSP/4567/2006. **4–137** Scottish cases are identified by an "S" after the "C", e.g. CSU/123/2007. The other letters indicate the type of case, see below. The first set of numbers represents the individual file number. The final digits identify the year in which the file was opened at the Commissioners' office.

The following abbreviations indicate the type of case: **4–138**

A   Attendance allowance
AF   War pensions and the armed and reserve forces compensation scheme
CR   Compensation recovery
CS   Child support
CTF   Child trust fund
DLA Disability living allowance
DWA Disability working allowance
F   Family allowance (now child benefit)
FC   Family credit
FG   Forfeiture—general (bereavement benefit and widow's benefit)
FP   Forfeiture—pension (retirement pension)
G   General (e.g. bereavement benefit, carer's allowance, death grant, maternity benefit)
H   Housing benefit and council tax benefit
HR   Home responsibilities protection
I   Industrial accidents and diseases and industrial injuries benefits
IB   Incapacity benefit
IS   Income support and social fund payments
JSA   Jobseeker's allowance
M   Mobility allowance
P   Pension (retirement pension)
PC   Pension credit
S   Sickness benefit and invalidity benefit
SB   Supplementary benefit
SSP   Statutory sick pay
TC   Tax credits
U   Unemployment benefit

When a decision is selected for reporting it is given a new number beginning with an "R": e.g. **4–139** CH/4306/2003 is reported as R(H) 2/05. The letters in brackets again identify the type of case. Scottish decisions are not expressly identified as such.

4–140 Details of decisions can be found at the decisions database on the website for the Social Security, Child Support and Pensions Appeal Commissioners (*http://www.osscsc.gov.uk/ decisions/decisions.htm*). The database contains over 2000 Great Britain Commissioners' decisions. It includes all reported commissioners' decisions from 1991 to date and all decisions from 2002. This database can be searched by adjudicator, subject category, file number, reported number. This database can be searched by word or phrase if accessed via *BAILII*, see, para.4.22.

4–141 Social Security and Child Support Commissioners Scotland website (*http://www.ossc-scotland. org.uk/index.shtml*) currently contains information about the Commissioners' Office in Scotland but has no decisions.

4–142 Neligan's Digest is a summary of important reported decisions (and some unreported) of the Social Security Commissioners. It is available on the Department of Work and Pension's website (*http://www.dwp.gov.uk/advisers/docs/neligans/volume1.asp*). It consists of two volumes which contain 32 chapters (although Chs 24–28 are spare) and appendices. Each chapter contains a contents list giving the subjects covered. Case summaries are arranged under the subject headings in chronological order. Appendix 2 contains a list of court decisions in proceedings against, or concerning or judicially considered in, Commissioners' decisions.

4–143 Decisions from other tribunals:

> The Stationery Office publishes Immigration Appeals and Value Added Tax Tribunals Reports.
> *Additional Support Needs Tribunals for Scotland* ⌖ free
> *http://www.asntscotland.gov.uk*
> This tribunal came into effect in 2005 and its decisions will be accessible via its website in due course.
> *Asylum Support Tribunal* ⌖ free
> *http://www.asylum-support-tribunal.gov.uk*
> This database can be searched by reference number, adjudicator, subject category, date and keyword.
> *Employment Appeals Tribunal* ⌖ free
> *http://www.employmentappeals.gov.uk*
> This has a searchable database which covers judgments since 1999. It can be searched by topic, EAT number, judge, party and date. Decisions of the Employment Appeal Tribunal (E.A.T.) are also published in the Industrial Cases Reports and the Industrial Relations Law Reports.
> *Finance and Tax Tribunals* ⌖ free
> *http://www.financeandtaxtribunals.gov.uk*
> This contains a decisions database where decisions since April 2003 can be searched by case number, topic, commissioner, date, category and party.
> *Transport Tribunal* ⌖ free
> *http://www.transporttribunal.gov.uk*
> This contains a searchable database of decisions from 2000. It can be searched by file number, category, date and party. It also contains a Transport Tribunal Digest which is a pdf where decisions appear under subject headings and in a chronological list.

Many tribunal decisions are available via the *BAILII* database, see para.4.22.

PUTTING CASES INTO CONTEXT

In order to put any case into context you need to appreciate where it lies in the development of **4–144** the law in whichever subject area. There are many different ways of locating material to facilitate your understanding of the relevance of a case:

> ➤ Examine your lecture notes.
> ➤ Text books.
> ➤ *The Laws of Scotland: Stair Memorial Encyclopaedia* or other major reference works.
> ➤ Some series of law reports contain commentaries on selected or all cases. Examples include Scottish Criminal Case Reports, Scottish Civil Law Reports, Green's Family Law Reports, Green's Housing Law Reports and the Environmental Law Reports.
> ➤ Journal commentaries or case notes. See paras 4.104–4.112 for how to find these articles about cases.
> ➤ The *Case analysis* section of *Westlaw* (see para.4.13) identifies and links to cases which have considered the case and relevant journal articles if available within *Westlaw*.
> ➤ *Current Law Case Citator* (see paras 4.34–4.38) gives references to any subsequent cases which have considered the case. The relevant case reports can then be examined.

Understanding the relevance of a very recent case (within the last month): **4–145**

> ➤ Check through daily newspapers and weekly published journals. You should also check journals published on the internet.
> ➤ If nothing has been written about it, you will have to make your own analysis of the case.

FURTHER READING

A. Bradney et al, *How to Study Law* 5th edn (London: Sweet & Maxwell, 2005).
P. Clinch, *Using a Law Library* 2nd edn (London: Blackstone Press, 2001) Chapter 12 covers Scottish case law.
G. Holburn and G. Engle, *Butterworths Legal Research Guide* (London: Butterworths, 2001).
J. Knowles and P. Thomas, *Effective Legal Research* (London: Sweet & Maxwell, 2006).
P.A. Thomas and J. Knowles, *Dane & Thomas How to Use a Law Library* 4th edn (London: Sweet & Maxwell 2001). This contains a separate Scottish chapter.
D.M. Walker, *The Scottish Legal System* 8th edn (Edinburgh: W. Green, 2001).

Chapter 5
Legislation

Introduction To Legislation

5–1 Legislation is the major source of Scots law today. You will encounter numerous pieces of legislation in your career at university and beyond. Familiarity with the concept of legislation and the various formats in which it appears is essential to the study of law. Chapter 5 will introduce you to the various types of legislation and the legislation process. It will also cover the skills of reading and understanding statutes and statutory instruments. Chapters 6 and 7 will concentrate on aids to tracing legislation and different search strategies which can be adopted.

Discussion of the sources of legislation which affect Scotland involves understanding some of the key events in Scottish history. Prior to 1707, Scotland was an independent country with its own Parliament which enacted legislation. The Treaty of Union of 1707 dissolved both the old English and Scottish Parliaments and created the new Parliament of Great Britain. This new Parliament became the only source of legislation for Scotland for several centuries. However, the Treaty of Union contained safeguards for the continuation of Scots law. It stated that no alteration was to be made in laws concerning "private right"—"except for the evident utility of the subjects within Scotland" (Article XVIII). The Court of Session and the High Court of Justiciary were to remain within Scotland 'in all time coming'. A new legislative influence began in 1972 with Britain's membership of the European Economic Community (now the European Union). A new source of legislation emerged in 1999—following a referendum in 1997 and the passing of the Scotland Act 1998—with the devolution of some legislative power from the UK Parliament to the new Scottish Parliament.

5–2 Today legislation affecting Scotland can emerge from the Scottish Parliament, the Westminster Parliament and the EC institutions. European legislation is dealt with in Chapter 10. The UK Parliament is the supreme legislator within the UK. Although the Scotland Act 1998 devolved some legislative powers to the Scottish Parliament it retained what are referred to as "reserved powers" to the UK Parliament. This means that the UK Parliament still enacts legislation for Scotland.

UK legislation can be divided into primary legislation, such as Acts of Parliament (sometimes referred to as statutes), and delegated (sometimes referred to as secondary or subordinate) legislation. The main form of delegated legislation is statutory instruments. Primary legislation is made by the UK Parliament and involves a process of parliamentary scrutiny. Delegated legislation can be made by an individual or a body who has been given the power to legislate by the UK Parliament. A key difference between the two types of legislation concerns challenges to their validity. The validity of Acts of the UK Parliament cannot be challenged in court. The validity of delegated legislation can be so challenged. The validity of legislation emerging from the Scottish Parliament is also open to challenge.

An Act of Parliament can alter the general law of the land, in which case it is called a Public General Act. However, it is also possible (although much less common) to affect only private interests by Act of Parliament. This type of Act is called a Local and Personal Act, see para.5.13.

5–3 Once an Act has become law it can be altered. The term used is "amended". An Act may be amended many times. The amendments may in turn be amended. An Act cannot be amended by something said by a judge in a case or by the comments of a member of the Government in the House of Commons. It can only be amended by later Acts of Parliament or statutory instrument.

Acts of Parliament do not cease to have the force of law just because they are old or have not been applied for a long period of time. An Act remains part of the law until it is repealed which means that it ceases to be part of the law. Whole Acts or parts of Acts can be repealed. An Act can be repealed in one part of the UK but remain law in another area. Acts can be repealed by later Acts or by delegated legislation (providing it is within its powers). You may encounter the term "desuetude". This doctrine held that there was implied repeal of an Act that was not used for a long period of time. If it applies at all now, it applies only to pre-1707 Scots Acts.

This chapter will briefly look at the pre-1707 Scots Parliament. It then moves on to the UK **5–4** Parliament and discusses the process by which laws are made, the anatomy of both a statute and a statutory instrument and provides advice on how to read and understand legislation. The chapter then turns to the Scottish Parliament and considers its process for making laws and the anatomy of both an Act of the Scottish Parliament and a Scottish statutory instrument.

Pre-1707 Scots Parliament

The earliest statutes which still affect the law of Scotland today emerged from the Scots Par- **5–5** liament which existed prior to the Treaty of Union in 1707. Not many of the statutes of the Scots Parliament are still in force and, unless you are undertaking a study of the history of Scots law, it is unlikely that you will come across them. The form of these statutes is very different from the layout and style of statutes today. They are usually very short and are obviously written in the language of the time which can make them difficult for the modern reader, especially those unfamiliar with the Scots language. Pre-1707 legislation is discussed in paras 7.3–7.7.

Modern Statutes from the UK Parliament Applying to Scotland

Bills

A Bill is a draft version of an Act before it is considered by Parliament. It is referred to as a Bill **5–6** throughout its passage through Parliament and it becomes an Act after it receives the Royal Assent. There are three types of Bills: public, private and hybrid.

Public Bills
Public Bills affect the general law of the land and every member of the population. A gov- **5–7** ernment Bill is a Public Bill which is presented to Parliament by a government Minister. It will have been drafted by parliamentary draftsmen who are civil servants. Private Members Bills are Public Bills (not Private Bills) which are introduced by an individual M.P. (or peer in the House of Lords) rather than by the government. Public Bills account for the majority of Bills today. Public Bills become Public General Acts.

Private Bills
Private Bills tend to be limited in effect to a certain area or organisation or even person. The **5–8** process is initiated by a promoter instead of an M.P. A promoter is someone who has an interest in the Bill. Historically there were large numbers of Private Bills but they are much less common today. They were used to facilitate major works such as the construction of the railways,

harbours and canals. They were also used for some personal matters such as divorce. Private Bills become Local and Personal Acts (also referred to as Private Acts). The procedure relating to Private Bills is different from Public Bills and is dealt with in para.5.15.

Hybrid Bills

5–9   As its name suggest, this is a Bill which contains elements of both Public and Private Bills. The procedure used is a mixture of Public and Private Bill procedures.

The procedure for a Public Bill in the UK Parliament

5–10   Most Bills may be introduced in Parliament in either the House of Lords or the House of Commons. A Bill must pass the stages detailed below in both Houses before it can be submitted for Royal Assent.

First Reading. This is the formal presentation of the Bill to Parliament. The name of the Bill is read out and a date set for the second reading. An order is made for the Bill to be printed and to become publicly available.

Second Reading. This is where the House considers the principles contained in the Bill. The debate is recorded in Hansard.

Committee Stage. This stage involves consideration of the Bill on a clause-by-clause basis. The whole House can consider a Bill at Committee stage but this usually only happens in exceptional circumstances, such as for Bills of constitutional importance. The norm is for a Bill to be considered by a Public Bill Committee (known as Standing Committees prior to the 2006–2007 session).

Report Stage. This consists of the whole House considering the amendments made in Committee. If the Bill was previously dealt with by a Committee of the Whole House and no amendments were made, it by-passes this stage and goes straight to third reading.

Third Reading. This is where the House takes an overview of the amended Bill. When a Bill has completed these stages it then goes to the House of Lords. It has to pass through similar stages in the House of Lords. When both Houses reach agreement about the Bill it goes forward for Royal Assent. Once a Bill receives the Royal Assent it becomes an Act. It does not automatically become law see para.5.16, section [8].

Citation of Bills

5–11   Each Bill is given a number. However, if the Bill is reprinted it will be given a new number. Bills may be amended many times as they progress through the various stages outlined above. They may be reprinted in a form that incorporates all the amendments. It is, therefore, very important that you are aware of which version of the Bill you are reading. The number of a Bill has no connection with the chapter number that will be allocated when it becomes an Act.

The elements of the citation of a Bill are:

1.   The initials of the House, e.g. H.C. or H.L.
2.   The session of Parliament, e.g. 2006–2007.
3.   The Bill number. If this is in square brackets it means that the Bill is being considered by the House of Commons. In the past round brackets meant that the Bill was being considered by the House of Lords however no brackets are now used.

Example of a Bill being considered by the House of Commons: Rating (Empty Properties) Bill HC 2006–2007 [102].

Example of a Bill being considered by the House of Lords: Forced Marriage (Civil Protection) Bill HL 2006–2007 70 (this is the Bill as reprinted following amendments, the Bill was originally introduced as the Forced Marriage (Civil Protection) Bill HL 2006–2007 3).

The divisions of a Bill are referred to as clauses and not as sections as in an Act of Parliament.

Citation of statutes

Acts of Parliament are normally referred to by their short title, e.g. Marriage (Scotland) Act **5–12** 1977. A complete citation would include the chapter number: Marriage (Scotland) Act 1977 c.15. It could also be cited by referring to the year in which it was passed and the chapter number, e.g. 1977 c.15.

Since 1963, the chapter number has been related to the sequence in which the Acts received the Royal Assent during a calendar year. The above Act was the 15th Act to receive the Royal Assent in 1977. Prior to 1963 the system was not as simple. Each Act was given a chapter number which related to its chronological place within the parliamentary session. Parliamentary sessions do not coincide with calendar years, they run from November to July. They will, therefore, span more than one calendar year. Each parliamentary session was numbered according to the regnal year. This means the years during which the sovereign had reigned. This was calculated from the month of accession to the throne. A table of the regnal years appears at the front of this book. You will notice that no Scottish monarchs are included in the list. This is because Acts of the pre-1707 Scottish Parliaments were referred to as stated in para.7.6 and not with reference to the regnal year.

The regnal year system means that Acts passed in the same calendar year can be in different regnal years and/or in different parliamentary sessions. This means that care has to be taken when checking the older volumes of statutes.

This cumbersome system was brought to an end by The Acts of Parliament Numbering and Citation Act 1962. Section 1 stated that chapter numbers were to be assigned by reference to the calendar year and not to the parliamentary session.

Local and Personal Acts

Private Bills become Local and Personal Acts. These Acts tend to be limited in effect to a certain **5–13** area or organisation or even person. There were large numbers of Private Acts in the past but they are much less common today. They were used to facilitate major works such as the construction of the railways, harbours and canals. They were also used for some personal matters such as divorce.

Citation
Local and Personal Acts are cited in the same way as Public General Acts, except that, in order **5–14** to differentiate them, the chapter number is printed differently.

The chapter numbers of Local Acts appear in lower case roman numerals, e.g. Peterhead Harbours Order Confirmation Act 1992 c xii.

The chapter numbers of Personal Acts appear in italicised arabic figures, e.g. John Francis Dare and Gillian Loder Dare (Marriage Enabling) Act 1982 *c.1*.

Procedure for Private Bills
The normal procedure involves the presentation of a petition to Parliament by the person or **5–15** organisation who is promoting the Bill. Information about the contents of the Bill has to be widely circulated and the petitioner has to appear before an examiner. Private Bills then go through the same stages as Public Bills.

Post devolution Scottish Private Bills which concern reserved matters are dealt with by the

UK Parliament. They are subject to a streamlined procedure laid down in the Private Legislation Procedure (Scotland) Act 1936. Application has to be made to the Secretary of State for Scotland for a Provisional Order. If an inquiry is deemed appropriate, it is undertaken by Commissioners and sits in Scotland. They make a report to the Secretary of State. If the Order has been approved, the Secretary of State will issue the Order. This does not become law until it has been confirmed by Parliament. The mechanism for this is an Order Confirmation Bill (which is a Public Bill) with the text of the Order appearing as the schedule to the Bill. If the Bill proceeds through a shortened parliamentary procedure, it emerges as a Local and Personal Act.

Anatomy of a statute

5–16 This is an example of a Public General Act. It has been chosen because of its brevity—not all Acts are as short as this one—they are usually much longer. While all Acts adopt the same format some, but not necessarily all, features will appear in all Acts. Different features are marked with numbers which correspond to the following list:

Local Government (Gaelic Names) (Scotland) Act 1997

1997 Chapter 6

Local Government (Gaelic Names) (Scotland) Act 1997 [1]

1997 Chapter 6 [2]

An Act to enable local authorities in Scotland to take [3] Gaelic names; and for connected purposes.

[27th February 1997] [4]

BE IT ENACTED by the Queen's most Excellent [5] Majesty, by and with the advice and consent of the Lords Spiritual and Temporal, and Commons, in this present Parliament assembled, and by the authority of the same, as follows:-

Power of council to change name into Gaelic and vice-versa. [7]

1. In section 23 of the Local Government (Scotland) Act [6] 1973 (change of name of local government area), there shall be inserted, after subsection (1), the following subsections-

> "(1A) Where a council so change the name of their area into Gaelic, they may also, by a resolution passed in accordance with subsection (1) above and notwithstanding sections 2(3) and 3(1)(a) of the Local Government etc. (Scotland) Act 1994, decide that their name shall be 'Comhairle' with the addition of the name of their area.
>
> (1B) A council which have so changed their name into Gaelic may, by a resolution passed in accordance with subsection (1) above, change it back into English.".

Short title, commencement and extent.

2.—(1) This Act may be cited as the Local Government [8] (Gaelic Names) (Scotland) Act 1997.

(2) This Act shall come into force on the expiry of the period of two months beginning with the day on which it is passed.

(3) This Act extends to Scotland only.

Key:

[1] The *short title* of the Act. This is the normal way to refer to the Act. The Short Titles Act 1896 and the Statute Law Revision Act 1948 gave short titles to many of the older Acts. Sch.2 of the Statute Law Revision (Scotland) Act 1962 gave short titles to many of the Acts of the pre-1707 Scottish Parliament.

[2] This is another way of referring to Acts—by their year and *chapter number*. The modern system of assigning chapter numbers dates from 1963. For the position before 1963, see para.5.12. A chapter number is assigned to each Act in chronological order throughout a calendar year. This means that this was the sixth Act of 1997.

[3] This is the *long title*. It sets out the purpose of the Act in very general terms. It will be more detailed than the short title. However, it is not a detailed guide to the background of the Act. It is no longer the practice for modern Acts to include a preamble but older Acts do contain an explanation of the reasons for the Act. Preambles could be quite detailed—far more so than the brief statement of purpose in modern long titles.

[4] The date which appears at the end of the long title in square brackets is the date of *Royal Assent*. This may or may not be the date that the Act comes into force. See section [8] below regarding commencement generally.

[5] This is the *standard enacting formula*. These words indicate that the Act has the full authority of Parliament.

[6] Acts are divided up into parts called *sections*. Sections are numbered consecutively throughout an Act. Sections can be subdivided into subsections. Subsections can be divided into paragraphs and further divided into sub-paragraphs.

If the Act is long or deals with separate things, it may be divided into parts and chapters, *e.g.* The Environment Act 1995 is divided into five parts:

> ➤ Part I The Environment Agency and The Scottish Environment Protection Agency
> ➤ Part II Contaminated Land and Abandoned Mines
> ➤ Part III National Parks
> ➤ Part IV Air Quality
> ➤ Part V Miscellaneous, General and Supplemental Provisions

Part I is then subdivided into three chapters:

Chapter I The Environment Agency
Chapter II The Scottish Environment Agency
Chapter III Miscellaneous, General and Supplemental Provisions Relating to the New Agencies

Chapter II contains ss.20–36:

"s34. general duties with respect to water
(1) It shall be the duty of SEPA—

(a) to promote the cleanliness of—
(i) rivers, other inland waters and ground waters in Scotland; and
(ii) the tidal waters of Scotland; and
(b) to conserve so far as practicable the water resources of Scotland."

The reference to SEPA's duty to promote the cleanliness of tidal waters is contained in the Environment Act 1995, s.34(1)(a)(ii). This means sub-paragraph (ii) of paragraph (a) of sub-section (1) of section 34 of the Act.

[7] *Marginal notes* are not technically part of the Act. They describe the content of the section in very brief terms.

N.B. The interpretation section is usually, but not always, to be found near the end of the Act. It sets out definitions of certain words which have been used in the Act. Words can be given a particular meaning for the whole of an Act or for a part of it. This Act does not have an interpretation section.

[8] The last section of an Act usually provides for citation of the short title, commencement and geographic extent. These are discussed in turn.

Short title. This also appears at the start of the Act. See comments above in section [1].

Commencement. If the Act contains no commencement provision there is a presumption that it comes into force at the beginning of the day on which it receives the Royal Assent. The commencement provisions in an Act can provide for it coming into force in one of three ways:

(a) The Act can specify a particular date.
(b) The Act can specify a period after the passing of the Act when the Act will come into force. This is the case with this Act. It came into force two months after it was passed, i.e. April 27, 1997.
(c) The Act can state that it is to come into force on a date to be set by a person, usually the relevant Secretary of State. It would be brought into force by a type of statutory instrument called a Commencement Order.

The whole of an Act can be brought into force at once or sections of it can become law at different times. This means that you need to check the commencement section carefully. There can be considerable time delay between an Act receiving the Royal Assent and becoming law. Some Acts never become law.

Some terminology can cause confusion. If an Act is referred to as "becoming law" or "coming into force" it has come into operation. If an Act has been "passed" or is referred to as "being on the statute books", it means that it has received the Royal Assent but has not necessarily become law.

Geographic extent. If an Act applies exclusively to Scotland the word "(Scotland)" will appear in the short title. However, finding Scottish legislation is not as straightforward as looking for Acts with "(Scotland)" in the short title as it is possible for legislation without "(Scotland)" in the short title to apply in Scotland. There is a presumption that Acts of the UK Parliament apply to the whole of the UK. If the Act is silent then it is taken to apply throughout the UK.

It is possible for only parts of an Act to apply to Scotland. If an Act applies only to part of the UK it has to state this expressly. Acts usually do this in the extent section. This means that you must always check the extent section of an Act.

N.B. Schedules may appear at the end of an Act. A large Act may contain numerous schedules. For instance, the Environment Act 1995 mentioned above contained 24 schedules. Schedules are not divided into sections, instead they are divided into paragraphs and sub-paragraphs. Schedules have equal force in law as the rest of the Act—they do not have a lower status just because they are added on to the end of the Act. Material is usually put into schedules because it is very detailed or technical and it is easier to present in tabular or list form. A common inclusion in schedules is a list of previous legislation which has been amended or repealed by the Act.

Reading legislation

Beware of making assumptions:

5–17

> ➢ You cannot presume that because you have found the text of an Act of Parliament that it constitutes the law. Firstly, you cannot assume that an Act is in force. All or part of it may not have been brought into force. See commencement in para.5.16 section [8]. Further, you cannot assume that it has not been amended or repealed. You need to check to see if any changes have taken place; see section starting at para.6.103.

> ➢ Another dangerous assumption is that an Act automatically applies to Scotland. It is safe to make this assumption if the word "Scotland" is included in the short title. If this is not the case, you should check the extent section. This will always be found at the end of the Act. See para.5.16 section [8]. Never assume that Acts without "Scotland" in the title do not apply to Scotland.

> ➢ You cannot assume that a word used in a statute will have the same meaning as it does in everyday usage. A word can have a special meaning for a section or for the whole Act. Make sure that you check to see if any special meaning has been given to the words of the statute. This involves looking for an interpretation section. This will normally be near the end of an Act. Remember that a definition given in one statute does not necessarily apply in other statutes. Only definitions in statutes which are *in pari materia* (of similar subject matter) can be used.

5–18 How do you read a statute?

Do not read an Act from beginning to end. They are not intended to be read in that way. Go straight to the section you are interested in or check the contents of the Act to locate a relevant section.

At first sight statutes bear little resemblance to normal English prose. They are set out in a very formal way and the language used can be difficult to comprehend. The most important piece of advice is to read statutes *carefully*. The exact wording is very important. Every word has been deliberately chosen. You need to be alert to the smallest of words as they can be crucial to your understanding of a provision. There is a huge difference between the word "may" which suggests that you can do something and the word "shall" which means that you must do something.

Pay particular attention to words at the beginning of a section, e.g. "subject to the provisions of section 10". This means that the current section is subordinate to the provisions of section 10. If there is any conflict between the two sections, section 10 will prevail.

5–19 If you want help in understanding a statutory provision you should consult:

> ⇒ Lecture notes, if relevant.

> ⇒ A textbook on the subject area. Check the Table of Statutes at the beginning of the book to see if any reference has been made to the Act. The table should give you page references where the Act has been discussed.

> ⇒ Annotations to the Act. Some versions of Acts contain annotations, e.g. *Current Law Statutes*. These are written by experts in the relevant area of law. There is usually a long introductory note at the beginning of the Act which explains its significance and places it in context. It will also refer you to the parliamentary debates on the Bill. Throughout the Act there will be shorter annotations which should help to explain the various sections and the effect they have on the existing law. Annotations can be very helpful but you should always remember that they are not authoritative. They are only the view of one person, albeit an expert.

> ⇒ Journal commentaries. These can be located by searching:

> (a) The Legal Journals Index is an index of articles which have appeared in UK legal journals since 1986. It is available via *Westlaw* and the advanced search function allows you to search for legislation cited in articles, see para.8.48.

(b) *Current Law*. Check under the appropriate subject headings in the Yearbooks and the latest Monthly Digest. See paras 8.15 and 8.21.

(c) The *Scots Law Times* and the *Journal of the Law Society of Scotland* often contain articles on recent legislation.

(d) Specialist journals may contain commentaries on recent relevant legislation.

⇒ Cases which have considered the legislation. *Westlaw* (electronic) and the *Current Law Legislation Citators* (paper) will give you references to any subsequent cases which have considered the legislation. See paras 4.92–4.103. The relevant case reports can then be examined.

Statutory interpretation

When trying to interpret the words of a statute you do not have a free hand. There are rules and **5–20** conventions governing how to interpret statutory provisions. What should you do if you cannot understand the wording of a statute? Below is a diagram of possible approaches. The detail of statutory interpretation is outwith the scope of this work, but see suggested further reading below for discussion of this topic.

Problem word/phrase: Has it been legally defined?	⇒ definitions section (located within Act itself)
	⇒ Interpretation Act 1978*
Have any cases interpreted this word/phrase as it occurred in this Act?	⇒ *Westlaw/Current Law Legislation Citators* —see para.4.92–4.103
Has it been defined in any statute that is *in pari materia?*	⇒ locate Acts which concern similar subject matter
Have the courts interpreted this word?	⇒ Judicial Dictionary, (para.4.85) updated by Words and Phrases Table in *Current Law Yearbooks* and *Monthly Digests* or *Westlaw* (para.4.90)

Note that this information may all be contained in an annotation to the Act.

If this search reveals nothing, try an English dictionary but remember, all that a dictionary can do is provide evidence of the ordinary meaning of a word. It cannot provide a definitive answer. Language is a very imprecise medium and a dictionary is likely to give several different definitions of the word which are equally valid. Dictionaries do not often solve legal problems.

If the word is ambiguous or unclear, use the rules of statutory interpretation	⇒ overall approach, e.g. purposive, literal
	⇒ grammatical context, e.g. *ejusdem generis*
	⇒ presumptions, e.g. legislation is presumed not to be retrospective

*Interpretation Act 1978. This is not as helpful as the name would suggest. It contains definitions of commonly used terms. It deals with matters such as words in the singular should include the plural and vice versa. It is unlikely to be of much help.

Further reading

Further reading on statutory interpretation: **5–21**

J.A. Holland and J.S. Webb, *Learning Legal Rules* 6th edn (Oxford: OUP, 2006) Chapter 8.

A.A. Paterson and T.St.J.N. Bates, *The Legal System of Scotland* 4th edn (Edinburgh: W. Green, 1999) Chapter 14.

W.A. Wilson, *Introductory Essays on Scots Law* 2nd edn (Edinburgh: W. Green, 1984), "Interpreting Statutes".

D.M. Walker, *The Scottish Legal System* 8th edn (Edinburgh: W. Green, 2001), pp.413–432.

R.M. White and I.D. Willock, *The Scottish Legal System* 3rd edn (Haywards Heath: Tottel 2003) Chapter 5.

DELEGATED LEGISLATION

5–22 The UK Parliament is the supreme law-maker within the UK but it is able to delegate its law-making powers to others. Delegated (sometimes called secondary or subordinate) legislation is legislation made by individuals or bodies other than Parliament, but with the authority of Parliament. Authority is given by the inclusion of a provision (known as an enabling provision) in an Act of Parliament. An example is s.245(1) of the Criminal Procedure (Scotland) Act 1995: "The Secretary of State may make rules for regulating the performance of work under community service orders or probation orders which include a requirement that the offender shall perform unpaid work."

Delegated legislation has been used increasingly throughout the twentieth century and is an important source of law. Acts of Parliament tend to provide only a broad framework. Delegated legislation is used to fill out the detail. Delegated legislation is used particularly for areas that change frequently and for detailed or technical matters. It is also used to implement a lot of EC legislation. According to the Office of Public Sector Information the numbers of statutory instruments in the UK series of statutory instruments (excluding Scottish statutory instruments) are: 3488 in 1999, 3424 in 2000, 4147 in 2001, 3271 in 2002, 3354 in 2003, 3452 in 2004, 3599 in 2005 and 3509 in 2006.

5–23 There are many different forms of delegated legislation. The most common is the statutory instrument. This is, in fact, not one type of delegated legislation but includes rules, regulations and orders. Before the Statutory Instruments Act 1946, the equivalent to modern statutory instruments were known as "statutory rules and orders". This chapter will concentrate on statutory instruments because they are the type of delegated legislation that you will encounter most frequently. Other types of delegated legislation include by-laws. Two peculiarly Scottish types of statutory instrument are Acts of Sederunt and Acts of Adjournal. They are pieces of legislation enacted by the Court of Session and the High Court of Justiciary respectively. Acts of Sederunt are rules which govern procedure in the civil courts while Acts of Adjournal concern procedure in Scotland's criminal courts. These were issued as statutory instruments prior to devolution but are now issued as Scottish statutory instruments.

5–24 A statutory instrument has the same force of law as a statute. However, there is a key difference between the two. Unlike an Act of Parliament, a statutory instrument can be challenged in court. It is only valid if the person making the legislation has been duly authorised by the "enabling" Act of Parliament and has acted within the limits of the powers laid down in that Act. If this is not the case the statutory instrument could be successfully challenged on the grounds that it was *ultra vires*.

5–25 Other than this point, there are many similarities with statutes:

➢ Statutory instruments can be general or local. All statutory instruments which have general application are required to be published. Local statutory instruments may not be published.

➢ There is a presumption that statutory instruments apply to the whole of the UK However, they may only be applicable to Scotland as in the example below.

➢ Statutory instruments can be amended or revoked (this means the same as repealed in respect of statutes). Statutory instruments remain in force until revoked or until the Act they were made under is repealed.

Greater discussion of delegated legislation will be found in texts such as: **5–26**

A.W. Bradley and K.D. Ewing, *Constitutional and Administrative Law* 14th edn (Harlow: Longman, 2006).
A. Carroll, *Constitutional and Administrative Law* 3rd edn (Harlow: Longman, 1998).
V. Finch and A. Ashton, *Administrative Law in Scotland* (Edinburgh: W. Green, 1997).

Citation of statutory instruments

Statutory instruments are cited either by title, year and number or, alternatively, by year and **5–27** running number, e.g. Control of Pollution (Silage, Slurry and Agricultural Fuel Oil) Regulations 1991/324 or SI 1991/324 (alternatively SI 1991 No. 324). The statutory instruments themselves frequently stipulate the citation by which they should be referred e.g. regulation 1 of the above regulations states "These Regulations may be cited as the Control of Pollution (Silage, Slurry and Agricultural Fuel Oil) Regulations 1991."

The fact that the number is followed by an "S" in brackets and another number shows that this statutory instrument applies only to Scotland, e.g. The Restriction of Liberty Order (Scotland) Amendment Regulations 1999 or SI 1999 No. 144 (S.6). If you are trying to find a statutory instrument ignore the Scottish number because the indexes for statutory instruments use the main number for the reference.

If the number is followed by a "C" it means that it is a Commencement Order. This is a particular type of statutory instrument which is used to bring an Act or part thereof into operation. They have additional information in their citation, e.g. The Environment Act 1995 (Commencement No. 12 and Transitional Provisions) (Scotland) Order 1998 or SI 1998 No. 781 (s.40) (c.16). If the number is followed by "NI" it applies only to Northern Ireland.

Anatomy of statutory instruments

This is an example of a statutory instrument. Different features are marked with numbers which **5–28** correspond to the list below.

STATUTORY INSTRUMENTS

1999 No. 144 (S. 6) **[1]**

CRIMINAL LAW, SCOTLAND **[2]**

The Restriction of Liberty Order (Scotland) Amendment Regulations 1999 **[3]**

Made	*21st January 1999*
Laid before Parliament	*28th January 1999* **[4]**
Coming into force	*19th February 1999*

The Secretary of State, in exercise of the powers conferred on him by sections 245A(8) and 245C(3) of the Criminal Procedure (Scotland) Act 1995[1] and of all other powers enabling him in that behalf hereby makes the following Regulations: **[5]**

[6]

Citation and commencement [7]

1.—(1) These Regulations may be cited as the Restriction of Liberty Order (Scotland) Amendment Regulations 1999.

(2) These Regulations shall come into force on 19th February 1999.

Interpretation

2. In these Regulations, unless the context otherwise requires—

"the Principal Regulations" mean the Restriction of Liberty Order (Scotland) Regulations 1998.

Amendment of Principal Regulations

3.—(1) The Principal Regulations shall be amended in accordance with the following paragraphs.

(2) In Reg.2(1), after the definition of "offender" insert the following—

" "Premier Geografix" means Premier Geografix Limited a limited company incorporated under the Companies Acts under number 3522659 having its registered office at Centennial Court, Easthampstead Road, Bracknell, Berkshire RG12 1YQ".

(3) In Sch.2, after para.3 insert the following—

"**4.** Devices manufactured by Premier Geografix and sold under the Premier Geografix name:

(a) GEM Transmitter;
(b) GEM Site Monitoring Unit;
(c) GEM Field Management Unit;
(d) GEM Monitoring Officers Transmitter,
(e) GEM Central Computer System."

Henry McLeish **[8]**
Minister of State, Scottish Office

St Andrew's House, Edinburgh
21st January 1999

EXPLANATORY NOTE **[9]**

(This note is not part of the Regulations)

These Regulations made under sections 245A(8) and 245C(3) of the Criminal Procedure (Scotland) Act 1995 as inserted by section 5 of the Crime and Punishment (Scotland) Act 1997 amend the Restriction of Liberty Order (Scotland) Regulations 1998 which regulate aspects of the monitoring by electronic and radio devices the compliance of offenders with requirements of restriction of liberty orders.

The amendment to Schedule 2 to the Restriction of Liberty Order (Scotland) Regulations 1998 specifies additional devices which may be used for monitoring.

Notes:

[1] 1995 c.46 sections 245A-245H were inserted by the Crime and Punishment (Scotland) Act 1997 (c.48), section 5.*back*.
[2] S.I. 1998/1802.*back*.

Statutory instruments can vary in length. This example is a particularly short one. Different **5–29**
features are marked with numbers which correspond to the following list:

[1] The citation consists of the year and number. The number refers to the number issued
   in a calendar year, e.g. this is number 144 for 1999. The fact that the number is followed
   by an "S" in brackets and another number shows that this statutory instrument applies
   only to Scotland. It is the sixth statutory instrument to apply to Scotland in 1999.
[2] This is not part of the name—it is a subject heading used in official editions of statutory
   instruments.
[3] This is the short title of the statutory instrument.
[4] This is a list of three dates relating to the parliamentary process involved in creating a
   statutory instrument. This is a requirement under s.4(2) of the Statutory Instruments
   Act 1946, which states that every statutory instrument should include details of when it
   is to come into force and when it was laid before Parliament. Statutory instruments also
   usually include details of the date on which they were made.
[5] This paragraph is a recital of the statutory authority and powers that enable the maker
   of the statutory instrument (here the Secretary of State for Scotland) to issue the
   statutory instrument. Here he has exercised powers under the provisions of the
   Criminal Procedure (Scotland) Act 1995, as amended.
[6] Statutory instruments are divided up into parts but these are not referred to as sections
   as in an Act of Parliament. The name given to the divisions depends on the type of
   statutory instrument. In this case the statutory instrument is a regulation and the
   divisions are called regulations, with further subdivisions called paragraphs and sub-
   paragraphs. If the statutory instrument is an order the divisions are called articles, but
   further subdivisions are called paragraphs and sub-paragraphs. If the statutory
   instrument is a rule, the divisions are called rules but further subdivisions are called
   paragraphs and sub-paragraphs.
[7] There are several types of regulation (article or rule) which tend to appear in most but
   not all statutory instruments:
   Citation and commencement. This will specify the correct citation to be adopted and
   give the date on which the statutory instrument will come into force.
   Interpretation. This states if particular meanings are to be given to words used in the
   statutory instrument.
[8] The signature of the person making the statutory instrument, along with their title and
   the date on which the statutory instrument was made.
   It is possible for statutory instruments to have schedules. As with statutes, material in
   the schedule will tend to be technical and/or very detailed. This statutory instrument
   does not have any schedules.
[9] In official editions of statutory instruments there is usually an explanatory note at the
   end of the statutory instrument. It is not technically part of the statutory instrument.
   They tend to be brief and do not add very much to your understanding of the
   legislation.

Reading statutory instruments

Reading statutory instruments raises the same issues as reading statutes. See paras 5.17–5.19. In **5–30**
addition you may find it helpful to read the enabling Act in conjunction with the statutory
instrument. The Act (and any annotations to it) may help your understanding of the broader
context of which the statutory instrument is part.

THE SCOTTISH PARLIAMENT (1999–)

Introduction

5–31 The Scottish Parliament was created by the Scotland Act 1998. It had its first meeting on May 12, 1999 and took up its legislative powers from July 1, 1999. The Scottish Parliament consists of 129 Members of the Scottish Parliament who are referred to as MSPs. Seventy-three are returned from constituencies elected by the "first past the post" system and 56 are returned under proportional representation (8 regions return 7 members). A Parliamentary session is for a fixed period of four years. This is different from the Westminster system where the maximum length of a parliament is five years. The Scottish Parliament has only one chamber (it is unicameral). Scottish legislation does not go to the House of Lords. Legislation is scrutinised by the Scottish Parliament as a whole and by its various committees.

5–32 Committees play a key role in the work of the Scottish Parliament. The Parliament may establish committees to deal with specific subject areas (known as subject committees) in addition to the mandatory committees. The mandatory committees are:

- ➢ Procedures Committee
- ➢ Standards Committee
- ➢ Finance Committee
- ➢ Audit Committee
- ➢ European Committee
- ➢ Equal Opportunities Committee
- ➢ Public Petitions Committee
- ➢ Subordinate Legislation Committee

5–33 Committees must have at least five but not more than 15 members. The composition of the committees reflects the balance of the parties in the Parliament. The committees can examine matters within their remit or matters referred to them by the Parliament. They may:

- ➢ Consider the policy and administration of the Scottish Administration;
- ➢ Consider proposals for legislation in the Scottish Parliament and the UK Parliament;
- ➢ Consider EC legislation and international Conventions;
- ➢ Consider the need for reform of the law;
- ➢ Initiate Bills;
- ➢ Consider the financial proposals and financial administration of the Scottish Administration.

5–34 The Presiding Officer (the equivalent of the Speaker in the House of Commons) is one of the important figures of the Parliament. The post is held by one of the MSPs and is elected by the Parliament. The Presiding Officer's role is to:

- ➢ Preside over meetings of the Parliament and exercise a casting vote in the event of a tie;
- ➢ Convene and chair meetings of the Parliamentary Bureau and exercise a casting vote in the event of a tie. The Parliamentary Bureau consists of representatives of the various parties who organise the business of the Parliament;
- ➢ Determine any question as to the interpretation or application of the rules governing parliamentary procedure; and
- ➢ Represent the Parliament in discussions and exchanges with any parliamentary, governmental, administrative or other body.

The Scottish Executive is the term used for the devolved Government in Scotland. Responsi- **5–35**
bility for all devolved matters was passed to the Scottish Executive from the Scottish Office and
other UK Government departments in 1999. The Scottish Executive is made up of: the First
Minister; Ministers appointed by the First Minister; the Lord Advocate and the Solicitor
General for Scotland. The First Minister is head of the Scottish Executive. He is nominated by
the Scottish Parliament and formally appointed by the Queen. Members of the Scottish
Executive are known collectively as "The Scottish Ministers" (Scotland Act 1998 s.44(2)). You
will come across this term frequently in your legal studies. When a power or duty relating to a
devolved function is conferred by an Act of Parliament it is exercisable by the "Scottish Ministers" (i.e. any member of the Scottish Executive). Prior to devolution the power would have
been exercisable by a specific Minister. Any legal challenges against the Scottish Executive are
also brought against the "Scottish Ministers" as opposed to a specific Minister.

In the Scottish Parliament, the term "session" refers to the period between the first meeting of
the Parliament after a general election and the dissolution of the Parliament before the next
election. The equivalent term in Westminster is a "Parliament".

Legislative competence

Any Act of the Scottish Parliament is not law if it is outside the legislative competence of the **5–36**
Parliament (Scotland Act 1998, s.29). A provision would be outside the Parliament's legislative
competence if it related to the reserved matters. The reserved matters are listed in Sch.5 of the
Scotland Act. General reservations include: the constitution, foreign affairs, defence, public
service, political parties and treason. There are also a range of specific reservations under the
following headings: financial and economic affairs, home affairs, trade and industry, energy,
transport, social security, regulation of the professions, employment, health and medicines,
media and culture and miscellaneous.

The matters which the Scottish Parliament can consider are not listed in the Act. They are to be **5–37**
implied by exception. They include: criminal justice and prosecution, civil and criminal courts,
legal aid, judicial appointments, the police and fire services, prisons, health services, education,
local government, the environment, agriculture, forestry, fisheries, social work services, liquor
licensing, housing, tourism, sport and the arts.

Acts of the Scottish Parliament can amend or repeal pre-devolution legislation from the UK **5–38**
Parliament but only if the subject matter of the legislation is within the legislative competence of
the Scottish Parliament.

Schedule 6 of the Scotland Act 1998 deals with "devolution issues". These are defined as
questions of whether:

    (a) The Act (or any of its provisions) is within the Parliament's legislative competence.
    (b) Any function being exercised is a function of the Scottish Ministers, First Minister or
        Lord Advocate.
    (c) A function being exercised by a member of the Scottish Executive is within the devolved
        competence.
    (d) The exercise of a function (or failure to act) by a member of the Scottish Executive
        would be incompatible with the rights under the European Convention of Human
        Rights or European Community law.

Devolution issues which arise in Scotland may be referred by a court to the Inner House (in
respect of civil cases) or to the High Court of Justiciary (in relation to criminal proceedings).
The issue may be further referred or appealed to the Judicial Committee of the Privy Council.

Legislation

Bills

5–39 As in the UK Parliament, proposed legislation starts off in the Scottish Parliament as a Bill. When a Bill is passed it becomes an Act of the Scottish Parliament. A Bill can be introduced by a:

> ➤ Member of the Scottish Executive, in which case it is referred to as an Executive Bill;
> ➤ Parliamentary Committee, in which case it is referred to as a Committee Bill; or
> ➤ Member of Scottish Parliament, in which case it is referred to as a Member's Bill.

The layout, structure and legislative drafting conventions adopted for Bills in the Scottish Parliament are very similar to Bills in the UK Parliament. The reason is that Acts of the Scottish Parliament form part of the UK "statute book". As in the UK Parliament legislation may be either general or private. The majority of the section below relates to Public General Bills.

Introduction

5–40 On introduction, a Bill must be accompanied by certain documents:

> ➤ A statement by the Presiding Officer indicating whether the provisions are within the legislative competence of the Parliament. Any provisions which are viewed as outside its competence have to be identified.
> ➤ A Financial Memorandum. This sets out a best estimate of the administrative, compliance and other costs arising from the provisions of the Bill. It must distinguish how such costs would fall on the Scottish Administration, local authorities and other bodies, individuals and businesses.
> ➤ Most Executive Bills must also be accompanied by:

(a) A statement by the Minister in charge of the Bill that in his view the provisions are within the legislative competence of the Parliament.
(b) Explanatory notes which summarise objectively each provision of the Bill.
(c) A Policy Memorandum which sets out:
   (i) Policy objectives of the Bill;
   (ii) Consideration of alternative methods of achieving these objectives and justification of the approach taken in the Bill;
   (iii) Details of any consultation on the objectives;
   (iv) Assessment of the effects, if any, of the Bill on: equal opportunities human rights, island communities, local government, sustainable development and any other matter which the Scottish Executive considers relevant.

If a Bill contains any provision charging expenditure on the Scottish Consolidated Fund, a report from the Auditor General must accompany the Bill. This report sets out whether the Auditor General views the charge as appropriate.

A Bill may be introduced on any sitting day by being lodged with the clerks. On the day of introduction, the Bill and accompanying documents are sent to RR Donnelley for publication, both in hard copy and on the Parliament's website, the following day.

The majority of Bills dealt with by the Scottish Parliament are Executive Bills. The procedure outlined below will generally apply to Executive Bills.

Stage 1—Consideration of the general principles of a Bill

Once a Bill has been printed it is referred to the committee within whose remit it falls. This **5–41** committee is known as "the lead committee". This committee considers the general principles and prepares a report for the Parliament. Parliament then considers the general principles of the Bill in the light of this report. It can:

> ➢ refer the Bill back to the lead committee for a further report; or
> ➢ fail to agree the general principles of the Bill (in which case the Bill falls); or
> ➢ agree to the Bill.

If the Bill is agreed, it can proceed to stage 2. There must be at least two weeks between the completion of stage 1 and the start of stage 2.

Stage 2—Consideration of the details of the Bill

This stage is either considered by the lead committee, another committee or a committee of the **5–42** whole Parliament. Each section and schedule are considered separately. A Bill may be amended at this stage. If the Bill has been amended, it will be reprinted. If it is amended in such a way as to affect powers to make subordinate legislation, the amended Bill must be referred to the Subordinate Legislation Committee for consideration.

If the Bill is amended at stage 2 there must be at least two weeks between completion of stage 2 and the start of stage 3.

Stage 3—Final consideration

The amended Bill is considered by the Parliament. The Bill can be further amended at this stage. **5–43** It is possible for up to half of the sections of the Bill to be referred back to committee for further stage 2 consideration. If this takes place, on resumption of stage 3 proceedings, amendments can only be made to the provisions which were referred back to committee.

If there is a final vote on the Bill, at least a quarter of all MSPs must vote or abstain. If this condition is not met, the Bill will be treated as rejected.

Royal Assent

If the Bill is passed, it will be submitted for Royal Assent by the Presiding Officer. Within four **5–44** weeks of the passing of the Bill the Advocate General, Lord Advocate or Attorney General can refer the question of whether the Bill is within the Parliament's legislative competence to the Judicial Committee of the Privy Council for a decision (Scotland Act 1998, s.33). The Secretary of State for Scotland has the power to intervene and prohibit the Presiding Officer from submitting the Bill for Royal Assent. He may do this if he has reasonable grounds to believe that the Bill is incompatible with any international obligations or the interests of defence and national security or will have an adverse effect on the law relating to reserved matters (Scotland Act 1998, s.35). Once the Bill receives Royal Assent, it becomes an Act of the Scottish Parliament. This does not necessarily mean that it becomes law see para.5.48, section [7].

Citation of Bills

Bills should be referenced by Scottish Parliament (SP) Bill number, title, [printing], Session, **5–45** (year), e.g.

> ➢ SP Bill 75 Rights of Relatives to Damages (Mesothelioma) (Scotland) Bill [as introduced] Session 2 (2006).
> ➢ SP Bill 58A Edinburgh Airport Rail Link Bill [as amended at Consideration stage] Session 2 (2007).

➢ SP Bill 59-ML2 Christmas Day and New Year's Day Trading (Scotland) Bill [Marshalled List of Amendments selected for Stage 3] Session 2 (2007).

Unlike UK Parliament Bills, Scottish Parliament Bills keep the original numbering. Subsequent revisions are indicated as follows:

SP Bill 1	Bill as introduced
SP Bill 1A	Bill as amended at Stage 2

Accompanying documentation and lists of amendments are given references which are linked to the citation of the Bill.

SP Bill 1-PM	Policy memorandum.
SP Bill 1-EN	Explanatory notes and other accompanying documents.
SP Bill 1-ML	Marshalled list of amendments to the Bill as introduced – if there are several marshalled lists of amendments then they are numbered SP Bill 1-ML1, SP Bill 1-ML2 etc.
SP Bill 1A-ML	Marshalled list of amendments to the Bill as amended at Stage 2.
SP Bill 1A-EN	Supplementary explanatory notes for the Bill as amended at Stage 2.
SP Bill 1A-FM	Supplementary financial memorandum for the Bill as amended at Stage 2.
SP Bill 1-G	Groupings of amendments—if there are several groupings then they are numbered SP Bill 1-G1, SP Bill 1-G2 etc.
SP Bill 1-DPM	Delegated powers memorandum.
SP Bill 1B	Bill as passed.

Citation of statutes

5–46 Acts of the Scottish Parliament are normally referred to by their short title, e.g. Aquaculture and Fisheries (Scotland) Act 2007. A complete citation would also include the asp number, e.g. Aquaculture and Fisheries (Scotland) Act 2007 asp 12.

Private legislation

5–47 In addition to public general legislation, the Scottish Parliament can also enact private legislation which deals with devolved issues. A private Bill "is a Bill introduced for the purpose of obtaining for an individual person, body corporate or unincorporated association of persons ("the promoter") particular powers or benefits in excess of, or in conflict with, the general law, and includes a Bill relating to the estate, property, status or style, or otherwise relating to the personal affairs, of the promoter" (Rule 9A.1.1 of the Standing Orders of the Scottish Parliament).

Private Bills are subject to substantially different procedures from public Bills. The procedure for private Bills is contained in *Guidance on Private Bills* (2005) available on the Scottish Parliament website. When enacted private Bills become Acts of the Scottish Parliament and are cited in the same way as public general Acts. Private Bills generally relate to development projects, the use of land, or the property or status of the promoter. An example of a private Act is the Stirling-Alloa-Kincardine Railway and Linked Improvements Act 2004.

Anatomy of an Act of the Scottish Parliament

5–48 This is an excerpt from a Public General Act. It has been chosen because of its brevity—not all Acts are as short as this one—they are usually much longer. While all Acts adopt the same format some, but not necessarily all, features will appear in all Acts. Different features are marked with numbers which correspond to the list below.

Tourist Boards (Scotland) Act 2006 (asp 15) **[1]**

[2] Tourist Boards (Scotland) Act 2006

[3] 2006 asp 15

[4] The Bill for this Act of the Scottish Parliament was passed by the Parliament on 24th October 2006 and received Royal Assent on 30th November 2006

[5] An Act of the Scottish Parliament to rename the Scottish Tourist Board, to increase the maximum number of members of that body and to abolish area tourist boards.

[6]

1. Scottish Tourist Board: change of name
    (1) The Scottish Tourist Board is renamed VisitScotland.
    (2) Accordingly, in the Development of Tourism Act 1969 (c.51), for "the Scottish Tourist Board", wherever that expression occurs, there is substituted "VisitScotland"

2. Scottish Tourist Board: increase in maximum number of members
    In section 1(3) of the Development of Tourism Act 1969 (which provides for the maximum number of members of the national tourist boards), for "six" where it secondly occurs, there is substituted "eleven".

3. Abolition of area tourist boards
    (1) Sections 172 to 175 of the Local Government etc. (Scotland) Act 1994 (c.39) (which make provision for area tourist boards) are repealed.
    (2) The following bodies are dissolved—
        (a) the Scottish Network 1 Tourist Board, and
        (b) the Scottish Network 2 Tourist Board.
    (3) Schedule 1 makes provision in connection with the dissolution of those bodies.

4. Consequential modifications
    Schedule 2 makes modifications of enactments in consequence of the preceding provisions.

5. Commencement and short title
    [7] (1) The preceding provisions come into force on such day as the Scottish Ministers may by order made by statutory instrument appoint.
    [8] (2) This Act may be cited as the Tourist Boards (Scotland) Act 2006.

Key:

[1] This is referred to as the running header. It tells you where in the Act you are and is useful if you are reading a long asp. Note that the coat of arms is different from a UK Parliament Act. Scottish Acts bear the Coat of Arms of the Scottish Crown.

[2] The short title of the Act. This is the normal way to refer to the Act. Acts of the Scottish Parliament normally (but not always) have Scotland in round brackets as part of the short title. The Act itself will usually provide details of the short title in a section at the end of the Act. In this Act this appears in s.5(2).

[3] This is another way of referring to Acts—by their year and asp number. The asp number is assigned to each Act in chronological order throughout a calendar year. This means that this was the 15th Act of 2006. This is the equivalent of the chapter number in an Act of the UK Parliament.

[4] This is the standard enacting formula. These words indicate that the Act has the full authority of the Scottish Parliament. It appears in bold and gives details of when the asp was passed and when it received the royal assent.

[5] This is the long title. It sets out the purpose of the Act in very general terms. It will be more detailed than the short title.

[6] Acts are divided up into parts called sections. Sections are numbered consecutively throughout an Act. Sections can be subdivided into subsections. Subsections can be divided into paragraphs and further divided into sub-paragraphs. The section number and section title appear in bold. There are no marginal notes.

[7] The last section of an Act usually provides for commencement. If the Act contains no commencement provision there is a presumption that it comes into force at the beginning of the day on which it receives the Royal Assent.

The commencement provisions in an Act can provide for it coming into force in one of three ways:

(a) The Act can specify a particular date;
(b) The Act can specify a period after the passing of the Act when the Act will come into force.
(c) The Act can state that it is to come into force on a date to be set by a person or persons, usually the Scottish Ministers. This means that the commencement of the legislation has been delegated to the Scottish Executive. This is the case with this Act. It would be brought into force by a type of statutory instrument called a Commencement Order. A search of sources which identify when Acts are brought into force (see paras 7.50–7.62) will show that this Act was brought into force on 31st January 2007 by the Tourist Boards (Scotland) Act 2006 (Commencement) Order 2007.

Note that the whole of an Act can be brought into force at once or sections of it can become law at different times. This means that you need to check the commencement section carefully. There can be considerable time delay between an Act receiving the Royal Assent and becoming law.

[8] The last section of an Act usually provides for citation of the short title. This is the formal statement of the short title. The short title also appears at the start of the Act. See comments above in section [2].

N.B. Schedules may appear at the end of an Act. Schedules are divided into paragraphs and sub-paragraphs. Schedules have equal force in law as the rest of the Act.

Delegated legislation

Following devolution a new type of delegated legislation was created: Scottish statutory **5–49** instruments. The power to make delegated legislation on a devolved matter may be contained in a pre-devolution Act of the UK Parliament (where the power has been transferred to the Scottish Ministers) or in an Act of the Scottish Parliament. Since devolution Acts of Sederunt and Acts of Adjournal have been created as Scottish statutory instruments. This is because their subject matter is devolved namely: procedure in the Scottish civil courts and criminal courts respectively. As with statutory instruments from the UK Parliament, Scottish statutory instruments can be general or local. The vast majority of the latter have related to roads, bridges, road traffic and rights of way.

The Scottish Parliament scrutinises delegated legislation. The procedure adopted will depend on **5–50** the enabling Act. Some instruments are subject to affirmative procedure. This means that the approval of Parliament is needed to allow the provisions to come into force. Alternatively an instrument could be subject to the negative procedure which means that its provisions could be annulled by the Parliament. In this case the instrument is laid before Parliament and will come into force after a period of 40 days unless Parliament annuls it. It is also possible for instruments to be subject to a "super-affirmative" procedure where the Parliament has an initial opportunity to comment on a draft before the final version is laid for approval. Some instruments are not subject to any parliamentary scrutiny and may not even be laid before Parliament. However, the majority of Scottish statutory instruments are considered by the Subordinate Legislation Committee and at least one other committee.

As with its UK counterpart the use of delegated legislation has proved a useful mechanism for **5–51** filling out the detail of statutes. According to the Queen's Printer for Scotland the numbers of Scottish statutory instruments are: 204 in 1999, 454 in 2000, 494 in 2001, 575 in 2002, 622 in 2003, 565 in 2004, 667 in 2005, 625 in 2006 and 269 up to March 31, 2007.

Citation of Scottish statutory instruments

Scottish statutory instruments are cited either by title, year and number or, alternatively, by year **5–52** and running number, e.g. The Number of Inner House Judges (Variation) Order 2007 (SSI 2007/258) or SSI 2007/258 (alternatively SSI 2007 No 258). The instruments themselves frequently stipulate the citation by which they should be referred, e.g. article 1 of the above order states "This Order may be cited as the Number of Inner House Judges (Variation) Order 2007."

Anatomy of a Scottish statutory instrument

This is an example of a Scottish statutory instrument. Different features are marked with **5–53** numbers which correspond to the list below.

SCOTTISH STATUTORY INSTRUMENTS

[1] 2007 No. 258

[2] COURT OF SESSION

[3] The Number of Inner House Judges (Variation) Order 2007

[4]　　　　　*Made*　　　　　　　　　　　　　　　　*21st March 2007*
Coming into force in accordance with article 1

[5] The Scottish Ministers, in exercise of the powers conferred by section 2(2A) and (2B) of the Court of Session Act 1988[1], hereby make the following Order, a draft of which has, in accordance with section 2(2D) of that Act, been laid before and approved by resolution of the Scottish Parliament:

[6] Citation and commencement
[7] **1.** This Order may be cited as the Number of Inner House Judges (Variation) Order 2007 and shall come into force on the day after the day on which it is made.

Variation of number of Inner House judges
2. Section 2(2) of the Court of Session Act 1988 (composition of court)[2] is amended by substituting for the word "four" where it second appears the word "five".

[8] *JOHANN M LAMONT*
Authorised to sign by the Scottish Ministers

St Andrew's House, Edinburgh
21st March 2007

---

[9] EXPLANATORY NOTE

(This note is not part of the Order)

This Order amends section 2(2) of the Court of Session Act 1988 to increase the number of senior judges in the Second Division of the Inner House of the Court of Session from four to five. The total number of judges in the Inner House, including the Lord President and the Lord Justice Clerk, will therefore be increased from ten to eleven.

Notes:

[1] 1988 c.36; subsections (2A) to (2D) were inserted into section 2 by the Bail, Judicial Appointments etc. (Scotland) Act 2000 (asp 9), section 5(a).

[2] The number of senior judges in each of the two Divisions of the Inner House of the Court of Session was increased from three to four by SSI 2001/41.

Key:

[1] The citation consists of the year and number. The number refers to the number issued in a calendar year, e.g. this is number 258 for 2007.

[2] This is not part of the name—it is a subject heading used in official editions of Scottish statutory instruments.

[3] This is the short title of the statutory instrument.

[4] This is a list of dates relating to the parliamentary process involved in creating a Scottish statutory instrument. The details will vary depending on the procedure to which it was subject. See para.5.50. This order has few details, others may contain additional details such as the date on which the instrument was laid before Parliament.

[5] This paragraph is a recital of the statutory authority and powers that enable the maker of the Scottish statutory instrument (here Johann Lamont has signed it on behalf of the Scottish Ministers) to issue the statutory instrument. Here she has exercised powers under the provisions of the Court of Session Act 1988, s.2(2A) and (2B).

[6] Scottish statutory instruments are divided up into parts but these are not referred to as sections as in an Act of Parliament. The name given to the divisions depends on the type of the instrument. In this case the instrument is an order and the divisions are called articles, with further subdivisions called paragraphs and sub-paragraphs. If the instrument is a regulation the divisions are called regulations, but further subdivisions are called paragraphs and sub-paragraphs. If the instrument is a rule, the divisions are called rules but further subdivisions are called paragraphs and sub-paragraphs.

[7] There are several types of article (regulation or rule) which tend to appear in most but not all instruments:

Citation and commencement. This will specify the correct citation to be adopted and give the date on which the instrument will come into force.
Interpretation. This states if particular meanings are to be given to words used in the instrument. There is no interpretation article in this order.

[8] The signature of the person making the instrument, along with their title and the date on which the statutory instrument was made. This will usually, as here, be a member of the Scottish Executive.

It is possible for instruments to have schedules. As with statutes, material in the schedule will tend to be technical and/or very detailed. This order does not have any schedules.

[9] In official editions of Scottish statutory instruments there is usually an explanatory note at the end of the statutory instrument. It is not technically part of the statutory instrument. They tend to be brief and do not add very much to your understanding of the legislation.

Reading Scottish Parliament legislation

The techniques for reading legislation and the principles of statutory interpretation are similar **5–54** to those for UK Parliament legislation see paras 5.17–5.21.

Chapter 6
Search Strategies for Finding UK Parliament Legislation

INTRODUCTION

6–1 This chapter discusses search strategies for finding legislation from the UK Parliament. It includes searching for Bills, Acts of Parliament and the main form of delegated legislation: statutory instruments. The information sources for legislation have developed over time and it is now easier than ever to search for legislation. The increased range and sophistication of online databases also means that it is now easier to locate some of the older materials as well as possible to access legislative changes more quickly than in the past. However, the greater availability of a range of electronic versions of legislation means that it is even more important to be aware of the qualities of the information source you are using and to have the ability to evaluate the information that it will retrieve for you.

With the onset of devolution many of the information sources for the UK Parliament expanded to include materials from the Scottish Parliament. Search strategies for Scottish Parliament legislation are discussed in Chapter 7. To avoid repetition the UK sources which have incorporated Scottish Parliament materials will be covered in this chapter while Chapter 7 will discuss how to search their content for Scottish Parliament materials and information sources unique to the Scottish Parliament.

UK PARLIAMENT BILLS

6–2 It is important to remember that Bills are amended to various degrees as they go through the different parliamentary stages. It is therefore essential to ensure that you find the most current version of the Bill. For more details on the parliamentary procedure for Bills see Chapter 5 from para.5.6 onwards.

Sources of the text of a recent Public Bill

Public Bills before Parliament website ᵔ free
http://www.parliament.the-stationery-office.co.uk/pa/pabills.htm

6–3 This website contains an alphabetical list of all Public General Bills currently before Parliament. The list indicates whether the Bill is in the House of Commons, House of Lords or whether it has been given the Royal Assent. There is a hypertext link to the homepage of the Bill. This provides the following information:

> ➢ Whether it is a Government or a Private Members' Bill and who introduced it.
> ➢ Details of the dates of the stages the Bill has completed.
> ➢ Links to debates on the Bill accessible by date.
> ➢ Links to marshalled lists of amendments.
> ➢ Links to full text versions of the Bill at the various stages at which it has been reprinted. These are produced in both pdf and html forms.
> ➢ A short summary of the content of the Bill.

> ➤ Links to Explanatory Notes.
> ➤ Links to any related research material.

It is possible to sign up for email alerts for the Bill homepage.

Individual Public Bills are published by The Stationery Office. They form part of a large group **6–4**
of documents known as Parliamentary Papers (see para.8.77). Bills may be printed many different times depending on the amount of changes made as they progress through Parliament.

Sources of the text of a recent Private Bill

Private Bills before Parliament website ⌂ free
http://www.publications.parliament.uk/pa/privbill.htm

This website provides information on current private bills and also gives an indication about **6–5**
how it is possible to take action to oppose the particular Bills.

The paper versions of Private Bills are more difficult to obtain and you may need to contact the **6–6**
promoter (or his agent) of the Bill.

Finding out which stage a Bill has reached

House of Commons Weekly Information Bulletin 📖 and ⌂ free
This is published weekly when the House of Commons is in session. The full text of the *House of* **6–7**
Commons Weekly Information Bulletin has been available via the internet since October 1996.
The online version is published on a Saturday and covers the previous week's events. It is
published in pdf and html form at (*http://www.publications.parliament.uk/pa/cm/cmwib.htm*).

The *House of Commons Weekly Information Bulletin* includes a huge amount of information
relating to the workings of Parliament, reports about past parliamentary business and gives
notice of future business. In addition it contains a section on legislation. In this section there is a
list of public Bills which appear in alphabetical order by title. Opposite the details of the Bill are
the dates of the various stages. All forthcoming, and therefore provisional, dates are italicised.
Government Bills are listed in bold type. There is also a list of private Bills before Parliament
which again provides details of the stages reached.

Public Bills before Parliament website ⌂ free
http://www.parliament.the-stationery-office.co.uk/pa/pabills.htm

The homepage for each Bill provides information about the stage the Bill has reached. See **6–8**
para.6.3.

Lawtel ⌂ subscription legal current awareness digest service
This service contains a search facility which allows you to search for Bills by keyword. Either **6–9**
use the *UK Search* section, enter search term and tick the *Parliamentary Bills* box or go to
legislation, enter search term and tick the *Parliamentary Bills* box. This takes you to details
about the Bill which include the stage that it has reached. There is a link to the full text of the
Bill if it is available on the Parliament website.

Parlianet ⌐ subscription service which is part of Justis

6–10 This is an index to the proceedings and publications of both Houses of Parliament in Westminster going back to 1979. The Bills before Parliament section is updated daily and provides a breakdown of the history of the Bill from when it was first introduced to when it either receives Royal Assent or when it fails.

Current Law Monthly Digest 📖

6–11 Information about the stages of a Bill is given in the Progress of Bills Table. To find out the stage a Bill has reached in the parliamentary process:

⇒ **Step 1**: Check the most recent Monthly Digest.
⇒ **Step 2**: Turn to the Progress of Bills Table. The bills are arranged in alphabetical order. Opposite the name of the Bill will be details of the stage it has reached.

!Example

6–12 Find out which stage the Digital Switchover (Disclosure of Information) Bill has reached.

⇒ **Step 1**: Go to the latest Monthly Digest.
⇒ **Step 2**: Turn to the Progress of Bills Table. Check under "D" and locate the entry for the Digital Switchover (Disclosure of Information) Bill. The name of the Bill is highlighted in bold as it is a Government Bill. It is followed by the word "(Commons)". This indicates that the Bill originated in the House of Commons. Opposite the entry is the stage the Bill has reached. In this case the entry is as follows:

"Commons, passed. Lords, Second reading, February 28, 2007 (*Committee, March 22, 2007*)"

The section in italics is provisional.

The Daily List 📖 and ⌐ free

6–13 This is published by The Stationery Office (*http://www.tsoshop.co.uk/parliament*). The information about a Bill that can be found in the *Daily List* includes the latest developments, the number allocated to a Bill, publication details and whether there have been any amendments moved. However, details only appear if the Bill has had to be reprinted or amendments printed.

Journals 📖

6–14 Journals may contain information about the progress of Bills. In each weekly issue of the *Scots Law Times* there is a news section which contains parliamentary news. This lists new Bills and provides a brief summary of the subject matter. There is also a Progress of Bills section.

Newspapers 📖 and ⌐ free

6–15 The broadsheets contain information about Bills and events in Parliament. This seldom makes the front page unless the Bill is particularly controversial.

6–16 Finding out about older bills

It is probably unlikely that you would need to look for information about older Bills unless you are carrying out some historical research.

Public Bills before Parliament in previous sessions back to 2002–2003 are available at: *http://www.publications.parliament.uk/pa/pubmenu.htm* ⌐ free

Private Bills before Parliament in previous sessions back to 2001–2002 are available at: **6–17**
http://www.publications.parliament.uk/pa/privmenu.htm ⌁ free

The House of Commons Weekly Information Bulletin and/or *The Sessional Information Digest* 📖 **6–18**
and ⌁ free
The House of Commons Weekly Information Bulletin (*http://www.publications.parliament.uk/pa/*
cm/cmwib.htm) and *The Sessional Information Digest* (which is the cumulative from of the
Weekly Information Bulletin) which is available in an annual from at *http://www. pub-*
lications.parliament.uk/pa/cm/cmsid.htm. These publications provide details of Bills back to
1996.

Parlianet ⌁subscription service which is part of *Justis*
This index to the proceedings and publications of both Houses of Parliament in Westminster **6–19**
goes back to 1979.

The Stationery Office website ⌁ free
The site (*http://www.tsoshop.co.uk/*) can be searched using the advanced search function for the **6–20**
publication details of Bills but its coverage is patchy although there are details of some Bills
from the late 1970s.

Finding out about parliamentary debates on a Bill

The House of Commons Weekly Information Bulletin 📖 and ⌁ free
This will alert you to the dates of parliamentary debates, see para.6.7. **6–21**

Current Law Statutes 📖
If the Bill has since become an Act, the annual volumes of *Current Law Statutes* should contain **6–22**
details of the parliamentary debates relevant to each Act. Look in the first annotation inserted
after the long title.

Explanatory Notes 📖 and ⌁ free
Since the start of 1999 *Explanatory Notes* are published for the majority of Public General Acts **6–23**
which result from Bills introduced into either House of Parliament by a government minister. At
the end of the *Explanatory Note* is a section called *Hansard References* which contains a table
setting out the dates and Hansard references for each stage of the Bill's passage through Parliament. Explanatory Notes are available in paper and via the *Office of Public Sector Infor-*
mation (OPSI) website (*http://www.opsi.gov.uk/acts.htm*).

Parliamentary Debates: Official Report (commonly referred to as *Hansard*) 📖 and ⌁ free and
CD Rom
Hansard contains an edited verbatim account of proceedings in Parliament. Commons Hansard **6–24**
covers proceedings in the Commons Chamber, Westminster Hall and General and Public Bill
Committees. Lords Hansard covers proceedings in the Lords Chamber and its Grand Com-
mittees. Both contain Written Ministerial Statements and Written Answers.
  The online version of *Hansard* is freely available at: *http://www.publications.parliament.uk/pa/*
pahansard.htm.
  It is available from 8am on the day following the sitting. Same-day access to speeches in the
Chamber and Westminster Hall is also available on a rolling basis on the internet. The production target is to have a member's speech available within three to four hours. Proceedings are
available from the 1988–1989 session of Parliament for Commons debates, the 1995–1996
session for House of Lords debates and Standing Committee debates are available from the
1997–1998 session. Note that from the beginning of the 2006–2007 session Standing Committees

have been known as General Committees and Standing Committees on Bills are to be known as Public Bill Committees.

Hansard is published daily while Parliament is sitting. It is also published weekly and in bound volumes by parliamentary session. The material appears in columns (like newspapers) and the columns are numbered. Each page contains two columns. References to *Hansard* are by column number not page number. Written answers to parliamentary questions are located in a separate section at the end of the bound volumes. Cumulative indexes are produced throughout the parliamentary session and there is a sessional index in the last bound volume for the session. The CD Rom version comprises the bound volumes of House of Commons debates from 1988–1989.

6–25 The way you search *Hansard* can depend on the particular part you are searching:

> ➤ The daily versions of House of Commons debates contain a table of contents which lists column numbers, headings, time lines and names of members. House of Commons debates which have been put into bound volumes can be searched online by date. However, if you are unsure of the date you can use the UK Parliament *advanced search* facility to which there is a link from each "bound" volume. This is an excellent search facility and can be used as an alternative to searching the specific sections of *Hansard*.
> ➤ House of Lords debates can be searched by date, member, category or by subject.
> ➤ General Committee debates for each parliamentary session are listed by committee. You can get information on the membership of the committee and reports of proceedings of its sittings.
> ➤ Public Bill Committee debates within each parliamentary session are listed by the title of the Bill being considered. When you click on the title of the Bill you are taken into details of the relevant Public Bill Committee. You can access the following information:

> ⇒ Membership of the committee.
> ⇒ Latest version of the Bill.
> ⇒ Reports of proceedings of the various sittings of the committee.

COLLECTIONS OF UK PARLIAMENT ACTS APPLYING TO SCOTLAND 1707–1948

There are several collections of statutes which applied to Scotland between 1707 and 1948:

6–26 *Scots Statutes Revised* (Vols 1–10) covered the period 1707–1900. It includes only Acts applicable to Scotland. Volume 10 includes a subject index to the whole collection. It was continued by *Scots Statutes* which covers the period 1901–1948. This, in turn, was continued from 1949 by *Scottish Current Law Statutes*, see below.

6–27 *Public General Statutes affecting Scotland* (1848–1947), known as Blackwood's Acts, was an annual publication. It included Acts with provisions which related to Scotland. In 1876 legislation from 1707–1847 which was still in force was published in three complementary volumes.

SOURCES OF MODERN UK PARLIAMENT ACTS

6–28 Acts of Parliament are published both electronically and in paper and in many different databases and series. The official electronic versions of Acts of Parliament are available from the *Office of Public Sector Information (OPSI)* website and the official paper versions are published by The Stationery Office (TSO). Printed Acts (known as the Queen's Printer copies) are published singly as they receive Royal Assent and subsequently appear in annual volumes called Public General Acts and Measures, see below. For information about the layout and structure of an Act, see para.5.16.

The fact that many different databases and series produce versions of Acts means that it is **6–29** possible for the same piece of legislation to appear in many different publications. The different versions of Acts may include additional information such as explanatory details called annotations and/or different search facilities for accessing legislation. Some gather together all legislation relating to a particular subject. Others cover specific periods in time. However, one vital feature which you must be aware of when reading legislation is whether it is the original version of the Act (i.e. the Act as passed by Parliament) or whether it is a revised version which includes any amendments which have been made to it. It is very important to be aware of the current law and therefore essential that you use a source which provides an **up-to-date revised version** of legislation. The original version of an Act should be treated with caution as it represents a historical document (one that is frozen in time). There may not have been any amendments since the original version was passed but unless you check the position, consulting the original version is worse than useless, it could lead to serious error.

Official versions

Public General Acts and Measures 📖
As soon as a Bill receives the Royal Assent it is published as an Act of Parliament by The **6–30** Stationery Office. Each Act is printed singly and these are known as Queen's Printer copies. Since the start of 1999 a separate book of Explanatory Notes has been published with Public General Acts which result from Bills introduced into either House of Parliament by a government minister.

At the end of each year the single Acts are produced together in a publication called *Public General Acts and Measures*. This is the official version of Acts of Parliament. Acts are arranged in chronological order (i.e. by chapter number). These do not contain annotations. Alphabetical and chronological lists are contained at the front of each volume. At the end of the final volume for each year are tables of derivations and destinations of the Consolidation Acts for the year. There is also a table called Effects of Legislation. This gives details of Acts (in chronological order) which have been repealed, amended or otherwise affected by legislation passed during the year.

Office of Public Sector Information (OPSI) ⌐ free
The official electronic original version of Acts of Parliament is available from the *Office of* **6–31** *Public Sector Information (OPSI)* website (*http://www.opsi.gov.uk/acts.htm*). *OPSI* has grown out of Her Majesty's Stationery Office (HMSO) which still exists within *OPSI*. All legislation is published on behalf of the Controller of HMSO. This site contains the full text of *all* Public General Acts from the beginning of 1988 and Local Acts from the start of 1991. The site aims to publish legislation simultaneously with their publication in printed form. Explanatory Notes are generally published at the same time as the Act but sometimes appear after the Act on this site. Acts of Parliament (and Explanatory Notes) are published in html and also importantly as pdfs which makes downloading the entire document and printing it straightforward. The Acts are grouped by year and within each year they can be viewed either alphabetically or chronologically by chapter number. The site also contains a *search legislation* function which links to an *advanced search* which allows you to search by keyword, type of legislation (e.g. Acts, Explanatory Notes or local Acts), jurisdiction or date. The material is published in its **original** form and amendments are not included. This means that this site is only of use if you particularly want the original form of an Act as opposed to the up-to-date form of the legislation.

Sources of revised versions of Acts

The following information sources contain revised versions of legislation and should therefore be used in preference to sources which contain original versions if you want to find out details of the current law.

6–32 *Westlaw* ⚘ subscription database
Westlaw UK contains all UK Public General Acts which were still in force in 1991, and all subsequent UK Public General Acts and Public General Acts of the Scottish Parliament. The archive dates back to 1267.

Features:

> ➤ Statutes are in **revised** form.
> ➤ *Westlaw* includes a lot of additional information such as details and links to the full text of amending legislation, secondary legislation made under an Act, cases citing an Act and the identification of journal articles discussing an Act.
> ➤ Access is provided to successive versions of statutes since February 1, 1991. You can view different versions of an Act back to *Westlaw's* "Table Top date" which is February 1, 1991. This is because a publication called Statutes in Force (published by HMSO) contained legislation which was fully consolidated up to February 1, 1991. These consolidated versions provide the earliest version of legislation contained on *Westlaw UK*.
> ➤ Prospective amendments are listed in the Analysis (see 6.41) and Overview Documents (see 6.42). They are not incorporated into the full text until they are in force.
> ➤ Concurrent versions of statutes. If a UK statute has been amended differently in different jurisdictions of the UK, the full text of the legislation will indicate details of the different forms. However, this is not the case with pdf versions of Acts, see para.6.103.

6–33 *Searching Westlaw for legislation. Westlaw* has three alternative ways of searching for legislation: basic search, advanced search and browsing.

6–34 *Basic search for legislation.* From the welcome page, click the *legislation* link from the navigation bar at the top of the screen. This will take you to the *legislation basic search* page, where you can search for statutes by typing the name of the piece of legislation, the year and provision number (if required). If you know the year, it is better to enter it as this will avoid retrieving multiple pieces of legislation. The basic search screen searches legislation currently in force. If you want to search historical legislation you need to use the *advanced search* facility.

The *free text* field allows you to enter terms or phrases and *Westlaw* searches for these within the text of statutes. Entering the title of a piece of legislation without quotation marks will retrieve all pieces of legislation with those words in the title. If you know the title of the Act you are looking for, enter it in quotation marks, e.g. "Civil Aviation Act 2006". If you know the year and chapter number, enter those into the title field to find the full text of the Act. For example: 2006 c.34 or 2006 c 34 (both will work). A space must be entered after the c or c. to retrieve the correct results.

If you enter the title of a piece of legislation without a provision number the whole of the legislation will be retrieved. The most efficient method of searching for a particular part of a piece of legislation is to enter, e.g. s.3 in the provision number box. If you enter solely a number, e.g. 3 the results you retrieve will include all parts of the legislation that have a provision number matching your entry. Another alternative is to click on the provision number menu and choose "section" as an option and then put 3 in the next box. However, unfortunately the menu of provisions is in alphabetical order which means that section is at the bottom of the list of options. This method is therefore cumbersome.

Searching can be improved if you use search techniques which *Westlaw* refer to as "Terms and Connectors" see para.2.33.

Advanced search for legislation. To access the *advanced search* facility, select *advanced search* in **6–35** the top right of the *legislation basic search* page. The advanced legislation search allows you to broaden your search to include legislation that is no longer in force. The default setting is *law in force* or you can select *law in force and historic law,* or *point in time.* The latter option allows you to look for legislation as it stood at a particular point in time. In order to do this you need to include the date in the format indicated by the date field.

Search results for legislation. The order of documents retrieved is primary legislation first, **6–36** followed by secondary legislation. If you search by legislation title only, the Arrangement of Act (see para.6.43) for that legislation will be returned. Searching for legislation using the *free text* function will return sections of legislation where those terms exist. The results list will show the name of the legislation as well as the title of the provision and the date when it came into force. Within a result list, status icons may display next to the title of the legislation indicating that either the provision has been repealed or superseded (⊟) or has pending amendments (⯑).To narrow down a long list of results, you can search for additional terms by entering your new search term(s) in the field at the top of the page and clicking *search within results.*

Browsing for legislation. You can browse for Acts by year, by title or by jurisdiction (either UK **6–37** or Scottish Parliament). The browse by year function allows you to select a time period (prior to 1990) from which to select the year you are looking for. From 1990 you can select a particular year. Within each year there is an alphabetical list of legislation that received its Royal Assent in that year. Browsing by title allows you to choose a letter and look at an alphabetical list of Acts. Select a title and you will be taken to the Arrangement of Act for that piece of legislation (see para.6.43).

Legislative materials. There are five types of legislation "document" available on *Westlaw:* full **6–38** text legislation, Legislation Analysis, Overview Document, Arrangement of Act and General Materials.

Full text legislation. The full text of legislation incorporates any amendments up to the "version **6–39** in force date". This date can be found in the entry for a specific part of legislation, e.g. a section. It is clearly displayed above the start of the section. The text contains links to other legislation cited and to footnotes describing amendments which themselves link through to the amending legislation. Within an Act you can navigate to *previous provision* or *next provision* by selecting the relevant link from above the legislation title.

If a provision has pending amendments that are not yet in force, a yellow exclamation flag (⯑) is **6–40** shown. To see the prospective change, select *legislation analysis* or *overview document* from the blue left-hand navigation bar. If you are viewing a historical version of legislation, you will see a red "no entry" flag (⊟) along with "superseded or repealed" indicating a more recent version is available. To see the most recent version, select *legislation analysis* from the blue left-hand navigation bar and click on the date beneath the *current law in force.*

6–41 *Legislation Analysis.* Legislation Analysis can be accessed from within a section of a piece of legislation by selecting *Legislation Analysis* from the blue left-hand navigation bar. It contains some or all of the following parts listed below. The relevant headings will appear in the blue left-hand navigation bar under *Legislation Analysis* and so you can easily get an impression of how much information there is about a specific section.

Current Law in Force	This includes a link to the current, consolidated version of a provision. It also lists the date that the provision came into force and gives details about what brought it into force and the scope of the amended version, for example if it takes effect on different days in different parts of the UK.
Commencement Information	This gives details about the initial commencement of the provision, including commencement date, scope of the commencement and links to any commencing legislation.
Amendments Pending	This details any prospective amendments to a provision, the date of the amendment (if known) and the legislation that will implement those changes.
Historic Law	This lists all previous versions of the legislation that are available in Westlaw (statutes back to 1991 and SIs from 1948). By selecting any of the entries listed, you can access legislation prior to amendment to see how the law read at a particular point in time. Each historical version also lists the date it came into force and the piece of legislation bringing it into force.
Extent	This shows the areas of the UK to which the provision extends.
SIs Made Under Act	This provides details of secondary legislation enacted with the authority of the legislation concerned.
Enabling Act	This details the Enabling Act or statutory instrument which gave authority for the statutory instrument to be enacted.
Modifications	This provides links to any legislation making non-textual amendments to the provision.
Related Legislation	This provides links to legislation applying, disapplying or referring to the provision.
Cases Citing	This lists the cases that cite the section of legislation in alphabetical order. If Westlaw provides a case analysis for any of these cases, clicking on the case citation underneath the case name will enable you to retrieve it.
Journal Articles	This lists citations to relevant materials taken from legal journals and law reviews. If *Westlaw* provides the full text of an article, there will be a link enabling access to it.

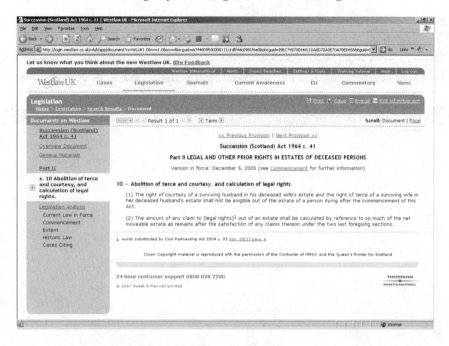

Diagram 6.1: Westlaw Legislation Analysis

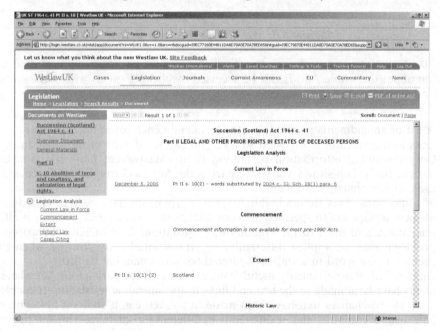

Diagram 6.2: Westlaw Legislation Analysis

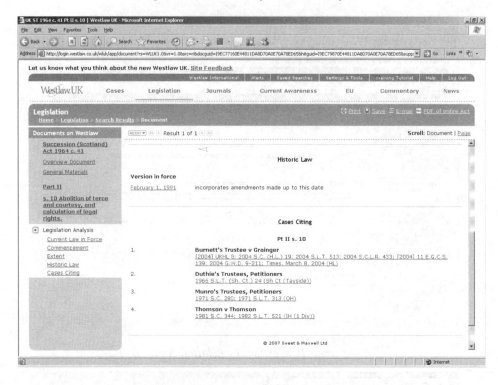

Diagram 6.3: Westlaw Legislation Analysis

6–42 *Overview Document*. This is a citator service which provides an extremely useful summary of information about the whole Act. It can be accessed by clicking on *Overview Document* on the left-hand side of the screen. It includes:

> ➤ A list of amendments pending (i.e. those amendments not applied to the full text) and links to the amending provision so that you can see details of the amendment.
> ➤ Commencement information pertaining to an Act (except pre-1991 commencement information). This shows when each part of the Act was brought into force and links to the commencement instrument.
> ➤ Modifications. This section highlights where provisions have been modified in relation to their application to specified areas or circumstances; however, the text itself remains unchanged and links to the "modifying" legislation. This includes occasions when a provision may be applied differently, e.g. transitional provisions or when the inter-pretation of a word in a statute is altered without changing its text.
> ➤ Citator. This is a particularly useful feature. It lists all the parts of an Act where amend-ments have been made to the text and links to the amending legislation. It enables you to trace all the changes that have been made to an Act, e.g. it shows if a section has been amended several times and/or differently in different jurisdictions. This can be very useful as the version in force (and the pdfs of Acts) only footnotes the most recent amendment to a section. Unfortunately citator information in not available for most pre-1990 Acts.
> ➤ All SIs enabled under authority of an Act which are listed in alphabetical order.
> ➤ Any EU Law implemented by an Act.

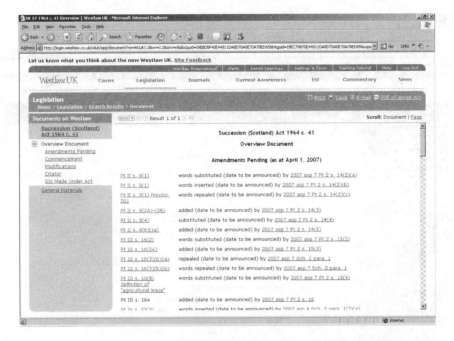

Diagram 6.4: Westlaw Overview

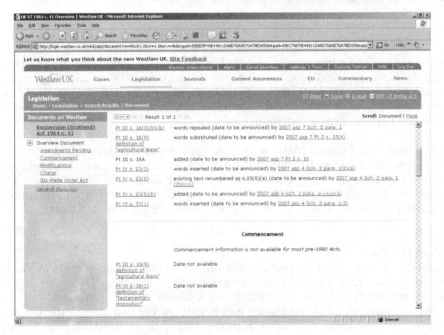

Diagram 6.5: Westlaw Overview

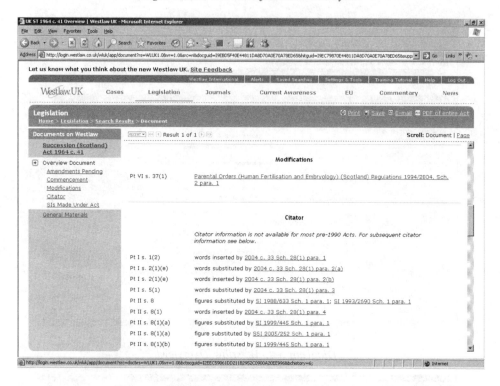

Diagram 6.6: Westlaw Overview

6–43 *Arrangement of Act.* The Arrangement of Act allows you to see the scheme of the Act and links, either directly or via part and chapter tables, to the provisions of an Act. This replicates the official table of provisions as published with every statute by *OPSI*. The fact that all the provisions within a piece of legislation are contained in one document means that you can easily navigate to any part or specific provision.

6–44 *General Materials.* The General Materials section provides information relating to the Act as a whole, as well as about major elements of the Act such as Parts, Chapters, Schedules, etc. It can be accessed by clicking on *General Materials* on the left-hand side of the screen. It includes information about: modifications, EU laws implemented, related legislation, disapplying legislation, referring legislation and cases and journal articles citing that Act, Part etc.

Statute Law Database free
6–45 The *Statute Law Database* (SLD) contains the official revised edition of Acts of Parliament in electronic form. This long awaited database was finally launched in December 2006 and is a welcome and important addition to free electronic legal information sources. It can be accessed at *http://www.statutelaw.gov.uk*. Its launch means that for the first time in the UK an official, authoritative online database of revised UK primary legislation is available free of charge to the public. This is seen by many as a fundamental right in a democratic society. The SLD was developed by the Statutory Publications Office which is part of the Department for Constitutional Affairs and contributes to the department's aims for improving access to justice. Unfortunately it has been launched before all the information on it has been brought completely up-to-date which means that caution must be exercised when using this database until the

updating process is complete. See para.6.47. However, it is planned that the database should be completely up to date by 2008.

The database contains the following primary legislation in **revised** form: UK Public General **6–46**
Acts; UK Local Acts 1991 to the present (Personal Acts are not included) and Acts of the Scottish Parliament 1999 onwards. Legislation repealed before February 1, 1991 is not included.

All legislation held in revised form has been updated at least to the end of 2001. The website **6–47**
claims that most of the legislation is up to date to the present but that some have effects outstanding from 2002 to the present. It is possible to update this information by checking the Update Status of Legislation page, see para.6.59. If amendments have not been applied a warning notice appears on the *results within legislation page* listing the years for which there are outstanding amendments. You must then check the Table of legislative effects to identify the missing amendments (see para.6.56). If there is no warning notice the user can assume the legislation has been revised to date.

It is possible to use the SLD to find details of amendments which have not yet been applied to an **6–48**
Act. All the amendments for 2002 to the present are listed in the tables of legislative effects. Taken together the SLD and the tables will enable the user to trace the effects to date. However, at the time of writing many important Acts still have a number of outstanding changes yet to be incorporated. This means that until the outstanding updating has been carried out it would be safer to use a completely revised database such as *Westlaw*.

Features: **6–49**

> ➢ Statutes are revised.
> ➢ Access to successive versions of statutes since February 1, 1991. You can view different versions of an Act back to the database's basedate which is February 1, 1991. This is the same date as for *Westlaw*.
> ➢ Access to prospective versions of statutes. If a provision has been amended but no date has been set for the change to come into force the database allows you to access a prospective version of the provision. You will be alerted to the existence of a prospective version when a 'P' icon appears alongside the section and in place of the version number in the table of attributes.
> ➢ Concurrent versions of statutes. This feature is available where the text of a provision is substituted but only in relation to part of its geographical extent, e.g. where a section which applies to Scotland, England and Wales is substituted by words which are only to apply to Scotland. Insertions and repeals do not give rise to concurrent versions. They will only be created where the amendment is a substitution so that there are different versions of the text for the different extents. Users are made aware of a concurrent version as the different sections will be listed after each other with the extent displayed in brackets, e.g. (S) or (E + W).

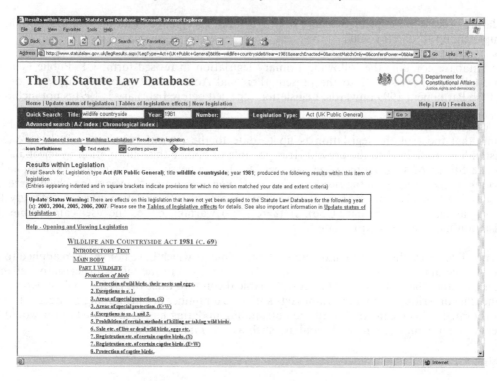

Diagram 6.7: The UK Statute Law Database

6–50 Presentational features:

> ➤ Insertions and substitutions that have been brought into effect appear in blue font inside square brackets.
> ➤ Prospective insertions and substitutions are in italicised blue font and inside square brackets.
> ➤ Repeals that have been made are signified by a row of dots. Prospective repeals are displayed in italicised text.
> ➤ If text is repealed only for a limited geographical extent, the text will not change colour but will remain in square brackets.
> ➤ Amendments to text as they appear in the amending legislation are in green font inside double quotes.
> ➤ When an amendment or other effect has been carried through, a purple arrow appears at the appropriate place in the text of the affecting legislation.

6–51 Annotation is the term used to describe features which give authority for amendments or other effects on legislation. They generally appear at the foot of a provision. Annotations citing authority from 2002 onwards may contain red hyperlinks which link to the relevant affecting legislation. When you navigate a link from affecting legislation to affected legislation, you will be taken to the version of the affected legislation in which the effect was **first** recorded. When you follow a link (e.g. to the affected provision when first recorded) the system is no longer constrained by your original search criteria. You may have to re-enter them.

Searching the Statute Law Database

Quick search. This facility is on a search bar towards the top of every page. This is the quickest **6–52** way to locate legislation based on details of the title, year, number, type of legislation or a combination of these criteria. You can use one or more of these criteria. If you specify criteria in more than one field, the search will return results that meet all the criteria specified, e.g. if you put "water" in the title field and "2005" in the year field, the search will bring up legislation with water in the title in 2005. Searches are not case sensitive.

The search results are displayed in chronological order with the most recent appearing first. **6–53** However, you can alter the list to appear in alphabetical order. If you click on one of the pieces of legislation listed, the *results within legislation* page will open. This will show you details of the Act and from there you can open the Act at various levels e.g. the whole Act, a particular section or paragraph of a schedule. *The results within legislation* page will alert you to any outstanding effects that have still to be applied to the Act by SLD.

If you open a particular section and scroll down to the bottom of the page, you will see a table of **6–54** attributes relating to the section. Attribute is the name SLD uses for items of information attached to different versions of legislation which denote properties of the legislative text. These include: version number, start date, end date, extent, confers power (i.e. if the Act confers the power to make secondary legislation) and blanket amendment (if the change is to affect legislation generally rather than the specific amendment).

Advanced search facility. This allows added functionality of searching. The additional features **6–55** include the ability to search by: a range of years and extent, e.g. you can narrow a search to legislation applicable to Scotland. The advanced search also allows text searching, searching for a version of legislation at a given date and searching for legislation which confers powers to make secondary legislation.

Table of legislative effects. The Table of legislative effects is located by clicking on the link in the **6–56** navigation bar at the top of the page. This is a list of all repeals, amendments and other effects (primary and secondary) enacted from 2002 to the current year. It can only be searched one year at a time but you can narrow that search by entering: the chapter/asp number of the affecting legislation; the year of the affected legislation; the chapter/asp number of the affected legislation; or any combination of these.

The results are displayed in ascending order ranked as follows: year of affected legislation; chapter/asp number of affected legislation; affected provision (letters then numbers); number of affecting legislation (year is fixed); affected provision (letters then numbers). For each entry, the type of effect is shown. A letter 'Y' in the 'Amendment Applied' column shows that the effect has been carried through on the database.

!Example of using the Table of legislative effects to find out about subsequent amendments

Use the Quick search to find the Railways and Transport Safety Act 2003. **6–57**
The *results within legislation* page shows a warning that there are outstanding amendments in 2003, 2004, 2005 and 2006.
Noting that the 2003 Act is Ch.20, go to the Table of legislative effects. In order to check for details of all the amendments from 2003 onwards:

> ➢ Enter 2003 in the year of affecting legislation box, 2003 in the year of affected legislation box and 20 in the number box opposite the year of affected legislation. Click Go. This brings up a table with details of amendments made in 2003.

> ➤ Enter 2004 in the year of affecting legislation box, 2003 in the year of affected legislation box and 20 in the number box opposite the year of affected legislation. Click Go. This brings up a table with details of amendments made in 2004.
> ➤ Repeat this exercise for the following two years by changing the year in the year of affecting legislation box to bring up lists of all the subsequent amendments.

This facility does alert you to all the amendments but it is cumbersome compared to obtaining the consolidated version on *Westlaw*. However, it is currently the only way to use SLD and ensure that you are aware of all the amendments to an Act which has not been fully updated in the database.

New legislation

6–58 This page shows all legislation newly published on the website over the previous seven days. New legislation will normally appear on the SLD within two weeks of receipt from The Stationery Office. If the interval is to be longer, a notice will appear in the homepage.

Update status of legislation

6–59 This page tells you how to determine the point in time to which any given item of legislation has been revised (i.e. its update status) and how to obtain details of any effects not yet applied. This page is particularly important as there are many statutes which do not contain recent changes.

Opening a whole Act

6–60 Go from the *results within legislation* page and click on the short title. If the Act is larger than 512 kilobytes a warning message tells the user it may take some time to open. Very large Acts (over two megabytes) cannot be opened in their entirety. This is a significant disadvantage compared to *Westlaw* where the user can easily access a pdf of any legislation.

Sources of original versions of Acts

BAILII free

6–61 The *BAILII* website which is operated by the British and Irish Legal Information Institute includes a large amount of legal information which is freely available on the web. It can be accessed at *http://www.bailii.org/*. The UK legislation material which it contains is reproduced from *OPSI* (i.e. all Public General Acts from 1988) with the addition of Magna Carta 1215 and the Bill of Rights 1689. The Acts are contained in the *United Kingdom Legislation* section of the site. The legislation search allows searching by keyword, dates and jurisdiction. The advanced search allows Boolean searching. Unlike the *OPSI* site it is possible to browse all the Acts in an alphabetical index. The Acts are available as continuous web pages as opposed to pdfs. The material is published in its original form and amendments are not included. This means that this site is only of use if you particularly want the **original** form of an Act as opposed to the up-to-date form of the legislation.

Justis UK Statutes subscription and CD Rom

6–62 This database contains the full text of all Acts of Parliament in England, Wales and Scotland as enacted, from 1235 to the present day. The UK Statutes is the only statute-law database to contain a full set of repealed legislation. It also has exact replica pdfs of the legislation. All Acts appear in their **original** form, with links to amending legislation. This means that you can trace the development of the law but if you want the current law you should use a source with a revised version of legislation.

Current Law Statutes 📖

Current Law Statutes (*Scottish Current Law Statutes Annotated* cover 1949–1990; *Current Law*   **6–63**
Statutes cover 1991 to the present) contain the full **original** text of every Public General Act
published since 1949. The English equivalent started one year earlier, in 1948. Private Acts have
been included since 1992. Acts of Sederunt and Acts of Adjournal were included until 1990. For
details of current sources, see para.7.130.

The Acts are published in annual volumes and within each volume the Acts are arranged in
chronological order. Each Act is annotated by an expert in the relevant field. This means that
notes (annotations) appear throughout the Act. The annotations are intended to clarify the
effect of the various sections. The number of annotations depends on the complexity of the Act.
In addition, there also tends to be a long introductory annotation which explains the Act's
purpose and puts it into context. It also refers to the dates of the parliamentary debates on the
Bill. The annotations are a very useful feature in that they provide an expert's insight into the
effect of a piece of legislation.

Acts from the current year appear singly in the looseleaf Statutes Service File. UK Public
General Acts are followed by Private Acts and Acts of the Scottish Parliament. After the end of
the year the material in the Statutes Service File is reissued in a bound volume.

The volumes of *Current Law Statutes* include:

- ➢ Chronological Table of Acts in the year.
- ➢ Alphabetical Index of Short Titles.
- ➢ Full text of Public General Acts passed by the UK Parliament in chronological order
  with annotations. The annotation after the long title is an introduction and a general
  note which will include reference to parliamentary debates on the Act. If appropriate,
  there may also be a more specific note after each or selected sections of the Act.
- ➢ Full text of Private Acts passed by the UK Parliament.
- ➢ Full text of Acts of the Scottish Parliament with its own subject index.
- ➢ Commencement Diary—an alphabetical table of the commencement of statutes in that
  year.
- ➢ Commencement Orders (full text) in chronological order.
- ➢ Alphabetical Table of UK statutory instruments in that year.
- ➢ Index by subject.

How to find details of an Act using Current Law

Check the volume of Statutes Annotated for the appropriate year. The full text (with annota-   **6–64**
tions) will appear in chronological order. Alternatively, a summary of the Act will be in the
relevant Yearbook or *Monthly Digest*.

!Example

Find the Local Government (Gaelic Names) Scotland) Act 1997.

⇒ **Step 1**:   Check the *Current Law Statutes* volumes for 1997. If you know the chapter
              number, you could check the spines of the volumes to locate the appropriate
              volume. Otherwise, start by checking the first volume.
⇒ **Step 2**:   Check the alphabetical list of short titles. Opposite the short title is the chapter
              number.
⇒ **Step 3**:   Turn to the page headed up with the chapter number. The chapter number
              appears in bold and is followed by a number corresponding to the section
              number of the Act which appears on that particular page.

Law Reports: Statutes 📖

6–65 These are published by The Incorporated Council of Law Reporting as part of the Law Reports. They include exclusively Scottish legislation. They are not annotated. The material is published in its **original** form and amendments are not included. This means that this source is only of use if you particularly want the original form of an Act as opposed to the up-to-date form of the legislation.

Sources of revised Acts which exclude exclusively Scottish legislation

LexisNexis Butterworths ⌨ subscription database

6–66 *LexisNexis Butterworths* includes all current Public General Acts for England and Wales. It provides the **revised** text of the legislation. Acts made by the UK Parliament which relate only to Scotland are not included, although provisions of Scottish Acts that apply or are relevant to England and/or Wales are included. Legislation from the Scottish Parliament is included. Public General Acts that are no longer in force do not appear in full text but, if the Act ceased to have effect on or after January 1, 1999, a note explains why the enactment no longer applies.

Halsbury's Statutes of England 📖 and ⌨ subscription

6–67 This publication provides comprehensive coverage of UK legislation but excludes statutes which relate only to Scotland and sections of UK statutes which relate to Scotland only. See para.9.5.

AIDS TO TRACING STATUTES

6–68 There are different types of aids to tracing statutes:

1. Full-text electronic databases such as *Westlaw* (see para.6.32), the *Statute Law Database* (see para.6.45) and *LexisNexis Butterworths* (see para.6.66).
2. Citators such as *Current Law Legislation Citators* (see para.6.69), *Current Legal Information* (see para.6.76) and *Justcite* (see para.6.77).
3. Digests of legislation contained in collections which are indexed in various ways such as *Lawtel* and the *Current Law Yearbooks* (see para.8.21).
4. Indexes contained in collections of legislation, reference works, encyclopaedias (such as the *Stair Memorial Encyclopaedia*) and textbooks.
5. Major collections of statutory material such as *Halsbury's Statutes of England* (although it should be remembered that this excludes exclusively Scottish legislation) (see para.9.5).
6. There is an increasing amount of recent material freely available via the internet. However, the text of legislation is not updated, which limits the usefulness of this as a source for research. The one exception to this is the *Statute Law Database* but this has not yet been fully updated (see para.6.45). The material freely available on the internet also suffers from the limitation that it only tends to be very recent (again with the exception of the SLD). This means that entering the title of a statute into Google or another search engine is *not* a wise research technique.

Current Law Legislation Citators

6–69 While the *Current Law Legislation Citators* are an efficient way of tracing statutes, they do require the user to have an appreciation of how the citators are organised and it is essential to adopt a systematic approach to searching them.

A *Legislation Citator* is a chronological list of all Acts passed since 1947 and includes mention of any Acts which have changed or been interpreted by the courts since 1947. The *Current Law*

Legislation Citators (formerly called Statute Citators) are in eight volumes and should be used along with the *Current Law Statutes Service File*. The proliferation of volumes in recent years is regrettable as it makes searching more cumbersome and means that you cannot carry out a systematic search if any of the volumes is missing from the library shelves.

The volumes are: 1948–1971, 1972–1988, 1989–1995, 1996–1999, 2000–2001, 2002–2004, 2005, **6–70** and 2006. The cumulative monthly updates of the Legislation Citator for the current year are to be found in the *Current Law Statutes Service File* (see para.8.23). The English version has a similar format except that the citators start in 1947.

The *Legislation Citators* list all amendments, modifications and repeals to primary and sec- **6–71** ondary legislation made in the years covered by the specific volume. Acts and statutory instruments passed by the Scottish Parliament are included. Since 1993 the *Legislation Citators* are in fact a combination of two citators—a *Statute Citator* and a *Statutory Instrument Citator*. Since 1999 legislation from the Scottish Parliament has been included.

Contents of the *Legislation Citators* are arranged as follows:

> ➢ Table of Abbreviations.
> ➢ Alphabetical Tables of Statutes cited in the *Statute Citator* and statutory instruments cited in the *Statutory Instrument Citator* (this includes Scottish statutory instruments).
> ➢ *Statute Citator*.
> ➢ *Statutory Instrument Citator*.

The *Statute Citator* is always listed first. It is arranged in the following order: **6–72**

1. Acts of the Scottish Parliament listed in chronological order by year and asp number.
2. Acts of the Northern Ireland Assembly listed in chronological order by year and reference to number.
3. Public General Acts of the UK Parliament since 1947 listed in chronological order by year and chapter number.

The *Statute Citator* contains:

⇒ Details of amendments and repeals since 1947 made to statutes of *any* date, including details of the amending or repealing provisions.
⇒ In respect of *any* Act, the names and citations of cases in which it has been judicially considered since 1947.
⇒ In respect of *any* Act, details of statutory instruments issued under its provisions.
⇒ In respect of *any* Act, where it has been consolidated by an Act passed since 1989.

The *Statutory Instrument Citator* is arranged in the following order:

1. Scottish statutory instruments listed in chronological order by year and number.
2. Statutory Rules issued by the UK Parliament listed in chronological order by year and number.
3. Statutory instruments made by the UK Parliament listed in chronological order by year and number.

The *Statutory Instrument Citator* contains:

⇒ Details of amendments and repeals since 1993 made to statutory instruments of *any* date.

⇒ In respect of *any* statutory instrument, the cases in which it has been judicially considered since 1993.
⇒ In respect of *any* statutory instrument, details of the statutory instruments issued since 1993 which have been made under its provisions.
⇒ In respect of *any* statutory instrument, where it has been consolidated by an Act passed since 1993.

Searching the *Statute Citators*

6–73 If you are trying to locate any possible changes, e.g. to an Act of Parliament, check the citator covering the period when the Act was passed. After you have found the reference to the Act in that volume, check all the subsequent citators right up to the latest citator in the *Current Law Statutes Service File*. This will ensure that you locate all subsequent developments relating to the Act in question. If there is no mention of the Act or the section, it means that there has been no alteration made to it within the time period covered by the citator.

Scottish Current Law
Statute Citator 1948–1971
↓
Scottish Current Law
Statute Citator contained in
Legislation Citator volume 1972–1988
↓
Current Law
Statute Citator contained in
Legislation Citator 1989–1995
↓
Current Law
Statute Citator contained in
Legislation Citator 1996–1999
↓
Current Law
Statute Citator contained in
Legislation Citator 2000–2001
↓
Current Law
Statute Citator contained in
Legislation Citator 2002–2004
↓
Current Law
Statute Citator contained in
Legislation Citator 2005
↓
Current Law
Statute Citator contained in
Legislation Citator 2006
↓
Statute Citator contained in the current year in the
Statutes Service File

Terms used to describe legislative effects

Current Law uses various terms to describe legislative effects. The following definitions are taken **6–74** from the latest edition of the *Legislation Citators*:

➢ "added" means that new provisions have been inserted by subsequent legislation;
➢ "amended" means that the text of the legislation is modified by subsequent legislation;
➢ "applied" means that it has been brought to bear or exercised by subsequent legislation;
➢ "consolidated" means that previous Acts in the same subject area have been brought together in subsequent legislation, with or without amendments;
➢ "disapplied" means that an exception has been made to the application of an earlier enactment;
➢ "enabling" means giving power for the relevant statutory instrument to be made;
➢ "referred to" means direction from other legislation without specific effect or application;
➢ "repealed" means rescinded by subsequent legislation;
➢ "restored" means that it has been reinstated by subsequent legislation;
➢ "substituted" means that the text of a provision is completely replaced by subsequent legislation;
➢ "varied" means provisions modified in relation to their application to specified areas or circumstances, however the text itself remains unchanged.

Excerpt from Statute Citator with features marked   **6–75**

---

[1] 26. Housing (Scotland) Act 1987 [2]
s.2, amended: 1989, c.42, s.161.
s.5A, added: 1993, c.28, s.149. **[3]**
s.5B, added: *ibid.*, s.151.
s.17, repealed in pt.: *ibid.*, s.157, Sch.22. **[4]**
ss.17A–17C, added: *ibid.*, s.153.
s.19, amended: *ibid.*, s.155. **[5]**
s.20, amended: *ibid.*, s.154.
s.21, see *Pirie v City of Aberdeen District Council* (O.H.), 1993 S.L.T. 1155. **[6]**
s.21, amended: 1993, c.28, s.155.
s.22A, added: *ibid.*, s.152.
s.24, amended: 1990, c.40, s.65.

Key:

[1] Chapter number
[2] Short title
[3] addition to the Act
[4] part of the Act repealed
[5] changes to the Act
[6] Case concerning a section of the Act

Current Legal Information ⌖ and CD Rom subscription legal research service
Current Legal Information contains an electronic version of the *Current Law Legislation Citator*. **6–76** It covers the period from 1989 to date. Searching the *Legislation Citator in Current Legal Information* enables you to access information by the year; words from the short title of an Act; sections of Acts or free text. The entry for a piece of legislation includes the same information

which is available in the paper version. The key advantage of the electronic version is the ease of use compared with checking through lots of different paper volumes.

Justcite ᛟsubscription legal citator

6–77 *Justcite* is an online legal citator which includes UK statutes (from 1235) and Scottish Parliament Acts (from 1999). The home page allows you to search for statutes by title or reference (which means, e.g. including the section number along with the short title of an Act). Acts can be searched separately by ticking the appropriate box on the right-hand side of the screen. Alternatively, you can search using the *index* tab. This allows you to browse through title indexes of statutes listed in alphabetical order. Scottish legislation is not listed separately.

6–78 The information retrieved can include:

> ➢ The status of the provision.
> ➢ A link to the particular reference. If you click on this link it will open a new window showing various sources of the full text of the entire Act or section which you may be able to access depending on the subscriptions held by your university library.
> ➢ Lists of sections which have been amended and the amending legislation.
> ➢ Lists of sections which have amended other legislation and the legislation amended.
> ➢ Cases which have interpreted the section.

SEARCH STRATEGIES FOR FINDING STATUTES

6–79 This section deals with the different ways which can be used to find legislation. This will allow you to find legislation from different starting points for instance you may want to explore a new area of law or your knowledge of the legislation's title may be incomplete. There are usually numerous ways of finding legal information. This section contains lists of various alternative sources along with comments as to their strengths and weaknesses. The most comprehensive sources for the Scottish researcher are listed first. This means that sources which exclude Scottish materials appear lower in the list even though they may be excellent information sources for UK (as opposed to Scottish) material. Sources which provide access to revised versions of legislation are given prominence because sources of original versions of Acts will require additional research to check for any amendments or repeals. Both electronic and paper sources are listed.

6–80 The following search strategies are considered:

> ➢ Finding statutes by subject. This should allow you to search where you may be interested in a specific subject area. See paras 6.81–6.91.
> ➢ Current status of a statute. It is vital to know whether a statute has been brought into force or whether it has been amended or repealed. See paras 6.92–6.102 and 6.103–6.110.
> ➢ Finding out about Local and Personal Acts. This is becoming much easier than in the past. However, it is something that you will rarely be expected to do at university. See paras 6.123–6.126.
> ➢ Finding whether courts have considered the legislation is discussed in paras 4.92–4.103. This covers the situation where you know of a specific legislative provision and you want to find out if any cases have discussed it or interpreted it in a particular way.
> ➢ Finding whether any articles have been written about the legislation is discussed in paras 6.112–6.118.

There is a summary of the alternative sources for each strategy in Appendix I.

Finding statutes by subject

Major textbooks/reference works and encyclopaedias 📖
Encyclopaedia or reference works are ideal starting points for research by subject. Unlike an **6–81** electronic database, they will not just identify a piece of legislation; they will place it in context. This means that they will explain its background and how it fits in to the whole area of law, how it has been interpreted and offer comment on it. Encyclopaedia or reference works can also provide you with the information necessary to refine your search terms which will make searching the full text databases manageable. If you try to conduct a subject search on a database with a broad subject term you will retrieve hundreds or even thousands of hits which it may take a long time to work through. Searching with a more relevant term will produce fewer more relevant hits.

When consulting an encyclopaedia or reference work look at the Table of Statutes which will be located at the beginning of the work. This will list statutes in chronological order.

The Laws of Scotland: Stair Memorial Encyclopaedia 📖
In the paper version check the Consolidated Index. This should lead you to the relevant volume **6–82** or reissued title. Each subject area has its own Table of Statutes. This information can be updated by checking the Annual Cumulative Supplement and the Service Binder. See para.8.2.

The Laws of Scotland Online (*Stair Memorial Encyclopaedia*) ⌖ subscription from *LexisNexis Butterworths*
It is possible to search the whole of Stair by free text or to limit your search to various titles. **6–83** You can also use a browse function to open up an alphabetical list of all the titles and link through to your chosen topic.

Westlaw ⌖ subscription database
From the welcome page, select the *legislation* heading from the navigation bar at the top of the **6–84** screen. This will take you to the *legislation basic search* page, where you can enter subject terms into the free text box. *Westlaw* will search for these within the short titles and the text of legislation. Searching can be improved by using the search techniques discussed in para.2.33.

Statute Law Database ⌖ free
The *Statute Law Database* allows searching for words in the title or, more useful for subject **6–85** searching, a free text search of the content of legislation in the database in its advanced search. There are facilities which enable you to restrict this by type of legislation, extent and date range. The results obtained will have the search terms highlighted in the text. However, this database is not completely up-to-date and should be used with caution. See paras 6.45–6.48.

Current Law Yearbooks and Monthly Digests 📖
Check the subject headings in the consolidated indexes in the master volumes of the Yearbooks, **6–86** and the more recent Yearbooks and *Monthly Digest*. See paras 8.15 and 8.21.

Justis UK Statutes ⌖ subscription and CD Rom
This database contains the full text of all Acts of Parliament in England, Wales and Scotland **6–87** from 1235 to the present day (including repealed legislation). All Acts appear in their **original** form with links to amending legislation.

Office of Public Sector Information (*OPSI*) ⌖ free
The *(OPSI)* website (*http://www.opsi.gov.uk/acts.htm*) contains the official electronic full text of **6–88** *all* Public General Acts but only from the beginning of 1988 and Local Acts from the start of 1991. The site contains a *search legislation* function which links to an *advanced search* which

allows you to search by keyword, type of legislation (e.g. Acts, Explanatory Notes or local Acts), jurisdiction or date. However, the material is published in its **original** form and amendments are not included.

BAILII [⊕] free

6–89   The *BAILII* website (*http://www.bailii.org/*) only contains Public General Acts from 1988. The legislation search allows searching by keyword, dates and jurisdiction. The advanced search allows Boolean searching. However, like *OPSI*, the material is published in its original form and amendments are not included.

LexisNexis Butterworths [⊕] subscription database

6–90   While *LexisNexis Butterworths* provides the revised text of the legislation Acts that were made by the UK Parliament and relate exclusively to Scotland are not included.

Halsbury's Statutes 📖 and [⊕] subscription

6–91   This is an excellent source of information about legislation which is accessed by subject. Unfortunately, it does not include exclusively Scottish legislation, see para.9.5.

Current status of a statute—Is It In Force Yet?

The Act itself

6–92   The date the Act comes into force may be the date of Royal Assent or it may be detailed in the commencement section at the end of the Act, see para.5.16, section 8. This means that you need to check the commencement section of the Act. If the Act is silent it comes into force on the date of the Royal Assent. If the Act stipulates a specific date or time period then that is the relevant date. Alternatively the Act (or part of it) may come into force at a time to be set by a Minister. If this is the case, you need to check if a commencement order has been issued and find out which part(s) of the Act have been brought into force.

Westlaw [⊕] subscription database

6–93   If you want to check whether a specific section of an Act has been brought into force you should search for the piece of legislation and section in the *basic search* box. This will retrieve the current version of the section. At the start of the entry underneath the section heading *Westlaw* UK provides details of commencement. The phrase "version in force:" will be followed by a date. This is the commencement date. It will be followed by the words "(see *Commencement* for further information)". Clicking on the word *commencement* will take you to a link to the relevant commencement order.

If there is no "version in force:" date, the words "(see *Commencement* for further information)" will still appear. This means that the section has not yet been brought into force. The word *commencement* will be a link which will take you to more details and a link to the legislative provision governing the commencement of that particular section.

If you want to see details about commencement for an entire Act, search for the piece of legislation and section in the *basic search* box. This will retrieve the arrangement of the Act. Click on the *overview document* link in the blue left hand navigation bar. This will retrieve a list of details of commencement for all the different parts of the Act. Commencement details will appear first unless there are any amendments pending in which case you will need to click on the Commencement link in the blue left hand navigation bar or scroll down to the commencement details. The commencement details show when each part of the Act was brought into force and link to the commencement instrument.

Is It in Force? 📖
This is an annual publication which covers all Public General Acts in England, Wales and **6–94**
Scotland (including Acts of the Scottish Parliament) over the previous 25 years. The current
edition is "*Is It in Force Spring 2007?*"

The years are presented in chronological order and within each year the statutes are listed
alphabetically. Opposite the short title are details of the relevant commencement provisions. If
the same Act applies to England/Wales and Scotland but there are differences in, e.g. commencement date, this is acknowledged by separating the Scottish information and following it
with an "(S)". See para.7.54 for an example.

The volume also contains *Statutes Not Yet in Force* which lists provisions of Acts for which
no commencement dates have yet been appointed. An example is the Easter Act 1928 which was
given the Royal Assent on August 3, 1928 but which has never been brought into force.

Note that this publication does not include full information on amendments and repeals. You
should use other publications to check this information, see paras 6.103–6.110. As it is an
annual publication it is always out of date so be sure to use another source to check from the
date of publication to the present unless you are using the electronic version—see below.

Is It in Force? 🖰 subscription service as part of *LexisNexis Butterworths*
The online version is updated daily and links through to the relevant commencement orders. **6–95**

Lawtel 🖰subscription legal current awareness digest service
Lawtel is updated daily and covers all statutes since 1984. On the *Lawtel UK* homepage click on **6–96**
statutory law. Enter your search terms in the box and click search. In the *search* results click on
the link to the details of the Act. From here, click on the link to the *statutory status table*. This
lists all the sections of the Act in a table, with entries relating to commencement, amendment
and repeal.

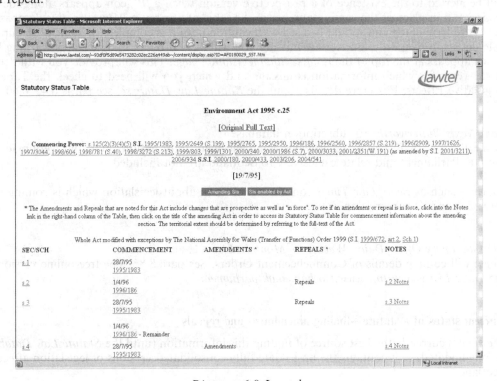

Diagram 6.8 Lawtel

Current Law Legislation Citators and Current Law Statutes 📖

6–97 The information in the *Current Law Legislation Citators* (see paras 6.69–6.75) is updated by the *Statutes Service File* (para.8.23) which contains a Commencement Diary. This notes, alphabetically by statute, the commencement of statutes from January of the current year as initiated by Orders and by statutory provisions. There is a Commencement Diary covering the year in the annual volumes of the *Current Law Statutes*. From 1992 Commencement Orders have been reprinted in the annual volumes. There is also a Dates of Commencement Table in the Monthly Digests.

How to find out if a Commencement Order has been issued in relation to an Act:

⇒ Check the Commencement Diary in the relevant volume of Statutes Annotated.
⇒ Check the Dates of Commencement Table in the latest Monthly Digest or the Commencement Diary in the Statutes Service File.

Current Legal Information 🖥 and CD Rom subscription legal research service

6–98 The legislation citator is available electronically as part of *Current Legal Information*. However, this only covers Acts from 1989 to date.

Statute Law Database 🖥 free

6–99 The *Statute Law Database* provides commencement information at the bottom of the text of a section of an Act. If a provision has been amended but no date has been set for the change to come into force the database allows you to access a prospective version of the provision. You will be alerted to the existence of a prospective version when a 'P' icon appears alongside the section and in place of the version number in the table of attributes. However, this database is not yet fully updated and should be used with caution until it is complete. If some of the up-to-date details in relation to an Act are missing you will alerted by an update status warning box which appears at the top of the *results within legislation page*. This will provide you with details of the years for which information is missing and which you will need to check the Table of Legislative Effects. For more details about the *Statute Law Database*, see paras 6.45–6.60.

LexisNexis Butterworths 🖥 subscription database

6–100 While *LexisNexis Butterworths* provides commencement information, Acts that were made by the UK Parliament and relate exclusively to Scotland are not included.

6–101 Journals such as *Scots Law Times* contain information about legislation which is coming into force. 📖 and 🖥 subscription

The Stationery Office Daily, Weekly or Monthly Lists 📖 and 🖥

6–102 These will contain details of Commencement Orders. See para.8.85. The free online version of the *Daily List* is at *http://www.tsoshop.co.uk/parliament*

Current status of a statute—finding amendment and repeals

Westlaw is currently the best source of finding this information (until the *Statute Law Database* is fully updated) as it contains the up-to-date fully consolidated versions of legislation affecting Scotland.

Westlaw ⚓subscription database

The legislation contained in *Westlaw* has incorporated any amendments or repeals. Words **6–103** which have been inserted or substituted are contained in square brackets and a footnote provides you with both details of and a link to the amending legislation. An ellipsis (...) indicates that text has been repealed and the repealing legislation is referenced and linked via a footnote.

⇒ **Note** that if a section has been amended several times the footnote only references the most recent amendment. To see details of all amendments select *overview document* from the blue left-hand navigation bar and then select the *citator* from the blue left-hand navigation bar. The citator lists all the amendments to an Act and provides links to the amending legislation.

⇒ **Note** that if a section of a UK Act has been amended differently in Scotland and in England you will be made aware of this when you are looking at the section itself. The section shown will be the most recent version of the Act with a footnote containing the version from the other jurisdiction. This means that, depending on timing, some sections may be those extant in Scotland and others may be those extant in England. This causes no problems when you are looking at the Act section by section as the footnotes will alert you if there are other versions of the section. However, if you create a pdf it will contain the most recent version of the Act, i.e. in these circumstances Westlaw will not create a pdf to show a Scottish or English version of an Act. This means that extreme care must be taken in relation to UK Acts which have been amended differently in different jurisdictions and involves checking the pdf against the citator in the *overview document*.

⇒ Prospective amendments are not incorporated into the text. If a provision has pending amendments that are not yet in force, a yellow exclamation flag (❗) is shown. To see the prospective change, select *legislation analysis* or *overview document* from the blue left-hand navigation bar.

⇒ Westlaw allows you to view versions of historic law back to 1991. To do this you have to use the *advanced search* facility by selecting *advanced search* in the top right of the *legislation basic search* page. The default setting is *law in force* or you can select *law in force and historic law*, or *point in time*. The latter option allows you to look for legislation as it stood at a particular point in time. In order to do this you need to include the date in the format indicated by the date field. If you are viewing a historical version of legislation, you will see a red "no entry" flag (⛔) along with "superseded or repealed" indicating a more recent version is available. To see the most recent version, select *legislation analysis* from the blue left-hand navigation bar and click on the date beneath the *current law in force*.

Statute Law Database ⚓ free

The *Statute Law Database* provides the revised form of legislation which incorporates **6–104** amendments and repeals. It indicates the authority for an amendment or other effect on legislation at the foot of the provision in an annotation. Annotations citing authority from 2002 onwards may contain red hyperlinks which link to the relevant affecting legislation. Insertions and substitutions that have been brought into effect appear in blue font inside square brackets. Repeals that have been made are signified by a row of dots. If text is repealed only for a limited geographical extent, the text will not change colour but will remain in square brackets.

However, this database is not yet fully updated and should be used with caution until it is complete. If some of the up-to-date details in relation to an Act are missing you will alerted by an update status warning box which appears at the top of the *results within legislation* page. This will provide you with details of the years for which information is missing and which you will need to check the Table of legislative effects. For more details about the *Statute Law Database* see paras 6.45–6.60.

Current Law Legislation Citator 📖

6–105 This is the best paper source for locating changes to Scottish legislation however while the legislation citators are an efficient way of tracing legislative changes, they do require the user to have an appreciation of how the citators are organised and it is essential to adopt a systematic approach to searching them, see paras 6.69–6.75.

Using *Current Law* to find out if an Act has been amended or repealed:

⇒ **Step 1**: Check the *Statute Citators* in the volumes of *Legislation Citators* in chronological order starting from the date of the Act. In order to locate the chapter number, check the alphabetical list of Acts at the beginning of the volume. Once armed with the chapter number you can turn to the Statute Citator itself. Under the entry for the Act, the citator will list any amendments that have been made.

⇒ **Step 2**: In order to be aware of all amendments (up to the last month) check through all the *Statute Citators* up to the most recent update for the citator in the *Statutes Service File*.

Current Legal Information 🖰 and CD Rom subscription legal research service

6–106 The legislation citator is available electronically as part of *Current Legal Information*. However, this only covers Acts from 1989 to date.

Lawtel 🖰 subscription legal current awareness digest service

6–107 *Lawtel* is updated daily and covers all statutes since 1984. On the *Lawtel UK* homepage click on *statutory law*. Enter your search terms in the box and click *search*. Click on the link in the search results to the details of the Act. Click on the link to the *statutory status table*. This lists all the sections of the Act in a table, with entries relating to commencement, amendment and repeal.

Halsbury's Statutes 📖 and 🖰 subscription

6–108 *Halsbury's Statutes* is a great source for UK legislation. It contains the amended text of legislation currently in force and has an effective updating service. Unfortunately, it does not include exclusively Scottish legislation, see para.9.5.

LexisNexis Butterworths 🖰 subscription database

6–109 *LexisNexis Butterworths* provides the revised form of legislation which incorporates amendments and repeals. An ellipsis (...) indicates that text has been repealed. Square brackets denote text that has been inserted or substituted. Italicised text means that the content is prospectively repealed or substituted. The notes section at the end of each document indicates the changes that have been made to the text. However, Acts that were made by the UK Parliament and relate exclusively to Scotland are not included.

Chronological Table of the Statutes 📖

6–110 This is published annually by The Stationery Office and is in two volumes. It is a chronological table of the statutes for the period 1235 to the year of publication. Statutes are listed chronologically by year and chapter number. When the title of the Act appears in italics it means it has been repealed. If it appears in bold type then the Act is still, at least in part, in force. Details of amendments and repeals are given. This is an annual publication but tends to be a couple of years out of date. The latest version was published in February 2007 and covers the period 1235–2005. This greatly reduces its usefulness. Another method would have to be employed to bring your search in the Chronological Table of Statutes up to date.

Finding whether the courts have considered an Act

This covers the situation where you know of a specific Act and you want to find out if any cases **6–111** have discussed it or interpreted it in a particular way. See paras 4.92–4.103.

Finding whether any articles have been written about an Act

Searching for journal articles generally is covered in the section starting at para.8.44.

Westlaw ⌐ⓣ subscription database
Westlaw UK is the best way of tracing this information as it contains the *Legal Journals Index* **6–112** within its journals section. This indexes legal articles and case summaries from over 1,000 journals and dates back to 1986. There are two different ways to obtain this information in *Westlaw*. One is to search the journals section and the alternative is to search the *legislation analysis* for the Act. To search the journals section access it by selecting *Journals* from the navigation bar at the top of the screen of the welcome page. This will take you to the *journals basic search* page, select *advanced search* in the top right of the screen. Enter the short title in the *legislation title* field and the provision details in the *legislation provision no.* field. Click search.
  Westlaw UK will also identify articles which have discussed legislation in the *legislation analysis* for the Act concerned. See para.6.41. Links will go to the full text (if available on *Westlaw*) or to an abstract of the article.

Current Legal Information ⌐ⓣ and CD Rom subscription legal research service
This, like *Westlaw*, also contains the Legal Journals Index. Click on the link to this database and **6–113** enter the short title in the *legislation* field.

LexisNexis Butterworths ⌐ⓣ subscription database
This is not as useful for tracing journal articles as it have the same coverage as the *Legal* **6–114** *Journals Index* on *Westlaw*. Choose the journals tab from the homepage. This opens up the journals search form. Enter the details of the Act in the *enter search terms* box.

HeinOnline ⌐ⓣsubscription database of legal journals
This increasingly popular database is expanding quickly and is changing its interface at the time **6–115** of writing. It holds a number of UK law journals in its Law Journal Library. The journals are in full text which can be searched for articles about legislation. However, its Scots law holdings are currently limited.

Current Law Yearbooks 📖
Check under the appropriate subject headings in the Yearbooks and the latest *Monthly Digest*. **6–116** See para.8.21.

Journals 📖
If you are aware of the date of the Act you could check relevant journal indexes. **6–117**

Lawtel ⌐ⓣ subscription legal current awareness digest service
Lawtel indexes fewer journals than the *Legal Journals Index* and the majority of its coverage of **6–118** journals dates from 1998. To locate articles about an Act, select the *articles index* on the home page, then choose the *focused search* option. Use the *statutes cited* box to enter the short title of the Act.

Finding whether any statutory instruments have been made under an Act

See paras 6.193–6.198.

LOCAL AND PERSONAL ACTS

Aids to tracing Local and Personal Acts

Chronological Tables of Local Acts and of Private and Personal Acts 📖 and ☞

6–119 The *Chronological Table of Local Acts* lists Local Acts passed between 1797 and the end of 2005 and the *Chronological Table of Private and Personal Acts* lists Private Acts passed between 1539 and the end of 2005. Both tables are based on work by the Law Commission and the Scottish law Commission. Printed versions are published by The Stationery Office and electronic versions are available from the *OPSI* website (*http://www.opsi.gov.uk/chron-tables/chron-index.htm*).

Index to Local and Personal Acts 1801–1947/Supplementary Index to Local and Personal Acts 1948–1966 📖

6–120 These volumes, published by HMSO, allow you to locate Local and Personal Acts by subject.

Public General Acts and Measures 📖

6–121 Local and Personal Acts are listed in alphabetical order in the bound volumes of *Public General Acts and Measures*. See para.6.30.

The Daily List 📖 and ☞ free

6–122 The *Daily List* and its cumulative versions list Local and Personal Acts. The online version is available at *http://www.tsoshop.co.uk/parliament*.

Sources of Local and Personal Acts

Current Law Statutes 📖

6–123 From 1992 the full text of Private Acts is published in the final volume of *Current Law Statutes* for the year.

Office of Public Sector Information (OPSI) ☞ free

6–124 The full text of Local Acts from the beginning of 1991 is freely available from the *OPSI* website (*http://www.opsi.gov.uk/acts.htm*). They appear in original format and do not take account of amendments.

Statute Law Database ☞ free

6–125 The *Statute Law Database* has UK Local Acts from 1991. Personal Acts are not included.

6–126 The texts of older Local and Personal Acts can be difficult to locate. Some can be purchased from The Stationery Office. However, you may have to consult one of the collections of Local and Personal Acts held at different libraries (see below) or approach a library local to the area covered by the Act or contact the organisation directly. Collections of Scottish Local and Personal Acts are held by: Aberdeen University library (Local Acts and Private Acts 1797 (38 Geo.3) onwards), the Advocates' Library (Local Acts and Private Acts 1797 (38 Geo.3) onwards), Edinburgh University library (Local Acts and Private Acts 1797 (38 Geo.3) onwards), Glasgow University (Local Acts and Private Acts 1797 (38 Geo.3) onwards, Scottish Acts only), Mitchell library (Local Acts and Private Acts 1895–1922, 1923–1956 (incomplete), 1957 onwards), St Andrews University library (Local Acts 1797 (38 Geo.3) onwards and Private Acts

1815–1885), Scottish Record Office (Local Acts 1797 (38 Geo.3) – 1884 (virtually complete) and Private Acts 1815–1884), Scottish Office Solicitors' library (Local Acts 1900 onwards, for the period 1900-1971 the holding is of Scottish Local Acts only) and the Signet library (Local Acts 1801 onwards. Private Acts 1815 onwards).

SOURCES OF STATUTORY INSTRUMENTS

Statutory instruments, like Acts of Parliament, are published both electronically and in paper **6–127** and in many different databases and series. The official electronic versions of statutory instruments are available from the *Office of Public Sector Information (OPSI)* website and the official paper versions are published by The Stationery Office (TSO). Not all statutory instruments are automatically published. All statutory instruments which are of general application will be published but local statutory instruments are not always published by The Stationery Office. An Explanatory Memorandum has been published with all statutory instruments which are subject to parliamentary procedure since the start of 2004. Although statutory instruments are not published with Acts of Parliament and there are separate publications which cover only statutory instruments, many of the major databases contain both Acts and statutory instruments. For information about the layout and structure of a statutory instrument, see para.5.28.

As with Acts, different databases and series produce different versions of statutory instruments **6–128** and it is vital that you are aware of whether you are reading the original version of a statutory instrument or whether it is an up-to-date revised version which includes any amendments which have been made to it. The original version should be treated with caution as it represents a historical document (one that is frozen in time). There may not have been any amendments since the original version was passed but unless you check the position, consulting the original version is worse than useless, it could lead to serious error.

Statutory instruments made by the UK Parliament and relating to Scotland have a main **6–129** number and an additional number which relates to its sequence in the issue of statutory instruments for Scotland made during a year. The Scottish number should be ignored when trying to trace an instrument. The indexes all use the main number for the reference.

Official versions

Statutory Rules and Orders and Statutory Instruments Revised 📖
This is an official consolidation which contains all statutory instruments in force up to the end **6–130** of 1948 and is arranged under subject headings.

Statutory Instruments (1949–) 📖
This is an official publication published by The Stationery Office. It contains the full text of **6–131** general statutory instruments. It is made up of annual volumes arranged in numerical order with a subject index. Before 1961 it was arranged by subject with a numerical index. It contains a list of local statutory instruments (both printed and non-printed).

General statutory instruments are published individually and can be purchased from The Sta- **6–132** tionery Office.

Office of Public Sector Information (OPSI) ⏚ free
The official electronic original version of statutory instruments is available from the *Office of* **6–133** *Public Sector Information (OPSI)* website (*http://www.opsi.gov.uk/stat.htm*). This site contains the full text of all published statutory instruments from the beginning of 1987. The site aims to

publish statutory instruments simultaneously with their publication in printed form. The statutory instruments are grouped by year and within each year they can be viewed chronologically by number.

Since their introduction in June 2004 Explanatory Memorandum have been included on the site. The statutory instruments and Explanatory Memorandum are grouped together by year and within each year they can be viewed chronologically by number. Explanatory Memorandum are generally published at the same time as the statutory instrument on this site. Statutory instruments are published in html and also importantly as pdfs which makes downloading the entire document and printing it straightforward. Explanatory Memorandum are published as pdfs.

From November 1, 1997, all new draft statutory instruments which are awaiting approval are available at this site. They are available until superseded by an official version or withdrawn. They are arranged by subject within each year. They are not available in printed form. The site also contains a *search legislation* function which links to an *advanced search* which allows you to search by keyword, type of legislation (e.g. statutory instruments and draft statutory instruments), jurisdiction or date. The material is published in its **original** form and amendments are not included. This means that this site is only of use if you particularly want the original form of a statutory instrument as opposed to the up-to-date form of the legislation.

Sources of revised versions

Westlaw ⌁subscription database

6–134 *Westlaw* contains a selection of UK statutory instruments of general application published between 1948 and 1991. All UK statutory Instruments are included from 1992 and all statutory instruments made by the Scottish Parliament from 1999. Draft statutory instruments are not included. Statutory instruments are in **revised** form. See paras 6.142–6.145 for tracing statutory instruments.

Sources of original versions

Justis UK Statutory Instruments ⌁ subscription and CD Rom

6–135 This database contains statutory instruments for England, Scotland and Wales from 1671 to the present in full text **original** form.

BAILII ⌁ free

6–136 The *BAILII* site (*http://www.bailii.org/*) includes statutory instruments reproduced from *OPSI* but *BAILII* only has statutory instruments from 2002. UK Statutory instruments are located in the UK legislation section. Statutory instruments from the Scottish Parliament are available from 1999 and located in the Scottish legislation section. The legislation search allows searching to be restricted by statutory instruments and to search by keyword, dates and jurisdiction. The advanced search allows Boolean searching. The statutory instruments are available as continuous web pages as opposed to pdfs.

Statute Law Database ⌁ free

6–137 The *Statute Law Database* (*http://www.statutelaw.gov.uk*) contains UK statutory instruments from January 1, 1991 but they are in the **original** (i.e. unrevised) form. Statutory instruments from the Scottish Parliament are available from 1999.

Specialist loose-leaf encyclopaedias and collections of legislation 📖

6–138 Specialist loose-leaf encyclopaedias (para.8.9) and collections of legislation (paras 6.199–6.200) may contain copies of selected statutory instruments relevant to their subject area.

Current Law Yearbooks 📖
Statutory instruments are digested in the *Yearbooks and Monthly Digests of Current Law*. The **6–139**
full text of Commencement Orders is printed in the Yearbooks (for each successive year since
1992) and in the looseleaf service file (for the current year). See para.8.21 for more details.

Sources of revised versions excluding exclusively Scottish material

LexisNexis Butterworths ⌁ subscription database **6–140**
The full text revised form of statutory instruments is available from *LexisNexis Butterworths* but
statutory instruments applying exclusively to Scotland are not included.

Halsbury's Statutory Instruments 📖 and ⌁ subscription
This contains information on every current statutory instrument of general application in **6–141**
England and Wales. It does not reprint *all* statutory instruments, many are only summarised. It
does not include exclusively Scottish statutory instruments. However, it does contain the **revised**
form of statutory instruments. This is covered in more detail in paras 9.12–9.14.

AIDS TO TRACING STATUTORY INSTRUMENTS

Westlaw ⌁ subscription database
Westlaw UK contains a selection of UK statutory instruments of general application published **6–142**
between 1948 and 1991. All UK statutory instruments are included from 1992 and all statutory
instruments made by the Scottish Parliament from 1999. Draft statutory instruments are not
included. Statutory instruments are in full text and in **revised** form.
   Westlaw UK has three alternative ways of searching for statutory instruments: basic search,
advanced search and browsing.

Basic search. From the welcome page, click the *legislation* link from the navigation bar at the **6–143**
top of the screen. This will take you to the *legislation basic search* page, where you can search for
statutory instruments by typing the name of the piece of legislation, the year and provision
number (if required.). If you know the year, it is better to enter it as this will avoid retrieving
multiple pieces of legislation. If you know the year and number, enter those into the title field,
e.g. 2007/927. If you know the title of the statutory instrument you are looking for, enter it in
quotation marks, e.g. "The Sea Fishing (Restriction on Days at Sea) Order 2007". Entering the
title of a piece of legislation without quotation marks will retrieve all pieces of legislation with
those words in the title.
   The *free text* field allows you to enter terms or phrases and *Westlaw* will search for these
within the text of statutory instruments. Searching can be improved if you use search techniques
which Westlaw refer to as "Terms and Connectors", see para.2.33. The basic search screen
searches legislation currently in force. If you want to search historical legislation you need to use
the *advanced search* (see para.6.35).

Search results for statutory instruments. If you search by legislation title only, the Arrangement **6–144**
of SI for that legislation will be returned. Searching for legislation using the *free text* function
will return sections of legislation where those terms exist. The results list will show the name of
the legislation as well as the title of the provision and the date when it came into force. Within a
result list status icons may display next to the title of the legislation indicating that either the
provision has been repealed or superseded (▣) or has pending amendments (❗). To narrow
down a long list of results, you can search for additional terms. Just enter your new search
term(s) in the field at the top of the page and click *search within results*.

6–145 *Browsing for statutory instruments.* You can browse for statutory instruments by year, by title or by jurisdiction (either UK or Scottish Parliament). The browsing by year function allows you to select a time period (prior to 1990) from which to select the year you are looking for. From 1990 you can select a year. Within each year there is an alphabetical list of legislation that received its Royal Assent in that year. Browsing by title allows you to choose a letter and look at an alphabetical list of statutory instruments. Select a title to see the Arrangement of SI for that piece of legislation.

The same legislative materials that are available for statutes are available for statutory instruments see paras 6.38–6.44.

Lawtel subscription legal current awareness digest service

6–146 *Lawtel's Statutory Instrument Database* indexes statutory instruments from 1984 and allows you to trace statutory instruments and check whether they have been amended or revoked. It provides links to the full-text where available. It is updated daily. To carry out a search: click on *statutory instruments* on the *Lawtel UK* homepage; enter your search terms in the box (or select *focused search* which allows you to search by title, number, enabling Act, date coming into force, and area of application) and click *search*. Click on the link in the search results to the details of the statutory instrument. The details shown will include the instrument's number, the enabling Act, coming into force date, a list of effects it has had on other legislation, its area of application and a link to the full original text of the instrument and the Explanatory Memorandum on the *OPSI* site.

Current Law Legislation Citators

6–147 The *Current Law Legislation Citators* list all amendments, modifications and repeals to primary and secondary legislation made in the years covered by the specific volume. Since 1993 the *Legislation Citators* have been a combination of two citators—a *Statute Citator* and a *Statutory Instrument Citator*. The *Statutory Instrument Citator* appears after the *Statute Citator*. It is arranged in the following order:

1. Scottish statutory instruments are listed in chronological order by year and number.
2. Statutory rules issued by the UK Parliament are listed in chronological order by year and number.
3. Statutory instruments made by the UK Parliament are listed in chronological order by year and number.

The *Statutory Instrument Citator* contains:

⇒ Details of amendments and repeals since 1993 made to statutory instruments of *any* date.
⇒ In respect of *any* statutory instrument, the cases in which it has been judicially considered since 1993.
⇒ In respect of *any* statutory instrument, details of the statutory instruments issued since 1993 which have been made under its provisions.
⇒ In respect of *any* statutory instrument, where it has been consolidated by an Act passed since 1993.

Searching *Current Law Statutory Instrument Citators* **6–148**

The 1972–1988 Legislation Citator contains a Table of Statutory Instruments
Affected 1947–1988. It is arranged chronologically and within each year numerically. It lists
amendments and revocations to Statutory Instruments made from 1947–1988

↓

1989–1995 Legislation Citator, which includes the Statutory Instrument Citator 1993–1995
contains a Table of Statutory Instruments Affected 1989–1992. This lists amendments and
revocations to Statutory Instruments made between 1989–1992

↓

Current Law Statutory Instrument Citator 1993–1995 contained in the Legislation Citator
Volume 1989–1995

↓

Current Law Statutory Instrument Citator contained in Legislation Citator volume 1996–99

↓

Current Law Statutory Instrument Citator contained in Legislation Citator volume 2000–01

↓

Current Law Statutory Instrument Citator contained in Legislation Citator volume 2002–04

↓

Current Law Statutory Instrument Citator contained in Legislation Citator volume 2005

↓

Current Law Statutory Instrument Citator contained in Legislation Citator volume 2006

↓

Statutory Instrument Citator updates for 2007 in the Statutes Service File

The material is arranged in chronological order by reference to the year and then within the
year, in *numerical order* according to the number of the statutory instrument. In order to locate
the number, check the alphabetical list of statutory instruments at the beginning of the volume.
Details on the Statutes Service File are at para.8.23.

Excerpt from a *Statutory Instrument Citator* with features marked: **6–149**

---

[1] 1956. Act of Sederunt (Sheriff Court Ordinary Cause Rules) 1993 [2]
amended: SI 96/2167 r.2, Sch. **[3]**
applied: SI 97/687 Sch.1.
Ch.33 Part II, applied: SI 96/125 art.3.
Form G13, see *Stewart v Callaghan* 1996 S.L.T. 12 (Sh Ct). **[4]**
r.33.22A, applied: SI 96/2444 Reg.18.
r.33.29, applied: SI 97/687 Sch.1 Table.
r.36.14, applied: SI 96/207 Sch.8, para.43.
r.128, applied: SI 96/207 Sch.8, para.43.
972. Advice and Assistance (Assistance by Way of Representation) (Scotland) Amendment Regulations 1993
revoked: SI 97/3070 reg.2, Sch. **[5]**

Key:

[1] SI Number
[2] Name of SI
[3] changes made to the SI
[4] case reference
[5] This SI has been revoked

6–150 How to find out if a statutory instrument has been amended or revoked:

> ⇒**Step 1**: Check the *Statutory Instrument Citators* in the volumes of *Legislation Citators* in chronological order starting from the date of the statutory instrument. In order to locate the number, check the alphabetical list of statutory instruments at the beginning of the volume. You can now turn to the appropriate entry for the statutory instrument, where the citator will list any amendments that have been made.
>
> ⇒**Step 2**: In order to be aware of all amendments (up to the last month) check through all the *Statutory Instrument Citators* up to the most recent update for the citator in the *Statutes Service File*.

How to find out if any cases have taken place concerning a particular statutory instrument:

> ⇒**Step 1**: Check through the *Statutory Instrument Citators* in chronological order. Look under the entry for the statutory instrument. If a case has taken place, it will appear opposite the entry.
>
> ⇒**Step 2**: You should then check the most recent update for the citator in the *Statutes Service File*.

How to find out about a statutory instrument:

> ⇒**Step 1**: If you know the year and name of the statutory instrument check the Alphabetical List of Statutory Instruments for the Year in the appropriate Yearbook. If you know the full citation and not the name of the statutory instrument, check the Numerical List of Statutory Instruments for the Year in the appropriate Yearbook. In both cases opposite the entry for the statutory instrument will be a reference to a paragraph number.
>
> ⇒**Step 2**: Turn to the appropriate paragraph and you will find a digest of the statutory instrument. It will provide details of its full title, a short summary of its content, details of the legislation it is made under and the date it was brought into force.

Current Legal Information ⌐ and CD Rom subscription legal research service

6–151 *Current Legal Information* contains an electronic version of the *Current Law Legislation Citator* which gives details of amendments and revocations made to statutory instruments by statutory instruments and statutes from 1994 to date. Searching the *Legislation Citator* in *Current Legal Information* enables you to access information by the year; words from the title of statutory instrument; the number of a statutory instrument or free text. The entry for a piece of legislation includes the same information which is available in the paper version. The key advantage of the electronic version is the ease of use compared with checking through lots of different paper volumes.

Justcite ⌐ subscription legal citator

6–152 *Justcite* is an online legal citator includes UK statutory instruments (from 1671) and Scottish Parliament statutory instruments (from 1999). The home page allows you to search for statutory instruments by title or reference (which means e.g. giving the year and number of a statutory instrument). Statutory instruments can be searched separately by ticking the appropriate box at the right hand side. Alternatively, you can search using the *index* tab. This allows you to browse through separate title indexes of statutory instruments listed in alphabetical order. Scottish legislation is not listed separately.

The information retrieved can include:

> ➢ The status of the provision.
> ➢ A link to the particular reference. If you click on this link it will open a new window showing various sources of the full text of the statutory instrument which you may be able to access depending on the subscriptions held by your university library.
> ➢ Lists of parts which have been amended and the amending legislation.
> ➢ Lists of parts which have amended other legislation and the legislation amended.

List of Statutory Publications 📖

The *List of Statutory Publications* is published monthly (albeit several months in arrears) by The **6–153** Stationery Office. It includes details of general and local statutory instruments (printed and non-printed) published during the previous month. They are arranged under subject headings and also listed numerically. The publication is consolidated at the end of a year and appears as an annual *List of Statutory Publications*.

Daily List 📖 and ⌁ free

The *Daily List* (paper and available at *http://www.tsoshop.co.uk/parliament/*) (see para.8.85) lists **6–154** statutory instruments published by The Stationery Office. It is the first official notice of the existence of a statutory instrument, giving details including the date of commencement.

Journals 📖 and ⌁ subscription

Information about very recent statutory instruments will also be available in journals such as **6–155** the *Scots Law Times* and in England the *New Law Journal* and the *Solicitors' Journal*.

Aids that contain the original version of statutory instruments

Justis UK Statutory Instruments ⌁ subscription and CD Rom

This contains the original form of UK statutory instruments for England, Scotland and Wales **6–156** from 1671 and Scottish statutory instruments made by the Scottish Parliament from 1999.

Statute Law Database ⌁ free

The *Statute Law Database* contains the original form of UK statutory instruments from 1991 **6–157** and Scottish statutory instruments made by the Scottish Parliament from 1999.

Office of Public Sector Information (OPSI) ⌁ free

OPSI contains the original form of UK statutory instruments from 1987 and Scottish statutory **6–158** instruments made by the Scottish Parliament from 1999.

BAILII ⌁ free

The *BAILII* website contains the original form of UK statutory instruments from 2002 and **6–159** Scottish statutory instruments made by the Scottish Parliament from 1999.

Aids that exclude exclusively Scottish material

LexisNexis Butterworths ⌁ subscription database

LexisNexis Butterworths has the full text revised version of statutory instruments in force in **6–160** England and Wales but excludes exclusively Scottish statutory instruments. It does contain Scottish statutory instruments made by the Scottish Parliament from 1999.

Halsbury's Statutory Instruments 📖 and ⌖ subscription

6–161 *Halsbury's Statutory Instruments* does not include exclusively Scottish statutory instruments. However, it does contain the revised form of statutory instruments. See paras 9.12–9.14.

Finding statutory instruments when only the title is known (i.e. the year and number are not known)

Westlaw ⌖subscription database

6–162 The *legislation* search in *Westlaw UK* allows you to search a title field. See para.2.33 for help with using *Westlaw's* terms and connectors. *Westlaw* also allows you to browse statutory instruments by title. This is one of the browse options available at the bottom of the legislation search screen, see paras 6.143–6.145.

Lawtel ⌖subscription legal current awareness digest service

6–163 This digest service only includes legislation from 1984. On the *Lawtel UK* homepage click on *statutory instruments*. Using the focused search allows you to search by title. Enter your search terms in the box and click *search*. Click on the link in the search results to the details of the statutory instrument.

Current law Yearbooks and Monthly Digests 📖

6–164 There are alphabetical lists of statutory instruments in the *Current Law Yearbooks* and in the *Monthly Digests*. The lists will provide you with the year and number of the statutory instrument. The *Current Law Yearbooks* and *Monthly Digests* will only contain a summary of the statutory instrument. In order to trace the full text you will need to take the additional details to one of the sources in paras 6.130–6.141.

Current Law Statutory Instrument Citator 📖

6–165 The *Current Law Statutory Instrument Citators* (1993–present) include an alphabetical list at the start of each volume. Using the citators will enable you to locate the year and number and to check if the statutory instrument has been amended or repealed. If you wish to trace the full text you will need to take the additional details to one of the sources in paras 6.130–6.141,

Current Legal Information ⌖ and CD Rom subscription legal research service

6–166 This contains an electronic version of the *Current Law Statutory Instrument Citator*.

The Laws of Scotland: Stair Memorial Encyclopaedia 📖

6–167 Check the Consolidated Table of Statutes or, if you know the subject area, go to the individual title. Each title has a list of legislation.

The Laws of Scotland Online (Stair Memorial Encyclopaedia) ⌖

6–168 Enter the title of the statutory instrument as your search term in the commentary search form. See para.8.5 for more details.

Subject specialist encyclopaedias and collections of legislation 📖

6–169 Specialist looseleaf encyclopaedias (para.8.9) and collections of legislation (paras 6.199–6.200) can be searched by Tables of Statutory Instruments or by the subject index. The amount of information you will be able to locate will depend on whether the work includes the full text of the particular statutory instrument.

Sources that contain the original version of statutory instruments

Justis UK Statutory Instruments ✒subscription and CD Rom
Justis UK Statutory Instruments contains the original form of UK statutory instruments for **6–170** England, Scotland and Wales from 1671 and Scottish statutory instruments made by the Scottish Parliament from 1999.

Statute Law Database ✒ free
The *Statute Law Database* contains the original form of UK statutory instruments from 1991 **6–171** and Scottish statutory instruments made by the Scottish Parliament from 1999. You can search by title or you can browse UK statutory instruments alphabetically.

Office of Public Sector Information (OPSI) ✒ free
OPSI contains the original form of UK statutory instruments from 1987 and Scottish statutory **6–172** instruments made by the Scottish Parliament from 1999. The site contains a *search legislation* function which links to an *advanced search* which allows you to search by keyword and to restrict your search to statutory instruments.

BAILII ✒ free
The *BAILII* website contains the original form of UK statutory instruments from 2002 and **6–173** Scottish statutory instruments made by the Scottish Parliament from 1999. The legislation search allows searching by keyword in the title, dates and jurisdiction. You can restrict your search to statutory instruments and/or Scottish statutory instruments. The advanced search allows Boolean searching.

Sources that exclude exclusively Scottish material

LexisNexis Butterworths ✒ subscription database
LexisNexis Butterworths has the full text revised version of statutory instruments in force in **6–174** England and Wales but excludes exclusively Scottish statutory instruments. It does contain Scottish statutory instruments made by the Scottish Parliament from 1999. It is possible to search by keyword in the title.

Halsbury's Statutory Instruments 📖 and ✒ subscription
This excellent resource excludes exclusively Scottish statutory instruments. See paras 9.12–9.14. **6–175**

Finding statutory instruments by subject

The Laws of Scotland: Stair Memorial Encyclopaedia 📖
Check the Consolidated Index. This lists detailed subject headings and will lead you to the **6–176** relevant volume or reissued title. You can update this information by checking the Annual Cumulative Supplement and the Service Binder. See para.8.2.

The Laws of Scotland Online (Stair Memorial Encyclopaedia) ✒
Enter details of the subject area as your search term in the commentary search form. See **6–177** para.8.5.

Subject specialist encyclopaedias and collections of legislation 📖
Specialist looseleaf encyclopaedias (para.8.9) and collections of legislation (paras 6.199–6.200) **6–178** can be searched by Tables of Statutory Instruments or by the subject index. The amount of information you will be able to locate will depend on whether the work includes the full text of the particular statutory instrument.

Westlaw ⁿ⁰ subscription database

6–179 The legislation search in *Westlaw UK* allows you to search by free text search. See, para.2.33 for help with using *Westlaw's* terms and connectors. *Westlaw* also allows you to browse statutory instruments by title.

Lawtel ⁿ⁰ subscription legal current awareness digest service

6–180 On the *Lawtel UK* homepage click on *statutory instruments*. Enter your search terms in the box and click *search*. (Alternatively use the *focused search* to search by title) Click on the link in the search results to the details of the statutory instrument. However, this digest service only includes legislation from 1984.

Current law Yearbooks and Monthly Digests ⊞

6–181 Check the Yearbooks under the appropriate subject heading (see para.8.21). This will provide you with a reference to a paragraph number. The *Current Law Yearbooks* and *Monthly Digests* will only contain a summary of the statutory instrument. In order to trace the full text you will need to take the additional details to one of the sources in paras 6.130–6.141.

Sources that contain the original version of statutory instruments

Justis UK Statutory Instruments ⁿ⁰ subscription and CD Rom

6–182 *Justis UK Statutory Instruments* contains the original form of UK statutory instruments for England, Scotland and Wales from 1671 and Scottish statutory instruments made by the Scottish Parliament from 1999. It is possible to search by keyword.

Statute Law Database ⁿ⁰ free

6–183 The *Statute Law Database* contains the original form of UK statutory instruments from 1991 and Scottish statutory instruments made by the Scottish Parliament from 1999. You can search all statutory instruments by title or you can restrict your search to UK or Scottish Parliament statutory instruments. You can use the advanced search to search the text by free text. The results obtained will have the search terms highlighted in the text.

Office of Public Sector Information (OPSI) ⁿ⁰ free

6–184 *OPSI* contains the original form of UK statutory instruments from 1987 and Scottish statutory instruments made by the Scottish Parliament from 1999. The site contains a *search legislation* function which links to an *advanced search* which allows you to search by keyword and to restrict your search to statutory instruments.

BAILII ⁿ⁰ free

6–185 The *BAILII* website contains the original form of UK statutory instruments from 2002 and Scottish statutory instruments made by the Scottish Parliament from 1999. The legislation search allows searching by keyword in the title, words in the text, dates and jurisdiction. You can restrict your search to statutory instruments and/or Scottish statutory instruments. The advanced search allows Boolean searching. The results obtained will have the search terms highlighted in the text.

Sources that exclude exclusively Scottish material

6–186 *LexisNexis Butterworths* ⁿ⁰ subscription database
LexisNexis Butterworths has the full text revised version of statutory instruments in force in England and Wales but excludes exclusively Scottish statutory instruments. It does contain Scottish statutory instruments made by the Scottish Parliament from 1999. It is possible to search by keyword.

Halsbury's Statutory Instruments 📖 and ᐟ᷇ subscription
This excellent resource excludes exclusively Scottish statutory instruments. See paras 9.12–9.14. **6–187**

Current status of statutory instruments—finding amendments and repeals

Westlaw ᐟ᷇ subscription database
Westlaw UK takes you to the amended text of the statutory instrument. This will incorporate **6–188**
any amendments and will show when the current version of the statutory instrument was
brought into force. It will also provide links to the amending legislation.

Lawtel ᐟ᷇ subscription legal current awareness digest service
On the *Lawtel UK* homepage click on *statutory instruments*. Enter your search terms in the box **6–189**
and click *search*, or alternatively use the *focused search* to search by title. Click on the link in the
search results to the details of the statutory instrument. The entry for the statutory instrument
has information about amendments and repeals from 1984.

Current Law Statutory Instrument Citator 📖 **6–190**
The citator has the disadvantage that it only dates from 1993 onwards. See paras 6.147–6.150
for more details.

Sources that exclude exclusively Scottish material

LexisNexis Butterworths ᐟ᷇ subscription database **6–191**
LexisNexis Butterworths has the full text revised version of statutory instruments in force in
England and Wales but excludes exclusively Scottish statutory instruments. It does contain
Scottish statutory instruments made by the Scottish Parliament from 1999.

Halsbury's Statutory Instruments 📖 and ᐟ᷇ subscription
The paper version is up to date to within a month and contains the amended versions of **6–192**
statutory instruments. The electronic version is updated daily (see paras 9.12–9.14).

Finding statutory instruments made under an Enabling Act

Westlaw ᐟ᷇ subscription database
Go to Legislation and search under the title of an Act, this will retrieve a link to the arrange- **6–193**
ments of the Act. Click on *overview document* which appears in the blue left hand navigation
bar. This brings up a list of information about the Act. Click on the link to *SIs made under the
Act*. This will retrieve a list of all the statutory instruments made under the Act which are linked
so that you can link thorough to view the full amended text of the statutory instruments. If *SIs
made under the Act* does not appear as an option in the *overview document* this means that no
statutory instruments have been made under the Act.

Lawtel ᐟ᷇ subscription legal current awareness digest service
Lawtel's disadvantage is that it only contains material after 1984. Search by title of the Act and **6–194**
then click on the link to the *statutory status table*. This will contain a link to *SIs enabled by Act*.
This will retrieve a list of all the statutory instruments made under the Act. You can then link
through to details about the statutory instrument and to its full original text.

Current Law Statute Citator 📖
The *Current Law Statute Citators* provide details of statutory instruments made under an Act. **6–195**
The details will be listed alongside entry for the Act. The *Current Law* system requires you to
start checking from the year the Act was passed in order to locate whether any statutory
instruments have been made under it. See paras 6.147–6.150 for more details.

Current Legal Information ⚲ and CD Rom subscription legal research service
6–196 This provides electronic access to the *Current Law Legislation Citators* but only back to 1989.

Sources that exclude exclusively Scottish material
6–197 *LexisNexis Butterworths* ⚲ subscription database.

6–198 *Halsbury's Statutes of England* 📖 (see paras 9.5–9.11).

Finding whether the courts have considered a statutory instrument

The techniques are very similar to tracing whether the courts have interpreted a statute, see paras 4.92–4.103.

Finding whether any journal articles have been written about a statutory instrument

The techniques are very similar to tracing articles about a statute, see paras 6.112–6.118.

COLLECTIONS OF LEGISLATION

Parliament House Book 📖
6–199 The *Parliament House Book* contains **revised** legislation covering selected areas of private law and court procedure. It includes both UK and Scottish Parliament legislation. It includes:

- ➢ Primary legislation
- ➢ Delegated legislation
- ➢ Practice notes
- ➢ Solicitors practice rules
- ➢ Notes for guidance issued by public departments

It is published in a looseleaf format consisting of six volumes. The *Parliament House Book* is arranged in different divisions. Within each division the material is arranged chronologically. Statutes are followed by statutory instruments and other regulations, then by tables and notes for guidance. The first page of each division lists its contents. The *Parliament House Book* is updated five times a year. The date at the foot of each page is the date when the page was last updated. The references given throughout the *Parliament House Book* are to the division and page number, e.g. The Sheriff Courts (Scotland) Act 1971 is referenced as D 74. This means that it is contained in Division D at page 74.

   N.B.: not all pieces of legislation are printed in full. Statutes may only be printed in part or the statute may be divided up and placed in different divisions of the *Parliament House Book*.

Contents of the *Parliament House Book*

Volume 1	Division B—Courts, Upper
	Division D—Courts, Lower
Volume 2	Division C—Greens Annotated Rules of the Court of Session
Volume 3	Division A—Fees, Stamps etc.
	Division F—Solicitors
	Division G—Legal Aid
Volume 4	Division H—Bankruptcy and other mercantile statutes
	Division I—Companies

Volume 5	Division K—Family Law
	Division M—Succession, Trusts, Liferents and Judicial Factors
Volume 6	Division E—Licensing
	Division J—Conveyancing, Land Tenure and Registration
	Division L—Landlord and Tenant

Specialised collections of legislation

An increasing number of subject-specific collections of legislation are now being produced. They **6–200** tend to be annotated. Examples include: *Renton & Brown's Criminal Procedure Legislation, Scottish Conveyancing Legislation, Scottish Family Law Legislation, Scottish Landlord & Tenant Legislation, Scottish Social Work Legislation* and *Scottish Trusts & Succession Service.*

There are numerous collections of legislation produced for the student market. They tend to contain a selection of subject-specific legislation; some include annotations but many do not. They are usually single-volume paperback works which are updated annually. Texts without annotations are sometimes allowed to be taken into open book exams.

Legislation may also be found in the growing number of looseleaf encyclopaedias. These tend to reprint the text of selected legislation. See para.8.9.

Further Reading

A. Bradney et al, *How to Study Law* 5th edn (London: Sweet & Maxwell, 2005).

P. Clinch, *Using a Law Library* 2nd edn (London: Blackstone Press, 2001) Chs 10 and 11 cover Scottish legislation.

G. Holburn and G. Engle, *Butterworths Legal Research Guide* (London: Butterworths, 2001).

J. Knowles and P. Thomas, *Effective Legal Research* (London: Sweet & Maxwell, 2006).

P.A. Thomas and J. Knowles, *Dane & Thomas How to Use a Law Library* 4th edn (London: Sweet & Maxwell, 2001). This contains a separate Scottish chapter.

Chapter 7
Search Strategies for Finding Scottish Parliament Legislation (Pre-1707 and Post 1999)

7–1 This chapter discusses search strategies for finding legislation from the pre-1707 Scottish Parliaments and from the new Scottish Parliament created in 1999. The pre-1707 Scottish Parliaments are discussed at the start of the chapter. This is followed by discussion of search strategies relevant for new Scottish Parliament legislation namely: Bills; Acts of the Scottish Parliament and Scottish statutory instruments.

The fact that the Scottish Parliament came into being as recently as 1999 has implications for the legal researcher. It means that the information sources for this modern institution were created in a world where use of electronic sources was the norm. This means that although many of the types of documentation are modelled on the UK Parliament an opportunity was taken to adopt a more modern style and format. The Scottish Parliament website (*http://www.scottish.parliament.uk*) contains a vast amount of information and is well laid out with quick search and advanced search facilities. It contains information designed for people with different levels of interest in the Parliament ranging from a casual visitor to an academic legal researcher. Once you are familiar with the site it is a mine of useful information about the workings of the Parliament and the legislation that it produces.

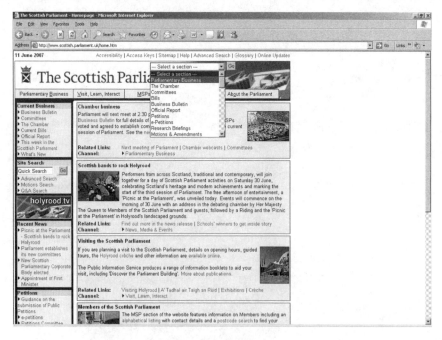

Diagram 7.1: The Scottish Parliament Homepage

The advent of the Scottish Parliament also resulted in many new publications being created to **7–2** cater for this new level of government. However, many of these publications have since ceased to publish and you find references to series which are now defunct. There was a period of uncertainty as to how many publications modelled on the UK Parliament would be needed and which UK-wide publications would expand to include Scottish Parliament materials. Now that the Parliament has been in existence for eight years the information sources have had a chance to settle down and it is now possible to see publication patterns becoming established.

While the use of modern technology and free availability of information on the internet is a positive development there is a cause for concern at the limited amount of paper collections of Scottish Parliament (and Scottish Executive) materials. While the official websites are key resources there are questions about online being the most appropriate place to store archive material. Websites are continually modernised and their material re-organised to reflect the latest organisational structure or agenda. This, and the fact that software developments can affect the compatibility of information, could lead to restrictions in access to materials in the future.

In order to avoid repetition, the UK information sources which have encompassed Scottish Parliament materials are fully covered in Chapter 6 and will be cross referenced as appropriate from this chapter. This chapter identifies the relevant sources and how to search their content for Scottish Parliament materials. It also discusses information sources unique to the Scottish Parliament.

PRE-1707 SCOTTISH LEGISLATION

Regiam Majestatem is the name of a work commonly regarded as containing the earliest col- **7–3** lection of Scottish legislation. It dates from either the late thirteenth or fourteenth century. The *Stair Memorial Encyclopaedia* (Vol.22, para.512) refers to it being "essentially a commentary on the procedures of the royal courts". It is not a completely Scottish document in that it is based on an English work (*Tractatus De Legibus et Consuetudinibus Regni Anglie* by Glanvill). However, it is not just a copy of the earlier work—it has adapted it to describe the legal system that was developing in Scotland. Another work of the period is the *Quoniam Attachiamenta*. It is a Scottish work and concerns procedure in the feudal courts. The two works are usually printed together. The modern edition of *Regiam Majestatem* is edited by Lord Cooper, Stair Society, vol. 11, 1947. There is a recent edition of *Quoniam Attachiamenta* edited by T.D. Fergus, The Stair Society, Edinburgh 1996.

There is a lack of information about early Scottish legislation due to "the loss of our public records, the most valuable of which were carried off into England, first by Edward I, and afterwards by an order of Oliver Cromwell, about the middle of the seventeenth century. Apart from six isolated rolls of 1292–3, 1368–9 and 1388–9, there are no original parliamentary records existing prior to 1466."—*An Introductory Survey of the Sources and Literature of Scots Law*, The Stair Society, Edinburgh 1936, p.4.

Sources of legislation from the pre-1707 Scottish Parliaments

Legislation from the pre-1707 Scottish Parliaments is usually referred to as Scots Acts. There are **7–4** two main sources of Scots Acts. *Acts of the Parliaments of Scotland 1124–1707*, edited by T. Thomson and C. Innes was published during the nineteenth century. This is known as the *Record edition*. It has been called the "authoritative edition" (P.G.B. McNeill "Citation of Scots Statutes" 1959 S.L.T. (News) 112). The other collection is *Laws and Acts of Parliament 1424–1707* by Murray of Glendook. The author of the above article goes on to refer to this as "a collection of statutes which is neither official nor authoritative, and which is full of inaccuracies". The content of the two works does not always agree and the numbering of Acts is different. The Registration Act 1579 referred to below could be referred to as A.P.S. III 142 in the *Record edition* or 1579, c.75 in Glendook's work. It is given the chapter number 13 in the *Record edition* but Glendook's work refers to it as Chapter 75.

7–5 Details of other early editions of Scots statutes are given in *An Introductory Survey of the Sources and Literature of Scots Law*, The Stair Society, Edinburgh 1936, Ch.1. Scots Acts which were still in force in 1908 were reproduced in a single volume called *Scots Statutes Revised 1424– 1707*. The Statute Law Revisions (Scotland) Act 1964 repealed many Acts of the old Scottish Parliament. Acts which were still in force following this Act were reprinted in *The Acts of the Parliaments of Scotland 1424–1707*, published in 1966.

There is now access to electronic versions of Scots Acts. The Statute Law Database (see para.6.45) contains the text of more than 100 Scots Acts. *Westlaw UK* has a much more limited number but has plans to include all Scots Acts currently in force in the near future. There is also a plan to make a new digital edition of the Acts of the Scottish Parliament from 1235 to 1707 freely available online. This is to include a number of Acts which have not been published before and some which have been translated to allow wider access. The new site (*http://www.rps.ac.uk/*) is called *The Records of the Parliaments of Scotland to 1707* and is due to become operational late in 2007.

Citation of Scots Acts

7–6 The correct citation of Scots Acts is by the short title or by the calendar year and chapter number or by the volume, page and chapter number of the Record edition. The Acts did not originally have short titles but all surviving Scots Acts were given short titles by Sch.2 of the Statute Law Revision (Scotland) Act 1964. An example from Sch.2 is the Act formerly known by "For pwnishment of personis that contempnandlie remanis rebellis and at the horne". It acquired the short title The Registration Act 1579.

Prior to 1964 Scots Acts were cited by calendar year and chapter number in the Glendook edition or by the volume and page number of the *Record edition*. This is still the case for Scots Acts which have been repealed.

Tracing Scots Acts that are still in force

7–7 There are still a number of Scots Acts which are still in force today. The *Statute Law Database* allows you to search by legislation type on its homepage. If you pull down the menu *Act (Old Scottish Parliament)* is an option. Click Go. This brings up a list of Scots Acts. You can then access the text of the individual Acts by clicking on the title. You could also search under the title or year of the Act. It is also possible to trace these Acts by checking the Chronological Table of Statutes where Acts of the pre-1707 Parliaments of Scotland are included in a separate table at the end of the second volume. You would then need to update your search by using the volumes of the *Current Law* Legislation Citators and the latest edition of the Citator in the Statutes Service File. *Current Law* is covered in more detail in paras 6.69–6.75.

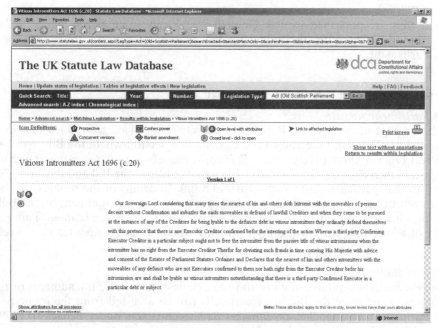

Diagram 7.2: Statute Law Database

SCOTTISH PARLIAMENT (1999–) BILLS

It is important to remember that Bills are amended to various degrees as they go through the different parliamentary stages. It is therefore essential to ensure that you find the most current version of the Bill. For more details on the parliamentary procedures for passing a Bill in the Scottish Parliament, see paras 5.39–5.44.

Sources of the text of a current Bill (public and private)

Scottish Parliament website 🖰 free

On the home page of the Scottish Parliament website (*http://www.scottish.parliament.uk*), click **7–8** on *Current Bills*. This will take you to *Current Bills* where the Bills will be listed in alphabetical order. (Alternatively, select *Bills* from the *select a section* menu at the top of the homepage and then click on *Current Bills*.) Click on the title of the Bill and this brings up a page dedicated to that particular Bill and you will find the current version of the Bill accessible as a pdf file.

Note that the following abbreviations are used: *Ex* denotes Executive Bill, *C* Committee Bill, *M* Member's Bill and *P* Private Bill.

The information available on the page dedicated to the Bill includes:

➢ Details of the progress of the Bill—follow the link and you can get details of which stage the Bill has reached.
➢ The content of the Bill at various stages i.e. as introduced and as amended.
➢ The accompanying documents (see para.5.40).
➢ SPICe briefings (briefings written by research specialists in the Scottish Parliament Information Centre).
➢ Details of amendments.

Individual Bills 📖

7–9 Individual Bills are published by RR Donnelley and appear on purple paper. Bills may be printed many different times depending on the amount of changes made as they progress through Parliament.

Finding out which stage a current Bill has reached

Scottish Parliament website ⌐ free

7–10 On the home page of the Scottish Parliament website (*http://www.scottish.parliament.uk*), click on *Current Bills*. This will take you to the *Current Bills* section where the Bills will be listed in alphabetical order. (Alternatively, select *Bills* from the *select a section* menu at the top of the homepage and then click on *Current Bills*.) Click on the title of the Bill and this brings up a page dedicated to that particular Bill which provides a link to details of the progress of the Bill.

    If you want to check on the progress of Bills generally at the Parliament, on the Bills section of the site, click on the link to a pdf of *Summary of Current Legislation*. This provides a summary of all the Bills currently going through Parliament and is updated on a weekly basis.

The Business Bulletin 📖 and ⌐ free

7–11 The Business Bulletin is produced daily and has details of new Bills, amendments or reprints of Bills along with the stage the Bill has reached. It can be accessed from the home page of the Scottish Parliament website, click on *Business Bulletin*. Business Bulletins back to 1999 can also be accessed from this section of the website.

Lawtel ⌐ subscription legal current awareness digest service

7–12 This service contains a search facility which allows you to search for Bills by keyword. Either use the *UK Search* section, enter search term and tick the *Parliamentary Bills* box or go to *legislation*, enter search term and tick the *Parliamentary Bills* box. This takes you to details about the Bill which include the stage that it has reached. There is a link to the full text of the Bill on the Scottish Parliament website.

Current Law Monthly Digest 📖

7–13 There is a separate Progress of Bills table covering the Scottish Parliament which indicates the latest stage in the parliamentary progress of Bills. For more details about the *Monthly Digest* see para.8.15.

Scottish Official Daily, Weekly and Monthly Listing ⌐ free

7–14 This lists the publication of Scottish Parliament Bills (and notes each version published), marshalled lists of amendments, explanatory notes and other accompanying documentation. The *Weekly Listing* is available at *http://www.lib.gla.ac.uk/swop/Astron/AstronWL.html*. It is possible to register to receive the listings by emailing your details to registerdetails@rrd.com.

Journals 📖

7–15 Journals may contain information about the progress of Bills. The *Scots Law Times* has a Parliamentary News (Scotland) section which notes the introduction and progress of Bills.

Newspapers 📖 and ⌐

7–16 The Scottish broadsheets contain information about Bills and events in the Scottish Parliament.

Finding out about older Bills—if the Bill was passed in the current session of the Parliament

Scottish Parliament website ⌐ free

On the Scottish Parliament website (*http://www.scottish.parliament.uk*) select *Bills* from the **7–17** *select a section* menu at the top of the homepage. If the Bill was passed in the current session of Parliament go to click Bills not in progress - enacted (E) or fallen (F) or withdrawn (W), the Bills are arranged in alphabetical order. Click on the Bill you are interested in and this brings up lots of information about the Bill including:

> ➤ Details of the progress of the Bill.
> ➤ The content of the Bill at various stages, i.e. as introduced and as amended.
> ➤ The accompanying documents.
> ➤ SPICe briefings.
> ➤ Details of the lead committee and a link to its site—if you follow this link you will be able to find the official report of the committees debates on the Bill by clicking on previous meetings and searching the relevant session for the Bill. Click on the official report for the relevant meeting which you can identify form the list of items discussed.
> ➤ Calls for evidence.
> ➤ Summary of the passage of the Bill.
> ➤ Details of the date it received the Royal Assent.
> ➤ A link to the Act in the *OPSI* site.

Finding out about older Bills—if the Bill was passed in a previous session of the Parliament

Scottish Parliament web site ⌐ free

On the Scottish Parliament website (*http://www.scottish.parliament.uk*) select *Bills* from the **7–18** *select a section* menu at the top of the homepage. Click on *Bill Summaries*. You then need to click through to the relevant session where the Bills are listed alphabetically. Click on the title of a Bill and the following information is provided: details of the date when the Bill was introduced, the name of person who introduced it, the date it was passed, the date of the Royal Assent, a link to the Act, a brief explanation of the purpose of the Act and some details of developments, e.g. if the Act has been subsequently repealed or is going to be consolidated.

Different information is provided if you click on the links on the left hand side to e.g. *Session 1 Bills*. The Bills for the session are again listed alphabetically. Click on the title of a Bill and the following information is provided by various links: a detailed timetable of the Bill's progress through Parliament; the Bills as introduced; the accompanying documents, a SPICe briefings; marshalled amendments; the Bill as amended; the Bills as passed; a summary of the passage of the Bill; the Act and the Explanatory Notes.

Passage of the Bill series 📖

This series is an excellent source of information about a Bill. It consists of a volume for each Bill **7–19** which contains all the relevant documentation from the passage of the Bill through to its enactment. The documentation includes: the various versions of the Bill, the accompanying documents, marshalled lists of amendments, committee reports and the relevant parts of the Official Report. The publication of this series has been slow—it has currently only been published up to 2002. However, it will provide a very useful resource for legal research.

Current Law Statutes 📖

Once the Bill is published in this series it will contain annotations which will contain infor- **7–20** mation about the background to the Act and the passage of the Bill.

Finding out about Parliamentary debates on a Bill

The Scottish Parliament Official Report 📖 and ᐦ free

7–21 The Official Report contains an edited substantially verbatim account of proceedings in Parliament (it is the equivalent of Hansard in the UK Parliament). It is published in three parts: plenary sessions, committee discussions which are held in public and written answers. The Official Report for plenary sessions of Parliament is published both on the Scottish Parliament website and in paper by 8am on the day following the meeting of Parliament. Reports of committee meetings are published to an agreed deadline which will always be before the next meeting of the committee. The written answers report is published weekly. There is a searchable database of written questions and answers on the Scottish Parliament website. There is no bound series of the Official Report.

7–22 If you do not know the date of the debate on the Bill you can search using the advanced search option. An easier option is to click on *Official Report* in the *Current Business* section of the Scottish Parliament homepage. Then click on *list of debates* in the *Official Report* section on the left hand side of the screen. This takes you to alphabetical lists of debates arranged in parliamentary sessions. The debate headings listed here are for substantive items of business considered at meetings of the whole Parliament. You will find discussions of Bills by clicking on the title of the Bill which will appear in the list. To search within the text on the alphabetical lists of debates page you can use the Find option (click on *edit* at the very top of the page and then *find on this page* or alternatively press the *Ctrl* key and the *F* key).

7–23 If you do not know the date of the committee discussion on the Bill you can search using the advanced search option. An alternative option is to click on *Official Report* in the *Current Business* section of the Scottish Parliament homepage. Then click on *committee meetings* in the *Official Report* section on the left hand side of the screen. Click on the name of the committee and then on the link to *meeting papers and official reports* which appears in the *Official Report* section on the left hand side of the screen. You can then scroll down and find the discussion of particular Bills.

7–24 The reference for the Official Report for meetings of the Parliament should include SP OR followed by full details of the date and column numbers e.g. SP OR 29 March 2007, col 33710–33712. The reference for the Official Report for Committee meetings should include SP OR followed by the appropriate committee abbreviation, the date and column numbers e.g. SP OR ERD 24 April 2006, col 3061–3104. The reference for the Official Report for written answers should include SP WA date, parliamentary question number, e.g. SP WA 28 March 2007, S2W-32485

Explanatory Notes 📖 and ᐦ free

7–25 All Acts of the Scottish Parliament which result from Bills introduced into the Parliament by the Scottish Ministers (except for Acts which result from Budget Bills), are accompanied by Explanatory Notes. At the end of the Explanatory Note is a section called *Parliamentary History* which contains a table setting out for each stage of the proceedings in the Scottish Parliament for the Act, the dates on which the proceedings at that stage took place, the references to the Official Report of those proceedings and the dates on which the Committee Reports and other papers relating to the Act were published, and the references to those Reports and other papers. Explanatory Notes are available in paper and via the *OPSI* website (*http://www.opsi.gov.uk/acts.htm*). From 2002 the references to the parliamentary debates in many Explanatory Notes have been hypertext linked to the Official Report. This is a particularly useful feature. The office of the Queen's Printer for Scotland (*http://www.oqps.gov.uk*) lists all the Explanatory Notes on one page by year and then alphabetically.

Current Law Statutes 📖

If the Bill has since become an Act, the annual volumes of *Current Law Statutes* should contain **7–26** details of the parliamentary debates relevant to each Act. Look in the first annotation inserted after the long title.

Passage of the Bill series 📖

This series consists of a volume for each Bill which contains all the relevant documentation from **7–27** the passage of the Bill through to its enactment. This documentation includes the relevant parts of the Official Report. The publication of this series has been slow—it has currently only been published up to 2002.

The Business Bulletin 📖 and ⌁free

The Business Bulletin is available from the homepage of the Scottish Parliament website and will **7–28** alert you to the dates of parliamentary debates.

SOURCES OF ACTS OF THE SCOTTISH PARLIAMENT

Acts of the Scottish Parliament, like their UK counterparts, are published both electronically **7–29** and in paper and in many different databases and series. For information about the layout and structure of an Act of the Scottish Parliament see para.5.48. The different versions of Acts may include additional information such as explanatory details called annotations and/or different search facilities for accessing legislation. However, one vital feature which you must be aware of when reading legislation is whether it is the original version of the Act (i.e. the Act as passed by Parliament) or whether it is a revised version which includes any amendments which have been made to it. It is very important to be aware of the current law and therefore essential that you use a source which provides an **up-to-date revised version** of legislation. The original version of an Act should be treated with caution as it represents a historical document (one that is frozen in time). There may not have been any amendments since the original version was passed but unless you check the position, consulting the original version is worse than useless, it could lead to serious error.

Official versions

Acts of the Scottish Parliament 📖

After a Bill receives the Royal Assent the official paper version is published by The Stationery **7–30** Office under the authority of the Queen's Printer for Scotland. Each Act is printed singly and these are known as Queen's Printer copies.

Explanatory Notes have been published with all Acts of the Scottish Parliament which result from Bills introduced into the Parliament by the Scottish Ministers (except for Acts which result from Budget Bills). The text of the Explanatory Notes is produced by the Scottish Executive Department responsible for the subject matter of the Act.

At the end of each year the single Acts are produced together in a publication called *Acts of the Scottish Parliament*. This is the official version of the Acts which are arranged in chronological order (i.e. by asp number). These do not contain annotations. Alphabetical and chronological lists are contained at the start of each volume. At the end of each volume are tables of derivations and destinations of the Consolidation Acts for the year. There is also a table called Effects of Legislation. This is in two parts. Part 1 gives details of Acts of the Scottish Parliament (in chronological order) which have been repealed, amended or otherwise affected by Acts of the Scottish Parliament, Scottish statutory instruments, Acts of the UK Parliament and statutory instruments made during the year. Part 2 gives details of Acts of the UK Parliament (in chronological order) which have been repealed, amended or otherwise affected by

Acts of the Scottish Parliament which received Royal Assent during the year. The index to the volume is organised alphabetically by short title and then by section.

Office of the Queen's Printer for Scotland website 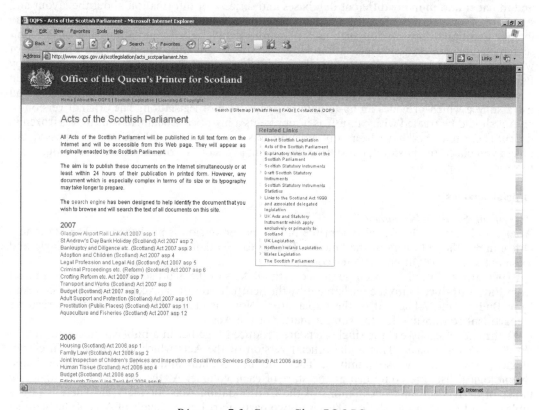 free

7–31 The official electronic original version of Acts of the Scottish Parliament is available from the *Office of the Queen's Printer for Scotland (OQPS)* website (*http://www.oqps.gov.uk/legislation/ acts*). This site contains links to the full original text of all Acts of the Scottish Parliament. The aim is to publish Acts on the site simultaneously or at least within 24 hours of their publication in printed form. Explanatory Notes are generally published at the same time as the Act. The Acts and Explanatory Notes are grouped together by year and within each year they can be viewed either alphabetically or chronologically by asp number. Acts are published in html and also importantly as pdfs which makes downloading the entire document and printing it straightforward. Explanatory Notes are only published as pdfs. The site also contains access to the full text of all UK Acts of Parliament (from 1988) and statutory instruments (from 1997) and any accompanying Explanatory Notes and Explanatory Memoranda, which apply exclusively or primarily to Scotland. The material is published in its original form and amendments are not included. This means that this site is only of use if you particularly want the original form of an Act as opposed to the up-to-date form of the legislation.

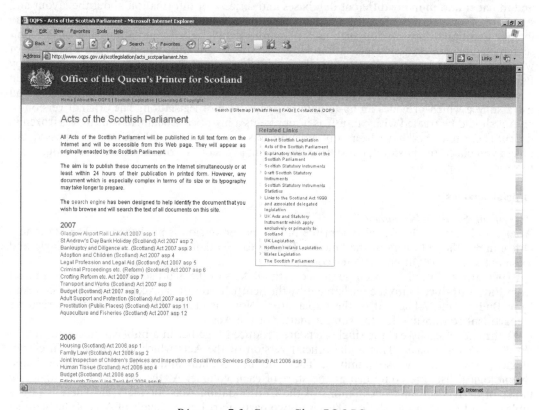

Diagram 7.3: Screen Shot 7OQPS

Office of Public Sector Information (OPSI) ⬦ free

The *Scotland Legislation* section of the *Office of Public Sector Information (OPSI)* website **7–32** (*http://www.opsi.gov.uk/acts.htm*) is managed by Her Majesty's Stationery Office on behalf of the Queen's Printer for Scotland. This site contains the full text of *all* Acts of the Scottish Parliament. The aim is to publish Acts on the site simultaneously or at least within 24 hours of their publication in printed form. Explanatory Notes are generally published at the same time as the Act. The Acts and Explanatory Notes are grouped together by year and within each year they can be viewed either alphabetically or chronologically by asp number. Both Acts (and Explanatory Notes) are published in html and also importantly as pdfs which makes downloading the entire document and printing it straightforward. The site also contains a *search legislation* function which links to an *advanced search* which allows you to restrict your search to Scotland and to search by keyword, type of legislation (e.g. Acts or Explanatory Notes) or date. The material is published in its **original** form and amendments are not included. This means that this site is only of use if you particularly want the original from of an Act as opposed to the up-to-date form of the legislation.

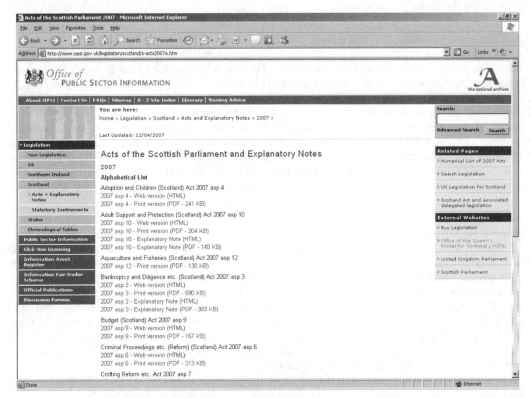

Diagram 7.4: OPSI

Sources of revised versions of Acts

The following information sources contain revised versions of legislation and should therefore be used in preference to sources which contain original versions if you are trying to find out details of the current law.

Westlaw ⌐ subscription database

7–33 *Westlaw UK* legislation contains the full text of all Public General Acts of the Scottish Parliament in **revised** form. For information on general searching for legislation, see paras 6.32–6.44 as the majority of search techniques are the same as for UK legislation. However, it is possible to restrict your searching to Scottish Parliament materials. From the welcome page, click the *legislation* link from the navigation bar at the top of the screen. Scroll down to the bottom of the screen and one of the browse options is to browse by *jurisdiction: Scottish Parliament*. If you click on this a new search page opens. This allows you to either carry out a basic search (see para.6.34) or to click through to an advanced search (see para.6.35) which will be restricted to Scottish Parliament legislation. You will be able to remind yourself that you are restricted to Scottish Parliament materials by looking at the breadcrumb trail in the blue area at the top of the search box. This is a useful feature as it is easy to forget that you are not in the main search area. If you would prefer to browse the Scottish Parliament legislation it is possible to do this. Follow the instructions above but instead of using the search box scroll down to the bottom of the screen to the browse options. These allow you to browse Acts of the Scottish Parliament by year or alphabetically by short title.

LexisNexis Butterworths ⌐ subscription database

7–34 *LexisNexis Butterworths Scottish Parliament Acts* contains the full text of all Public General Acts of the Scottish Parliament in **revised** form. To search for an Act of the Scottish Parliament choose the legislation tab from the homepage. This opens up the legislation search form. Select *Scottish Parliament Acts* from the Select Sources drop-down list. Go to the *type* field and select Statute from the drop-down list. If you do not know the name of the Act you can enter words or phrases in the *enter search terms* box. You can use Boolean connectors to show the relation of the terms, see para.2.33. If you know the title or part of the title, enter search terms in the *legislation title* field, giving the year if known. If you only enter part of the title, use Boolean connectors to link your search terms (see para.2.33). If you want to search for a particular section, enter the number in the *provision* field. You can retrieve your results by clicking on *search*.

Statute Law Database ⌐ free

7–35 The *Statute Law Database* (SLD) contains the official revised edition of Acts of the Scottish Parliament in electronic form. This database was launched in December 2006 and is a welcome and important addition to free electronic legal information sources. It can be accessed at *http:// www.statutelaw.gov.uk*. The database contains all Acts of the Scottish Parliament in **revised** form. Unfortunately it has been launched before all the information on it has been brought completely up-to-date which means that caution must be exercised when using this database until the updating process is complete. However, it is planned that the database should be completely up to date by 2008. See paras 6.45–6.60 for more details about the *Statute Law Database* and searching techniques for legislation.

It is possible to restrict your search to Acts of the Scottish Parliament using the Quick search or advanced search functions by choosing *Act (Scottish Parliament)* from the *Legislation Type* menu. You can browse Acts of the Scottish Parliament by clicking on the *A-Z index* option from the SLD's homepage and then choosing *Act (Scottish Parliament)* from the *Legislation Type* menu. You can similarly restrict the chronological index (again available from the homepage) by choosing the same option.

7–36 As indicated earlier, this database is not fully up-to-date. This means that if an update status warning appears at the start of a piece of legislation you must consult the table of legislative effects to obtain details of any effects not yet applied by the database. The table of legislative effects is located by clicking on the link in the navigation bar at the top of the page. This is a list of all repeals, amendments and other effects (primary and secondary) enacted from 2002 to the current year. It can only be searched one year at a time but you can narrow that search by entering: the asp number of the affecting legislation; the year of the affected legislation; the asp number of the affected legislation; or any combination of these.

The results are displayed in ascending order ranked as follows: year of affected legislation; asp number of affected legislation; affected provision (letters then numbers); number of affecting legislation (year is fixed); affected provision (letters then numbers). For each entry, the type of effect is shown. A letter "Y" in the "Amendment Applied" column shows that the effect has been carried through on the database.

!Example of using the Table of Legislative Effects to find out about subsequent amendments

Use the Quick search to find the Title Conditions (Scotland) Act 2003.   **7–37**

The *results within legislation* page shows a warning that there are outstanding amendments in 2003, 2004, 2006 and 2007.

> ➤ Noting that the 2003 Act is asp 9 go to the table of legislative effects. In order to check for details of all the amendments from 2003 onwards.
> ➤ Enter 2003 in the year of affecting legislation box, 2003 in the year of affected legislation box and 9 in the number box opposite the year of affected legislation. Click Go. This brings up a table with details of amendments made in 2003.
> ➤ Enter 2004 in the year of affecting legislation box, 2003 in the year of affected legislation box and 9 in the number box opposite the year of affected legislation. Click Go. This brings up a table with details of amendments made in 2004.
> ➤ We know that there are no outstanding amendments for 2005 and so continue the search by:
> ➤ Entering 2006 in the year of affecting legislation box, 2003 in the year of affected legislation box and 9 in the number box opposite the year of affected legislation. Click Go. This brings up a table with details of amendments made in 2006; and finally
> ➤ Entering 2007 in the year of affecting legislation box, 2003 in the year of affected legislation box and 9 in the number box opposite the year of affected legislation. Click Go. This brings up a table with details of amendments made in 2007.

This process identifies all amendments but until it is fully up-to-date *Westlaw* or *LexisNexis Butterworths* are much easier to use as they provide the current revised form of legislation.

Sources of original versions of Acts

BAILII ⚙ free

The *BAILII* website (*http://www.bailii.org/*) contains Acts of the Scottish Parliament reproduced **7–38** from *OPSI*. The Acts are contained in the Scottish Legislation section of the site. The legislation search allows you to restrict a search to Acts of the Scottish Parliament and to search by keyword and date. The advanced search allows Boolean searching. Unlike the *OPSI* site, it is possible to browse all the Scottish Parliament legislation in an alphabetical index. From the homepage go to *A-Z legislation title index* and then click on *Scotland*. The Acts are available as continuous web pages as opposed to pdfs. The material is published in its original form and amendments are not included. This means that this site is only of use if you particularly want the **original** from of an Act as opposed to the up-to-date form of the legislation.

Current Law Statutes 📖

7–39 *Current Law Statutes* include the full **original** text of all Acts of the Scottish Parliament. They appear after Public General Acts and Private Acts of the UK Parliament. Within the Scottish section, the Acts are arranged in chronological order. Each Act is annotated by an expert in the relevant field. This means that notes (annotations) appear throughout the Act. The annotations are intended to clarify the effect of the various sections. The number of annotations depends on the complexity of the Act. There tends to be a long introductory annotation which explains the Act's purpose and puts it into context. It will also refer to the dates of the parliamentary debates on the Bill. The annotations are a very useful feature in that they provide an expert's insight into the effect of a piece of legislation. More details about the *Current Law Statutes* are in para.6.63.

Acts from the current year appear singly in the looseleaf Statutes Service File where similarly the Acts of the Scottish Parliament follow after UK Public General Acts and UK Private Acts. After the end of the year the material in the Statutes Service File is reissued in a bound volume.

Justis UK Statutes 🖱 subscription and CD Rom

7–40 This database contains the full text of all Acts the Scottish Parliament as enacted. All Acts appear in their **original** form, with links to amending legislation. This means that you can trace the development of the law but if you want the current law you should use a source with a revised version of legislation.

SEARCH STRATEGIES FOR FINDING ACTS OF THE SCOTTISH PARLIAMENT

7–41 This section deals with the different ways which can be used to find Scottish Parliament legislation. This will allow you to find legislation from different starting points: for instance you may want to explore a new area of law or your knowledge of the legislation's title may be incomplete. There are usually numerous ways of finding legal information. This section contains lists of various alternative sources along with comments as to their strengths and weaknesses. The most comprehensive sources are listed first. Sources which provide access to revised versions of legislation are given prominence because sources of original versions of Acts will require additional research to check for any amendments or repeals.

Although private Bills are subject to different procedures from public Bills on enactment all Bills become Acts of the Scottish Parliament (asps) and private asps are numbered in the same single series as public asps and can therefore be searched for in the same way.

7–42 The following search strategies are considered:

> ➤ Finding statutes by subject. This should allow you to search where you may be interested in a specific subject area. See paras 7.43–7.49.
> ➤ Current status of a statute. It is vital to know whether a statute has been brought into force or whether it has been amended or repealed. See paras 7.50–7.62 and 7.63–7.69.

There is a summary of the alternative sources for each strategy in Appendix I.

Finding whether courts have considered the legislation is discussed in paras 4.92–4.103. This covers the situation where you know of a specific legislative provision and you want to find out if any cases have discussed it or interpreted it in a particular way. Finding whether any articles have been written about legislation involves the same techniques as for UK Parliament legislation and is discussed in paras 6.112–6.118.

Finding Acts of the Scottish Parliament by subject

Major textbooks/reference works/encyclopaedias
As with UK Acts, the *Stair Memorial Encyclopaedia* (see para.8.2), major textbooks or reference **7–43**
works are ideal starting points for research by subject. Unlike an electronic database, they will
not just identify a piece of legislation; they will place it in context. This means that they will
explain its background and how it fits in to the whole area of law, how it has been interpreted
and offer comment on it. Encyclopaedias or reference works can also provide you with the
information necessary to refine your search which will make searching the full text databases
manageable. If you try to conduct a subject search on a database with a broad subject term you
will retrieve hundreds or even thousands of hits which it may take a long time to work through.
Searching with a more relevant term will produce fewer more relevant hits.

   Note that Acts of the Scottish Parliament will normally be referenced in the same tables of
statutes as Acts from the UK Parliament. Acts will be listed in chronological order rather than
by jurisdiction.

Westlaw ⊕ subscription database and *LexisNexis Butterworths* ⊕ subscription database **7–44**
Both these databases have the **revised** form of Acts of the Scottish Parliament and can be
searched using sophisticated search techniques including searching for words in the title or free
text searching of the content of legislation. For *Westlaw* see para.7.33 and for *LexisNexis
Butterworths* see paras 7.34 and 9.3.

Statute Law Database ⊕ free
The *Statute Law Database* allows searching for words in the title or, more useful for subject **7–45**
searching, a free text search of the content of legislation on the database in its advanced search.
There are facilities which enable you to restrict this to Acts of the Scottish Parliament by
choosing the appropriate type of legislation (see further para.7.35). The results obtained will
have the search terms highlighted in the text. However, this database is not completely up-to-
date and should be used with caution, see paras 6.45–6.48.

Office of Public Sector Information (OPSI) ⊕ free
The *OPSI* website (*http://www.opsi.gov.uk/acts.htm*) contains the official electronic full text of **7–46**
all Acts of the Scottish Parliament in their **original** form. The site contains a *search legislation*
function which links to an *advanced search* which allows you to restrict your search to Scotland
and to search by keyword, type of legislation (e.g. Acts or Explanatory Notes) or date.

BAILII ⊕ free
The *BAILII* website (*http://www.bailii.org/*) contains the full text of all Acts of the Scottish **7–47**
Parliament in their **original** form. The legislation search allows you to restrict a search to Acts of
the Scottish Parliament and to search by keyword and date. The advanced search allows
Boolean searching. Unlike the *OPSI* site it is possible to browse the all the Scottish Parliament
legislation in an alphabetical index. From the homepage go to *A-Z legislation title index* and
then click on *Scotland*.

Justis UK Statutes ⊕ subscription and CD Rom
This database contains the full text of all Acts of the Scottish Parliament in their **original** form **7–48**
with links to amending legislation.

Current Law Yearbooks and Monthly Digests 📖
Check the subject headings in the consolidated indexes in the master volumes of the Yearbooks, **7–49**
and the more recent Yearbooks and Monthly Digests. See paras 8.15 and 8.21.

Current status of an Act of the Scottish Parliament—is it in force yet?

The Act itself

7–50 As with UK Acts, the date the Act comes into force may be the date of Royal Assent or it may be detailed in the commencement section at the end of the Act, see para.5.48, section [7]. This means that you need to check the commencement section of the Act. If the Act is silent it comes into force on the date of the Royal Assent. If the Act stipulates a specific date or time period then that is the relevant date. Alternatively the Act (or part of it) may come into force at a time to be set by the Scottish Ministers. If this is the case, you need to check if a commencement order has been issued and find out which part(s) of the Act have been brought into force.

Westlaw subscription database

7–51 The searching technique is the same as for UK Acts, see para.6.93.

LexisNexis Butterworths subscription database

7–52 In *LexisNexis Butterworths* commencement notes appear in the legislation.

Is It in Force?

7–53 This annual publication includes Acts of the Scottish Parliament and covers the previous 25 years. The current edition is "Is It in Force Spring 2007?" The years are presented in chronological order and within each year the statutes are listed alphabetically (they are not separated out by jurisdiction). Opposite the short title are details of the relevant commencement provisions. The volume also contains Statutes Not Yet in Force which lists provisions of Acts for which no commencement dates have yet been appointed.

Note that this publication does not include full information on amendments and repeals. You should use other publications to check this information, see para.7.63 onwards. As it is an annual publication it is always out of date so be sure to use another source to check from the date of publication to the present unless you are using the electronic version, see para.7.55.

!Example

7–54 Using the paper version of *Is It in Force*?

Has s.25 of the Title Conditions (Scotland) Act 2003 been brought into force?

Check the latest edition of *Is It in Force*? Turn to the entries for 2003. The statutes are listed in alphabetical order, so check under "T". You will find the title of the Act and the sections listed underneath. Opposite s.25 is the information that it came into force on November 28, 2004. The authority is SSI 2003 No. 456.

Is It in Force? subscription

7–55 There is an online version which is available from *LexisNexis Butterworths*. The online version is updated daily and links through to the relevant commencement orders.

Lawtel subscription legal current awareness digest service

7–56 *Lawtel* is updated daily. To search generally for commencement information, see para.6.96. If you want to restrict your search to legislation from the Scottish Parliament, on the *Lawtel UK* homepage click on *statutory law*. Click on *focused search* tab, enter your search terms and then click on *Edinburgh* in the *origin* box. Click on the link in the search results to the details of the Act. From here, click on the link to the *statutory status table*. This lists all the sections of the Act in a table, with entries relating to commencement, amendment and repeal.

Current Law Legislation Citators and Current Law Statutes

7–57 The searching technique is the same as for UK Acts, see para.6.97.

Current Legal Information ⌐ and CD Rom subscription legal research service
The legislation citator is available electronically as part of *Current Legal Information*. **7–58**

Statute Law Database ⌐ free
The *Statute Law Database* provides commencement information at the bottom of the text of a **7–59**
section of an Act. However, this database is not yet fully updated and should be used with
caution until it is complete. For more details about the *Statute Law Database* see para.7.35.

Journals ⌐
Journals such as *Scots Law Times* contain information about legislation which is coming into **7–60**
force.

The Daily List ⌐ free
The Daily List (*http://www.tsoshop.co.uk/parliament/*) and its weekly and monthly consolidated **7–61**
forms contain details of Commencement Orders, see para.8.85.

Scottish Official Daily, Weekly and Monthly Listing ⌐ free
This listing contains details of Commencement Orders. The *Weekly Listing* is available at *http://* **7–62**
www.lib.gla.ac.uk/swop/Astron/AstronWL.html It is possible to register to receive the listings by
emailing your details to registerdetails@rrd.com.

Current status of an Act of the Scottish Parliament—finding amendments and repeals

Westlaw ⌐ subscription database
Westlaw UK provides the revised form of legislation which incorporates amendments and **7–63**
repeals, see para.6.103.

LexisNexis Butterworths ⌐ subscription database
LexisNexis Butterworths provides the revised form of legislation which incorporates amend- **7–64**
ments and repeals. An ellipsis (...) indicates that text has been repealed. Square brackets denote
text that has been inserted or substituted. Italicised text means that the content is prospectively
repealed or substituted. The notes section at the end of each document indicates the changes
that have been made to the text.

Statute Law Database ⌐ free
The same issues arise as with UK legislation, see para.6.104. **7–65**

Current Law Legislation Citators ⌐
This is the best paper source for locating changes to legislation. The principles of searching are **7–66**
covered in paras 6.69–6.75. The only additional issue is to remember that Acts of the Scottish
Parliament are listed separately in the legislation citators; they make up the first part of the
statute citator. It can be easy to miss this section which is currently very short.

Current Legal Information ⌐ and CD Rom subscription legal research service
The legislation citator is available electronically as part of *Current Legal Information*. **7–67**

Lawtel ⌐ subscription legal current awareness digest service
Lawtel is updated daily. To search generally for amendments see para.6.107. If you want to **7–68**
restrict your search to legislation from the Scottish Parliament, on the *Lawtel UK* homepage
click on *statutory law*. Click on *focused search* tab, enter your search terms and then click on
Edinburgh in the *origin* box. Click on the link in the search results to the details of the Act. From

here, click on the link to the *statutory status table*. This lists all the sections of the Act in a table, with entries relating to commencement, amendment and repeal.

Chronological Table of the Statutes 📖
7–69   This work is published annually by The Stationery Office. It is a chronological table of the statutes for the period 1235 to the year of publication. The latest version was published in February 2007 and covers in the period 1235–2005. It includes a Table of Acts of the Scottish Parliament which lists Acts of the Scottish Parliament from 1999 to the end of 2005 in chronological order and reflects the effects of all new legislation on those Acts. The work tends to be a couple of years out of date and this greatly reduces its usefulness. Another method would have to be employed to bring your search up to date.

Finding whether the courts have considered an Act of the Scottish Parliament

7–70   This covers the situation where you know of a specific Act and you want to find out if any cases have discussed it or interpreted it in a particular way. See paras 4.92–4.103.

Finding whether any articles have been written about an Act of the Scottish Parliament

The same techniques are required as for UK legislation, see paras 6.112–6.118.

Finding whether any statutory instruments have been made under an Act of the Scottish Parliament

The same techniques are required as for UK legislation, see paras 6.193–6.197.

SCOTTISH STATUTORY INSTRUMENTS

7–71   This section relates to Scottish statutory instruments from the Scottish Parliament and not statutory instruments for Scotland from the UK Parliament: they are dealt with in Chapter 6.
   Scottish statutory instruments, like Acts of the Scottish Parliament, are published both electronically and in paper and in many different databases and series. Not all Scottish statutory instruments are automatically published. All Scottish statutory instruments which are of general application will be published but local statutory instruments are not usually published. For information about the layout and structure of a Scottish statutory instrument see para.5.28. Since July 2005 Scottish statutory instruments laid before the Scottish Parliament have been accompanied by Executive Notes which set out a brief statement of the purpose of the instrument and provide information about its policy objective and policy implications. The Executive Notes are only available electronically they are not produced in printed form.

7–72   Although statutory instruments are not published with Acts of Parliament and there are separate publications which cover only statutory instruments, many of the major databases contain both Acts and statutory instruments. As with Acts, different databases and series produce different versions of statutory instruments and it is vital that you are aware of whether you are reading the original version of a statutory instrument or an up-to-date revised version which includes any amendments which have been made to it. The original version should be treated with caution as it represents a historical document (one that is frozen in time). There may not have been any amendments since the original version was passed but unless you check the position, consulting the original version is worse than useless, it could lead to serious error.

SOURCES OF SCOTTISH STATUTORY INSTRUMENTS

Official versions of Scottish statutory instruments

Individual Scottish statutory instruments 📖
General Scottish statutory instruments are published individually and can be purchased from 7–73
The Stationery Office.

Annual Volumes of Scottish statutory instruments 📖
Annual volumes of Scottish statutory instruments are published by The Stationery Office. They 7–74
contain:

> ➢ A copy of all general Scottish statutory instruments for the period arranged in number
>   order.
> ➢ A classified list of local instruments.
> ➢ Tables showing the effect on enactments and previous statutory rules or statutory
>   instruments (whether Scottish or not) of the Scottish statutory instruments included in
>   the edition.
> ➢ An annual numerical and issue list of Scottish statutory instruments.
> ➢ An index which is arranged by subject heading and then alphabetical within the subject
>   heading.

Office of the Queen's Printer for Scotland website ᐰ free
The official electronic original version of *all published* Scottish statutory instruments is available 7–75
from the *Office of the Queen's Printer for Scotland* (*OQPS*) website (*http://www.oqps.gov.uk/
legislation/ssi/*). The aim is to publish them simultaneously with their publication in printed
form. The Scottish statutory instruments and Executive Notes (since July 2005) are grouped
together by year and within each year they can be viewed chronologically by number. Scottish
statutory instruments are published in html and as pdfs. Executive Notes are only published as
pdfs. The full text of all draft Scottish statutory instruments awaiting approval is available at
http://www.oqps.gov.uk/legislation/ssi/dssi-index They are arranged by subject within each year.
The site also contains access to the full text of all UK statutory instruments (from 1997
onwards) and accompanying Explanatory Memoranda, which apply exclusively to Scotland.
The material is published in its **original** form and amendments are not included. This means that
this site is only of use if you particularly want the original form of an Act as opposed to the up-
to-date form of the legislation. The site also contains statistics about the numbers and content of
Scottish statutory instruments.

Office of Public Sector Information (OPSI) ᐰ free
The *Scotland Legislation* section of the *Office of Public Sector Information (OPSI)* website 7–76
(*http://www.opsi.gov.uk/legislation/scotland/s-stat.htm*) is managed by Her Majesty's Stationery
Office on behalf of the Queen's Printer for Scotland. This site contains the full text of *all*
published Scottish statutory instruments. The aim is to publish Scottish statutory instruments
on the site simultaneously or at least within 24 hours of their publication in printed form. The
statutory instruments are grouped by year and within each year they can be viewed chronologically by number. Since July 2005, Executive Notes prepared by the Executive have been
published on the site. The Scottish statutory instruments and Executive Notes are grouped
together by year and within each year they can be viewed chronologically by number. Scottish
statutory instruments are published in html and also importantly as pdfs which makes downloading the entire document and printing it straightforward. Executive Notes are published as
pdfs.

7–77 The full text of all draft Scottish statutory instruments awaiting approval are available on the *OPSI* site at *http://www.opsi.gov.uk/legislation/scotland/s-stat-draft.htm* They will remain on this site until they are superseded by a Scottish statutory instrument or until they are withdrawn. They are arranged by subject within each year. They are not available in printed form. The site also contains a *search legislation* function which links to an *advanced search* which allows you to restrict your search to Scotland and to search by keyword, type of legislation (e.g. statutory instruments and draft statutory instruments) or date. The material is published in its **original** form and amendments are not included. This means that this site is only of use if you particularly want the original from of an Act as opposed to the up-to-date form of the legislation.

Sources of revised versions of Scottish statutory instruments

Westlaw ✋ subscription database

7–78 *Westlaw UK* legislation contains all published Scottish statutory instruments made by the Scottish Parliament in **revised** form. Draft statutory instruments are not included, see para.7.85 for tracing Scottish statutory instruments.

LexisNexis Butterworths ✋ subscription database

7–79 The full text revised form of all published Scottish statutory instruments is available from *LexisNexis Butterworths*, see para.7.86 for tracing Scottish statutory instruments.

Sources of original versions of Scottish statutory instruments

7–80 *Statute Law Database* ✋ free

BAILII ✋ free

7–81 Scottish statutory instruments are located in the Scottish legislation section, see para.7.38.

7–82 *Justis UK Statutory Instruments* ✋ subscription and CD Rom database.

Specialist encyclopaedias and collections of legislation 📖

7–83 Specialist looseleaf encyclopaedias (para.8.9) and collections of legislation (paras 6.199/6.200) may contain copies of selected Scottish statutory instruments relevant to their subject area.

Current Law Yearbooks and Monthly Digests 📖

7–84 Scottish statutory instruments are digested in the Yearbooks and Monthly Digests. The full text of Commencement Orders is printed in the Yearbooks and in the looseleaf service file (for the current year). See paras. 8.15 and 8.21.

Aids to tracing Scottish statutory instruments

Westlaw ✋ subscription database

7–85 *Westlaw UK legislation* contains all published Scottish statutory instruments made by the Scottish Parliament in **revised** form. Draft statutory instruments are not included.

For information on general searching for statutory instruments see paras 6.142–6.145 as the majority of search techniques are the same as for UK legislation. However, it is possible to restrict your searching to Scottish Parliament materials. From the welcome page, click the *legislation* link from the navigation bar at the top of the screen. Scroll down to the bottom of the screen and one of the browse options is to browse by *jurisdiction: Scottish Parliament*. If you click on this a new search page opens. This allows you to either carry out a basic search (see para.6.143) or to click through to an advanced search (see para.6.35) which will be restricted to Scottish Parliament legislation. You will be able to remind yourself that you are restricted to Scottish Parliament materials by looking at the breadcrumb trail in the blue area at the top of the search box. This is a useful feature as it is easy to forget that you are not in the main search area. If you would prefer to browse the Scottish Parliament legislation it is possible to do this. Follow the instructions above but instead of using the search box scroll down to the bottom of the screen to the browse options. These allow you to browse Scottish statutory instruments by year or alphabetically by title.

LexisNexis Butterworths ⁀ subscription database
LexisNexis Butterworths Scottish Parliament SIs contains all published Scottish statutory **7–86** instruments made by the Scottish Parliament in **revised** form.

Choose the legislation tab from the homepage. This opens up the legislation search form. Select *Scottish Parliament SIs* from the Select Sources drop-down list. Go to the *type* field and select Statutory Instrument from the drop-down list. If you do not know the name of the instrument you can enter words or phrases in the *enter search terms* box. You can use Boolean connectors to show the relation of the terms see para.2.33 If you know the instrument number, enter the year in the *legislation title* field and the series number in the *series number* field. If you know the title or part of the title, enter search terms in the *legislation title* field, giving the year if known. If you only enter part of the title, use Boolean connectors to link your search terms (see para.2.33). You can retrieve your results by clicking on *search*.

Lawtel ⁀ subscription legal current awareness digest service
Lawtel is updated daily. To search generally see para.6.146. To search for Scottish statutory **7–87** instruments click on *statutory instruments* on the *Lawtel UK* homepage. Click on *focused search* tab, enter your search terms including "Scotland" in the *title* field, enter an "s" in the *application* field and then click on search. Note: if you just put 's' in the application field this will not restrict your search to Scottish statutory instruments; it will include all statutory instruments which apply in Scotland. The next step is to click on the link in the search results to the details of the instrument. The details shown will include the instrument's number, the enabling Act, coming into force date, a list of effects it has had on other legislation, its area of application and a link to the full original text of the instrument and the Executive Note on the *OPSI* site.

Current Law Legislation Citators 📖
This is the best paper source for locating changes of Scottish statutory instruments. The prin- **7–88** ciples of searching are covered in paras 6.147–6.150. The only additional issue is to remember that Scottish Statutory Instruments issued by the Scottish Parliament are listed separately in the legislation citators; they make up the first part of the statutory instrument citator. It can be easy to miss this section which is currently very short compared to the UK section of the citator.

Current Legal Information ⁀ and CD Rom subscription legal research service
The *Current Law Legislation Citator* is available electronically as part of *Current Legal Information*. It enables you to access information by the year; words from the title of instrument; the **7–89** number of an instrument or free text. The key advantage of the electronic version is the ease of use compared with checking through lots of different paper volumes.

Justcite ⁀subscription legal citator
Justcite is an online legal citator which includes Scottish Parliament statutory instruments from **7–90** 1999. Scottish legislation is not listed separately. See para.6.77.

List of Statutory Publications 📖
The *List of Statutory Publications* is published monthly (albeit several months in arrears) by The **7–91** Stationery Office. It includes details of general and local statutory instruments (printed and non-printed) published during the previous month. They are arranged under subject headings and

also listed numerically. The publication is consolidated at the end of a year and appears as an annual *List of Statutory Publications*.

Scottish Parliament and Statutory Publications 📖 and ⌖ free

7–92   This is a bibliography of the Scottish Parliament. It is published by The Stationery Office and available on the Scottish Parliament website. It is intended to be published twice a year (although it is currently behind) and lists both TSO and other publications.

Daily List 📖 and ⌖ free

7–93   The *Daily List* (available at *http://www.tsoshop.co.uk/parliament/*) lists Scottish statutory instruments published by The Stationery Office, see para.8.85.

Scottish Official Daily, Weekly and Monthly Listing ⌖ free

7–94   This lists the publication of Scottish statutory instruments. The *Weekly Listing* is available at *http://www.lib.gla.ac.uk/swop/Astron/AstronWL.html* It is possible to register to receive the listings by emailing your details to registerdetails@rrd.com.

Journals

7–95   Information about very recent Scottish statutory instruments will also be available in journals such as the *Scots Law Times*.

Aids that contain the original version of Scottish statutory instruments

Office of Public Sector Information (OPSI) ⌖ free

7–96   *OPSI* contains the original form of Scottish statutory instruments, see para.7.32.

Statute Law Database ⌖ free

7–97   The *Statute Law Database* contains the original form of Scottish statutory instruments, see para.7.35 for accessing Scottish legislation.

BAILII ⌖ free

7–98   The *BAILII* website contains the original form of Scottish statutory instruments which are located in the Scottish legislation section, see para.7.38.

Justis UK Statutory Instruments ⌖ subscription and CD Rom database

7–99   This contains the original form of Scottish statutory instruments.

Finding a Scottish statutory instrument when only the title is known (i.e. the year and number are not known)

Westlaw ⌖subscription database

7–100   The *legislation* in *Westlaw UK* allows you to search a title field. See para.2.33 for help with using Westlaw's terms and connectors. *Westlaw* also allows you to browse Scottish statutory instruments by title. To do this from the *legislation* search page, scroll down to the bottom of the screen and one of the browse options is to browse by *Jurisdiction: Scottish Parliament*. If you click on this a new search page opens, scroll down to the bottom of the screen to the browse options one of which allows you to browse Scottish statutory instruments alphabetically by title.

LexisNexis Butterworths ⌖ subscription database

7–101   *LexisNexis Butterworths Scottish Parliament SIs* database allows you to search using the *legislation title* field. See para.2.33 for help with using this database's terms and connectors.

Lawtel ⌁ subscription legal current awareness digest service
Lawtel allows you to search by title using the focused search see para.7.87.   **7–102**

Current Law Yearbooks and Monthly Digests ▢
There are alphabetical lists of statutory instruments in the *Current Law Yearbooks* and in the **7–103**
Monthly Digests. The lists will provide you with the year and number of the statutory instrument. The *Current Law Yearbooks* and *Monthly Digests* will only contain a summary of the statutory instrument. In order to trace the full text you will need to take the additional details to one of the sources detailed in the section starting at para.7.73.

Current Law Statutory Instrument Citator ▢
The *Current Law Statutory Instrument Citators* have an alphabetical list at the start of each **7–104**
volume which includes Scottish statutory instruments. Using the citators will enable you to locate the year and number and to check if the instrument has been amended or repealed. If you wish to trace the full text you will need to take the additional details to one of the sources detailed in the section starting at para.7.73.

Current Legal Information ⌁ and CD Rom subscription legal research service
This contains an electronic version of the *Current Law Statutory Instrument Citator*.   **7–105**

The Laws of Scotland: Stair Memorial Encyclopaedia ▢
Check the Consolidated Table of Statutes or, if you know the subject area, go to the individual **7–106**
title. Each title has a list of legislation. See para.8.2.

The Laws of Scotland Online (*Stair Memorial Encyclopaedia*) ⌁
Enter the title of the Scottish statutory instrument as your search term in the commentary search **7–107**
form. See para.8.5.

Subject specialist encyclopaedias ▢
Specialist looseleaf encyclopaedias (para.8.9) and collections of legislation (paras 6.199/6.200) **7–108**
can be searched by Tables of Statutory Instruments or by the subject index. The amount of information you will be able to locate will depend on whether the work includes the full text of the particular instrument.

Sources that contain the original version of Scottish statutory instruments

Office of Public Sector Information (OPSI) ⌁ free
The site contains a *search legislation* function which links to an *advanced search* which allows **7–109**
you to search by keyword and to restrict your search to statutory instruments and to the area being Scotland. See para.7.32.

Statute Law Database ⌁ free
You can search by title or you can browse Scottish statutory instruments alphabetically, see **7–110**
para.7.35.

BAILII ⌁ free
The legislation search allows searching by keyword in the title, dates and jurisdiction. You can **7–111**
restrict your search to Scottish statutory instruments. The advanced search allows Boolean searching. See para.7.38.

Justis UK Statutory Instruments ⌁ subscription and CD Rom database.   **7–112**

Finding Scottish statutory instruments by subject

The Laws of Scotland: Stair Memorial Encyclopaedia 📖

7–113 Check the Consolidated Index. This lists detailed subject headings and will lead you to the relevant volume or reissued title. You can update this information by checking the Annual Cumulative Supplement and the Service Binder. See para.8.2.

The Laws of Scotland Online (Stair Memorial Encyclopaedia) ⏣

7–114 Enter details of the subject area as your search term in the commentary search form. See para.8.5.

Subject specialist encyclopaedias and collections of legislation 📖

7–115 Specialist loose-leaf encyclopaedias (para.8.9) and collections of legislation (paras 6.199/6.200) can be searched by Tables of Statutory Instruments or by the subject index. The amount of information you will be able to locate will depend on whether the encyclopaedia includes the full text of the particular statutory instrument.

Westlaw ⏣ subscription database

7–116 The legislation search in *Westlaw UK* allows you to search by free text search. See para.2.33 for help with using *Westlaw's* terms and connectors. *Westlaw* also allows you to browse Scottish statutory instruments by title, see para.7.100.

LexisNexis Butterworths ⏣ subscription database

7–117 *LexisNexis Butterworths Scottish Parliament SIs* database allows you to search by free text search, see para.7.101. For help with using this database's terms and connectors, see para.2.33.

Lawtel ⏣ subscription legal current awareness digest service

7–118 On the *Lawtel UK* homepage click on *statutory instruments*. Enter your search terms in the box and click *search*. (Alternatively use the *focused search* to search by title.) Click on the link in the search results to the details of the statutory instrument.

Scottish Statutory Instruments 📖

7–119 The index to these annual volumes is arranged by subject. See para.7.74.

Current Law Yearbooks and Monthly Digests 📖

7–120 Check the Yearbooks under the appropriate subject heading. This will provide you with a reference to a paragraph number, see para.8.21. The *Current Law Yearbooks* and *Monthly Digests* will only contain a summary of the statutory instrument. In order to trace the full text you will need to take the additional details to one of the sources detailed in the section starting at para.7.73.

Sources that contain the original version of Scottish statutory instruments

Office of Public Sector Information (OPSI) ⏣ free

7–121 The site contains a *search legislation* function which links to an *advanced search* which allows you to search by keyword and to restrict your search to statutory instruments and to the area being Scotland. See para.7.32.

Statute Law Database ⏣ free

7–122 You can search all statutory instruments by title or you can restrict your search to Scottish statutory instruments. You can use the advanced search to search the text by free text. The results obtained will have the search terms highlighted in the text. See para.7.35.

BAILII ⌖ free
The legislation search allows searching by keyword in the title, dates and jurisdiction. You can **7–123** restrict your search to Scottish statutory instruments. The advanced search allows Boolean searching. The results obtained will have the search terms highlighted in the text. See para.7.38.

Justis UK Statutory Instruments ⌖ subscription and CD Rom database. **7–124**

Current status of Scottish statutory instruments—finding amendment and repeals

Westlaw ⌖ subscription database
Westlaw UK provides the revised form of Scottish statutory instruments which incorporates **7–125** amendments and repeals. It shows when the current version of the instrument was brought into force and provides links to the amending legislation. See para.6.103 for more information about amended legislation in *Westlaw*.

LexisNexis Butterworths ⌖ subscription database
LexisNexis Butterworths Scottish Parliament SIs provides the revised form of legislation which **7–126** incorporates amendments and repeals. An ellipsis (...) indicates that text has been repealed. Square brackets denote text that has been inserted or substituted. Italicised text means that the content is prospectively repealed or substituted. The notes section at the end of each document indicates the changes that have been made to the text.

Lawtel ⌖ subscription legal current awareness digest service
On the *Lawtel UK* homepage click on *statutory instruments*. Enter your search terms in the box **7–127** and click *search*. (Alternatively use the *focused search* to search by title.) Click on the link in the search results to the details of the Scottish statutory instrument. The entry for the instrument has information about amendments and repeals.

Current Law Statutory Instrument Citator 📖
This is part of the *Current Law Legislation Citator* and is the best paper source for locating **7–128** changes to legislation. The principles of searching are covered in paras 6.147–6.150. The only additional issue is to remember that Scottish statutory instruments are listed separately in the citators; they make up the first part of the statutory instrument citator. It can be easy to miss this section which is currently very short in comparison with the UK Parliament section.

Scottish Statutory Instruments 📖
The annual volumes contain tables showing the effect on enactments and previous statutory **7–129** rules or statutory instruments (whether Scottish or not) of the Scottish statutory instruments included in the edition. However, you would also need to check one of the above sources to update your search.

Finding Scottish statutory instruments made under an enabling Act

The sources and search techniques are the same as for UK Parliament statutory instruments, see the section starting at para.6.193.

Finding whether the courts have considered a Scottish statutory instrument

The principles are the same as for UK legislation. See paras 4.92–4.103.

Finding whether any journal articles have been written about a Scottish statutory instrument

The principles are the same as for UK legislation, see section starting at para.6.112.

ACTS OF SEDERUNT AND ACTS OF ADJOURNAL

7–130 Two peculiarly Scottish types of statutory instrument are Acts of Sederunt and Acts of Adjournal. They are pieces of legislation enacted by the Court of Session and the High Court of Justiciary respectively. Acts of Sederunt are rules which govern procedure in the civil courts while Acts of Adjournal concern procedure in Scotland's criminal courts. Prior to devolution they were enacted as statutory instruments by the UK Parliament. Since devolution they have been created as Scottish statutory instruments. This is because their subject matter is devolved namely: procedure in the Scottish civil courts and criminal courts respectively.

Sources of Acts of Sederunt, Acts of Adjournal

Given that they are enacted as types of statutory instruments the relevant sources are the same as for UK statutory instruments prior to devolution (see the section starting at para.6.130) and Scottish statutory instruments from 1999 onwards (see the section starting at para.7.73). In addition, an annotated version of Acts of Sederunt which are currently in force is contained in the vol.2 of the *Parliament House Book* and an annotated version of Acts of Adjournal currently in force is contained in *Renton & Brown's Criminal Procedure Legislation*. Acts of Sederunt and Acts of Adjournal also appear in the *Scots Law Times* when they are enacted. Acts of Sederunt and Acts of Adjournal made after May 2002 can be accessed by the Scottish Courts website. They were included in *Current Law Statutes Annotated* but this ceased from 1991 onwards. The cumulative indexes in *Current Law Yearbooks* and *Monthly Digests* can be searched under 'Act of Sederunt' and 'Act of Adjournal' and this would lead you to a summary of the instrument's content.

COLLECTIONS OF LEGISLATION

Parliament House Book

The *Parliament House Book* contains **revised** legislation covering selected areas of private law and court procedure. It includes both UK and Scottish Parliament legislation. See para.6.199.

Specialised Collections of Legislation

An increasing number of subject-specific collections of legislation which include both UK and Scottish Parliament legislation are now being produced. See para.6.200.

Chapter 8
Information Sources of Relevance to the Scots Lawyer

This chapter contains short sections on a range of information sources of relevance to the Scots lawyer. Some of the sources could be described as exclusively legal but other sources cover many different areas, including law. Many of the information sources are UK–wide and, where this is the case, the Scottish element has been stressed.

INSTITUTIONAL WRITERS

Institutional writings are a closed class of works which have considerable authority. They are **8–1** regarded as the third formal source of Scots law, after legislation and case law. As you will see from the dates of the works given below they were all written a considerable time ago. However, you should not infer that they are unimportant today. They are still taken to represent the law if there is no statute or case law on a point in an area where society's norms have undergone little fundamental change. While it is no longer true to say that the Scots lawyer frequently turns to the works of the Institutional Writers in day to day practice, the influence of these works is still very much with us. In the past they have had considerable influence on the development of case law and the doctrine of judicial precedent means that this will endure long into the future.

The list of Institutional Writers is a closed list in that no new works may be added to it. However, there is no unanimity as to the complete list and you will find that it varies. The most widely accepted institutional works are:

Civil law:
➤ Sir Thomas Craig, *Jus Feudale*, 1603
➤ Andrew McDouall, Lord Bankton, *An Institute of the Laws of Scotland*, 1751
➤ James Dalrymple (Viscount Stair), *The Institutions of the Law of Scotland*, 1681
➤ John Erskine, *An Institute of the Law of Scotland*, 1773
➤ George Joseph Bell, *Commentaries on the Law of Scotland*, 1804 and *Principles of the Law of Scotland*, 1829

Criminal law:
➤ Sir George Mackenzie, *The Laws and Customs of Scotland in Matters Criminal*, 1678
➤ David Hume, *Commentaries on the Law of Scotland Respecting Crimes*, 1797
➤ Archibald Alison, *Principles of the Criminal Law of Scotland*, 1832 and *Practice of the Criminal Law of Scotland*, 1833

LEGAL ENCYCLOPAEDIAS

The Laws of Scotland: Stair Memorial Encyclopaedia

Although there are several encyclopaedias on specific subject areas *The Laws of Scotland: Stair* **8–2** *Memorial Encyclopaedia* (usually referred to as the Stair Memorial Encyclopaedia) is the only modern encyclopaedia which provides a comprehensive narrative statement of the law of

Scotland. It is an important source of information which includes more than 130 titles by over 300 authors. This is a modern work and has no connection with Viscount Stair other than being named in his memory.

The commentary is arranged alphabetically in broad areas of the law and consists of substantial articles (referred to as "titles") on each area. The style of the titles varies as they are written by many different contributors. Each contributor has specialist knowledge of the area of law discussed. Within each area of law, the titles are divided into numbered paragraphs. These are the basis of the referencing system for the encyclopaedia. It is important to remember that references are to the paragraph number not the page number e.g. the European Community dimension to customs and excise law is discussed in Vol.7, paras 1003-1030.

The encyclopaedia is available in both paper and online. The paper version of the encyclopaedia originally consisted of 25 paper volumes which were published between 1986 and 1996. Each volume contains several titles on different topics. Since 1999, 41 titles from the original volumes have been updated and issued as separate booklets. These are stored in binders as opposed to bound volumes. The system of reissuing may cause confusion as the re-issued titles supersede the title in the original bound volume but the bound volume still remains on the library shelf until all titles within it are re-issued. This means that two versions of the same title are available so you have to be careful to check that you are using the most up-to-date version. The material in the reissued booklets is referred to within Stair by the abbreviated form of its title and the paragraph number e.g. the nature of offences against the state is discussed in Crim 531.

Each volume and reissued booklet consists of the following:

> List of Abbreviations;
> Table of Statutes;
> Table of Orders, Rules and Regulations;
> Table of Other Enactments;
> Table of Cases;
> Title(s). In the bound volumes the titles are in alphabetical order of the subject area with each title having its own table of contents;
> Index. At the back of each volume and reissued booklet there is an index. There is one index for each subject title covered.

8–3 The encyclopaedia is kept up to date by an annual Cumulative Supplement published in March. This brings all the volumes up to date to December 31 of the previous year. The Cumulative Supplement contains:

> Table of Statutes;
> Table of Orders, Rules and Regulations;
> Table of Cases;
> Updates on a volume by volume basis followed by updates on the reissued titles in alphabetical order.

Further updating is provided by the looseleaf Service Binder. It contains a Noter-up which amends the Cumulative Supplement and is published in July and November. Changes are listed by volume number and then by subject within the volume followed by the reissued titles. This does not contain new commentary but notes the effects of new case law or legislation. The Service Binder also contains glossaries of Scottish and EC legal terms.

There is a Consolidated Index which is now being published on an annual basis. It is organised in alphabetical order of subject. References are to volume (or reissue abbreviation) and paragraph number. Volume numbers/reissue abbreviations are in bold.

In addition, there are annual volumes of Consolidated Tables of Cases and Consolidated

Tables of Statutes etc. The Table of Cases is listed by first party's name. This is useful for tracing Scottish cases. The Consolidated Tables of Statutes etc. consist of consolidated tables of: Statutes, Orders, Rules and Regulations, EC legislation, Treaties and Conventions and other enactments.

The necessary updating of the encyclopaedia has meant that the paper version is rather cumbersome in comparison to its online form (see para.8.5).

Using the Stair Memorial Encyclopaedia   **8–4**
To search by subject:

Consolidated Index

or

Reissued title or relevant volume (if not reissued)
(identified from contents listed on the spines of volumes or reissue binders)

Update this information by checking

Annual Cumulative Supplement

and update further by checking
Service Binder

➢ Remember that the reissued titles supersede the titles in the volumes and that references are always to paragraph number and not page number.

To access information from a case name:

Consolidated Table of Cases

Relevant title

➢ Remember to check in the Service Binder as it may include more recent cases

To access information by title of statute:

Consolidated Table of Statutes etc.

Relevant title

➢ Remember to check in the Service Binder as it may include more recent legislation.

The Laws of Scotland Online (Stair Memorial Encyclopaedia) 🖰 subscription

8–5 The online version is available from *LexisNexis Butterworths*. The user has the original volumes and reissued titles together with the text of the most recent annual cumulative supplement which is updated bi-monthly. Updating material and original text are on screen together–the updating material appears at the bottom of your screen.

It is possible to search the whole of *Stair* by free text or to limit your search to various titles. You can also use a browse function to open up an alphabetical list of all the titles and link through to your chosen topic.

The online version contains hypertext links that enable you to link between narrative, cases and legislation.

Citation of the Laws of Scotland: Stair Memorial Encyclopaedia

8–6 The style of reference to the *Stair Memorial Encyclopaedia* depends on whether the material is from one of the original volumes or a reissue.

Material in a title in one of the original volumes should be styled: *The Laws of Scotland: Stair Memorial Encyclopaedia,* Vol 6 paras 896-922.

Material in a title that has been reissued should be styled: *The Laws of Scotland: Stair Memorial Encyclopaedia* Criminal Procedure Re-issue, para 183.

Note that there is no need to cite the date of publication given that this encyclopaedia is updated on an ongoing basis.

Halsbury's Laws of England

8–7 *Halsbury's Laws of England* is the equivalent of the *Stair Memorial Encyclopaedia* for English law in that it provides a comprehensive guide to the Law of England—see paras 9.33–9.42.

The Encyclopaedia of the Laws of Scotland (originally known as Green's Encyclopaedia of the Laws of Scotland)

8–8 There were three editions of *The Encyclopaedia of the Laws of Scotland.* The first edition (1896-1904) was published ten years before *Halsbury's Laws of England*. This encyclopaedia drew its inspiration from *Bell's Dictionary and Digest*. The first edition was edited by J. Chisholm. According to the preface of a later edition the aim of the work was to "help the practitioner, and especially the country practitioner who has not at his hand an extensive law library, to see exactly how the law stands on any particular subject." It states that the 2nd edition greatly augmented and enlarged the first edition: "'Noting up' is a process which is beyond all but the laborious and meticulous few. The ordinary practising lawyer has neither the heart nor the leisure for such as task."

The second edition (1909-14), also edited by J. Chisholm, ran to 12 volumes and contained short sections on topics which ran in alphabetical order. An example of the different topics is: accounts; accretion; accumulation; accumulation of prisoners; accusation, false; acids, throwing; acknowledgement; *a coelo usque ad centrum* etc. The third edition (1926–35) was edited by Viscount Dunedin and ran to 15 volumes. This edition gathered topics together to a greater extent e.g. "acids, throwing" now appeared under "crime". Following its publication there were a number of supplementary volumes issued. The final updating was an appendix to the supplement published in 1949 and it brought the law up to 30th June 1952.

Looseleaf Encyclopaedias

8–9 There are now an increasing number of specialist encyclopaedias covering a variety of subjects. They tend to contain a mixture of legislation and narrative and can be extremely useful sources of information. They also tend to be produced as looseleaf publications which are updated regularly. They, therefore, have an advantage over books. However, you should always make sure that you check the date of the most recent update. This is usually indicated at the beginning of the work. Looseleaf publications are updated by the removal of out-of-date pages and the insertion of new pages. It is not uncommon to find that pages have been misfiled. Great care should therefore be taken when consulting such publications to ensure that you are looking at the most current edition issued. Examples of specialist encyclopaedias include: Armour on Valuation for Rating; Butterworth's Scottish Family Law Service; Employment Tribunal Practice in Scotland; Encyclopaedia of Health & Safety at Work; Garner's Environmental Law; Harvey on Industrial Relations and Employment; McEwan & Paton on Damages for Personal Injuries in Scotland; Renton & Brown's Criminal Procedure; Scottish Planning Encyclopedia; and Sentencing Practice.

REFERENCE WORKS

Reference works can provide a useful starting point for your research. They tend to cover a **8–10** broad area and therefore will not contain too much detail on each subject. However, they are ideal for providing a context to your research even though they may only mention the particular issue briefly. The text (and accompanying footnotes) should provide you with sufficient material to act as a launch pad for your research and point you in the right direction. You will probably need to update the information they contain as these major works do not tend to be updated that frequently.

Reference works tend to run to many editions and it is important to make sure that you use the most up to date edition. Examples are Gloag & Henderson, *An Introduction to the Laws of Scotland* 12th edn (Edinburgh: W.Green due to publish in 2007) and D.M. Walker, *Principles of Scottish Private Law* 4th edn (Oxford: Clarendon Press, 1988). D.M. Walker's *Legal History of Scotland* runs to seven volumes and is a detailed narrative account of the history of the Scottish legal system. D.M. Walker's earlier work, the *Oxford Companion to Law* (Oxford: Clarendon Press, 1980), is a single volume work which is becoming increasingly dated but is still useful, particularly as a starting point for a literature search.

CURRENT LAW DATA RETRIEVAL SYSTEM

Current Law has the most comprehensive range of information available in one paper data- **8–11** retrieval system and is widely available throughout Scotland. It is an important and useful source of information. It covers legal developments since 1948 and is updated monthly.

Using *Current Law* can be confusing at first because of all the component parts but it is worth persevering and mastering the system. When you become familiar with it, it becomes a very efficient way of checking certain types of legal information. However, it does require the user to have an appreciation of how the various component parts organised and it is essential to adopt a systematic approach to searching them. If you do, you will find that you can retrieve information faster with this paper source than with many of the electronic databases.

That is not to say that the system is without its faults. Over the years as the system has expanded **8–12** and incorporated more information, the format has changed in minor but significant ways. There is very little information about the various changes and this can be confusing. The proliferation of volumes in recent years is regrettable as it makes searching more cumbersome and means that you can not carry out a systematic search if any of the volumes is missing from the library shelves. Another criticism is that the classification of material into subject headings can sometimes leave a lot to be desired. You often need to check under several different headings, e.g. water pollution material could be classed under water, environmental protection, pollution or utilities. It is also true to say that the subject headings are not used consistently. If there is no relevant material for that month then the heading disappears. However, despite these criticisms *Current Law* is an invaluable tool to the legal researcher.

8–13 Prior to 1991 the *Current Law* service was provided in two formats: (a) Scottish *Current Law* and (b) *Current Law*. The Scottish *Current Law* service included the English and Welsh service. The *Current Law* service excluded all purely Scottish material. From 1991 the service has been called *Current Law* and now covers the law of England and Wales, Northern Ireland, Scotland and the EC.

    Current Law is referred to throughout this book in the appropriate chapters and these are shown in relation to the various component parts of this system:

> ➢ Monthly Digests (see paras 8.15–8.20)
> ➢ Yearbooks (see paras 8.21–8.22)
> ➢ Case Citators (see paras 4.34–4.38)
> ➢ Legislation Citators (see paras 6.69–6.75)
> ➢ *Current Law* Statutes (see paras 6.63–6.64)
> ➢ Statutes Service Files (see paras 8.22–8.23)
> ➢ European *Current Law*: European *Current Law* Monthly Digest (see para.10.28)
> ➢ European *Current Law*: Yearbook (see para.10.28)

Points of note:

> ➢ Matters applicable to the UK generally are included in the English section of *Current Law*. Scots lawyers should not just look at the Scottish section.
> ➢ *Current Law* uses a system of references to apply to its various constituent parts. The references appear in the form, *e.g.* 82/4292. The numbers represent the year/paragraph number and not the page number.

8–14 Some components of the *Current Law* service are available as parts of *Current Legal Information* which is an online and CD Rom subscription legal research service. The CD Rom version is updated monthly while the on-line version is updated on a daily basis. *Current Legal Information* cannot at present be regarded as a replacement for the paper version of *Current Law* as it only has a limited number of components and the time periods covered are different e.g. the legislation citator section only covers back to 1989 compared to the paper version which covers back to 1948.

MONTHLY DIGESTS

8–15 Monthly Digests provide a monthly updating service. Each issue is divided into two parts, Cases, Legislation, Books and Materials and Tables:

Cases, Legislation, Books and Materials

The subject headings covered in *Current Law* are listed at the beginning of each Monthly Digest. Not every subject heading will appear in every issue. The subject areas covered in the issue are printed in bold type.

➢ *Table of Abbreviations.* This is a good place to look for new abbreviations. It covers whatever is included in that issue of the Monthly Digest.

➢ *Current Law Notes.* These are brief notes arranged under subject headings. They are designed to provide an overview of recent developments in different fields of law. There is a separate section of *Current Law* Notes (Scotland).

➢ *Digest.* The material is arranged alphabetically by subject. The material consists of summaries of developments in the law such as cases, legislation, government department circulars, books and articles. The subject headings are divided into three sections:

⇒ UK, England & Wales and the EU
⇒ Northern Ireland
⇒ Scotland

Tables

A series of tables cover the following:

➢ *Quantum of damages* provides cumulative information on quantum of damages in personal injuries cases reported in the current year. Information is given in tabular form under five headings: injury, age, case, award and reference. Scottish cases are in a separate table, following the table relating to English cases.

➢ *European law* details subject areas covering cases heard in the European Court of Justice and the Court of First Instance and European legislation which is digested in that month's digest.

➢ *Words and phrases judicially considered* is a cumulative guide to words and phrases which have been judicially considered throughout the year.

➢ *Guide to civil proceedings fees* relates to the English High Court and the County Court.

➢ *Guide to family proceedings fees* relate to the English High Court and the County Court.

➢ *Progress of Bills* covers Bills in the current parliamentary session at the UK Parliament and is complete to a date given at the top of the page. Government Bills are given in bold. The word "Commons" or "Lords" appears after the Bill's name to show where the Bill originated.

➢ *Scottish Progress of Bills* covers Bills in the current parliamentary session at the Scottish Parliament and is complete to a date given at the top of the page. Government Bills are given in bold.

➢ *Progress of Bills (Northern Ireland).*

➢ *Royal Assent.* There are separate tables for England/Wales, Scotland and Northern Ireland.

➢ *Dates of commencement* gives dates of commencement and details of the instrument that brought the statute into force.

➢ *Alphabetical Table of Statutory Instruments* is a cumulative alphabetical list of statutory instruments digested in the current year.

➢ *Alphabetical Table of Scottish Statutory Instruments* is a cumulative alphabetical list of Scottish statutory instruments digested in the current year.

➢ *European legislation implemented by Statutory Instrument* European legislation implemented by statutory instruments issued in the current year is listed in chronological order.

➢ *European legislation implemented by Scottish Statutory Instrument* European legislation implemented by Scottish statutory instruments issued in the current year is listed in chronological order.

➢ *Table of Transcripts subsequently reported* is a cumulative list of cases recently digested in *Current Law* as transcripts and subsequently reported elsewhere.

➢ *Table of cases* is cumulative and is in alphabetical order. It covers cases which have been digested or judicially considered in the current year. Cases which have been digested are in CAPITAL LETTERS. Cases which have been judicially considered or commented on are in normal print.

➢ *Cumulative index arranged alphabetically within subject headings.* Scottish entries are followed by an "S". The subject headings used here are greater in number and more specific than the broad subject headings in the Cases, Legislation, Books and Materials section.

➢ *Legal publications* (reference to books can also be found under relevant subject headings) includes books published that month which are arranged in alphabetical order of author.

8–16 Excerpt from Monthly Digest Sept 1998 P. 198–199, Legal Aid, with features marked

---

[1]
LEGAL AID
693. Criminal legal aid — solicitors — employment [2]
SCOTTISH LEGAL AID BOARD (EMPLOYMENT OF SOLICITORS TO PROVIDE CRIMINAL LEGAL ASSISTANCE) REGULATIONS 1998, SI 1998 1938 (S.101); **[3]**
[4]   **[5]**
made under the Legal Aid (Scotland) Act 1986 s.28A, s.37. In force: October 1, 1998; £1.10. These Regulations provide for solicitors to be employed by the Scottish Legal Aid Board to give criminal legal assistance and to be used in the Sheriff Court district of Edinburgh. **[6]**

694. Expenses — modification — personal liability of legal aided person — competency of appeal [7]
[Legal Aid (Scotland) Act 1986 (c.47) s.18(2).] **[8]**
In an action between two legally aided parties G was found liable in expenses.
The sheriff also refused G's motion under the Legal Aid (Scotland) Act 1986 s.18(2) to modify his personal liability for expenses. G appealed seeking an order that the matter of modification be remitted to the sheriff for reconsideration. **[9]**
Held, refusing the appeal, that (1) where a sheriff might have erred in law it was incompetent for a sheriff principal to remit the case to the sheriff, and (2) it was not competent for an appellate court to review a decision on the modification of expenses, *Todd v. Todd* 1966 S.L.T. 50, [1966] C.L.Y. 13387 followed. **[10]**
Observed, that *Todd v. Todd* was not consistent with sound policy or the terms of the statute and ought to be reviewed by a larger court. ORTTEWELL v. GILCHRIST 1998 S.C.L.R. 451, CGB Nicholson Q.C., Sheriff Principal, Sh Ct. **[11]**

695. Articles [12]
[13] No entry! No access! No justice!: J.L.S.S. 1998, 43(7) Supp, 2–3. (Proposed changes to civil legal aid scheme and implications of alternative means of funding litigation). **[14]**

Key:

[1] Subject heading
[2] Subject matter, catchphrases appear in bold
[3] Title and citation of a statutory instrument
[4] Enabling legislation
[5] Date brought into force

[6] Digest of contents
[7] Subject matter, catchphrases appear in bold
[8] Relevant legislation [in square brackets]
[9] Facts
[10] *Ratio decidendi*
[11] Case name and citation
[12] Subject matter in bold
[13] Title of article and reference
[14] Summary of contents

Searching the Monthly Digest

Points to note: 8–17

> ➢ All indexes are cumulative and they refer to the relevant paragraph in the Monthly Digest in which the item is mentioned. This means that you should always check the most recent issue of the Monthly Digest as it will contain information which will allow you to access all the material for the current year.
> ➢ Scottish items are identified by the letter "S" after the *Current Law* paragraph number.
> ➢ Matters applicable to the UK generally are included in the English section of *Current Law*.
> ➢ Not all digest headings are used in each Monthly Digest. They are not used if there is no current information.
> ➢ You will notice that the Monthly Digests use two different referencing systems. This can result in the same reference being given in two different ways in the same volume. The Monthly Digest index refers to previous Monthly Digests as, e.g. Mar 442, i.e. month and paragraph number, whereas other indexes in the Monthly Digest, e.g. alphabetical list of statutory instruments refer to them as 373 3CL, i.e. paragraph and volume number for the Monthly Digest.

How to find out about recent developments on a particular subject

To find out about developments over the last month: 8–18
   Check the relevant subject heading in the latest Monthly Digest. This will tell you if anything has happened over the last month. If the subject heading does not appear it means that there have been no developments in the area for that month.

To find out about developments over the current year: 8–19

⇒ **Step 1**: Check the relevant subject heading in the cumulative index at the back of the latest Monthly Digest. This will refer you to the month and paragraph number, *e.g.* Mar 403. If you are looking for Scottish information the references will be followed by the letter "S".
⇒ **Step 2**: Turn to the March monthly Digest at para.403 and you will find the information.

How to find a recent Scottish article on a subject   8–20

⇒ **Step 1**: Go to the latest issue of the Monthly Digest.
⇒ **Step 2**: Check the cumulative index under the subject heading. Various sub-headings will exist and will be listed alphabetically. Check under "articles". You will see various references. If any of the references is followed by an "S", you know that the article is Scottish.

⇒ **Step 3**:   Turn to the entry referred to and you will find details of the article.

!Example

Find the latest Scottish article on administration of justice.

⇒ **Step 1**: Check the latest Monthly Digest (April 2007);

⇒ **Step 2**: Check the cumulative index under the subject heading "administration of justice". Within the heading "administration of justice." locate the sub-category "articles". Check at the end of the list to find the latest items. You are looking for the latest reference followed by the letter "S". The reference given is Apr510S.

⇒ **Step 3**: Check para.510S in the April issue of the Monthly Digest. It gives details of an article by Robert Shiels called "The Demise of Lord Glenalmond", S.L.T. 2007 8, 49-52.

CURRENT LAW YEARBOOKS

8–21 These are annual volumes which revise and consolidate the Monthly Digests. Items may be regrouped and re-edited. They are not usually available until the middle of the following year. The Yearbooks are arranged by subject and contain summaries of all legal developments for that year. Over the years the format of the Yearbooks has changed, the current format (published in two volumes since 1995) is detailed below:

➢ Digest Headings in Use
➢ Table of Cases
➢ Table of Quantum of damages cases (with a separate table for Scottish cases)
➢ Alphabetical List of Statutory Instruments for the Year
➢ List of Statutory Instruments arranged alphabetically by subject headings
➢ Numerical Table of Statutory Instruments for the Year
➢ Alphabetical Table of Northern Ireland Statutory Rules and Orders
➢ Numerical Table of Northern Ireland Statutory Rules and Orders
➢ Alphabetical Table of Scottish Statutory Instruments
➢ Numerical Table of Scottish Statutory Instruments
➢ Table of Abbreviations
➢ The Law summarised under Subject Headings—UK, England and Wales and EU
➢ The Law summarised under Subject Headings—Northern Ireland
➢ The Law summarised under Subject Headings—Scotland
➢ Words and Phrases Table
➢ Law Books published during the Year
➢ Index

Searching in the Yearbooks

8–22 If you are searching for a particular topic you should check under the appropriate subject heading. Under the subject heading you will find a reference consisting of a year and a paragraph number, *e.g.* 96/6674S. You would locate the material in the 1996 Yearbook at para.6674. The "S" denotes that it is Scottish material.

If you know the approximate date you can check the appropriate Yearbook. If you do not know the date then you do not have to check every Yearbook—in some key volumes the subject index has been consolidated at various times. Unfortunately it is now some time since the last consolidation:

1956 Scottish *Current Law* Yearbook Master Volume	contains entries for 1948–56
1961 Scottish *Current Law* Yearbook Master Volume	contains entries for 1957–61
1966 Scottish *Current Law* Yearbook Master Volume	contains entries for 1962–66
1971 Scottish *Current Law* Yearbook Master Volume	contains entries for 1967–71
1986 Scottish *Current Law* Yearbook	contains entries for 1972–86
1990 Scottish *Current Law* Yearbook	contains entries for 1987–90
From 1991 onwards each Yearbook should be checked.	contain entries for each year
You should then check the latest Monthly Digest.	contains entries for current year

N.B. The English version has been consolidated at different times.

!Example

Find out if there have been any developments in the law of succession in Scotland since 2003.

⇒ **Step 1**: Check the 2004 Yearbook in the Scottish section under "Succession".
⇒ **Step 2**: Check the 2005 Yearbook in the Scottish section under "Succession".
⇒ **Step 3**: Check the December issue of the Monthly Digest for 2006 in the index under the subject heading "Succession" and look for references followed by an "S". Once the 2006 Yearbook is issued you would check in there instead of this step.
⇒ **Step 4**: Check the latest issue of the Monthly Digest for the current year in the index under the subject heading "Succession" and look for references followed by an "S".

CURRENT LAW STATUTES SERVICE FILES

The Statutes Service Files allow access to a vast amount of information about recent legislative **8–23** developments. They are structured as follows:

➤ *Contents* section which includes:
⇒ Chronological table of Public General Acts which have received Royal Assent in the current year.
⇒ Chronological table of Private Acts which have received Royal Assent in the current year.
⇒ A list of recent White Papers and Green Papers.
⇒ Separate cumulative Progress of Bills Tables for Public General Bills and Private Bills.
⇒ A cumulative Table of Hansard references for Public Bills and Private Members' Bills currently before Parliament.
➤ *Legislation Not Yet in Force.* This table lists alphabetically statutes which have been published in *Current Law* and remain on the statute book but which, in whole or in part, are not yet in force and for which no coming-into-force date has yet been fixed.
➤ *Subject index* covering all Acts in the current year.
➤ *Statute Citator cumulative monthly updates.* Acts of the Scottish Parliament followed by Acts of the UK Parliament. This is the part you should use to update a search in the Statute Citator part of the Legislation Citator volumes.
➤ *Statutory Instrument Citator cumulative monthly updates.* Statutory Instruments issued by the Scottish Parliament followed by Statutory Instruments issued by the UK Parliament. This is the part you should use to update a search in the Statutory Instrument Citator part of the Legislation Citator volumes.

> *Alphabetical Table of Public General Acts* 1700–present. This table is cumulative and is updated each year.
> *Chronological Table of Statutes* (1267–present).
> *Table of Parliamentary Debates* (1950–present). This lists Hansard references for substantive debates in both the House of Commons and the House of Lords for Public General Acts 1950–present.
> *Commencement* Orders. This section includes the Commencement Diary which notes alphabetically by statute the commencement of statutes from January of the current year as initiated by Orders and by statutory provisions. This section also includes a chronological table of European legislation implemented by statutory instrument. Commencement Orders issued appear in chronological order.
> *Alphabetical Table of Statutory Instruments*. This table lists all statutory instruments published in the current year.
> *The full text of Public General Acts.*
> *The full text of Private Acts.*
> *The full text of Acts of the Scottish Parliament.*

DICTIONARIES

8–24 Language is the everyday tool of the lawyer and the precise meaning of words is very important. General English dictionaries are used but there are two types of dictionary which are more important for lawyers. Judicial dictionaries of words and phrases contain definitions given to words by the judiciary and legislation. You would consult a judicial dictionary to find out how a certain word has been legally defined. A legal dictionary (often referred to as a glossary) seeks to explain technical legal terms in a way that can be understood by the student or lay person. It is important to remember that while legal dictionaries provide guidance they are not authoritative.

Judicial dictionaries

8–25 Scottish
   Scottish Contemporary Judicial Dictionary of Words & Phrases by W.J. Stewart (Edinburgh: W.Green, 1995). This is a dictionary of words and phrases interpreted by the Scottish courts. It claims to cover every case in which a word has been judicially considered between 1946 and 1993.
   Scottish Judicial Dictionary: Dictionary of Words & Phrases by A.W. Dalrymple and A.D. Gibb (Edinburgh: W.Green, 1946). This work is a dictionary of words and phrases interpreted by the Scottish supreme courts (not the sheriff court) between 1800–1944.

8–26 United Kingdom
   Stroud's Judicial Dictionary of Words and Phrases 7th edn (London: Sweet & Maxwell, 2006). This work consists of three volumes which are updated by annual cumulative supplements.
   Words and Phrases Legally Defined. The third edition of this work was published in four volumes in 1988/89 and it is also updated by supplements.

Tip: you should update any search carried out in the above dictionaries by checking their date of publication and using the Words and Phrases Tables in the *Current Law Yearbooks* and *Monthly Digests*, *Halsbury's Laws* or *The Law Reports Index* to bring the search up to the present.
   It is now possible to search electronic databases for particular words and phrases (see paras 4.90–4.91). However, when searching a database you will retrieve results of every time a word or phrase occurs in a case which will be considerably greater than the number of times when they are actually considered by the courts.

Legal dictionaries/glossaries

Scottish   **8–27**

The classic dictionary of Scots law is *Bell's Dictionary and Digest of the Law of Scotland* 7th edn (1890). More modern works include:

> ➤ *Glossary of Legal Terms* by S.R. O'Rourke 4th edn (Edinburgh: W. Green, 2004)
> ➤ *Glossary: Scottish and European Union Legal Terms and Latin Phrases* S. Styles (ed) 2nd edn (Edinburgh: Law Society of Scotland, LexisNexis UK, 2003)
> ➤ *Latin Maxims & Phrases* by J. Trayner 4th edn (Edinburgh: W. Green, 1993).

Online dictionaries include:

> ➤ *Scottish Courts website* (*http://www.scotcourts.gov.uk*) contains a useful glossary of more common Scottish legal terms. It is contained in a pdf file accessible by going to the professional section of the site, clicking on *leaflets and guidance materials* on the top left of the page, and then scroll down to the link to the glossary.
> ➤ *Oxford Reference Online* is a subscription service through which many libraries subscribe to the online *A Dictionary of Law*.
> ➤ *Collins Dictionary of Law* W.J.Stewart & R. Burgess 3rd ed (London: Harper Collins, 2006) covers in the law in England, Wales, Scotland and Ireland and is available in paper and as an e-book.
> ➤ *Lawdictionaries.com* (*http://www.lawdictionaries.com/*) contains links to various free online legal dictionaries arranged under the headings: general law; commercial law; crime/human rights; family law/alternative dispute resolution; and international law & other. The general law section includes a Scots law glossary.

English   **8–28**

Jowitt's Dictionary of English Law 2nd edn (London: Sweet & Maxwell 1977) consisted of two volumes published in 1977. There is a 1985 supplement. Other, shorter dictionaries include: *Osborn's Concise Law Dictionary*, M. Woodley 10th edn (London: Sweet & Maxwell, 2005); *Mozley and Whiteley's Law Dictionary*, J.E. Penner 12th edn, (2001); *Dictionary of Law*, L.B. Curzon 6th edn (Harlow: Longman, 2002); and *A Dictionary of Law,* Elizabeth A. Martin and Jonathan Law 6th edn (Oxford: OUP, 2006).

Online dictionaries include:
Her Majesty's Court Service (*http://www.hmcourts-service.gov.uk/infoabout/glossary/index.htm*) contains two glossaries. One contains English legal terms and the other is an explanation of common Latin terms.

LAW BOOKS AND SEARCH STRATEGIES FOR LAW BOOKS

Different types of law books

There are several different types of law books:

Textbooks

Textbooks aim to provide the student with an introduction to an area of law. They are designed **8–29** to be user friendly and to make the law accessible. They explain key concepts and put the law in context with discussion of the background of the current law and usually discuss possible future developments. Textbooks tend to be produced in several editions in order to keep up with changes in the law. It is very important to ensure that you have the most up-to-date text. A second hand book may seem like a bargain but if it is an out-of-date edition it is useless to you. If you use out-of-date information sources as a solicitor you will be negligent and as a student you will lose marks.

Casebooks (sometimes called Cases and Materials texts) are a type of textbook. These books contain excerpts from legal materials such as cases, legislation, articles, books and official reports accompanied by commentary which discusses the excerpts and places them in context. They are designed to be portable "mini libraries" about a specific subject. However, when you are recommended to read cases or other materials it is better practice to read the primary materials themselves as casebooks only contain short excerpts from the materials.

In recent years there has been an increase in the publication of revision guides designed to help students prepare for exams. There are currently two series dedicated to Scots law: *Law-Basics* and *Essentials*. These types of book will not contain sufficient depth to serve as a main text for a course but can be useful as an aid to revision for exams especially for students who are short of time. It is however, far better practice to prepare your own revision notes from which to revise. This is because they will be based on the actual course as taught and will contain the relevant emphasis and nuances.

Monographs

8–30 Monographs are different from textbooks in that they assume a certain amount of knowledge and will discuss an area of law in greater depth. They vary but they will tend to move away from black letter law and consider policy issues or theoretical debates in the area of law. You would consult a monograph to obtain detailed information after an initial literature search.

Practitioner texts

8–31 Practitioner texts are designed principally for use by the legal profession. They will therefore assume a certain amount of prior knowledge. They contain detailed discussion of the particular area of law and tend to adopt a more practical, rather than theoretical, approach. A particular type of practitioner text is a styles book. These are works which contain "styles" (templates) for different types of legal documents commonly encountered by solicitors. These are also relevant to students studying for the Diploma in Legal Practice. Styles are now contained in many different works e.g. *Greens Practice Styles*.

Features of law books

8–32 Law books contain certain unique features which help the researcher find information. These features include:

> ➢ A statement (usually in the *preface*) of a date up to which the law can be taken as accurate. It is very important that you are aware of this date. It alerts you to the period from which you will have to update your research. The timescale of the publishing process means that most law books are at least six months out of date on the day they are published. You will always need to update information found in a book.
> ➢ *Table of abbreviations.* This will give you the meaning of any abbreviations used in the text.
> ➢ *Table of cases.* This lists all the cases referred to in the text in alphabetical order of the first named party. If you want to find discussion of a case, check this table and it will refer you to the relevant part of the text.
> ➢ *Tables of legislation.* This is a chronological list of all the statutes/ statutory instruments referred to in the text. This means that if you want to search for discussion of a specific piece of legislation, you can check this table and it will refer you to the relevant page of the text.

Finding legal books

The first source of details about law books will be your course materials. They will identify and **8–33** recommend particularly relevant reading for your course. As you research more material for yourself you should find details of books from textbooks, general reference works and ency- clopaedias. Their details will be contained in bibliographies at the end of the book, lists of further reading at the end of chapters or in footnotes throughout the book. In order to search beyond this level you can find out about books on a certain subject by searching your library catalogue using a keyword search. It is also now easy to search other university libraries via the internet. COPAC (*http://www.copac.ac.uk/*) provides free access to the merged online catalogues of major UK and Irish academic research libraries as well as the British Library and the National Library of Scotland.

Some libraries are libraries of deposit which means that by law they receive a copy of every book **8–34** that is published in the UK. These libraries will have even more comprehensive collections than university libraries. The National Library of Scotland (see para.8.37) is one of the libraries of deposit under the Legal Deposit Libraries Act 2003. The Advocates Library was the precursor of the National Library of Scotland and has retained its copyright privileges for law publica- tions when it gifted its non-law collections to the nation. The Advocates Library (which was inaugurated in 1689) therefore has a copy of every law book published in the UK. It is possible to search the catalogue of the Advocates library online at *http://voyager.advocates.org.uk/*. It can be searched by title, author, subject and journal title. This is a very useful source of information about legal materials.

Other useful online sources of information about legal books are websites of legal booksellers **8–35** and publishers. Legal booksellers online catalogues include: Avizandum (*http://www. avi- zandum.com/absHome.htm*); Hammock's Legal Bookshop (*http://www.hammickslegal. com/*) and Wildy & Sons Ltd (*http://www.wildy.com/*). Amazon (*http://www.amazon.co.uk/*) is a good source of information about books in general which has a particularly useful feature of allowing the table of contents to be browsed on selected books. Individual publishers' catalogues can also be helpful e.g. W.Green (*http://www.wgreen.co.uk/*), Tottel (*http://www.tottel publishing.com/*) and Oxford University Press (*http://www.oup.co.uk/*). However, the advantage of searching libraries instead of bookshops is that they include books which may be out of print as compared with bookshops/publishers who will only list in print titles.

Legal bibliographies

Another way of finding out about books on legal topics is to search a legal bibliography. They **8–36** contain lists of books grouped under subject headings. Examples of legal bibliographies are:

➢ D. Raistrick, *Lawyers' Law Books* 3rd edn (London: Bowker Saur, 1997). This contains bibliographical listings by subject. It includes encyclopaedias, periodicals and texts. It concentrates on UK legal literature but does include material relating to other legal jurisdictions. There is a section on Scots law and various Scots terms appear, *e.g.* delict. However, this book is obviously becoming out of date.

➢ *Information Sources in Law*, J. Winterton and E.M. Moys (eds.) 2nd edn (London: Bowker Saur, 1997). This book is designed to provide a starting point for research in an unfamiliar area. It contains chapters written by information specialists in many dif- ferent areas ranging from the law of the EU, Albania, Austria to Turkey and the states of the former Yugoslavia.

➢ *Scottish Current Law Yearbooks* and *Monthly Digests* contain details of books and articles. There is a list of law books published during the year at the end of the

Yearbooks. The Monthly Digests are a useful way of finding out about recent publications.

➤ For information about older Scottish material: *An Introductory Survey of the Sources and Literature of Scots Law*, Publication of the Stair Society, No. 1, Stair Society, Edinburgh, 1936. Information on older UK material: Sweet & Maxwell's *Legal Bibliography of the British Commonwealth of Nations* 2nd edn (London: Sweet & Maxwell, 1957). Volume 5 covers Scots law up to 1956.

➤ *Law Books and Serials in Print.* This three volume work gives details of books published in English and currently in print. It currently includes 131,706 titles.

The Stair Society was instituted in 1934 to encourage the study and to advance the knowledge of the history of Scots law. The society publishes legal history materials which are listed on their website (*http://www.stairsociety.org/pubs.htm*). The website also contains a useful section of legal history links (*http://www.stairsociety.org/links.htm*).

There are many specialist legal bibliographies, *e.g.* E. Beyerly, *Public International Law: A Guide to Information Sources* (London: Mansell, 1991) (see para.11.19).

General bibliographic sources

8–37 The following works are sources of general bibliographic information including legal materials:

➤ *Bibliography of Scotland.* This is a database of material that has been written about Scotland. It excludes material published in Scotland if it has no Scottish content. It includes books, serials and periodical articles. It is possible to search by author, title, subject and keyword. Information from 1976–1987 is available in annual printed volumes. It is available online (free access) from 1988 onwards:
http://sbo.nls.uk/cgi-bin/Pwebrecon.cgi?DB=local&PAGE=First

➤ *National Library of Scotland* Main *Catalogue.* It is possible to search the catalogue of printed books online. The site currently contains over three million records and covers printed material acquired by the library since 1801. It is possible to search by author, title, subject and keyword. *http://main-cat.nls.uk/cgi-bin/Pwebrecon.cgi?DB=local&PAGE=First*

➤ *British National Bibliography.* This is a complete listing of all books published in the UK since 1950 which have been received and catalogued by the British Library. UK and Irish publishers are obliged by law to send a copy of all new publications, including serial titles, to the British library and this is therefore a comprehensive listing. It references all books regardless of whether or not the work is in print. Note that official publications are not included. It is available as a weekly paper publication or a monthly CD Rom. The CD Rom has sophisticated search facilities and you can search by names, titles and keywords.

➤ *British Books In Print* This lists all books published in the UK and still in print. The current edition is 2006, lists 1.9 million titles and consists of six bound volumes.

➤ *Global Books In Print* is a US online subscription service (*GlobalBooksInPrint.com*) and features over 14.8 million English and Spanish-language titles.

➤ *Books in Print* features books currently published or distributed in the United States. The current edition is 2006-07. It is published in eight bound volumes and is also available on CD Rom and online by subscription (*BooksInPrint.com*)

THESES

Theses which have been awarded by your university will usually be available to look at in the **8–38** library.

You can locate theses by checking the *Index to Theses* which is a subscription website (*http://www.theses.com/*). This contains details and abstracts (from 1986 and where provided by the institution) of theses accepted for higher degrees in Great Britain and Ireland. The online version now covers the period from 1716 to the present. In order to read a copy of a thesis you will have to apply to borrow it through the inter-library loan scheme. An alternative is to contact the relevant university directly.

Legal Research in the United Kingdom 1905–1984 is a classified list of postgraduate legal theses and dissertations accepted by UK institutions (published in 1985 by the Institute of Advanced Legal Studies, London).

LEGAL JOURNALS

There are many different types of legal journals (sometimes called periodicals) and they are **8–39** available in different formats and produced at different times and frequencies. Journals tend to be aimed at different audiences (e.g. practitioner, academic and student) and tailored accordingly. The practitioner journals tend to be published frequently and aim to provide a current awareness service as well as practical information about the law. Academic journals tend to be published less frequently and contain lengthy articles about more theoretical issues. Student journals contain short articles on recent legal developments.

Some journals are general in that they contain information on all areas of law. Others are restricted to one area. Journals also cater for different legal jurisdictions. There are Scottish legal journals, UK legal journals and journals which cover European and International law.

There is no standard format for a legal journal. Some journals are produced as a collection of **8–40** scholarly articles and are reasonably large publications, while others are slim updating services. Most of the journals are published in parts (called issues) which are subsequently consolidated into annual volumes. Some legal journals are only published electronically but the majority are still paper-based although an increasing number are available electronically from different sources.

In the law library, legal journals will be stored in alphabetical order. Usual practice is to separate the current edition from back issues of the journal. The latest editions will be placed where they are designed to be browsed. Older editions will be shelved elsewhere.

Scottish journals aimed at the profession:

Journal of the Law Society of Scotland (J.L.S.S.) (1956–)	published monthly	*Contents*: professional information, articles, book reviews, news features, letters and interviews.
Scots Law Times (S.L.T.) (1893–)	published weekly	*Contents*: Articles, Acts of Adjournal/Sederunt, appointments, book reviews, business changes, case commentaries, coming events, general information, law reports,

		letters, parliamentary news, and taxation.
Scottish Law Gazette (S.L.G.) (1933–)	published every second month by the Council of the Scottish Law Agents Society	*Contents*: articles, news, book reviews and book information.

English journals aimed at the profession

These include: *New Law Journal, Solicitors' Journal* and the *Law Society Gazette*. These are all published weekly.

Scottish academic journals include:

Juridical Review (J.R.) (1889–)	published four times a year	*Contents:* articles, analysis of current legal developments and notes on cases.
Edinburgh Law Review (EdinLR) (1996–)	published three times a year	*Contents:* articles, significant developments in the law and book reviews.

English academic journals include:

Law Quarterly Review (L.Q.R.) (1885–)	published six times a year
Modern Law Review (M.L.R.) (1937–)	published six times a year
Cambridge Law Journal (C.L.J.) (1921–)	published every four months
Oxford Journal of Legal Studies (O.J.L.S.)	published quarterly

Specialist journals published in Scotland include:

Scottish Planning and Environmental Law (S.P.E.L.) (1993–) (formerly Scottish Planning Law and Practice)	published six times a year	
SCOLAG (Scottish Legal Action Group) (1975–)	published monthly	This monthly journal contains articles, law updates and book reviews.
Green's Business Law Bulletin Green's Civil Practice Bulletin, Green's Criminal Law Bulletin, Green's Employment Law Bulletin, Green's Family Law Bulletin, Green's Property Law Bulletin,	All published every two months	These are short updating bulletins which contain commentary about recent cases and legal developments.

UK-wide specialist journals include: *British Journal of Criminology, Journal of Law and Society,* and the *Criminal Law Review*.

There are legal journals which are aimed at students. There include: the *Cambridge Student Law Review* (*http://www.cslr.org.uk/*); and the *Student Law Journal* (*http://www.studentlaw journal.com/home.htm*).

An example of an electronic legal journal is the *Journal of Information Law & Technology*

(J.I.L.T.) (1996–). This is available free: *http://www2.warwick.ac.uk/fac/soc/law/elj/jilt/*. It covers topics relating to information technology law and IT applications in law.

Finding articles in legal journals

Finding legal journal articles can cause students problems. This is because university holdings of **8–41** journals are, by necessity, selective and there is no one electronic source of legal journal articles. Although searching has been made easier by the linking of many of the online sources directly to university library catalogues, some of the main sources (such as *Westlaw* and *LexisNexis Butterworths*) do not link at present. Most of the online providers of full text journal articles only reference their own holdings and the majority of the journal indexing services are US based with limited UK (let alone Scottish) materials included. While it is a useful habit to become familiar with the contents of recent issues of relevant journals, wandering the shelves of the journals section of a library is not productive use of your time. However, there is one excellent source which makes tracing articles in UK legal journals since 1986 easy. This is the *Legal Journals Index* which is part of *Westlaw* and also available but less widely used in *Current Legal Information*.

Westlaw and *LexisNexis Butterworths* both have large collections of full text journals which do **8–42** not overlap. The choice of database is therefore dependent on the subject matter of the journals which they contain. This is not a static list as both databases are constantly expanding their holdings so you will need to check to see their contents at any given point in time.

Law students do not just need to be aware of legal journals. Studying law will also involve **8–43** looking at journals aimed at social scientists generally. This is particularly true if you are studying criminology, jurisprudence or socio-legal studies however they are also relevant to many substantive law subjects. A short section on finding what might best be described as "law-related" articles in included below at paras 8.62–8.67.

SEARCH STRATEGIES FOR FINDING ARTICLES IN JOURNALS

Finding journal articles in a law library if you have a full reference

If you have been referred to an article in a lecture or found its details in a reference in a textbook **8–44** you should have the full journal reference. A full reference for a journal article will include:

- ➢ Name of the author(s);
- ➢ Title of the articles;
- ➢ Reference with details of the date, volume number, title of the journal (usually in abbreviated form) and a page number.

If you know the full name of the journal you can check your library catalogue or proceed to the journals section to browse the shelves. Journals are generally shelved in alphabetical order. Remember that current issues are normally stored in a different part of a library from older editions of journals.

If the reference to the journal title is in abbreviated from and you do not know what it means, **8–45** your library should have a list of abbreviated forms beside its journal holdings. If this is not available you can check the *Cardiff Index to Legal Abbreviations* (*http://www.legalabbrevs. cardiff.ac.uk*) which is a free website. If this does not contain the reference try looking in D. Raistrick, *Index to Legal Citations and Abbreviations* 2nd edn (London: Bowker-Saur, 1993).

This work is particularly useful for older references. Once armed with the name of the journal you can proceed as above.

If your library does not have the journal concerned you may be able to access it online or you may be able to get a copy of the article through the inter-library loan scheme.

8–46 If you do not have the complete reference you may still be able to find the article. If you have the full reference details but are missing the author and title details this should not be a problem as the reference details will be sufficient to trace the article. However, if you are missing part of the reference you may have more difficulty. If you know the name of the journal and approximate year then you could check through the tables of contents in the issues in the library. If you do not know the journal title you will have to use an online source to search for the missing details. If the article is in a UK journal and has been published since 1986 the best place to search is the journals section of *Westlaw UK*, see para.8.48.

Finding journal articles online if you have a full reference

8–47 Check your library catalogue for the journal series. Many university libraries now link directly from their catalogue to particular series of journals if they have the appropriate subscription. The password arrangements will depend on your particular library.

If the journal series does not appear in your university catalogue, check the journals section of *Westlaw UK* see para.8.48 and other online sources to which you have access. If this is unsuccessful you may be able to get a copy of the article through the inter-library loan scheme.

Finding journal articles on a particular subject

8–48 The best source for tracing articles UK legal journals since 1986 is *Westlaw UK* which includes the excellent *Legal Journals Index*.

Westlaw subscription database

Westlaw UK Journals contains the *Legal Journals Index* and a number of full-text articles. The *Legal Journals Index* currently indexes over 800 legal journals from the UK and English language European journals. This represents the most efficient way of searching for UK legal journal articles. *Westlaw* also includes the *Financial Journals Index* (which ceased to be updated as of March 31, 2006) which indexes over 45 journals in areas such as insurance, financial services, banking, construction, employment, property and health and safety.

In addition to the *Legal Journals Index*, *Westlaw* also contains full-text articles from journal titles published by Sweet & Maxwell and Tottel Publishing. This includes selected coverage of *Scots Law Times* articles from 1997. However, it is a common experience to be able to trace an article's existence through the Legal Journal s Index and then to be unable to locate its full text within Westlaw. In this circumstance you should print off/email/note the details and then look in other databases or use the inter library loan system to obtain the article.

You can search for articles by using the basic search, advanced search or by browsing.

Basic search

8–49 From the Welcome page, click the Journals link from the navigation bar at the top of the screen. This will take you to the Journals basic search page, where you can search for articles by entering the *article title* or *author*, or key subject terms into *free text*. Searching can be improved if you use search techniques which Westlaw refer to as "Terms and Connectors". See para.2.23.

Advanced search

To access the advanced search facility, select *advanced search* in the top right of the *journals* **8–50** basic search page. In addition to the free text, article title and author search fields you can also search:

➢ For subject headings or keywords. However, note that this field only searches the article title and the abstract not the full text of the article.
➢ By journal title.
➢ Search for articles discussing a particular case by entering the names of one or more parties in the *cases cited* field.
➢ Search for articles referring to a particular Act or statutory instrument by entering its name in the *legislation title* field. You can restrict your search to individual sections of legislation (where abstracts or articles refer to a specific provision number) by entering the title, then additionally entering the section number in the *legislation provision no.* field.
➢ Restrict your search by year of publication.

The results list will show the name of the article title, its citation and the subject and keywords applied to the abstract. There will also be a link to the *Legal Journals Index* abstract and full text if available.

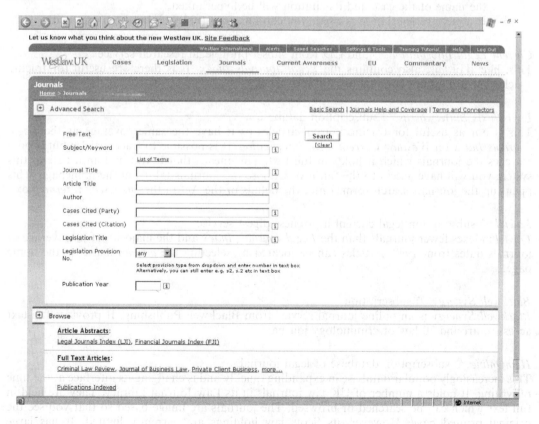

Diagram 8.1: Westlaw Journals Advanced Search Page

8–51 **Browsing journal articles.** From the basic search page you can browse journals (which are indexed in the Legal Journals Index or which appear in full text) alphabetically and by issue number or article title. You can use this function to restrict your search to one series e.g. if you want to restrict your search to the *Scots Law Times* you could choose S.L.T. from the list of full text articles accessed by the link on the search page. Once you have made this choice a new search box appears and this enables you to search within a single publication. It is easy to do this and forget that you have limited your search in this way but you can check by looking at the breadcrumb trail in blue near the top of the screen. This makes your research route clear.

8–52 The Legal Journals Index abstract contains:

> ➤ Title of the article,
> ➤ Author(s),
> ➤ If the full text is available in *Westlaw* you can access it by clicking on the citation immediately following the author's name,
> ➤ Full reference to the article,
> ➤ The name of the journal. Clicking on it will display the publisher's details.
> ➤ The subject and keywords used to index articles,
> ➤ A brief abstract (this is very brief—usually only a couple of lines) about the subject of the article,
> ➤ If a case is referred to in the article, and there is a Case Analysis available for that case, the name of the case and its citation will be hyperlinked,
> ➤ If a piece of legislation is cited, you can link to it (unless it has been repealed).

Current Legal Information ⌐ and CD Rom subscription legal research service
8–53 This, like *Westlaw*, also contains the *Legal Journals Index*. It is therefore useful for tracing articles but it does not contain any full text articles.

LexisNexis Butterworths ⌐ subscription database
8–54 This is not as useful for tracing journal articles as it have the same coverage as the *Legal Journals Index* on *Westlaw/Current legal Information*. It is possible to trace articles but it only searches the journals which it holds in full text. This means that if you find an article in this system you will have access to the full text. Choose the journals tab from the homepage. This opens up the journals search form. Enter the details of the Act in the *enter search terms* box.

Lawtel ⌐ subscription legal current awareness digest service
8–55 *Lawtel* indexes fewer journals than the *Legal Journals Index* and the majority of its coverage of journals dates from 1998. Articles can be located by selecting the *articles index* on the home page.

Blackwell Synergy ⌐ subscription
8–56 *Blackwell Synergy* is an online journal service from Blackwell Publishing. It provides full-text access to around 20 law or criminology journals.

HeinOnline ⌐ subscription database of legal journals
8–57 This increasingly popular database in expanding quickly and is changing its interface at the time of writing. It holds a number of UK law journals in its Law Journal Library. They are held in full text which can be searched or browsed. The journals are image-based so that you see the original printed page. However, its Scots law holdings are currently limited. It has large amounts of North American materials.

Index to Legal Periodicals 📖 and ᵔᵔ subscription indexing service
This index references legal periodicals and books which are published in Great Britain, Ireland,   **8–58**
US, Canada, Australia and New Zealand. It is an American publication and the majority of
material is American. The online version goes back to 1982 and now allows access to some
journals in full text. It has good search facilities and is updated daily. Pre-1981 articles are
referenced in the bound volumes.

Index to Foreign Legal Periodicals 📖 and ᵔᵔ subscription indexing service
This is another US based index. It covers selected international law and comparative law   **8–59**
periodicals and collections of essays. The paper volumes go back to 1960 and the online version
contain material back to 1985.

Current Law Index 📖 and ᵔᵔ subscription indexing service
This is also a US based index. It covers more than 900 law journals, legal newspapers and   **8–60**
specialty publications from the United States, Canada, the United Kingdom, Ireland, Australia
and New Zealand.

Current Law Yearbooks
Current Law Yearbook and *Monthly Digests* contain details of articles under subject headings.   **8–61**
See para.8.21.

Finding journal articles on a case

See paras 4.104–4.112.

Finding journal articles on a piece of legislation

See paras 6.112–6.118.

Finding "non-law" journal articles

Periodical Index Online ᵔᵔ subscription indexing service
This is an electronic index to millions of articles published in the arts, humanities and social   **8–62**
sciences. It is a useful way of searching information contained in back issues of older journals,
e.g. the *Juridical Review*.

Zetoc ᵔᵔ indexing service which is free to some higher education institutions
Zetoc provides access to the British Library's Electronic Table of Contents database, containing   **8–63**
details of approximately 20,000 current journals and 16,000 conference proceedings published
per year. The database includes science, technology, medicine, engineering, business, law,
finance and the humanities. The database covers the years from 1993 to date and is updated
daily.

British Humanities Index 📖 and ᵔᵔ subscription indexing service
The online version of the *British Humanities Index* provides abstracts from over 400 daily   **8–64**
newspapers, weekly magazines and academic journals of international standing, with over
667,000 records dating back to 1962. It is updated monthly, covering the latest material on the
arts, literature, cinema, economics, history, current affairs, popular science, religion, music, and
architecture.

Applied Social Sciences Index and Abstracts (ASSIA) ⤶ subscription indexing service
8–65 This is an abstracting and indexing tool for health and social science professionals which provides abstracts from around 650 UK, US and international journals. Coverage includes all branches of the applied social sciences, with over 240,000 records dating back to 1987.

Social Sciences Citation Index/Arts & Humanities Citation Index ⤶ subscription indexing service
8–66 Both of these indexes are available as part of the Web of Knowledge. Both these indexes include not only the content of the articles, but also the reference lists and bibliographies included by the author. They also list how many times an article has been referenced or cited in another paper.

CSA Sociological Abstracts Database ⤶ subscription indexing service
8–67 The database draws information from an international selection of over 2,600 journals and other serials publications, plus conference papers, books, and dissertations. Records added after 1974 contain abstracts of journal articles.

NEWSPAPER ARTICLES

8–68 The law is an important part of society and you will find that there are hardly any sections of newspapers where the law is irrelevant. As a law student you should ensure that you are aware of current events and legal developments. It is a good idea to read a quality newspaper on a regular basis and to ensure that you read any features on the law. The Scotsman currently features legal articles on a Monday.

Newspapers are not only useful for current events. They can be useful to read about past issues as a way of understanding the development of the law or society's reaction to a particular law. Most newspapers have websites that allow you to search back into their archives. However, the period available for free access is not usually very extensive and tends to be only a couple of years. A useful feature is available from the Independent newspaper website (*http://news. independent.co.uk/uk/legal/*) which has a legal section listing legal stories over the last six months and links to the full stories.

8–69 Both *Westlaw* and *LexisNexis Butterworths* have the ability to search UK newspapers. Both allow searching of the majority of the broadsheets. *Westlaw* includes the following Scottish newspapers: Aberdeen Press & Journal (from May 2004), Dundee courier (from July 2002), Evening News (October 1999), Evening Times (July 2002) Herald (from January 2000) and Scotsman (from 1996). *The British Humanities Index* (see para.8.64) indexes articles and features but not news items and editorials. The papers it covers are the Independent, Guardian, Financial Times, Observer, Times (and supplements), and Sunday Times.

8–70 The following are free sites that provide access to the current issues of newspapers:

> ➢ Onlinenewspapers.com (*http://www.onlinenewspapers.com/*) has links to a large number of newspaper worldwide including a large number of Scottish newspapers.
> ➢ ABYZ News Links (*http://www.abyznewslinks.com/*) is another site that links to a large number of newspapers in Scotland and the world.
> ➢ BUBL Link (*http://bubl.ac.uk/link/n/newspapers.htm*) This site will link you to a number of newspapers and news organisations worldwide.
> ➢ The Hero site (*http://www.hero.ac.uk/uk/reference_and_subject_resources/index.cfm*) has a useful collection of links to newspapers around the world.

8–71 News services on the web include:

> ➤ BBC News (*http://news.bbc.co.uk/*)
> ➤ Reuters UK (*http://uk.reuters.com/*)
> ➤ NewsNow (*http://www.newsnow.co.uk/*) This contains a lot of web only new material.
> ➤ Ananova (*http://www.ananova.com/*)
> ➤ Behind the Headlines (*http://www.intute.ac.uk/behindtheheadlines.html*)

CURRENT AWARENESS OF LEGAL DEVELOPMENTS

Westlaw ⌁ subscription database
Westlaw has a Current Awareness service which can be accessed by clicking the Current **8–72**
Awareness link at the top of the Welcome Screen. It contains daily updates and notices of cases,
legislation, and legal developments contained in or represented by official publications, press
releases (including from the Scottish Executive) and legal news (including from the Scotsman
and Herald) relating to the UK. It is updated three times daily at 9am, 11am and 2pm, with new
information. The information remains in Current Awareness for 90 days and can then be found
by searching the Current Awareness Archive. This includes over 10 years of content. If you wish
to restrict your search to Scotland you should include the word "Scotland" in the *subject/
keyword* box in the basic search. Searching can be improved if you use search techniques which
Westlaw refer to as "Terms and Connectors" see para.2.33. There is also a browse facility which
allows you to browse within various date ranges e.g. today or the last four days.

LexisNexis Butterworths ⌁ subscription database
LexisNexis Butterworths also has a Current Awareness service which can be searched by clicking **8–73**
on the Current Awareness tab on the homepage.

Current Legal Information ⌁ and CD Rom subscription legal research service
One of the databases is the LRDI Grey Paper Index which references information about legal **8–74**
developments. It can be searched within various date ranges e.g. last seven days and can be
restricted to Scotland by entering "Scotland" in the subject field.

The following free sites from information about Scottish legal developments: **8–75**

> ➤ *Scots Law News* (*http://www.law.ed.ac.uk/sln/*) provides short topical news items on
> aspects of Scots law. It is published by Hector MacQueen Professor of law, University
> of Edinburgh. It has a searchable archive beginning in 1996.
> ➤ *Thejournalonline* (http://www.journalonline.co.uk/) The online Journal of the Law
> Society of Scotland is updated daily and has an searchable archive back to August
> 2004.
> ➤ Scottish Executive site (*http://www.scotland.gov.uk/News/News-Today*) This site has
> news headlines and news by topic. The news can also be search under *this week's news*
> and *last week's news*. There is also a news archive back to 1997 which can be searched.
> ➤ Scottish Parliament What's new (*http://www.scottish.parliament.uk/business/whats-
> New.htm*) provides information about the day's events along with links to information
> sources about the events of the past seven days.
> ➤ The Scottish Courts site (*http://www.scotcourts.gov.uk/*) can be searched under 50 most
> recent opinions for the Supreme Courts or the Sheriff court. Go to the professional
> section of the site and click on the appropriate link in the grey opinions section. See
> para.4.21 for other sources of recent opinions.
> ➤ The Scotland Office site (*http://www.scotlandoffice.gov.uk*) has a latest news section.

> *Absolvitor* (*http://www.absolvitor.com/*) provides links to a selection of legal stories from the news.
> *The Firm* (*http://www.firmmagazine.com/*) has news and gossip covering Scotland's legal profession.
> UK Parliament pages (*http://www.parliament.uk/*) have a latest news section.
> Government News Network (GNN) (*http://www.gnn.gov.uk/*) provides UK, regional and Scottish news releases from Government departments and agencies.
> Inner Temple Current Awareness Weblog (*http://innertemplelibrary.wordpress.com/*) This selective current awareness weblog provides up-to-date information regarding new case law, changes in legislation, and legal news designed to be of interest to lawyers practising in the UK. The content is selected and updated daily by information professionals on the staff of the Inner Temple Library in London.
> ePolitix.com (*http://www.epolitix.com/EN/Legislation/*) is an impressive site which provides a useful way of keeping track of Bills going through the UK Parliament. The site also includes up-to-the-minute politics and parliamentary news (including the Scottish Parliament).
> The Lawyer (*http://www.thelawyer.com/*) This site has legal news along over 35,000 articles from The Lawyer magazine. It is free but you have to register.

UK OFFICIAL PUBLICATIONS

8–76 In recent years there have been many changes in the way official publications have been published. An increasing amount of information is published on the internet which has greatly improved access although finding the information is often not as straightforward as might be imagined. The ease of locating information has not been helped by the fact that the number of different publishers of official information has increased since the privatisation of Her Majesty's Stationery Office (HMSO) in 1996. UK official publications includes a vast amount of information and can be divided into two distinct categories: parliamentary papers and non-parliamentary publications.

Parliamentary papers

8–77 Bills and parliamentary debates (Hansard) are both classed as parliamentary papers and have already been covered in Chapter 6. Other parliamentary papers which you are likely to encounter at university are:

> Command Papers
> House of Commons papers
> House of Lords papers

Command Papers

8–78 A Command Paper is technically presented to Parliament "by the Command of Her Majesty" but in practice is presented on the initiative of a person or body other than Parliament. They are usually presented by Government Ministers. They are documents which have been produced for Parliament to consider; they have not been produced by Parliament. There are many different types of Command Papers:

> White Papers (proposal for legislation which is put forward by the Government)
> Green Papers (consultation documents)
> Reports of Royal Commissions

> ➤ Reports of Committees of Enquiry
> ➤ Annual reports and statistics produced by certain bodies
> ➤ State Papers including treaties
> ➤ Some Law Commission reports are Command papers

There are six series of Command Papers. Each Command Paper has a number; they are all **8–79** numbered less than 10,000 and (apart from the first series) preceded with a different form of abbreviation for Command:

1833–1866	1–4222
1870–1899	C.1 – C.9550
1900–1918	Cd.1 – Cd.9239
1919–1956	Cmd.1 – Cmd.9889
1956–1986	Cmnd.1 – Cmnd.9927
1986–	Cm.1 –

As the same numbers are used in the different series, it is very important to note the precise abbreviation so that you can locate the appropriate Command Paper.

All Command Papers which originate in government departments are available at the Stationery **8–80** Office's Official Documents website (*http://www.official-documents.co.uk/menu/browse Documents.htm*) from the 2005-2006 parliamentary session. It also includes a selection of material from 2004. The search feature enables you to search by free text, title, department, subject, type and number. The site also allows you to browse by department or subject.

The Office of Public Sector Information (OPSI) (*http://www.opsi.gov.uk/official-publications/* **8–81** *command-papers/index.htm*) has a list of all command papers since 2001 with links to the Command Papers where known. You can view the list alphabetically by department or if you know the Command Paper number you can view the list numerically.

House of Commons and House of Lords Papers

House of Commons and House of Lords Papers are documents that result from the work of **8–82** both Houses and that of their committees. They include: Votes and Proceedings (Commons) and the Minute (Lords) which are the formal, authoritative record of the decisions taken by each House; Select Committee reports and evidence; Register of Members' interests; Standing Orders (which are the rules for conducting business in both Houses); and Sessional Returns (which include statistics on the work of the Commons for each parliamentary year).

House of Commons Papers are given a reference which consists of H.C., the relevant parliamentary session (*e.g.* 2006/07) and the number of the paper. House of Lords Papers are numbered in a similar way but with H.L. as the prefix.

Many House of Commons Papers are available on the parliamentary web site (*http://* **8–83** *www.parliament.uk*). From the homepage, click on *Publications and Records*. If you click into the *Commons publications* section you will find: all select committee reports from the beginning of the 1997-1998 session; Standing Orders; the Sessional Returns (from 1997-1998); and the Register of Members' Interests.

House of Commons Papers which originate in government departments are available at the **8–84** Stationery Office's Official Documents website (*http://www.official-documents.co.uk/menu/ browseDocuments.htm*) from the 2005-2006 parliamentary session. It also includes a selection of material before then. The search feature enables you to search by free text, title, department, subject, type and number. The site also allows you to browse by department or subject.

Aids to tracing official publications

Specific sources of the full text of the various parliamentary papers have been covered in the dedicated sections: Bills (para.6.3), Hansard (para.6.24), Command Papers (para.8.78), and House of Commons and House of Lords Papers (para.8.82). The sources below are general tracing aids to official publications.

The Stationery Office (TSO) is the provider of different means of tracing official publications.
8–85 It has an online bookshop (*http://www.tsoshop.co.uk/*) which contains details not only of TSO publications but also of publications which TSO sell. This is a useful source of information and contains a search facility that allows you to limit your search to various options including: Commons; Lords; and Command Papers.

TSO publishes the *Daily List* which is available in paper format and free on the parliamentary section of the TSO bookship site (*http://www.tsoshop.co.uk/parliament/*). The *Daily List* is divided into several sections:

> ➤ Parliamentary publications which includes details of House of Commons and House of Lords Papers, Bills, Command Papers, Acts and debates;
> ➤ Statutory instruments which are listed separately;
> ➤ Official publications which includes non-parliamentary publications;
> ➤ Separate sections for Scottish Parliament Acts, Scottish Parliament publications, Scottish statutory instruments and Scottish official publications;
> ➤ Northern Ireland publications;
> ➤ Agency publications which include agency publications which TSO sells but does not publish e.g. International Court of Justice and the UN.

The online version also contains a link to previous issues which are available back to 2000. The Daily Lists for a week are published in paper format together as a *Weekly List*. The information is also published as monthly catalogues and again as an annual catalogue.

Collections of parliamentary publications 📖
8–86 Some libraries will hold a full set of parliamentary papers. These can be searched by a Sessional Index. The National Library of Scotland holds House of Commons Papers since 1715 and House of Lords papers since 1801.

The United Kingdom Official Publications Database (UKOP) subscription
8–87 UKOP (*http://www.ukop.co.uk/*) is the official catalogue of UK official publications. It combines the official catalogue of The Stationery Office with the Catalogue of Official Publications Not Published by the Stationery Office. It is published by The Stationery Office. UKOP contains over 450,000 bibliographic records of official publications from 1980 onwards and is updated daily. It catalogues all parliamentary and statutory publications (including Acts and statutory instruments), and the publications of over 2500 official bodies including central government departments, the devolved administrations, agencies, quangos and other bodies. UKOP has the benefit of allowing users to trace government publications without having any knowledge of the departments that might have been involved in their production.

British Official Publications Current Awareness Service (BOPCAS) subscription
8–88 This database allows access to publications emanating from Government published since July 1995. It includes Acts, Bills, Command Papers, House of Commons Papers, House of Lords Papers, departmental publications and Standing Committee Reports.

LRDI Grey Paper Index (formerly BADGER) part of *Current Legal Information* ⌒ and CD
Rom subscription legal research service

This is an index to the following from 1994 onwards: press releases, newspaper articles, par- **8–89**
liamentary publications, Command Papers, English, Welsh and Scottish statutory instruments,
progress of Bills, White and Green Papers and European Commission documents. This index
can be searched by field (this includes subject, author, title, document type) or by free text.

Lawtel ⌒subscription legal current awareness digest service

Lawtel has the facility to search for Command Papers including White and Green Papers. Its **8–90**
holdings go back to 1984. It is updated daily and contains hypertext links to full text when this is
available from Government websites.

Parlianet ⌒ subscription service which is part of Justis

This is an index to the proceedings and publications of both Houses of Parliament in West- **8–91**
minster going back to 1979.

British Official Publications Collaborative Reader Information Service (BOPRIS) ⌒ free

BOPRIS (*http://www.bopcris.oc.uk*) allows access to older official publications. It is a biblio- **8–92**
graphic database covering the period 1688–1995. It can search approximately 39,000 selected
British official publications within this period. It can be searched by subject but this is likely to
retrieve a large number of hits. The advanced search allows you to search by date, title or key
word.

Non-parliamentary publications

These are basically official publications which are not presented to Parliament. This is not a **8–93**
particularly helpful definition but this group of government publications is enormous and
emerges from a large number of official bodies. Problems of searching for this material can be
exacerbated by the fact that these bodies can change name of be reorganised. Much of the
information is available via the internet and when such organisational change takes place it can
affect the location of publications and can even result in the disappearance of publications. In
the past many of these were published by HMSO but this is no longer the case.

Finding non-parliamentary publications

Non-parliamentary publications are included in The Stationery Office Daily List and bookshop **8–94**
(para.8.85), UKOP (para.8.87), BOPCAS (para.8.88), and BOPCRIS (paras 8.92).

If you know the name of the body you can carry out a search of their website. They will usually **8–95**
have a link to *publications*. To find the relevant website carry out a Google search or go to
http://www.direct.gov.uk, click on *directories*. This section of the site contains a listing of A-Z of
central government and the devolved administrations.

Catalogue of British Official Publications Not Published by the Stationery Office 📖

Many libraries may have the *Catalogue of British Official Publications Not Published by the* **8–96**
Stationery Office which is issued bi-monthly and bound into annual volumes. This includes
references to a large amount of material emerging from over 500 different organisations. UKOP
(see above para.8.87) includes this catalogue.

Sources of additional information about the workings of the UK Government

UK Parliament pages ᛒ free

8–97   The Parliament pages (*http://www.parliament.uk/*) contain a large amount of information about the UK Parliament's role and history, the day to day workings of Government and parliamentary procedures, MPs, and details the business of the day.

The Civil Service Yearbook ☐ and ᛒ subscription

8–98   This is published annually and is the official reference for central government in the UK providing the most authoritative source of up-to-date information on the Civil Service. (*http://www.civil-service.co.uk/*)

The Directory of Westminster and Whitehall, 2006/07 ☐

8–99   This directory gives information about M.P.s, their staff and constituencies, contact details for Government departments, listings of subject responsibility in Government departments and contact details for "quangos".

Press releases from UK Government Departments and the Scottish Executive

8–100 Press releases are available from the websites of the Scottish Executive (*http://www.scotland.gov.uk/Topics/*) and the various UK Government departments. There is a listing of public bodies with links to their website available at *http://www.scotland.gov.uk/Topics/Government/public-bodies/directory*. In addition, there are several sources which allow you to search several departments or offer other facilities.

Government News Network (GNN) ᛒ free

8–101 This website (*http://www.gnn.gov.uk/*) allows you to search Government press releases by department and also by regions (which includes a Scottish section). The advanced search allows you to search historical departments (i.e. departments that no longer exist in the same form). It also allows you to narrow a search by department, region, keywords and date range. This impressive site has made tracing Government press releases easy.

Westlaw ᛒ subscription database

8–102 *Westlaw UK* allows you to search for press releases with a legal connection from UK Government departments, the European Commission and the European Parliament. Choose *current awareness* from the homepage and click on *document type* and then enter your search terms and choose *press releases*. This will retrieve press releases from the last 90 days.

LRDI Grey Paper Index (formerly BADGER) part of *Current Legal Information* ᛒ and CD Rom subscription legal research service

8–103 This indexes press releases which can be searched by choosing press releases as your document type and searching by free text or keyword.

HERMES ᛒ subscription database which is provided by *Justis*

8–104 This database contains press releases and announcements from most of the major government departments in England and Scotland from 2000.

SCOTTISH OFFICIAL PUBLICATIONS

Scottish official publications comprise Scottish Parliament and Scottish Executive publications. All of these are issued electronically and appear on their respective websites and some are only issued electronically.

Scottish Parliament publications

Scottish Parliament publications include: Bills (discussed in para.7.8), the Official Report **8–105** (discussed in paras 7.21–7.24), Minutes of proceedings (which formally record all items of business taken and the results of any decisions), Business Bulletin (this contains full details of current and future business), SPICe research publications (research produced by the Scottish Parliament Information Centre). They previously included WHISP (What's Happening in the Scottish Parliament) which was published from May 15, 1999 to July 3, 2004 and still can be searched on the Scottish Parliament website (*http://www.scottish.parliament.uk*).

Most Scottish Parliament papers are reports of a Committee enquiry into a subject, e.g. sub- **8–106** ordinate legislation, or Bills of the Scottish Parliament. Scottish Parliament papers also include other publications produced by the Parliament, such as annual reports of the Scottish Parliamentary Corporate Body and Scottish Parliament statistics. Guidance on citing Scottish Parliament materials can be found in paras 13.44–13.52.

A bibliography of the Scottish Parliament, *Scottish Parliament and Statutory Publications*, is **8–107** published by The Stationery Office and is published on the Scottish Parliament website. It is intended to be published twice a year (although it is currently behind) and lists both TSO and other publications.

Scottish Parliament publications are listed in the Scottish Official Listings (see para.8.113) while **8–108** The Stationery Office Daily List (see para.8.85) contains a more limited listing.

Scottish Executive publications

The Scottish Executive publications include a large range of documents. The documents that **8–109** you are most likely to use in your studies are policy documents, consultation papers, annual reports of Executive Agencies and Scottish Law Commission documents. Many Scottish Executive publications are laid before the Scottish Parliament. The process for laying documents is set out in Ch.14 of the Parliament's Standing Orders. Documents may have to be laid before the Parliament because they require parliamentary scrutiny, such as Scottish statutory instruments. Alternatively, legislation may require that documents such as the annual reports of certain public bodies be brought to the attention of the Parliament

If a Scottish Executive document is laid before the Parliament it becomes part of the "SE series" **8–110** of papers (these are the equivalent of Command Papers in the UK Parliament). They are numbered sequentially in a year and are cited e.g. SE/2006/123. Confusingly some documents (e.g. some Scottish law Commission Reports which are published jointly with the Law Commission) are laid before both Parliaments and therefore have both a Command Paper number and an SE series number.

Scottish Executive publications are available from the Scottish Executive website (*http://* **8–111** *www.scotland.gov.uk/Publications/Recent*) which currently holds full-text publications from 1997 onwards. From 2001, all publications are available in both HTML and PDF formats. On the website publications are listed under *publications* and *consultations*. The *publications archive* allows searching by date, subject, topic and keyword. The consultations are searchable by *current* and *closed* consultations. Note that not all SE series (i.e. documents that have been laid before Parliament) are available on the site: only documents prepared by one of the Scottish Executive core departments are on its site. You may therefore have to search for the homepage of the relevant body.

8–112 The Scottish Executive Information and Library Services produce an annual register of bibliographic details of Scottish Executive publications which is available in paper and on their website (*http://www.scotland.gov.uk*): The Scottish Executive Publications List.

Listings of Scottish official publications

8–113 Two listings produced by RR Donnelley are particularly useful for tracing Scottish official publications.

They produce a listing of Scottish official material on a daily, weekly and monthly basis. The weekly listing is available at *http://www.lib.gla.ac.uk/swop/Astron/AstronWL.html* It is divided into several sections: Scottish Executive/Agency print publications; Scottish Executive/Agency online publications; Scottish Parliament publications; and Scottish legislation. The listing provides brief details about the publications and where they can be sourced. This includes a link to all the free electronic publications listed.

RR Donnelley also produce a monthly listing of Scottish Executive Web only documents. This is available at *http://www.lib.gla.ac.uk/swop/Astron/AstronWebonlyList.html*

It is possible to register to receive the listings by emailing your details to registerdetails@rrd.com.

8–114 The Stationery Office Daily List (see para.8.85) contains details of some Scottish official publications.

8–115 Details of Scottish official publications are available on UKOP (see para.8.87).

Sources of additional information about the workings of the Scottish Parliament

8–116 Information about MSPs, their constituencies along with the details of the working of the Parliament and the legislative process is available free via the Scottish Parliament website (*http://www.scottish.parliament.uk/home.htm*). A particularly useful part of the site is the *research briefings* section which can be accessed via the drop down menu on the homepage. Research briefings are written by research specialists in the Scottish Parliament Information Centre (SPICe). SPICe research briefings are for use by MSPs in support of parliamentary business in the Committees and in the Chamber and are always impartial. Briefings can be browsed either by subject or by date of publication. Briefings can be searched back to 1999. Fact sheets are also available in the research briefing section of the site: choose the *fact sheet* option from the list at the left hand side of the screen. These contain information about various aspects of parliamentary business and about MSPs past and present.

Law Commission Papers

8–117 The Scottish Law Commission and the Law Commission were both created by the Law Commissions Act 1965. The Chairman of the Scottish Law Commission is a Senator of the College of Justice. He is assisted by four Commissioners. Its purpose is to promote the reform of the law of Scotland. It proposes reforms in the law, prepares Consolidation and Statute Law Repeals Bills. The Law Commission publishes consultation papers and at a later stage it prepares a report with recommendations. These usually include a draft Bill. The Law Commission does not have the power to alter the law, merely to contribute to debate and to make proposals. The Government makes the final decision whether to adopt the proposals.

The Scottish Law Commission website (*http://www.scotlawcom.gov.uk/*) contains details of current projects being undertaken, discussion papers since 1997, a listing of all its reports and full text reports since 1999 (as well as some earlier ones) are available. The website has a basic search facility. Scottish Law Commission reports are laid before the Scottish Parliament and this means that they are Scottish Executive publications. Confusion can sometimes be caused by the fact that some Scottish Commission reports are published jointly with the English Law Commission and therefore also UK parliamentary papers.

The English Law Commission website (*http://www.lawcom.gov.uk/*) contains a listing of consultation papers and reports and information about current consultations. Full text reports are available on the site back to 1995.

Statistical information about Scotland

The Scottish Executive website allows access to much statistical information about Scotland at: **8–118** *http://www.scotland.gov.uk/Topics/Statistics/* This page allows you to access statistics under various subject headings. Crime and Justice is one of the subject headings along with Agriculture and Fisheries, Businesses, Children and Young People, Economy, Environment, Health and Community Care, Housing and Regeneration, Labour Market, Lifelong Learning, Local Government Finance, Planning, Population and Migration, School Education, Social and Welfare, Tourism, Culture and Sport and Transport and Travel. The site also contains information about new and forthcoming statistical publications. There is also access to ScotStat which is a network for users and providers of Scottish official statistics. It aims to improve communication amongst those interested in particular statistics and facilitate the setting up of working groups on specific statistical issues.

Other statistical information about Scotland available online includes: **8–119**

> ➢ General Register Office for Scotland (*http://www.gro-scotland.gov.uk/statistics/ index.html*). This provides information about Scotland's population, including the 10-yearly census.
> ➢ Information on health statistics is available from *http://www.isdscotland.org/isd/ CCC_FirstPage.jsp.*
> ➢ UK statistical information is available from the Office for National Statistics (*http:// www.statistics.gov.uk/*).

Other sources of official information of interest to the legal researcher

Details of research carried out for the Scottish Executive publications is available free at *http://* **8–120** *www.scotland.gov.uk/Topics/Research* The site lists recent research publications and presents research under various subject headings: Agriculture, Arts & Culture, Business and Industry, Economy, Education and Training, Environment, Fisheries, Government, Health and Community Care, Housing and Regeneration, Justice, People and Society and Planning Research.

Many official bodies produce information either in the form of annual reports or via a website. **8–121** These include:

> ➢ The Scottish Legal Services Ombudsman. Her role is to investigate complaints about how the relevant professional body (Law Society of Scotland or Faculty of Advocates) has dealt with a complaint against a practitioner. Annual reports are produced and more information is available on the website: *http://www.slso.org.uk/*

> ➢ The Scottish Legal Aid Board also produces annual reports and has a website: *http://www.slab.org.uk/*
> ➢ The Scottish Committee of the Council of Tribunals produces annual reports. They oversee, on behalf of the Council, the procedures of those UK-wide tribunals which take place in Scotland. Their annual reports are available at *http://www.council-on-tribunals.gov.uk/scottish/scottish.htm*
> ➢ The Crown Office and Procurator Fiscal Service *http://www.crownoffice.gov.uk/* provides information about the operation of the criminal justice system.
> ➢ The recently constituted Scottish Criminal Cases Review Commission website: *http://www.sccrc.org.uk/* has information about the workings of the Commission.
> ➢ Scottish Prison Service website *http://www.sps.gov.uk/* contains access to its annual report and information about Scotland's prisons.
> ➢ Police Forces in Scotland have a website *http://www.scottish.police.uk/mainframe.htm* which provides information about the various forces, news and campaigns.

8–122 Many agencies have their own websites which provide much useful information, *e.g.* Scottish Environment Protection Agency (*http://www.sepa.org.uk/*).

LEGAL DIRECTORIES

8–123 The Scottish Law Directory: The White Book. This is an annual publication, the 116th edition of which is due to publish in this year. It contains an official list of certificated solicitors and is accompanied by a Fees Supplement which contains details of fee rates. There was a similar directory called The Blue Book: the Directory of the Law Society of Scotland but it has not been published for a couple of years.

8–124 The Law Society of Scotland provides an online directory of Scottish solicitors at *http://www.lawscot.org.uk/find/* It can be searched by name, location and category of legal practice work. *Scots law Online* contains a Scots law firm directory at *http://www.scottishlaw.org.uk/lawfirms/index.html* The Legal 500.com website (*http://www.legal500.com/*) includes some of the larger Scottish firms.

8–125 INFORMATION AIMED AT PRACTITIONERS

> ➢ The Law Society of Scotland (*www.lawscot.org.uk/*) is the professional body for solicitors and contains information about the profession and links to the daily updates of the Journal of the Law Society of Scotland at *http://www.journalonline.co.uk/*
> ➢ Scottish Young Lawyers Association (*http://www.syla.co.uk/*) is an association for lawyers up to 10 years qualified.
> ➢ WS Society (*http://www.thewss.co.uk/*) The Society of Writers to Her Majesty's Signet is an independent association for lawyers.
> ➢ The Scottish Law Agents Society (*http://www.slas.co.uk/*) is a society of solicitors who publish the Memorandum Book (a pocket size reference book which is updated and issued every year) and the Scottish Law Gazette which is issued quarterly.
> ➢ Faculty of Advocates site (*http://www.advocates.org.uk/*) is the professional body for Scotland's advocates. The well laid out site contains information about current advocates and also guidance on how to become an advocate.
> ➢ The Society of Solicitor Advocates (*http://www.solicitoradvocates.org/*) was formed in 1990 and represents the interests of Scottish Solicitor Advocates. This site can be used

to obtain information about becoming a solicitor advocate or instructing a solicitor advocate.

➢ Scottish Paralegal Association (*http://www.scottish-paralegal.org.uk/*) contains useful information for the growing number of paralegals .
➢ Society of Specialist paralegals (*http://www.specialistparalegals.co.uk/*) is also aimed at paralegals and provides information about continual professional development.

Practical information about Scottish courts

The Scottish Courts website (*http://www.scotcourts.gov.uk*) has a professional section which **8–126** contains a great amount of very useful information about all the Scottish courts. As well as opinions from the Court of Session, High Court of Justiciary and the sheriff court (see para.4.21) the site also contains links to Rules of Court for the various courts and rules governing different types of actions. It also contains practice notes for the Court of Session, High Court of Justiciary and sheriff court.

In addition to this large amount of legal information, the site also contains very useful practical information for solicitors. It contains the Rolls of Court (schedule of daily business) for the Court of Session, High Court of Justiciary (both Trial and Appeal) and the sheriff courts. The *locations* section of the site (accessible from the blue bar on the homepage) contains an impressive array of practical information for visiting the Supreme Courts or any of the sheriff courts. You can select a court from a menu or a map. You can then access the following information which you print (apart from the daily court lists) to take with you on your visit:

➢ Contact details—telephone numbers and addresses.
➢ Getting there—public transport and parking information.
➢ Customer information—what to do on arrival, who to report to, what to expect.
➢ Local facilities—e.g. disabled access to the court house, refreshments available on site or locally.
➢ Court opening times and local holidays.
➢ Local notices and public information.
➢ Searchable Daily Court Lists which are held for five business days.
➢ Local street map.
➢ Court photograph—colour picture of the Sheriff Court House.

Styles

There are many books which provide styles for various documents commonly encountered by **8–127** solicitors. These books are referred to as "styles" in Scotland and "precedents" in England. The idea of a styles book is not new. The *Scots Style Book* was published between 1902–1905 and ran to seven volumes with an eighth volume of sheriff court styles appearing in 1911 largely complied from earlier volumes. The styles were arranged in alphabetical order according to subject. In 1935, the 10 volume *Encyclopaedia of Legal Styles* was published. Again, the styles were arranged alphabetically according to subject. These works are now largely of historical interest however there are an increasing amount of styles publications. Examples include S.A. Bennett, *Style Writs for the Sheriff Court* 3rd edn (Edinburgh: Barnestoneworth, 2001) and A. Barr *et al., Drafting Wills in Scotland,* 2nd edn (Edinburgh: Butterworths, 2005).

There are an increasing number of packages which allow the practitioner to download styles and adapt them for his own use. *Green's Litigation Styles* is a collection of styles for use in the Court of Session and the sheriff court. It is a looseleaf publication in two volumes and includes a CD containing styles which can be downloaded. The service is updated twice a year. Green's also publish *Practice Styles*. This is also a two-volume looseleaf publication with a CD. It covers the following areas: agriculture and crofting, commerce, commercial conveyancing, court, domestic conveyancing, executry, family law, intellectual property, moveable property, trusts and wills. Another example of a modern styles package is *Express Wills for Scotland*. This is a CD which generates wills automatically from a styles bank when you type in information on an individual client. You input information through an interactive questionnaire, you then have the ability to edit and print, allowing you to complete complex personalised wills.

INFORMATION AIMED AT LAW STUDENTS

8–128 This section identifies information sources which are aimed specifically at law students.

> H.L. MacQueen, *Studying Scots Law* 3rd edn (Haywards Heath: Tottel, 2006) is a useful book which provides information about studying law as well as about becoming a solicitor tailored for Scottish law students.

> There are many websites aimed at law students in the UK but few have much information specifically for the Scottish law student. The Law Society of Scotland site has a useful section on becoming a solicitor (*http://www.lawscot.org.uk/training*). Likewise, the Faculty of Advocates also provides information about becoming an advocate (*http://www.advocates.org.uk/training/index.html*).

> *The Scottish Council of Law Reporting site* (*http://www.scottishlawreports.org.uk/*) has links to some key Scottish cases and also to *Donoghue v Stevenson: The Paisley Snail MiniTrial*. This is an educational initiative from Scottish Lawyers supported by The Faculty of Advocates, the Law Society of Scotland, and The W.S. Society. It is a collection of materials to allow the trial of *Donoghue v Stevenson* (one of the most famous Scottish cases) to proceed. In reality the case never went to court on its facts. The materials are designed to allow students and others to conduct their own civil trial.

> *The Scots Law Online Student Zone* (*http://www.scottishlaw.org.uk/student/index. html*) has career advice and tips. It also has recreational sites but you should be careful using its shared essay facilities. While students can learn from sharing ideas you have to be very careful not to "borrow" ideas which could lead to an accusation of plagiarism (see para.14.6).

> Delia Venables' site has a student section (*http://www.venables.co.uk/students.htm*) which provides details of law courses, information about careers in the law, links to resources for students and a section of practical information for lawyers. This is an impressive gateway of legal information.

> *Absolvitor* has a student part of its site (*http://www.absolvitor.com/students/?index.html*) which includes various drinking games!

> *Mooting* is a site for those interested in mooting (*http://www.mootingnet.org.uk/*).

Predominantly English student resources:

> *The Incorporated Council of Law Reporting* (*http://www.lawreports.co.uk/Newsletter/ home.htm*) has a student newsletter which contains articles by law reporters, academics and students, in addition to selected case summaries from The *WLR Daily* (see Chapter 9). The ICLR also have a student forum (*http://www.lawreports.co.uk/StudentForum/ home.htm*).

> *Cambridge Student Law Review* (*http://www.srcf.ucam.org/cslr/index.html*) is a law review written by students and it is open to students from UK universities to contribute articles and case notes.

> *Student Law Journal* (*http://www.studentlawjournal.com/home.htm*) contains book reviews and articles.

➤ *Consilio* (*http://www.spr-consilio.com/*) is published by Semple Piggott Rochez and is an online magazine designed for law students. It includes articles, law reports, net radio and television interviews and a selection of English course materials. There is a member's area for which you can register at no cost. *The Legal Practitioner* (*http://www.thelegalpractitioner.com/*) is a new site also published by Semple Piggott Rochez which is designed in a similar format to *Consilio* but is aimed at practitioners.

➤ *Chambers and partners student guide*—information about training in English law firms: *http://www.chambersandpartners.com/chambersstudent/*

➤ *The Lawyer* has a student section to its website (*http://www.thelawyer.com/l2b/*) which has a lot of information aimed at English law students.

➤ *LawBore* (*http://www.lawbore.net/*) This site is hosted by City University, London and is designed as the law student's guide to the web. There are lots of links organised by subject.

➤ Some of the bigger legal publishers have student sections on their web sites e.g. *Lexis Nexis Law Campus* at *http://www.lexisnexis.co.uk/lawcampus/* and Sweet and Maxwell have a student section at *http://www.sweetandmaxwell.co.uk/academic/index.aspx*

ACCESS TO LIBRARY CATALOGUES

Information about law libraries can be gained from: **8–129**

➤ *HERO Online catalogues*
http://www.hero.ac.uk/sites/hero/uk/reference_and_subject_resources/institution_facilities/online_catalogues_alphabetic3793.cfm This is an alphabetical listing with links to all UK higher education library catalogues.

➤ COPAC
http://copac.ac.uk/ is a union catalogue, giving free access to the merged online catalogues of members of the Consortium of Research Libraries (CURL). There are over 32 million records on COPAC representing the merged holdings of most CURL member institutions. This includes the British Library, the National Library of Scotland and the university libraries of Aberdeen, Edinburgh, Glasgow.

➤ *Co-operative Academic Information Retrieval Network for Scotland* (CAIRNS) (*http://cairns.lib.gla.ac.uk/*). The aim of this project is to produce single searching of major academic research collections throughout Scotland. At present the service is not complete.

Chapter 9
UK-Wide Legal Information Sources which Exclude Scots Law

9–1 This chapter looks at some legal information sources which are relevant for UK-wide legal information but which exclude Scots law (either wholly or partially). The sources covered have been limited to those which are widely available in Scotland. The chapter starts by discussing *LexisNexis Butterworths* which is a major legal database which excludes exclusively Scottish legislation from the UK Parliament although it does include legislation from the Scottish Parliament and a selection of Scottish law reports. The chapter then considers the major collections of English and Welsh legislation: *Halsbury's Statutes of England and Wales* (annotated full amended text of statutes currently in force) and *Halsbury's Statutory Instruments* (annotated full amended text of statutory instruments currently in force) along with explanations of how to search them. The principal series of English law reports are discussed followed by sources of recent English cases. The chapter concludes with a description of the major English legal encyclopaedia: *Halsbury's Laws of England*.

LexisNexis Butterworths ⌨ Subscription Database

9–2 *LexisNexis Butterworths* is a major legal database which excludes exclusively Scottish legislation from the UK Parliament although it does include a selection of Scottish law reports. It is made up of many different databases which can be subscribed to in a series of packages. *UK Parliament Acts* contains the revised form of all Acts of the UK Parliament relating to England and Wales currently in force. Coverage is from 1266. Public General Acts that are no longer in force do not appear in full text but, if the Act ceased to have effect on or after January 1, 1999, a note explains why the enactment no longer applies. Acts that were made by the UK Parliament and relate to Scotland only are not included, although provisions of Scottish Acts that apply or are relevant to England and/or Wales are included. There is a separate database, *Scottish Parliament Acts*, which contains the revised form of Acts of the Scottish Parliament from 1999. *UK Parliament Statutory Instruments* contains the revised form of UK statutory instruments but does not include provisions that extend exclusively to Scotland. Another *LexisNexis Butterworths* database, *Scottish Parliament SIs*, contains the revised form of Scottish statutory instruments from 1999. Other databases which are available via *LexisNexis Butterworths* are *Halsbury's Statute Citator* which provides details of the current status of statutes included in the Halsbury's Statutes series (see para.9.5) and *Halsbury's Statutory Instrument Citator* which does the same for statutory instruments covered in the *Halsbury's Statutory Instrument* series (see para.9.12).

Searching LexisNexis Butterworths

Searching for an Act of Parliament

Choose the *legislation* tab from the homepage. This opens up the legislation search form. Select **9–3**
UK Parliament Acts from the Select Sources drop-down list. Go to the *type* field and select
Statute from the drop-down list. If you do not know the name of the Act you can enter words or
phrases in the *enter search terms* box. You can use Boolean connectors to show the relation of
the terms, see para.2.33. If you know the title or part of the title, enter search terms in the
legislation title field, giving the year if known. If you only enter part of the title, use Boolean
connectors to link your search terms. If you want to search for a particular section, enter the
number in the *provision* field. You can retrieve your results by clicking on *search*.

Searching for a statutory instrument

Choose the *legislation* tab from the homepage. This opens up the legislation search form. Select **9–4**
UK Parliament SIs from the Select Sources drop-down list. Go to the *type* field and select
Statutory Instrument from the drop-down list. If you do not know the name of the statutory
instrument you can enter words or phrases in the *enter search terms* box. You can use Boolean
connectors to show the relation of the terms see para.2.33. If you know the statutory instrument
number, enter the year in the *legislation title* field and the series number in the *series number*
field. If you know the title or part of the title, enter search terms in the *legislation title* field,
giving the year if known. If you only enter part of the title, use Boolean connectors to link your
search terms. You can retrieve your results by clicking on *search*.

   LexisNexis Butterworths is discussed in paras 2.20–2.26 and is also included where relevant in
relation to specific search activities throughout the book.

LEGISLATION

Halsbury's Statutes of England and Wales (4th edn) 📖

This work is a collection of statutes which are arranged in broad subject headings. It consists of **9–5**
50 volumes along with an updating service which has three parts: Cumulative Supplement, a
Noter-up and Current Statutes Service. It contains statutes which relate to England and Wales
or to the UK as a whole. Sections of UK statutes which relate to Scotland only are not included
and statutes which relate only to Scotland are not included.

   The full text of each statute is given along with annotations which clarify the legislation and
refer to relevant case law. The text of the statute incorporates subsequent amendments (it is not,
as in *Current Law*, the original version). From 1993 onwards reference to parliamentary debates
is given. The volumes are arranged in alphabetical order, Vol.1 starts with Admiralty and Vol.50
ends with Wills. The volumes are re-issued periodically. At the start of each volume there is a
statement that it represents the law up to a certain date. You should ensure that you always
check this date and then use the updating service to check for changes since that date. You may
also need to check a very up to date source (e.g. *Lawtel*, *LexisNexis Butterworths* or *Westlaw*) to
ensure that your knowledge is current.

   Each bound volume conforms to the same format. At the start:

> ➤ List of headings in all the volumes.
> ➤ Table of contents for this volume.
> ➤ References and abbreviations.
> ➤ Tables of statutes covering all the statutes printed in the volume in both alphabetical
>   and chronological order.
> ➤ Table of statutory instruments in alphabetical order.
> ➤ Table of cases.

Within each subject heading there is:

> ➢ Table of contents.
> ➢ Cross references. This indicates where material has been categorised under a different heading and is therefore contained in a different volume.
> ➢ Preliminary note. This explains the legislative background to the subject area.
> ➢ Annotated and amended version of legislation.

At the end of the volume there is a subject index.

In addition to the volumes there is the *Current Statutes Service* which is contained in six loose-leaf binders. It includes the text of Acts passed since January 1, 1985, other than those included in the published volumes. It is arranged by volume number and subject.

9–6 The updating service consists of:

> ➢ *Annual Cumulative Supplement.* This records change which affect the published volumes. It is arranged by volume, subject and page order in the same way as the bound volumes. Updating material relating to Acts in the Current Statutes Service is given at the end of material for the corresponding volume title and is indicated by "(S)" following the volume number at the top of the page.
> ➢ *Noter-up.* This records the effect of changes in the material in the volumes and Current Service Binders which have occurred since the publication of the last cumulative supplement. It is arranged by subject in the same way as the volumes and Cumulative Supplement. Again, the letter "S" indicates that the legislation is contained in one of the Current Service Binders. The Noter-up also contains an update for the publication *Is It in Force?* (see below). The Noter-up is updated four times a year.

Halsbury's Statutes includes a biannual publication *Is It in Force?* 📖
9–7 This contains the commencement dates of Acts of general application to England, Wales and Scotland passed in the previous 25 year period. The Acts are listed in alphabetical order in the year in which they were passed. The publication also contains a Table of Statutes Not Yet in Force, which lists provisions of Acts passed prior to the 25 year period for which no commencement dates have yet been made. More information is contained in para.6.94.

Is it in Force? 🖱 subscription service as part of *LexisNexis Butterworths*
9–8 The online version of *Is It in Force?* is updated daily and contains links to the relevant commencement orders.

9–9 *Halsbury's Statutes* also includes the following paperback volumes:

Statutes Citator. Part 1 contains an alphabetical list of statutes published in *Halsbury's Statutes*. It does not include statutes repealed before 1929. Part 2 shows the current status of these statutes and is arranged chronologically and then alphabetically within each year. An online version of the citator is available via *LexisNexis Butterworths.*

Consolidated Index which contains alphabetical and chronological lists of all statutes contained in *Halsbury's Statutes*. It also contains a consolidated index to the current volumes and Current Statutes Service up to November 1, 2006. Volumes published subsequently will be covered by their own indexes which will supersede this index.

Consolidated Table of Statutory Instruments. This is a guide to secondary legislation which has been made or has effect under any Act in *Halsbury's Statutes.*

Consolidated Table of Cases. This contains both an alphabetical list of cases that appear in *Halsbury's Statutes* and a listing of the cases under the statutes to which they relate. Volumes reissued after June 1, 2006 will be covered by their own Tables of Cases which will supersede this index.

Destination Tables. These cover all Consolidation Acts passed between 1983 and 2005 and a selection of important Consolidation Acts back to 1957. These are useful when you want to find the provision which is currently in force where you only know the pre-consolidated legislative provision.

How to use *Halsbury's Statutes* 9–10

Using Halsbury's Statutes to find an Act on a specific subject

Consolidated Index
↓
Relevant volume (you could start from here if you know the subject area)
↓
Update by checking Cumulative Supplement
↓
Update by checking the Noter-up

!Example

You want to find out about cruelty to badgers. 9–11

⇒ **Step 1**: Either browse the spines of the hardback volumes which list the subject headings contained in each volume or look in the Consolidated Index. This will allow access under several different routes, *e.g.*

Index heading: badgers   Entry: cruelty to, offences of, 2 590

⇒ **Step 2**: Use the reference to locate the information. 2 590 means Vol. 2 p.590.
This leads to the text of the Badgers Act 1992 (c.51), s.2 which is headed "Cruelty".

⇒ **Step 3**: Check whether this information is still current. Check the beginning of the volume for a reference to a date. On one of the first pages will be a statement: "This volume states the law as at ... ." You need to update your information to cover the period from this date to the present. Volume 2 states the law as at February 1, 2003.

⇒ **Step 4**: Go to the Cumulative Supplement. This includes updated information from the bound volume to the date of the Cumulative Supplement. Check what it says about currency, *e.g.* the 2006 version says that it is "includes the effect of legislation published up to 1 March 2006". Turn to the entry for Vol.2—Animals. In this section any changes appear in the page order of Vol.2. The original reference was to p.590. The entry in the Cumulative Supplement relates to other sections of the Act but not s.2. This means that s.2 had not been changed at this stage.

⇒ **Step 5**: Again you have to ask, is this the most up to date information? No. This will only be up to date to the date of the last Cumulative Supplement. In order to include later developments you need to check the Noter-up. Turn to the entry for Vol.2—Animals. Check at the end of the section for Vol.2.There is no mention of s.2 and so you can assume it is still law unless a very recent change has been made.

⇒ **Step 6**: Having established that the current law covering cruelty to badgers is contained in the Protection of Badgers Act 1992 s.2, you will want to look at the text of the Act to establish what the current rule is. This is contained in 2, 590. You can now find out about the law regarding cruelty to badgers.

N.B. You may also need to check a very up to date source (e.g. *Lawtel, LexisNexis Butterworths* or *Westlaw*) to ensure that your knowledge is current.

Halsbury's Statutory Instruments 📖

9–12 This service provides information about every statutory instrument of general application in England and Wales. It does not include provisions that extend exclusively to Scotland. It does not reproduce every statutory instrument in full text. Those which are regarded as of little general importance are summarised. This can be the cause of frustration when you need to look at the full text.

Halsbury's Statutory Instruments consists of 22 volumes. They are arranged by subject in a similar format to *Halsbury's Laws* (para.9.33) and *Halsbury's Statutes* (para.9.5). Volume 1 starts with a section about statutory instruments. The rest of the work is alphabetical by subject from agriculture to wills. At the beginning of each volume is the date at which the law is stated in that volume. It is very important to check this date so that you can update your search accordingly.

If you want to find a statutory instrument on a specific subject then you can go to the relevant volume, *e.g.* Vol.9 for health and safety. Alternatively, if you are unsure of the relevant subject heading, you can check the detailed subject index in the separate paperback Consolidated Index. This will direct you to the relevant volume. Turn to the health and safety section. It has a table (referred to as an "arrangement") showing contents of the section. In this case the section is large and is split into three parts. There is a list of cross-references to allow you to see where material has been categorised under a different subject heading, *e.g.* slaughterhouses are dealt with under animals and food.

A preliminary note explains the legislative background to the subject area. This is followed by cross-references to *Halsbury's Statutes*. The next part of the volume is a chronological list of statutory instruments. This shows instruments in the subject area. It lists: year and number of the instrument, full title, remarks indicating if it is an amending instrument and a reference to a page number where the instrument is either printed in full or summarised. There is also a *Table of Instruments No Longer in Operation*. This lists instruments which have ceased to have effect since the last re-issue of the volume.

The texts of the statutory instruments are printed in amended form. Where amendments have been printed the added or substituted words appear in square brackets. Omissions are indicated by three dots. Each volume has a subject index at the end.

9–13 The service is kept up to date by re-issuing the volumes periodically. Between re-issues it is updated on a monthly basis through the Service. This is a looseleaf work that consists of two binders. Binder 1 contains the following information:

➢ Chronological list of all statutory instruments in the main volumes and in the Service and the subject heading under which they can be found.
➢ Table of Statutes which lists all the enabling legislation under which statutory instruments in *Halsbury's Statutory Instruments* have been made.

➤ Annual Cumulative Supplement. This updates the bound volumes and contains changes made since they were published. It contains a chronological list of new instruments, table of instruments no longer in operation, noter-up to pages of the main volumes and summaries of new instruments.

➤ Monthly Survey. This contains updates subsequent to the last Annual Cumulative Supplement. It is divided into two sections: summaries of statutory instruments which are arranged numerically and a key which relates the numbers to subject headings.

There is a separate paperback Annual Consolidated Index and Alphabetical List of Statutory Instruments which is published each year. This contains a consolidated version of all the subject indexes to the current volumes. It also covers information in the current Annual Supplement. This means that the Consolidated Index is never more than a year out of date. The Alphabetical List contains references to all statutory instruments which are included in the Service in alphabetical order. This is very useful if you want to find the number for a statutory instrument when you only know the title.

There are different ways of locating statutory instruments, by: **9–14**

⇒ Subject matter

> Start at either the Annual Consolidated Index or the volume subject index
> ↓
> relevant volume and page reference
> ↓
> update by using Annual Cumulative Supplement and the Monthly Survey.

⇒ Number

Start by looking at the chronological list in Binder 1 of the Service. This lists all statutory instruments in *Halsbury's Statutory Instruments*. This will give you the relevant heading.

↓

Turn to the relevant volume. Check the chronological list in this volume. This will lead you to the statutory instrument. If the instrument is very recent, check the Monthly Survey and the additional texts in Binder 2.

⇒ Title

Use the Alphabetical List of Statutory Instruments. This will indicate the number of the instrument and the relevant subject heading. The bound volume can then be consulted and the statutory instrument located by checking the chronological list at the beginning of the subject area.

⇒ Enabling power

To find out if any statutory instruments are made under an Act, check the Table of Statutes in Binder 1. This lists all the enabling powers under which the instruments included in *Halsbury's Statutory Instruments* have been made. It also references the appropriate subject heading. This allows you to access the statutory instruments in the bound volumes.

LAW REPORTS

9–15 South of the border, the *Law Reports* are the most authoritative series of law reports. Publication has traditionally tended to be slow and weekly law reports appeared to fill in the gap. The two most widely used weekly series are the *Weekly Law Reports* and the *All England Law Reports*.

9–16 A system of media neutral citation was introduced from January 11, 2001. This means that judgments deriving from the High Court (all divisions), the Court of Appeal (civil and criminal divisions), the House of Lords, and the Privy Council have been issued with unique judgment numbers. Cases are referenced to case number and paragraph number (instead of page number). This system means that case references are completely independent of published reports. The reason it has been adopted is to make it easier to cite and trace unreported judgments.

The judgments are numbered in the following way:

> ➢ Court of Appeal (Civil Division) [2001] EWCA Civ 1, 2, 3, etc.
> ➢ Court of Appeal (Criminal Division) [2001] EWCA Crim 1, 2, 3, etc.
> ➢ High Court (Administrative Court) [2001] EWHC Admin 1, 2, 3, etc. (pre-January 12, 2002)*
> ➢ House of Lords [2001] UKHL 6
> ➢ Privy Council [2001] UKPC 5
> ➢ Privy Council (for Devolution cases) [2001] UKPC D3

Each of these unique judgment numbers represents a case number allocated by the court, and must appear as the first in any string of citations, e.g. para.23 in *Green v Blue*, the tenth numbered judgment of the year in the Criminal Division of the Court of Appeal and the second reported case in Cr.App.R. in 2001, would be cited:

Green v Blue [2001] EWCA Crim 10 at [23]; [2001] 1 Cr.App.R. 2 [23]

*From January 12, 2002, all High Court judgments were provided with a media neutral citation by virtue of the allocation of a unique number from a central register. This applies to: Administrative Court, Admiralty Chancery Division, Commercial Court, Family Division, Patents Court, Queen's Bench Division, Technology and Construction Court. After this date, no suffix will be added after the EWHC abbreviation as the numbering is sequential. However, the Admin suffix will be retained for legacy material, i.e. judgments delivered between January 11, 2001 and January 12, 2002.

The Law Reports 📖

9–17 This series started in 1865 and is published by the Incorporated Council of Law Reporting. It is the most authoritative series of English law reports and should be cited in preference to other reports where there is a choice. The judge is given the opportunity to check the text before publication. They are also the only reports to include a summary of the argument of counsel. It was originally published in several different series but is now published in four series:

> ➢ Appeal Cases (A.C.)
> ➢ Queen's Bench (Q.B.). This becomes Kings Bench if a King is on the throne.
> ➢ Chancery Division (Ch.)
> ➢ Family Division (Fam.)

All these different parts usually appear together under "L" for Law Reports in a law library.

The Law Reports cover cases heard in:

> ➤ House of Lords
> ➤ Privy Council
> ➤ The Court of Appeal (Criminal and Civil Divisions)
> ➤ Chancery Division
> ➤ Family Division
> ➤ Queen's Bench Division
> ➤ Employment Appeal Tribunal
> ➤ European Court of Justice

The Law Reports ☜ subscription
Electronic versions of the Law Reports are available on three subscription online databases: **9–18**
LexisNexis Butterworths, Justis UK and *Irish Primary Case Law* and *Westlaw UK*.

The Law Reports Index 📖
The *Law Reports Index* provides a continuous indexing system from 1951 to date. This includes **9–19**
all cases reported in: *Law Reports, Weekly Law Reports* and *Industrial Case Reports*. It also
includes references to cases reported in: *All England Commercial Cases; All England European
Cases; All England Law Reports; Criminal Appeal Reports; Lloyd's Law Reports; Local Government Reports; Road Traffic Reports;* and *Simon's Case Cases.*

There are currently six volumes. They are referred to as the "Red Indexes". The six volumes
are: 1951–60, 1961–70, 1971–80, 1981–90, 1991–00, 2001–05. There is also a Red Book for 2006.

The Red Index is a very useful way of finding cases using a paper source. It consists of the
following tables of information:

> ➤ Cases reported
> ➤ Subject matter—includes "Words and Phrases" as a heading
> ➤ Cases judicially considered
> ➤ Statutes judicially considered
> ➤ Statutory Instruments judicially considered
> ➤ Standard forms of Contract judicially considered
> ➤ EC enactments judicially considered
> ➤ Overseas enactments judicially considered
> ➤ International Conventions judicially considered

The Red Index is updated by periodic pink indexes which are published several times a year.
Further updates of the Index can be found at the beginning of each issue of the *Weekly Law
Reports*.

Red Index
↓
Pink Index
↓
Weekly Law Reports

The Weekly Law Reports (WLR) 📖
This series started in 1953. It is published 45 times a year. The *Weekly Law Reports* for each year **9–20**
are in four volumes. Vols 1a and 1b contain cases which do not merit inclusion in *The Law
Reports*. vol.2 (January–June) and Vol.3 (July–December) cover cases which will be subsequently published in the *Law Reports*.

The annual volumes contain the following information:

> ➢ List of judges
> ➢ Cases—accessible by either party's name
> ➢ Subject Matter Index which includes a "Words and phrases" heading
> ➢ Case reports

The weekly parts additionally contain the update of The Law Reports Index, namely:

> ➢ Cases judicially considered
> ➢ Statutes judicially considered
> ➢ Statutory Instruments judicially considered
> ➢ EC enactments judicially considered
> ➢ Overseas enactments judicially considered

The Weekly Law Reports (WLR) ⌁ subscription

9–21 Electronic versions of the *Weekly Law Reports* are available in *Justis UK* and *Irish Primary Case Law* and *Westlaw UK*. Also see the *WLR Daily* at para.9.31.

All England Law Reports (All ER) 📖

9–22 This series began in 1936. It is published 48 times a year in weekly parts. The annual volumes contain the following information:

> ➢ List of judges
> ➢ Table of cases—accessible by either party's name
> ➢ Digest of cases accessible via subject matter
> ➢ House of Lords Petitions—details of the results of any petitions for leave to appeal

The case reports contain references to *Halsbury's Laws of England*, *Halsbury's Statutes of England and Wales*, and *Halsbury's Statutory Instruments*.

There are two subseries:
All England Commercial Cases 1999–present. This series is in the same format as the general series but contains cases of interest to lawyers who specialise in commercial law.
All England European Cases 1995–present. This series contains judgments with headnotes and catchwords from the European Court of Justice and the Court of First Instance.

There are three volumes of Consolidated Tables and Index covering from 1936–2006. These include Commercial Cases and European Cases. Vol.1 contains:

> ➢ Table of cases reported and judicially considered.
> ➢ Table of practice directions and notes.
> ➢ Table of statues judicially considered.
> ➢ Table of words and phrases judicially considered.

Volumes 2 and 3 contain a subject index.

All England Law Reports (All ER) ⌁ subscription

9–23 An electronic version of the *All England Law Reports*, *All England Commercial Cases* and *All England European Cases* is available in *LexisNexis Butterworths*.

The Times Law Reports 📖
The Times Law Reports were published from 1884 until 1952, when the *Weekly Law Reports* **9–24** started publication. The early reports were based on those published in the *Times* while later reports were transcripts of the judgments. These were published in annual volumes.

The *Times* publishes law reports today however these are just summaries of cases. These modern reports are published in annual volumes from 1990. In addition to the reports the volumes contain:

> ➢ Cumulative table of cases reported,
> ➢ Cumulative table of cases referred to,
> ➢ Cumulative table of legislation,
> ➢ Cumulative subject index.

The Times Law Reports ⌃ subscription
Online versions of the *Times Law Reports* are available from *Justis UK* and *Irish Primary Case* **9–25** *Law* (from 1990) and *LexisNexis Butterworths* from 1988.

The daily reports can be viewed on *http://business.timesonline.co.uk/tol/business/law/reports* at no cost.

The Digest (formerly The English & Empire Digest) 📖
The *Digest* covers case law of England and Wales and has a selection of cases from Scotland, **9–26** Ireland, Canada, Australia, New Zealand and other Commonwealth countries. The current edition consists of 116 volumes. It contains annotated summaries of over 500,000 cases. The *Digest* tends to be the most widely available source of information about Scottish cases in England.

The *Digest* is a sister publication to *Halsbury's Laws* and the arrangement is similar. Cross-references are given to *Halsbury's Statutes* and *Halsbury's Laws*. It is updated by volumes being re-issued, an Annual Cumulative Supplement and a Quarterly Survey of recent developments. In order to facilitate searching there are Consolidated Tables of Cases and a Consolidated (Subject) Index.

SOURCES OF RECENT ENGLISH CASES

BAILII ⌃ free
The *BAILII* site (*http://www.bailii.org/*) is a full text searchable database which includes a large **9–27** amount of English cases, for more details about *BAILII* see para.4.22. It contains the following UK/English cases:

> ➢ House of Lords decisions November 14, 1996 onwards.
> ➢ Privy Council judgments 1996 onwards and selected earlier judgments.
> ➢ Court of Appeal (Civil Division) and High Court (Administrative Court and Crown Office List), all cases from 1996 to August 1999, all significant handed down decisions September 1999 to December 2002, and all substantive judgments from January 2003 onwards.
> ➢ Court of Appeal (Criminal Division), all decisions from 1996 to August 1999 and some significant handed down decisions from August 1999 onwards.
> ➢ Other divisions of the High Court, selected decisions from 1997 onwards.

House of Lords website ⌃ free
House of Lords Judgments appear on a section of the United Kingdom Parliament web pages **9–28** *http://www.publications.parliament.uk/pa/ld/ldjudgmt.htm* For more details see para.4.23.

Judgments of the Privy Council ⊕ free

9–29 All judgments of the Privy Council from 1996 onwards along with some selected earlier judgments are available at *http://www.privy-council.org.uk/output/page31.asp*.

The Register of Judgments, Orders and Fines ⊕ search fee payable

9–30 *The Register of Judgments, Orders and Fines is available* at *http://www.registry-trust.org.uk/* This has three sections which can be searched for a fee:

> ➢ County Court Judgments, Administration Orders and Child Support Agency Liability Orders.
> ➢ High Court Judgments.
> ➢ Magistrates Courts Fines defaults.

The WLR Daily ⊕ free

9–31 The *WLR Daily* is a free case summary service from The Incorporated Council on Law Reporting's service (ICLR) and can be accessed at (*http://www.lawreports.co.uk/WLRD/AboutWLRD.htm*). The cases reported are cases deemed to be worthy of inclusion in The *Weekly Law Reports*, *The Law Reports* or *The Industrial Cases Reports*. You can view daily summaries of *Latest Cases* as they appear or navigate via the *Monthly Archive*. Alternatively, you can search by subject matter using the *Subject Matter Search*. The cases are summarised and appear within 24 hours of judgment being handed down.

Daily Cases ⊕ subscription

9–32 *Daily Cases* is a subscription service provided by *Justis*. It is a fully searchable web version of *The WLR Daily* (above). It includes judgments of the House of Lords, the Privy Council, the Court of Appeal, all Divisions of the High Court, the Courts-Martial Appeal Court, the Restrictive Practices Court, the Employment Appeal Tribunal and the European Court of Justice. Only cases that develop or clarify a point of law or that set legal precedent are included. Practice Directions, Practice Notes and Practice Statements are also covered. Its coverage is from 1999 to the present and it is updated most working days.

HALSBURY'S LAWS OF ENGLAND 📖

9–33 This is a major encyclopaedia covering all areas of English law. It is the English equivalent of *The Laws of Scotland: Stair Memorial Encyclopaedia*. It has been in existence for far longer than its Scottish counterpart and is widely regarded as the best starting point for research on a UK-wide or English problem. It does not include exclusively Scottish material. This work should be distinguished from *Halsbury's Statutes*, which contains annotated versions of the text of Acts of Parliament. *Halsbury's Laws* does not contain primary material, it is a commentary on the law of England.

The current edition (4th) of *Halsbury's Laws* was completed in 1987. It consists of 57 main volumes. It is kept up to date by the re-issue of individual volumes. There are now few volumes which date from 1986. In addition there is an annual Cumulative Supplement (two volumes) and a monthly Current Service (two binders). References used throughout are to volume and paragraph number.

There are many component parts to *Halsbury's Laws*.

Component parts

Individual volumes

9–34 The following information is given at the beginning of each volume:

➢ The date at which the law is stated
➢ Table of contents
➢ Table of references and abbreviations
➢ Table of statutes
➢ Table of statutory instruments
➢ Table of cases

At the end of the volume there is a detailed index for each subject covered by that volume and a words and phrases index. This lists words and phrases which have been explained or defined in the volume.

Annual Cumulative Supplement

The two-volume Annual Cumulative Supplement brings the work up to date to within a year. It **9–35** provides an account of the changes which have taken place since publication of the bound volumes. Each annual Cumulative Supplement supersedes the previous supplement. Unfortunately libraries often leave out-of-date editions sitting on the shelves. This means that you should ensure that you are using the most recent edition. The Cumulative Supplement is arranged in the same way as the volumes.

The Current Service

This is contained in two binders and is updated monthly. It details developments in the law **9–36** which have taken place since the date of the last Cumulative Supplement. Binder 1 contains the following information:

➢ The *Monthly Review*. This is published in a journal format. Its prime function is to update *Halsbury's Laws* on a monthly basis but it is designed so that it can be read on its own as a digest of recent developments.
➢ Tables of cases (includes a quantum of damages table), statutes and statutory instruments.
➢ A cumulative index to the monthly reviews. This cross-references the reviews to the bound volumes and the Cumulative Supplement.

Binder 2 contains the following information:

➢ Commencement of Statutes Table. This lists statutes which were not in force (wholly or partially) when the latest Cumulative Supplement was published. It specifies commencement dates for statutes or states "no date" as appropriate.
➢ Destination Tables for Consolidation Acts.
➢ Personal Injury Section which includes various model letters.
➢ Practice Directions relating to the English courts.
➢ Table of Articles which relates recent articles to the *Halsbury* subject headings.
➢ Words and Phrases Judicially Interpreted.
➢ EC materials.
➢ Noter-up. This sets out the latest developments in the same format as the Cumulative Supplement.

The Annual Abridgement

This has been published annually since 1974. The *Monthly Review* contains numerous sum- **9–37** maries of cases and legislation which (for reasons of space) are not included in the Cumulative Supplement. The Cumulative Supplement only contains details of the effects of these developments on the previous law. The summaries of the cases and legislation are consolidated from the *Monthly Reviews* into an Abridgement volume.

Volume 53 (1) and (2) Consolidated Tables of Statutes etc.

9–38 This includes consolidated tables of statutes, statutory instruments, procedural materials, European material, treaties and conventions, non-statutory rules and regulations, Codes of practice and reports. These list the piece of legislation and the relevant reference for it in *Halsbury's Laws.* This allows you to access *Halsbury's Laws* when you know the title of a piece of legislation but are unsure about the subject area.

Volume 54 (1) and (2) Consolidated Table of Cases

9–39 This lists all the cases (including cases from the European Court of Justice) referred to in *Halsbury's Laws* in alphabetical order of claimant (previously referred to as plaintiff). There is also a chronological table of European cases. This allows access to *Halsbury's Laws* when you only know the name of a case.

Consolidated Index Volume 55 (A–E), Volume 56 (F–O) and Volume 57 (P-Z)

9–40 This is a very detailed subject index allowing you to key into the system of categorisation used throughout *Halsbury's Laws.* At the end of Vol.57 is a Words and Phrases Table. This includes words which are defined or explained in *Halsbury's Laws.* This is a very useful feature. Say, for example, you want to find out about how "marine pollution" has been defined. Check this table under "M" and there is an entry:

"marine" (pollution)   **43(1), 39n1**"

Turn to Vol.43(1), para.39 and note 1 discusses the definition of "marine pollution".

N.B. The information in Vols 53–57 will quickly become out of date so you need to check the date of publication. A volume of the main work which has been re-issued since these index volumes were last updated will have more up-to-date information for its own subject area.

9–41 Using *Halsbury's Laws*

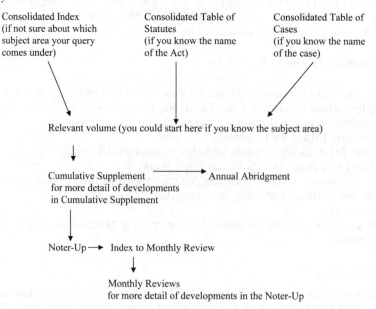

Diagram 9.1: Using Halsbury's Laws

N.B. Halsbury's Laws is always being updated. It is important to make sure that you are looking at the most up-to-date version. There is a check list of materials at the beginning of Binder 1 of the Current Service.

Halsbury's Laws of England ⌐♱ subscription

Halsbury's Laws of England are also available online as part of *LexisNexis Butterworths*. From **9–42** the home page select *Commentary* from the tab along the top of the page. This opens up the *Commentary search* page. Click on the downward arrow beside the Select Source box and click on *Halsbury's Laws*. Use the *enter search terms* box to do a free text search. This will search the whole encyclopaedia. Alternatively if you select *browse* on the *Commentary search* page, you will then be able to click on *Halsbury's Laws* and browse an alphabetical list of the subject headings used in the paper version. You could go straight to a subject or you could tick one or more subjects and then enter words into the *Quick search* box or return to the *commentary search* box where your search will be restricted to your chosen subject areas. The text from the original paper volume will appear on the screen with any updates appearing at the end of the main text. It is updated on a monthly basis.

Further information

Further information on English legal information sources will be found in: **9–43**

A. Bradney et al *How to Study Law* 5th edn (London: Sweet & Maxwell, 2005).
P. Clinch, *Using a Law Library* 2nd edn (London: Blackstone Press, 2001).
G. Holburn and G. Engle, *Butterworths Legal Research Guide* (London: Butterworths, 2001).
J. Knowles and P. Thomas *Effective Legal Research* (London: Sweet & Maxwell, 2006).
P.A. Thomas and J. Knowles, *Dane & Thomas How to Use a Law Library* 4th edn (London: Sweet & Maxwell, 2001).

INTRODUCTION

10–1 European law makes up an increasingly important part of our body of law. It is, therefore, essential to be aware of the European dimension to our legal system. This chapter is not intended to provide an overview of the European institutions and the law-making process. Further information on these areas can be found in one of the large number of dedicated European texts (see para.10.60). It is intended to draw your attention to features of the European system which are of relevance to the legal researcher, to introduce you to the key documents of European law and to suggest search strategies for finding information about European law.

There is a vast amount of material published on European law and it is not possible to cover all of it in one chapter. This chapter is designed to introduce you to the principal sources and to make you aware of some of the many alternative ways of locating material. Particular attention will be paid to sources which are official, widely available and those which are free.

For many years the sources used were almost exclusively dedicated European sources however over time many of the principal UK information sources have incorporated European elements. European cases are also increasingly reported in UK law reports. However, it is still the case that the information sources are largely different from UK material. This is principally because of the high standard of some of the European databases both in range of information and search functionality. The provision of free information has always been an important concept in the European institutions. This means that there are excellent free electronic sources of European law. This, together with the large amount of information produced by the Community institutions, means that the majority of information sources are electronic as opposed to paper in this area.

Although there are large numbers of official Community publications this does not mean that it is easier to research EC law than our own domestic law. Problems can be caused by several factors: the sheer volume of material emerging from centralised institutions; significant time delays in publication of some key sources; and a lack of user-friendly indexes to *all* the information (although this is improving). Another problem relates to terminology. The indexing systems tend to use Euro-terminology, which can be confusing.

10–2 One initial point of confusion is the difference between the EEC, EC and EU. The term "Community law" originally referred to the three communities set up by the Treaty of Paris 1951 and the Treaty of Rome 1957: the European Coal & Steel Community (ECSC), the European Atomic Energy Community (EURATOM) and the European Economic Community (EEC). There are now only two communities following the expiry of the ECSC in 2002. The Treaty on European Union (the "Maastricht Treaty") came into force in November 1993. It renamed the EEC, "EC" (European Community) and established the European Union. The European Union consists of three "pillars": the first pillar is the "Communities pillar" and it is the only pillar to be governed by European Community law. The other pillars (Common Foreign and Security Policy and Co-operation in Justice and Home Affairs) are not subject to the jurisdiction of the Community institutions and the European Court. Those second and third pillars function by way of intergovernmental co-operation.

LEGISLATION

EC laws are made by a completely different process and are different in format to UK legis- **10–3** lation. See anatomy section, para.10.6. Some forms of legislation (Regulations) are effective immediately on all Member States; others (Directives) are generally only effective after implementation by Member States into their own national law.

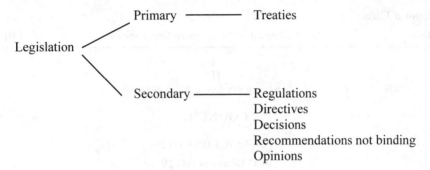

Diagram 10.1: European Legislation

Primary legislation—Treaties

The EC Treaty (previously the European Community Treaty) 1957 and the Euratom Treaty are **10–4** primary sources of Community law. However, there have been many other subsequent treaties some of which (including the Treaty on European Union 1992: the Maastricht Treaty) have amended these founding treaties. For the legal researcher a particularly significant change was made by the Treaty of Amsterdam 1997 which came into force in 1999. As a result of article 12 of the Treaty of Amsterdam the articles, titles and sections of the Treaty on European Union and the EC Treaty have been renumbered. This can cause for confusion and many texts now include tables of equivalences which list the previous and new numbering.

Citation convention

The citation convention for secondary legislation comprises: **10–5**

- ➢ The institutional origin (Commission or Council or European Parliament and Council)
- ➢ The form (Regulation or Directive etc.)
- ➢ The number
- ➢ The year of enactment
- ➢ The institutional treaty basis (EC, ECSC, EURATOM)
- ➢ Date passed

Note that Regulations are cited by number first followed by the year whereas Directives and Decisions cite the year followed by the number.

!Examples

Council Regulation (EC, Euratom) No.337/2007 of March 27, 2007 adjusting from January 1, 2007 the scale applicable to missions by officials and other servants of the European Communities in Bulgaria and Romania.

Directive 2006/7/EC of the European Parliament and of the Council of February 15, 2006 concerning the management of bathing water quality and repealing Directive 76/160/EEC.

2007/323/EC: Council Decision of September 18, 2006 on the signing and provisional application of the Agreement between the European Community and the Republic of Paraguay on certain aspects of air services.

ANATOMY OF A DIRECTIVE

10–6 Excerpt from a Directive

31. 12 91 **[2]**   Official Journal of the European Communities   **[1]** No L375/1

II
(Acts whose publication is not obligatory)

COUNCIL

COUNCIL DIRECTIVE
of 12 December 1991 **[3]**

concerning the protection of waters against pollution caused by nitrates from agricultural sources

(91/676/EEC) **[4]**

COUNCIL OF THE EUROPEAN COMMUNITIES,
      [5]

Having regard to the Treaty establishing the European Economic Community, and in particular Article 130s thereof, **[6]**

Having regard to the proposal from the Commission (¹)

Having regard to the opinion of the European Parliament (²)

Having regard to the opinion of the Economic and Social Committee (³), **[7]**

Whereas the nitrate content of water in some areas of Member States is increasing and is already high as compared with standards laid down in Council Directive 75/440/EEC of 16 June 1975 concerning, the quality required of surface water intended for the abstraction of drinking water in the Member States (⁴), as amended by Directive 79/869/EEC (⁵), and Council Directive 80/778/EEC of 15 July 1980 relating to the quality of Crater intended for human consumption (⁶), as amended by 1985 Act of Accession;

Whereas the fourth programme of action of the European Economic Communities on the environment (⁷) indicated that the Commission intended to make a proposal for a

Directive on the control and reduction of water pollution resulting from the spreading or discharge of livestock effluents and the excessive use of fertilizers; **[8]**

Whereas the reform of the common agricultural policy set out in the Commission's green paper 'Perspectives for the common agricultural policy' indicated that, while the use of nitrogen-containing fertilizers and manures is necessary for Community agriculture, excessive use of fertilizers constitutes an environmental risk, that common action is needed to control the problem arising from intensive livestock production and that agricultural policy must take greater account of environmental policy;

Whereas the Council resolution of 28 June 1988 of the protection of the North Sea and of other waters in the Community (⁸) invites the Commission to submit proposals for measures at Community level;

Whereas the main cause of pollution from diffuse sources affecting the Community's waters in nitrates from agricultural sources;

Whereas it is therefore necessary, in order to protect human health and living resources and aquatic ecosystems and to safeguard other legitimate uses of water, to reduce water pollution caused or induced by nitrates from agricultural sources and to prevent further such pollution; whereas for this purpose it is important to take measures

---

(¹) OJ No C 54, 3. 3. 1989, p. 4 and OJ No C 51, 2. 3. 1990, p. 12.
(²) OJ No C 158, 26. 6. 1989, p. 487.
(³) OJ No C 159, 26. 6. 1989, p. 1.
(⁴) OJ No L 194, 25. 7. 1975, p. 26.

(⁵) OJ No L 271, 29. 10. 1979, p. 44.
(⁶) No L 229, 30. 8. 1980, p. 11.
(⁷) OJ No C 328, 7. 12. 1987, p. 1.
(⁸) OJ No C 209, 9. 8. 1988, p. 3.

concerning the storage and the application on land of all nitrogen compounds and concerning certain land management practices;

Whereas since pollution of water due to nitrates on one Member State can influence waters in other Member States, action at Community level in accordance with Article 130r is therefore necessary;

Whereas, by encouraging good agricultural practices, Member States can provide all waters with a general level of protection against pollution in the future;

Whereas certain zones, draining into waters vulnerable to pollution from nitrogen compounds, require special protection;

Whereas it is necessary for Member States to identify vulnerable zones and to establish and implement action programmes in order to reduce water pollution from nitrogen compounds in vulnerable zones;

Whereas such action programmes should include measures to limit the land-application of all nitrogen-containing fertilizers and in particular to set specific limits for the application of livestock manure;

Whereas it is necessary to monitor waters and to apply reference methods of measurement for nitrogen compounds to ensure that measures are effective;

Whereas it is recognized that the hydrogeology in certain Member States is such that it may he many years before protection measures lead to improvements in water quality;

Whereas a Committee should be established to assist the Commission on matters relating to the implementation of this Directive and to its adaptation to scientific and technical progress;

Whereas Member States should establish and present to the Commission reports on the implementation of this Directive;

Whereas the Commission should report regularly on the implementation of this Directive by the Member States, HAS ADOPTED THIS DIRECTIVE: **[9]**

Article 1 **[10]**

This Directive has the objective of:

— reducing water pollution caused or induced by nitrates from agricultural sources; and
— preventing further such pollution.

Article 2

For the purpose of this Directive:

(a) 'groundwater': means all water which is below the surface of the ground in the saturation zone an direct contact with the ground or subsoil;

(b) 'freshwater': means naturally occurring water having a low concentration of salts, which is often acceptable as suitable for abstraction and treatment to produce drinking water;

(c) 'nitrogen compound': means any nitrogen-containing substance except for gaseous molecular nitrogen;

(d) 'livestock': means all animals kept for use or profit;

(e) 'fertilizer': means any substance containing a nitrogen compound or nitrogen compounds utilized on land to enhance growth of vegetation; it may include livestock manure, the residues from fish farms and sewage sludge;

(f) 'chemical fertilizer: means any fertilizer which is manufactured by an industrial process;

(g) 'livestock manure': means waste products excreted by livestock or a mixture of litter and waste products excreted by livestock, even in processed form;

(h) 'land application': means the addition of materials to land whether by spreading on the surface of the land, injection into the land, placing below the surface of the land or mixing with the surface layers of the land;

(i) 'eutrophication': means the enrichment of water by nitrogen compounds, causing an accelerated growth of algae and higher forms of plant life to produce an undesirable disturbance to the balance of organisms present in the water and to the quality of the water concerned;

(j) 'pollution': means the discharge, directly or indirectly, or nitrogen compounds from agricultural sources into the aquatic environment, the results of which are such as to cause hazards to human health, harm to living resources and to aquatic ecosystems, damage to amenities or interference with other legitimate uses of water;

(k) 'vulnerable zone': means an area of land designated according to Article 3(2).

Article 3

1. Waters affected by pollution and waters which could be affected by pollution if action pursuant Article 5 is not taken shall be identified by the Member States in accordance with the criteria set out in Annex I.

2. Member States shall, within a two-year period, following the notification of this Directive, designate as vulnerable zones all known areas of land in their territories which drain into the waters identified according to paragraph 1 and which contribute to pollution. They shall notify the Commission of this initial designation within six months.

3. When any waters identified by a Member State in accordance with paragraph 1 are affected by pollution

from waters from another Member State draining directly or indirectly in to them, the Member States whose waters affected may notify the other Member States and the Commission of the relevant facts.

The Member States concerned shall organise, where appropriate with the Commission, the concentration necessary to identify the sources in question and the measures to be taken to protect the waters that are affected in order to ensure conformity with this Directive.

4. Member States shall review if necessary revise or add to the designation of vulnerable zones as appropriate, and at least every four years, to take into account changes and factors unforeseen at the time of the previous designation. They shall notify the Commission of any revision or addition to the designations within six months.

5. Member States shall be exempt from the obligation to identify specific vulnerable zones, if they establish and apply action programmes referred to in Article 5 in accordance with this Directive throughout their national territory.

Article 12 **[11]**

1. The Member States shall bring into force the laws, regulations and administrative provisions necessary to

---

(¹) This Directive was notified to the Member States on 19 December 1991.

comply with this Directive within two years of its notification (¹). They shall forthwith inform the Commission thereof.

2. When Member States adopt these measures, they shall contain a reference to this Directive or shall be accompanied by such reference on the occasion of their official publication. The methods of making such a reference shall be laid down by the Member States.

3. Member States shall communicate to the Commission the texts of the provisions of national law which they adopt in the field governed by this Directive.

Article 13

This Directive is addressed to the Member States.

Done at Brussels, 12 December 1991.

For the Council
The President
J.G.M. ALDERS

ANNEX 1 **[12]**

CRITERIA FOR IDENTIFYING WATERS REFERRED TO IN ARTICLE 3(1)

A. Waters referred to in Article 3 (1) shall be identified making use, *inter alia*, of the following criteria:

  1. whether surface freshwaters, in particular those used or intended for the abstraction of drinking water, contain or could contain, if action pursuant to Article 5 is not taken, more than the concentration of nitrates laid down in accordance with Directive 75/440/EEC;

  2. whether groundwaters contain more than 50 mg/1 nitrates or could contain more than 50 mg/1 nitrates if action pursuant to Article 5 is not taken;

  3. whether natural freshwater lakes, other freshwater bodies, estuaries, coastal waters and marine waters are found to be eutrophic or in the near future may become euthropic if action pursuant to Article 5 is not taken.

B. In applying these criteria, Member States shall also take account of:

  1. the physical and environmental characteristics of the waters and land;

  2. the current understanding of the behaviour of nitrogen compounds in the environment (water and soil);

  3. the current understanding of the impact of the action taken pursuant to Article 5.

10–7 Different features of the Directive are marked with numbers which correspond to the following list:

  [1] Official Journal series, issue and page—note the title has now changed to the *Official Journal of the European Union*.
  [2] Date of publication.
  [3] Date of adoption.

[4] Number of the Directive which comprises the year of enactment, running number and the institutional treaty basis of the Directive.

[5] The enacting authority.

[6] The legal basis (treaty) for the Directive.

[7] The legislative procedure.

[8] The series of paragraphs beginning with the word "whereas" are referred to as recitals. They state the main policy considerations that lie behind the Directive.

[9] This is usually printed in capital letters and represents the end of the first part of the Directive.

[10] The substantive part of the Directive. The parts of European legislation are referred to as articles and not as sections.

[11] Provision concerning when the Directive is to be brought into force.

[12] Additional information at the end of a Directive will be contained in annexes (the equivalent of schedules in UK legislation).

A Directive has been used as an example of European legislation. Regulations are similar in format.

CASES

There are two courts which interpret and enforce EC law. The European Court of Justice **10–8** (E.C.J.) was established in 1952 and the Court of First Instance (C.F.I.), which gave its first judgment in 1990. Both are situated in Luxembourg. Points to note:

⇒ Avoid using the term the "European Court". This can cause confusion as there are several courts this title could refer to: European Court of Justice, Court of First Instance, the EFTA (European Free Trade Association) Court and the European Court of Human Rights.

⇒ European cases are reported in a different format from UK cases, see anatomy of a case, para.10.10.

⇒ There is no equivalent to the role played by the Advocate General in our legal system. At present there are eight Advocates General who assist the Court of Justice. The Advocate General's role is independent. He has no connection with either of the parties to a case and yet he is not one of the judges. He delivers an Opinion for the court to consider. In the Opinion he reviews the legal issues and puts forward a proposal as to how the case should be decided. The purpose of the Opinion is to help the court come to their decision. The court is not bound to follow the Opinion, but in practice it does so frequently. The Advocate General's Opinion can be persuasive in later cases. The Opinion will consider the legal issues whereas the judgment of the court will tend to be short and concise. Greater understanding of the legal issues of a case can be gleaned from the Opinion.

⇒ There is no strict doctrine of *stare decisis* in the European Court of Justice.

⇒ Statutory interpretation in the European Court of Justice is different from in the UK. The European Court of Justice has tended to adopt a purposive approach to statutory interpretation. It has been criticised for taking this too far and attempting to create law.

⇒ Nicknames for cases. It is common for European cases to be referred to by nicknames. This has arisen because the names tended to be long and difficult to remember. This habit can be useful to distinguish similar cases. However, it can cause problems in locating a case as the nickname is seldom referred to in indexes of cases. Problems can also arise if the same nickname has been given to more than one case. An example of a nickname being used is the Bosman case, Case C-415/93 *Union Royale Belge de Societes de Football Association ASBL v Jean-Marc Bosman* [1995] E.C.R. I-4921.

Case Citation

10–9 The full case citation is made up as follows:

> ➤ case number/year*
> ➤ names of the parties
> ➤ [year of judgment]
> ➤ citation of the report

!Example

Case 6/64 *Costa v ENEL* [1964] E.C.R. 585.

*The year referred to is the year that application was made to the court. It does not necessarily mean that it will appear in the case reports of that year.

In 1990, the Court of First Instance started to issue judgments. In order to distinguish cases from the two courts, the letter "C" was added to cases from the Court of Justice and the letter "T" added to cases from the Court of First Instance. If the letter "P" appears after the year it denotes that the case has been appealed from the Court of First Instance to the European Court of Justice.

!Example

Case C-200/02 *Zhu v Chen* [2004] E.C.R. I-9925

Case T-93/02 *Confédération nationale du Crédit mutuel v Commission of the European Communities* [2005] E.C.R. II-00143

Case C-113/04 P *Technische Unie BV v Commission of the European Communities* [2006] E.C.R. I-08831

Note: while the above is the full style of citation it is common to see citations of European cases omitting the case number altogether or placing it after the names of the parties.

Anatomy of a European Case Report

10–10 The following case appears in the format used by the European Court Reports.

Case C-83/97 [1]

Commission of the European Communities [2]

v

Federal Republic of Germany

(Failure to fulfil obligations—Failure to transpose Directive 92/43/EEC)

Opinion of Advocate General Fennelly delivered on 23 October 1997 .... I—7192
Judgment of the Court (Fifth Chamber) 11 December 1997 .... I—7195

Summary of the Judgment [3]

Acts of the institutions — Directives — Implementation by the Member States — Mere administrative practices not sufficient
(EC Treaty, Art. 189, third para.)

Mere administrative practices, which by their nature are alterable at will by the administration and are not given the appropriate publicity, cannot be regarded as constituting the proper fulfilment of a Member State's obligations under Article 189 of the Treaty.

I—7191 [4]

OPINION OF MR FENNELLY — CASE C-83/97

OPINION OF ADVOCATE GENERAL [5] FENNELLY

delivered on 23 October 1997*

1. Council Directive 92/43/EEC of 21 May 1992 on the conservation of natural habitats and of wild fauna and flora[1] (hereinafter 'the Directive') was notified to the Federal Republic of Germany on 5 June 1992. Article 23(1) required Member States to 'bring into force the laws, regulations and administrative provisions necessary to comply with this Directive within two years of its notification [and] forthwith [to] inform the Commission thereof'. For Germany, this deadline therefore expired on 5 June 1994.

2. In the absence of any indication that the Directive had been transposed into German law, the Commission opened the pre-litigation stage of the procedure provided by Article 169 of the Treaty establishing the European Community ('the Treaty') by sending a letter of formal notice on 9 August 1994. Germany did not contest the complaint in its reply of 6 October 1994. The Commission issued a reasoned opinion on 28 November 1995, to the effect that in failing to adopt the necessary provisions, Germany was in breach of its obligations under the Directive, and setting a two-month deadline for compliance. The present proceedings were initiated pursuant to Article 169 of the Treaty by an application registered at the Court on 24 February 1997.

3. In its application, the Commission observes that, as far as it is aware, not all the provisions necessary to comply with the Directive have been adopted or notified, and that the defendant neither answered nor complied with the reasoned opinion. On this ground, it requests the Court to hold that Germany is in breach of its obligations under the Treaty, and in particular the third paragraph of Article 189 and the first paragraph of Article 5 thereof.

4. In its defence, Germany admits that it has not adopted all the necessary measures to comply with its obligations under the Directive. It adds by way of complementary information that the Directive is directly applied by the competent public authorities, and that the existing national provisions are interpreted in conformity therewith. Furthermore, a bill to amend the Bundesnaturschutzgesetz (Federal law on nature protection) has

been submitted to the Bundestag (Federal Assembly, lower house of parliament); the legislative procedure was scheduled to be completed by Autumn 1997.

5. The Directive is predicated on the statement in the first recital in the preamble that, 'the preservation, protection and improvement of the quality of the environment, including the conservation of natural habitats and of wild fauna and flora, are an essential objective of general interest pursued by the Community'. The fourth recital notes that, as 'the threatened habitats and species form part of the Community's natural heritage and the threats to them are often of a transboundary nature, it is necessary to take measures at Community level in order to conserve them'. This Directive is closely linked to Council Directive 79/409/EEC of 2 April on the conservation of wild birds[2] (hereinafter 'the Birds Directive').[3] The definition of the obligation to transpose the Birds Directive laid down by the Court from its earliest judgments in this area seems to me to be applicable, *mutatis mutandis*, to the obligation to transpose the present Directive. In *Commission v Belgium*, for example, the Court held that transposition 'does not necessarily require the provisions of the directive to be enacted in precisely the same words in a specific express legal provision national law; a general legal context may be sufficient if it actually ensures the full application of the directive in a sufficiently clear and precise manners'.[4] It added a proviso to this general statement which is especially relevant in the present proceedings, to the effect that 'a faithful transposition becomes particularly important in a case such as this in which the management of the common heritage is entrusted to the Member States in their respective territories'.[5]

6. Germany has expressly admitted its failure to adopt all of the necessary provisions to comply with the Directive; it has not contended that the action of the public authorities, or the interpretation of the relevant national provisions, ensures such compliance, and, indeed, the Court has consistently held that '[mere] administrative practices, which by their nature are alterable at will by the authorities and are not given the appropriate publicity, cannot

he regarded as constituting the proper fulfilment of obligations under the Treaty'.[6] In these circumstances, I am of the opinion that the Commission should be granted the declarations which it has requested both on the merits and as regards costs.

* Original language: English
[1] — OJ 1992 L 206, p. 7.
[2] — OJ 1979 L 103, p. 1.
[3] — See paragraph 70 of my Opinion in Case C-44/95 *Royal Society for the Protection of Birds* [1996] ECR I-3802, at pp. I-3832 and I-3833.

[4] — Case 247/85 [1987] ECR 3029, paragraph 9 of the judgment.
[5] — Loc. Cit.
[6] — Case C-334/94 *Commission v France* [1996] ECR I-1307, paragraph 30 of the judgment.

Conclusion

7. In the light of the foregoing, I recommend to the Court that it:

(1)   Declare that, by failing to adopt the laws, regulations and administrative provisions necessary to comply with Council Directive 92/43/EEC of 21 May 1992 on the conservation of natural habitats and of wild fauna and flora within the deadline set, the Federal Republic of Germany has failed to comply with its obligations under the EC Treaty;

(2)   Order the Federal Republic of Germany to pay the costs.

COMMISSION v GERMANY

JUDGMENT OF THE COURT (Fifth Chamber) [6]

11 December 1997*

In Case C-83/97,

Commission of the European Communities, represented by Götz zur Hausen, Legal Adviser, acting as Agent, with an address for service in Luxembourg at the office of Carlos Gómez de la Cruz, of its Legal Service, Wagner Centre, Kirchberg, [7]

applicant,

v

Federal Republic of Germany, represented by Ernst Rösder, Ministerialrat in the Federal Ministry of Economic Affairs, and Bernd Kloke, Oberregierungsrat in the same ministry, acting as Agents, D-53107 Bonn,

defendant,

APPLICATION for a declaration that, by failing to adopt within the prescribed period the laws, regulations and administrative provisions necessary to comply with Council Directive 92/43/EEC of 21 May 1992 on the conservation of natural habitats and of wild fauna and flora (OJ 1992 L 206, p. 7), the Federal Republic of Germany has failed to fulfil its obligations under the EC Treaty, [8]

* Language of the case: German. [9]

COMMISSION v GERMANY

THE COURT (Fifth Chamber)

composed of. C. Gulmann (Rapporteur), President of the Chamber, M. Wathelet, J. C. Moitinho de Almeida, J.-P. Puissochet and L. Sevón, Judges, [10]

Advocate General: N. Fennelly,
Registrar. R. Grass, [11]

having regard to the report of the Judge-Rapporteur, [12]

after hearing the Opinion of the Advocate General at the sitting on 23 October 1997, gives the following

Judgment [13]

1. By application lodged at the Registry of the Court of justice on 24 February 1997, the Commission of the European Communities brought an action under Article 169 of the EC Treaty for a declaration that, by failing to adopt within the prescribed period the laws, regulations and administrative provisions necessary to comply with Council Directive 92/43/EEC of 21 May 1992 on the conservation of natural habitats and of wild fauna and flora (OJ 1992 L 206, p. 7, 'the directive'), the Federal Republic of Germany has failed to fulfil its obligations under the EC Treaty.

2. In accordance with Article 23 of the directive, the Member States were to bring into force the laws, regulations and administrative provisions necessary to comply with it within two years of its notification, and forthwith to inform the Commission thereof. Since the directive was notified to the Federal Republic of Germany on 5 June 1992, the period allowed for its implementation expired on 5 June 1994.

3. On 9 August 1994, not having been notified or otherwise informed of any measures to transpose the directive into German law, the Commission give the Federal Government formal notice under Article 169 of the Treaty to submit its observations in that regard within two months.

4. By letter of 25 October 1994 the Federal Government replied that the German authorities were drafting the provisions necessary to comply with the directive and that, pending their adoption, the directive was to be applied under the legal rules in force. However, the Federal Government asserted that the provisions of the directive concerning the conservation of natural habitats were not yet relevant for areas of Community interest, that the provisions relating to protection of species had already been to a large extent transposed by the federal law on the protection of nature then in force and, generally, that in certain places the directive was unclear, which complicated its transposition.

5. On 28 November 1995, not having received any communication of the promised transposition measures, the Commission sent the Federal Government a reasoned opinion requesting it to take the necessary measures to comply therewith within two months from its notification. That reasoned opinion went unanswered.

6. Accordingly, the Commission decided to bring the present action.

7. The Federal Government does not deny that it has not adopted all the measures necessary for implementation of the directive. It states, however, that since the passing of the deadline for transposition, the directive has been directly applied by the competent authorities and existing national provisions have been interpreted in accordance with Community law. It goes on to say that a law designed *inter alia* to implement the directive is in the process of being adopted.

8. Since the directive has not been transposed into national law by the Federal Republic of Germany within the prescribed period, the action brought by the Commission must be held to be well founded.

9. It has consistently been held that mere administrative practices, which by their nature are alterable at will by the administration and are not given the appropriate publicity, cannot be regarded as constituting the proper fulfilment of a Member State's obligations under Article 189 of the EC Treaty (see, *inter alia*, Case C-242/94 *Commission v Spain* [1995] ECR I-3031, paragraph 6).

10. It must therefore he held that, by failing to adopt within the prescribed period the laws, regulations and administrative provisions necessary to comply with the directive, the Federal Republic of Germany has failed to fulfil its obligations under Article 23 of the directive.

Costs

11. Under Article 69(2) of the Rules of Procedure, the unsuccessful party is to be ordered to pay the costs if they have been applied for in the successful party's pleadings. Since the Commission has applied for costs and the defendant has been unsuccessful, the Federal Republic of Germany must be ordered to pay the costs.

COMMISSION v GERMANY

On those grounds, **[14]**

THE COURT (Fifth Chamber)

hereby:

1. Declares that, by failing to adopt within the prescribed period the laws, regulations and administrative provisions necessary to comply with Council Directive 92/43/EEC of 21 May 1992 on the conservation of natural habitats and of wild fauna and flora, the Federal Republic of Germany has failed to fulfil its obligations under Article 23 of that directive;

2. Orders the Federal Republic of Germany to pay the costs.

Gulmann   Wathelet   Moitinho de Almeida

Puissochet   Sevón

Delivered in open court in Luxembourg on 11 December 1997.

R. Grass   C. Gulmann

Registrar   President of the Fifth Chamber

10–11 Different features of the case report are marked with numbers which correspond to the following list:

[1] Case number.
[2] Names of the parties.
[3] Summary of Judgment. This is similar to the headnote in UK cases. It can be a useful guide to the subject matter of the case but it has no binding force of law.
[4] The page number in the E.C.R. The full citation for this case in Case C-83/97: *Commission of the European Communities v Federal Republic of Germany* [1997] E.C.R. I-7191.
[5] Opinion of the Advocate General, see para.10.8.
[6] The current composition of the E.C.J. is 27 judges. The court can sit as a full court, in plenary session with 13 judges or it can also sit with smaller numbers of judges in groups which are referred to as "Chambers".
[7] The parties and their legal advisers.
[8] The section beginning with "APPLICATION" outlines the legal issue(s). The wording would depend on the type of case e.g. a reference or an action.
[9] The authentic version of the case is in the language used in the case itself. The E.C.J. identifies the original language in a footnote.
[10] Details of the composition of the court in this case.
[11] The Registrar is a close equivalent to the clerk of court in the UK system except that he is considered as more important. He deals with the procedure and administration of the court.
[12] Until 1994 the Report of the Judge-Rapporteur was published with the rest of the case in the E.C.R. It is a report for the hearing which gives the background to the dispute,

the legislative framework, details of the procedure adopted and a summary of the written observations submitted to the court.

[13] Judgment. Single judgments are given in all decisions. There is no publication of dissenting judgments. Judgments are brief (by UK standards) consisting of a series of short paragraphs.

[14] The actual ruling of the court is always at the end of the judgment and usually starts with the words "On those grounds". As in this case, the rulings tend to be short.

SOURCES OF EC LEGISLATION

Official sources of EC legislation

The Official Journal of the European Union (previously *Communities*) *(O.J.)*

The OJ is the official gazette of the EC. It is published every working day and contains a vast **10–12** amount of material. It is published in all the official languages. It contains all secondary legislation in full text along with proposed legislation and official announcements and information about the activities of the European Union's institutions. The Official Journal is available in paper, CD ROM and online. Parts of it are only available electronically.

There are separate series within the Official Journal:

The L series contains the full authoritative text of *all* legislation whose publication is obligatory and virtually all adopted legislation. In addition, the *Directory of Community Legislation in Force* is published as part of the OJ L series. This directory lists references to the initial texts and to any subsequent amendments.

The C series, "Information and Notices", covers a wide range of information including summaries of judgments of the Court of Justice and the Court of First Instance; minutes of parliamentary meetings; reports of the Court of Auditors; parliamentary written questions and answers from the Council or Commission; and statements from the Economic and Social Committee and the Committee of the Regions. The CE series, an electronic sub-series, currently contains the preparatory acts in the legislative process and this material is only available electronically. Full authoritative case reports from the European Court of Justice and the Court of First Instance are *not* published in the Official Journal. They appear in the Reports of Cases before the Court of Justice and the Court of First Instance (usually known as the European Case Reports see para.10.42).

The S series is a supplement to the OJ and contains invitations to tender for public works, services and supply contracts. This series is only available online via the Tenders Electronic Daily database (TED) or on CD Rom.

The debates of the plenary sessions and oral questions from the European Parliament are published in the *Official Journal: Annex-Debates of the European Parliament* which, since 2000, has only been available electronically.

Monthly indexes to the L and C series are subsequently cumulated into an annual index. The alphabetical index is organised by subject and the methodological index is listed by number. These indexes are not particularly useful for locating material.

10–13 **Citation**. Each issue of the L, C and S series is numbered sequentially beginning with 1 at the start of every calendar year. There is no standard citation convention for references in the O.J. A commonly used format is:

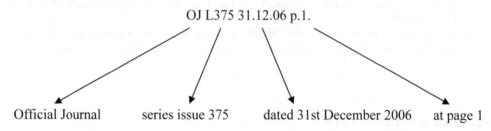

Diagram 10.2: Example of a Citation

However, OSCOLA (see para.13.27) recommends [year] OJ series number/page e.g. [2006] OJ L375/1.

Eur-lex ⬦ free

10–14 The *Eur-lex* site (*http://eur-lex.europa.eu/en/index.htm*) is a very impressive database and there are still further features to be added in the near future. It is the product of the merging of the original *Eur-lex* site and *Celex* (which was previously the EC's official legal database) in 2005. It allows free access to a large amount of information and is arranged by collections:

> ➢ Official Journal L and C series since 1998 in full text.
> ➢ EC primary legislation—the Treaties (including consolidated versions of the EC Treaty and the Treaty of European Union) in full text.
> ➢ International agreements. All the instruments generated by the European Communities in the exercise of their international responsibilities in full text.
> ➢ Legislation in force. The full consolidated version of secondary legislation is contained in the Directory of Community Legislation in Force. It is grouped into 20 classification categories with further subcategories.
> ➢ Preparatory acts. Legislative proposals and other Commission communications to the Council and other institutions (COM documents). This section is to be expanded in the future to include a greater number of preparatory documents.
> ➢ Case law from 1954.
> ➢ Parliamentary questions. There is a link to the European Parliament site, where the texts of the questions and answers of the three most recent legislative terms are available.

The site has a *simple search* function which is very easy to use. It has various options:

> ➢ General search with options to search by free text, date/time span, author, classification heading or keywords.
> ➢ Document number using natural numbers or Celex numbers.
> ➢ File category with options to search by Treaties, legislation, preparatory acts, cases or parliamentary questions.
> ➢ Publication reference from the Official Journal or the European Court Reports.

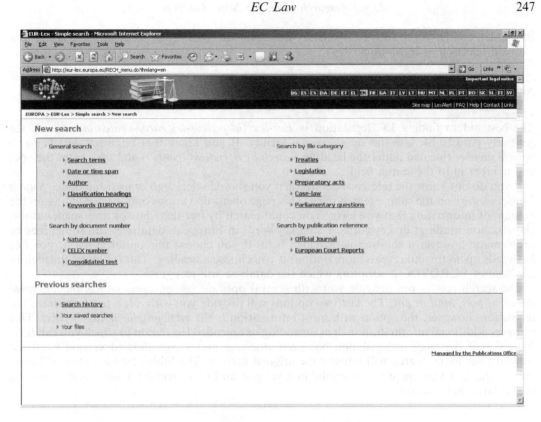

Diagram 10.3: Eur-lex Simple Search

Commercial sources of EC legislation

Commercial databases

There are several commercial databases which contain EC legislation: **10–15**

> ➢ *Justis Celex* 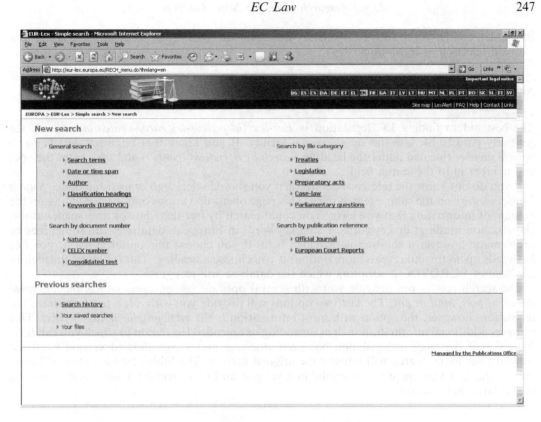 and CD Rom subscription database
> ➢ *LexisNexis Butterworths* subscription database
> ➢ *Westlaw* subscription database

European Legislation Service

This service is made up of two encyclopaedias. *The Encyclopaedia of European Union Law* **10–16** contains primary legislation and is published in five loose-leaf volumes. *The Encyclopaedia of European Community Law* is a collection of secondary legislation and is published in 11 loose-leaf volumes. The service contains the full text of legislation and is updated four times a year.

Single volume collections of legislation

These include: **10–17**

N. Foster, *Blackstone's EC Legislation* 17th edn (Oxford: OUP, 2006). This is an annual publication which contains a selection of primary and secondary legislation. There are no annotations.

B. Rudden and D. Wyatt, *Basic Community Laws* 8th edn (Oxford: OUP, 2002). This contains a broad selection of legislation.

Aids to finding EC legislation

Eur-lex ⌂ free

10–18 The best aid to finding EC legislation is *Eur-lex* (*http://eur-lex.europa.eu/en/index.htm*), see generally para.10.14. Use the *simple search* facility. If you know that reference details go to *natural number* (located under the heading *Search by document number*) and then enter the year and number in to the search field.

  If you do not know the reference details then you should select *legislation* listed under *Search by file category* on the simple search page. This page opens up various options depending on the amount of information that you have. You could search by free text, date or time span, author, classification headings or keywords. Using keywords in European databases can sometimes be problematic however a solution is provided here. If you choose this option a list of possible keywords opens up and reveals more options if you choose a heading. This is linking through to a system of EUROVOC descriptors which the database will recognise.

  The search results will provide you with several options: *bibliographic notice, bibliographic notice + text, html* or *pdf*. The last two options will provide you with a full text version of the legislation, however, the option with most information is the *bibliographic notice + text*. This retrieves additional information such as amending or amended legislation to which you can link. Note that if the piece of legislation has been amended and a consolidated version has been created your initial search will retrieve the **original** version. The bibliographic notice will alert you to the fact that there is a consolidated version and there will be a link to it. This is a particularly useful feature.

10–19 *Commercial databases*

  ➢ *Justis Celex* ⌂ and CD Rom subscription database
  ➢ *LexisNexis Butterworths* ⌂ subscription database
  ➢ *Westlaw* ⌂ subscription database

European Communities Legislation: Current Status 📖

10–20 This contains reference to every piece of EC legislation both in force and repealed. Annotations beside each entry indicate the status of the legislation, its Official Journal reference and how it has been amended. It consists of two annual volumes, quarterly supplements and a fortnightly updating newsletter. It lists secondary legislation in chronological/numeric order and also has an alphabetical subject index.

The Index to the Official Journal of the European Union 📖

10–21 This index is issued monthly and annually. It is in two parts: an alphabetical subject index and a methodological index which references legislation in numerical order and cases by number. It is not a particularly useful research tool.

The Official Journal of the European Communities: Directory of Community Legislation in Force 📖 and ⌂ free

10–22 This is published twice a year. It lists legislation in force (and references any amending legislation) by subject and by reference number. It is available online as part of *Eur-lex*, see para.10.14.

Finding EC legislation on a subject

Eur-lex 🖰 free
Once again *Eur-lex* (*http://eur-lex.europa.eu/en/index.htm*) is the best search option, see **10–23**
para.10.18.

Commercial databases   **10–24**

 ➢ *Justis Celex* 🖰 and CD Rom subscription database
 ➢ *LexisNexis Butterworths* 🖰 subscription database
 ➢ *Westlaw* 🖰 subscription database

European Communities Legislation: Current Status 📖
Use the alphabetical subject index.   **10–25**

The EU's General Report on the Activities of the European Union 📖 and 🖰 free
This is an annual publication arranged by subject matter. It is also available on Europa (*http://* **10–26**
europa.eu/generalreport/en/welcome.htm). Update by checking the monthly *Bulletin of the Eur-*
opean Union. This is also available on *Europa* (*http://europa.eu/bulletin/en/welcome.htm*).

Loose-leaf encyclopaedias and texts: **10–27**

 ⇒ *European Legislation Service* (see para.10.16)
 ⇒ D. Vaughan *Law of the European Communities Service*
 ⇒ *Butterworths Annual European Review*
 ⇒ *The Laws of Scotland: Stair Memorial Encyclopaedia* (see para.8.2)

N.B. Once you know the year you can use The *Index to the Official Journal of the European*
Communities which is an annual index.

European Current Law Yearbooks 📖
European *Current Law* started in 1993 and provides a guide to legal developments in Europe. It **10–28**
consists of Monthly Digests which are subsequently consolidated into Yearbooks. Information
can be accessed by subject or by country.
    The information contained in European *Current Law* is divided into four sections:

 ➢ Focus. This contains short articles about developments in a specific subject area or
   jurisdiction.
 ➢ The European Union. This section contains details of legislation, cases (from the
   European Court of Justice and the Court of First Instance), books and articles
   arranged under subject headings. Each annual volume contains information for that
   one year.
 ➢ National Jurisdictions. Digests of legislation and cases and lists of legislation recently
   passed are arranged under subject headings and referenced to particular Member
   States.
 ➢ Reference Section. This includes a glossary of courts covering all Member States, a list
   of abbreviations, Treaty provisions referred to in cases and legislation digested in the
   volume, cumulative lists of legislation digested and cases reported and a cumulative
   subject index.

Current status of EC legislation

Eur-lex ⌁ free

10–29 Once again *Eur-lex* (*http://eur-lex.europa.eu/en/index.htm*) is the best search option. The *legislation in force* option from the homepage retrieves current legislation grouped into 20 classification categories with further subcategories from which to make your choice.

Alternatively status details are provided in the bibliographic notice which will appear in your results after searching for legislation. See para.10.18.

If you use the simple search facility and *search by category* and *legislation* options you can tick a box at the bottom of the search template which will restrict your search to legislation in force.

10–30 *Commercial databases*

> ➢ *Justis Celex* ⌁ and CD Rom subscription database
> ➢ *LexisNexis Butterworths* ⌁ subscription database
> ➢ *Westlaw* ⌁ subscription database

10–31 *European Communities Legislation: Current Status.* See para.10.20.

Tracing if a Directive has been implemented in national law

N-Lex ⌁ free

10–32 At the time of writing, *N-Lex* (The web address for *N-Lex* is *http://eur-lexeuropa.eu./n-lex/pays.html?lang=en*) was still in the experimental stage. It is to be a common access portal for sources of national law and has been developed by the Office for Official Publications of the European Communities in conjunction with the Member States of the European Union. It allows users to search national sites using a single uniform search template. Once this site is fully operational it should be much easier to trace details of implementation of directives.

Westlaw ⌁ subscription database

10–33 When you open a Directive in the EU section of *Westlaw* you will see a section on the left of the screen headed *Document outline*. Click on the option below this heading for *national measures*. A list of countries will appear and you can click on *Great Britain* to obtain details of the implementing legislation.

EC Legislation Implementator 📖

10–34 This is part of *Halsbury's Statutory Instruments* and is a guide as to whether EC directives/decisions relevant to the UK have been implemented by national law. It is divided into two parts, the first of which provides a chronological list of relevant EC directives or decisions and an indication of when, how and if they have been implemented in the UK. The second part is a chronological list of UK legislation, indicating the EC directives or decisions that that legislation implemented.

Current Law Monthly Digest 📖

10–35 *Current Law Monthly Digests* contain tables of European legislation implemented by statutory instruments and Scottish statutory instruments. However, the consolidated versions of these tables only appear sporadically in the *Current Law Legislation Citators*.

OFFICIAL DOCUMENTS

10–36 Working documents are published as COM documents. Legislative proposals will first be published as COM documents and will later appear in the C series of the Official Journal.

COM documents are available in *Eur-lex* in the *preparatory acts* collection accessible from the **10–37** homepage. At the time of writing legislative proposals and other Commission communications to the Council and other institutions are available but there are plans to increase this part of the site.

Information about legislative proposals and their progress can be found in a site called *OEIL* **10–38** (*http://www.europarl.europa.eu/oeil/index.jsp*). It is the Legislative Observatory and is produced under the auspices of the European Parliament. It is updated daily. From the homepage, click on *procedures*. This opens up a simple search which allows searching by various options including by subject or words in title. This will allow you to identify whether proposals have been made into legislation.

Pre-lex (*http://ec.europa.eu/prelex/apcnet.cfm?CL=en*) is a site that monitors the decision- **10–39** making process between institutions. This allows you to track a proposal through different stages and provides links to relevant documents.

COM documents can also be located by checking: **10–40**

- ➢ *Bulletin of the European Union* ⌁ free, see para.10.69
- ➢ *House of Commons Weekly Information Bulletin* 📖 and ⌁ free, see para.6.7
- ➢ *LexisNexis Butterworths* ⌁ subscription database
- ➢ *Justis Celex* ⌁ and CD Rom subscription database
- ➢ *LRDI Grey Paper Index* (part of Current Legal Information ⌁ subscription, see para.8.89)
- ➢ *Westlaw* ⌁ subscription database

A useful source of information about the EU is the House of Lords European Union Com- **10–41** mittee. This Committee has considered Community proposals and reported on them since 1974. Its reports are available through the House of Lords website: *http://www.publications.parliament. uk/pa/ld/ldeucom.htm*

EC CASE LAW

Sources of EC case law

Law Reports

There are two main series of law reports: **10–42**

Title	**European Court Reports**
	Formal title: Reports of Cases before the Court of Justice and the Court of First Instance.
Abbreviation	E.C.R.
Citation	Case C-41/93 *French Republic v Commission of the European Communities* [1994] E.C.R. I-1829.
Period covered	1954 to present.
Publisher	Office for Official Publications of the European Communities.
Comments	This is the official series of European law reports.

The reports are published in all the official languages of the EC. The authentic text is that of the language of the case.

The production of multiple translations of every case means that the series is slow to appear.

The reports include the Advocate General's Opinion beside the decision. This is particularly useful as it is the Advocate General's Opinion which tends to contain the reasoned legal argument in EC cases.

Available in	Paper.
Coverage	Originally *all* cases from the European Court of Justice and the Court of First Instance were reported, but, since 1989, some may be in summary form. From 1/05/2004 the following are not published in the ECR: judgments delivered, other than in preliminary ruling proceedings, by Chambers of three Judges, judgments delivered, other than in preliminary ruling proceedings, by Chambers of five Judges ruling without an Advocate General's Opinion and orders.
Format	Indexed by subject matter and in the final volume of the year there is a chronological table of cases. Since 1990 the reports have been divided into two sections: section I for the Court of Justice and section II for the Court of First Instance.
Title	**Common Market Law Reports**
Abbreviation	C.M.L.R.
Citation	T-194/94 *Carvel & Guardian Newspaper Ltd v Council* [1995] 3 C.M.L.R. 359. Since 2001 a case number as opposed to a page number as the citation e.g. C-321/03 *Dyson Ltd v Registrar of Trade Marks* [2007] 2 C.M.L.R. 14 refers to case number 14 of the 2nd volume of the 2007 Common Market Law Reports.
Period covered	1962 to present.
Publisher	Sweet & Maxwell.
Comments	Although they are not official reports, this series has the big advantage of appearing much quicker than the E.C.R. It is published weekly.
Available in	Paper, CD-ROM and online via *Westlaw*.
Coverage	Decisions from the European Court of Justice and the Court of First Instance, Commission decisions and decisions of national courts, including the UK, relevant to EC law. It does *not* report every case but it does report all cases of significance.
Format	Indexed alphabetically by case name, subject and Community legislative provisions. It also contains tables of Treaties and regulations judicially considered, cases judicially considered, statutes cited and abbreviations.

These have been joined by a more recent introduction:

Title	**All England Law Reports European Cases**
Abbreviation	All ER (EC)
Citation	C-280/00 *Altmark Trans GmbH v Nahverkehrsgesellschaft Altmark GmbH* [2005] All ER (EC) 610.
Period covered	1995 to present.

Publisher	LexisNexis.
Available in	Paper, and online via *LexisNexis Butterworths*.
Coverage	Decisions from the European Court of Justice and the Court of First Instance.

European Court of Justice website (Curia)

The "official" electronic version of opinions and judgments is the European Court of Justice **10–43** website (*http://curia.europa.eu/en/transitpage.htm*) Note: The definitive version of European cases is that published in the *European Court Reports*, the Reports *of European Community Staff Cases* or the *Official Journal*. If there is any difference in the text between the electronic versions and the above list, the latter are authoritative.

There are many sections of this useful site:

➢ The *institution* provides background information about the European Court of Justice and the Court of First Instance. It also allows access to their annual reports.
➢ *Texts governing procedure* provides direct links to relevant legislation and practice notes
➢ *Case-law* contains:

  o Numerical access to case law 1953–present;
  o Search form for case law after 17/06/1997. This allows you to search by names of parties, subject and words in the text as well as by number and date;
  o Digest of case law which contains summaries of judgments which is only available in French;
  o Alphabetical table of subject matter also only available in French;
  o Annotations to judgments also only available in French.

➢ *News* which contains:

  o *Judicial proceedings* which has listings for the current week and future week and an archive back to 1997.
  o *Press releases* which gives very brief details about recent judgments and opinions. It is a useful current awareness service. It can alert you to the existence of a new case which you can then read by clicking on the link to the full text.

➢ *European Union law in Europe* which has link to Dec.Nat which is a database containing national decisions which contains over 18,800 references to national decisions concerning Community law from 1959 up to the present day and an impressive search engine.

Eur-lex ⏱ free

Opinions and judgments since 1998 can be searched on this site (*http://eur-lex.europa.eu/en/* **10–44** *index.htm*).
There are different search options:

➢ Recent cases are listed in the *case law* section accessible via a link from the homepage.
➢ Search by number—follow the *case law* link on the homepage. The search boxes at the bottom of the screen allow you to search by number and year. This can also be achieved by choosing the *simple search* from the homepage, choosing *natural number* and then choosing *European Court Case* and entering the number and year.

> ➤ Search by subject. Choose *simple search* from the homepage, choose *case-law* under the *search by file category* option. This allows you to choose to search by court, date range or type of procedure.

Westlaw ⟨ᵗ⟩ subscription database

10–45 *Westlaw* allows access to EC case law and also to the *Common Market Law Reports*.

LexisNexis Butterworths ⟨ᵗ⟩ subscription database

10–46 *LexisNexis Butterworths* allows access to EC case law and also to the *All England Law Reports European Cases*.

Finding EC cases

10–47 The information source which is by far the best for speed of access to recent materials and range of information is the *European Court of Justice website (Curia)*, see para.10.43.

⇒ If you have the number and year of a case use the numerical access option to search cases back to 1953, alternatively you can use the search form to search for cases from 1997.
⇒ If you want to search by subject, use the search from but note that this will only search back to 1997.

10–48 *Other sources for finding EC cases*

> ➤ *Eur-lex* can be used to search for EC cases from 1998, see para.10.44
> ➤ *LexisNexis Butterworths* ⟨ᵗ⟩ subscription database
> ➤ *Westlaw* ⟨ᵗ⟩ subscription database

Finding recent EC cases

European Court of Justice website (Curia) ⟨ᵗ⟩ free

10–49 The *judicial proceedings* and *press releases* sections are useful, see para.10.43.

Eur-lex ⟨ᵗ⟩ free

10–50 The *Case-law* section has a list of recent cases see para.10.44.

SOURCES OF INFORMATION ABOUT RECENT DEVELOPMENTS

What's New on Europa? ⟨ᵗ⟩ free

10–51 This is a very useful general awareness site covering all kinds of developments. It is updated on a daily basis. *http://europa.eu/geninfo/whatsnew.htm*

What's New EU Institutions and Agencies? ⟨ᵗ⟩ free

10–52 This allows you to click on the press release sites for all the different Community institutions and agencies. *http://europa.eu/geninfo/whatsnew_inst.htm*

What's New Commission ⟨ᵗ⟩ free

10–53 This page provide links to the What's New pages of many of the Commission's main activities. *http://ec.europa.eu/geninfo/whatsnew.htm*

European Court of Justice site 🖰 free
This part of the European Court of Justice website allows you to see details of the current week's **10–54**
cases: *http://curia.europa.eu/en/actu/activites/activite.htm*

Eur-lex 🖰 free
The homepage of *Eur-lex* (*http://eur-lex.europa.eu/en/index.htm*) has a news section. This also **10–55**
has a link, *selection of documents*, which takes you to a list of new documents which you can
access by pdf. These are cumulated each month and appear under subject headings in the
dossiers by topic link from the homepage.

EU Press Room and *RAPID* 🖰 free
This is a daily press release page (*http://europa.eu/press_room/index_en.htm*) link to the *RAPID* **10–56**
database which contains all the Press Releases of the Commission since 1985. It also contains
Press Releases of some of the other European institutions, particularly the Council of the
Union. It is useful for providing a daily view of EU activities. The *RAPID* site is free but you
have to register: *http://europa.eu/rapid/*

EU Observer 🖰 free
This site (*http://euobserver.com/*) is an excellent source of EU related news. **10–57**

Newspapers **10–58**
The EU is covered in many newspapers. The most in-depth coverage is to be found in:

> ➤ *The European Voice* (a weekly newspaper which covers recent events in the EU) 📖 and
>   🖰 free (*http://www.europeanvoice.com/*)
> ➤ *The Financial Times* 📖 and 🖰 free (*http://www.ft.com/home/uk*)
> ➤ *BBC World Service Europe Today* 🖰 free
>   *http://www.bbc.co.uk/worldservice/programmes/europetoday/index.shtml*
> ➤ *EuroNews* 🖰 free (*http://www.euronews.net/create_html.php?page = home*)
> ➤ *European Current Law Monthly Digest* 📖
> ➤ This categorises recent legal developments, books and articles by subject heading. See
>   para.10.28.

Current awareness strategy

To keep up with the latest legal developments, check the following free services daily: **10–59**

> ➤ *What's New on Europa? http://europa.eu/geninfo/whatsnew.htm*
> ➤ *Eur-lex http://eur-lex.europa.eu/en/index.htm* homepage and selection of documents.
> ➤ European Court of Justice, judicial proceedings *http://curia.europa.eu/en/actu/   acti-*
>   *vites/activite.htm*

SECONDARY SOURCES OF EC LAW

Texts

There are numerous texts on European law. The following are some examples: **10–60**

> ➤ The entry in *The Laws of Scotland: Stair Memorial Encyclopaedia* "European Com-
>   munity Law and Institutions".

> ➤ D. Vaughan, *Law of the European Communities Service*. This is a four-volume loose-leaf work which is updated five times a year.
> ➤ *Butterworth's Annual European Review*.
> ➤ P. Craig and G. De Burca, *EU Law: Text, Cases & Materials* 3rd edn (Oxford: OUP, 2003).

Shorter, more introductory texts include:

> ➤ A.M. Arnull et al., *Wyatt & Dashwood's European Union Law* 5th edn (Oxford: OUP, 2006).
> ➤ K. Davies, *Understanding EU Law* 3rd edn (Oxford: Routledge, 2006).
> ➤ J. Hanlon, *European Community Law* 3rd edn (London: Sweet & Maxwell, 2003).
> ➤ T. Kennedy, *Learning European Law* (London: Sweet & Maxwell, 1998).

10–61 A selection of journals containing legal information about the EC

> ➤ *Common Market Law Review* (C.M.L.Rev.) Published bi-monthly.
> ➤ *European Law Review* (E.L.Rev.) Published bi-monthly.
> ➤ *Journal of Common Market Studies* (J.C.M.S.) Published four times a year.
> ➤ *The International and Comparative Law Quarterly* (I.C.L.Q.) Published four times a year.
> ➤ *European Law Journal* (E.L.J.) Published four times a year.
> ➤ *The Yearbook of European Law* (Y.E.L.) This is an annual publication which contains tables of abbreviations, articles, annual surveys, book reviews, tables of cases, decisions and communications, legislation, treaties and rules of procedure, international conventions and agreements, national legislation and an index.

Journals concentrating on specific aspects of EC law include:

> ➤ *European Business Law Review* (E.B.L.R.) Published 11 times a year.
> ➤ *European Competition Law Review* (E.C.L.R.) Published eight times a year.
> ➤ *European Environmental Law Review* (E.E.L.R.) Published 11 times a year.
> ➤ *European Intellectual Property Review* (E.I.P.R.) Published monthly.
> ➤ *European Public Law* (E.P.L.) Published four times a year.

Finding journal articles about EC law

Westlaw ⌖ subscription database
10–62 *Westlaw UK Journals* contains the Legal Journals Index and a number of full-text articles. The Legal Journals Index currently indexes over 800 legal journals from the UK and English language European journals. See para.8.48.

Current Legal Information ⌖ and CD Rom subscription legal research service
10–63 This, like *Westlaw*, contains the Legal Journals Index. It is therefore useful for tracing articles but it does not contain any full text articles.

European Commission Library catalogue (ECLAS) ⌖ free
10–64 You can use ECLAS (*http://ec.europa.eu/eclas/F*) to search for articles on European law and policy.

European integration current contents ⌾ free
This online service (*http://centers.law.nyu.edu/jmtoc/index.cfm*) provides access to the tables of **10–65** contents of journals relevant in European Integration research. It includes law, human rights, economics, history and political sciences. Currently it covers 108 journals published in nine languages and 14 countries.

European Current Law 🕮
Check the subject index at the end of the Yearbooks. There is also an alphabetical list by title. **10–66** See para.10.28.

SOURCES OF INFORMATION ABOUT THE EU, ITS ACTIVITIES AND POLICIES

Europa ⌾ free
Europa is the portal site of the European Union (*http://europa.eu/index_en.htm*). It provides up- **10–67** to-date coverage of European Union affairs and allows access to a vast amount of information. It is an essential site. It can be accessed by several entry points on the homepage:

> ➤ Under the *EU day by day* section there is a link to *All the news* which takes you to the *Europa press room* containing press releases and links to background information.
> ➤ *Activities* lists 32 "activities" or subject areas. Each subject area which has a portal page and an overview page. If you click on one of the links, you will reach links to various sources of information collated for the particular subject chosen: the relevant pages of all the institutions, latest developments, related legal texts and other documents (e.g. press releases categories under the subject and the relevant section of the *Bulletin of the European Union*). The *legal texts* section is very impressive. It links directly with the relevant section of legislation in force in *Eur-lex* and recent case law categorised under the subject heading.
> ➤ *Institutions* provides direct links to the EU institutions.
> ➤ *Documents* provides easy access to the various documents available in the different EU databases.
> ➤ *Services* provides links to the different services available e.g. the central library, statistics and opinion polls.

There is an advanced search function which allows you to narrow a search by various fields but searching from this first point of access may be rather ambitious given the sheer volume of information available on this site.

General Report on the Activities of the European Communities 🕮 and ⌾
This is an annual publication produced by the Secretariat—General of the Commission. It **10–68** reviews the previous year's developments. It is available on paper and via the internet: *http://europa.eu/generalreport/en/welcome.htm*. The reports from 1997 are available in full text.

Bulletin of the European Union ⌾
This is a monthly review of the work of the EU, published by the EU publisher. Latest issue and **10–69** issues from 1996 are available online: *http://europa.eu/bulletin/en/welcome.htm*

SCADPLUS ⌾ free
This site (*http://europa.eu/scadplus/info_scad_en.htm*) provides user-friendly fact sheets which **10–70** summarise EU legislation. The fact sheets are divided into 32 subject areas. There are summaries of existing measures and also follow-up information about legislative proposals. The dates that

appear at the bottom of each summary correspond to the date of the last substantial modification, for example, the introduction of an amending or a related act. It has almost 2,500 fact sheets and the site is updated daily.

European Parliament Factsheets ⌐

10–71 Useful factsheets are provided in this site (*http://www.europarl.europa.eu/facts/default_en.htm*) which have been updated numerous times (last time was 2005). They are designed to provide a general view of the process of European integration. It has a useful section on *how the European Community works*.

European Union in the World ⌐ free

10–72 This site (*http://ec.europa.eu/world/index_en.htm*) provides information on the EU's external relations, trade policy, humanitarian aid and other areas of the EU's global role.

European Information Network: Europe in the UK ⌐ free

10–73 This website (*http://www.europe.org.uk/info/*) is maintained by the European Commission Representation in the UK It brings together contact details for organisations and individuals in the United Kingdom that provide EU information and advice for the general public, business, and the academic community. It also has news items.

EU for Journalists ⌐ free

10–74 This website (*http://www.eu4journalists.eu/*) aimed at journalists contains lot of background information about the European Union.

OTHER SOURCES OF INFORMATION ABOUT EUROPE

Britain in the EU ⌐ free

10–75 The Foreign and Commonwealth Office site has a link on its homepage (*http://www.fco.gov.uk/*) to Britain in the EU which provides news and information from a UK perspective.

EC Representation offices

10–76 These are located in all EU countries. Their purpose is to represent the Commission. In addition, they are a good source of information about the EU and EU policy. The website for the European Commission Representation in the UK is: *http://ec.europa.eu/unitedkingdom/* The Scottish office is at 9 Alva Street, Edinburgh EH2 4PH. It is a drop-in information centre.

Europe in the UK ⌐ free

10–77 This site provides information and news about the EU in the UK and also has culture and youth/education sections. (*http://www.europe.org.uk/*)

European Information Network in Scotland ⌐ free

10–78 (*http://www.europe.org.uk/regions/scotland/*). This site includes information about EU institutions in Scotland, EU information in Scotland and sources of EU funding.

Intute:Euro Studies ⌐ free

10–79 This site (*http://www.intute.ac.uk/socialsciences/eurostudies/*) has a large number of links which are grouped under Europe, European Union and UK and EU. It also contains links to resources for the various regions of Europe.

European Documentation Centres
Certain libraries have been designated as European Documentation Centres (EDCs). This **10–80**
means that they will have copies of every publicly available document produced by the EC
EDCs in Scotland are the university libraries of Edinburgh, Glasgow, Dundee and Aberdeen.

Further resources

Internet for European Studies "teach yourself" tutorial ⌁ free   **10–81**
(*http://www.vts.intute.ac.uk/tutorial/eurostudies*)

European Information sources
This is an impressive collection of annotated links for those researching European law: (*http://
www.library.ex.ac.uk/internet/eurostudies.html*)

J. Knowles and P. Thomas, *Effective Legal Research* (London: Sweet & Maxwell, 2006) Ch.8.

Chapter 11
International Law

11–1 There is a distinction between public international law and private international law. Private international law is also known as "conflict of laws". It is in essence an area of Scots law but with international dimensions. It involves examining the relationship between two or more legal systems. An example of a private international law dispute would be a couple who wished to divorce. They were married in Iceland and the man now lives in France and works in the Netherlands and the wife is Scottish but lives in England.

The sources involved in private international law are principally the same as other areas of Scots law, with the addition of being able to locate international conventions. This subject will not be dealt with separately. Searching for international conventions will be dealt with under public international law.

The purpose of this chapter is to highlight the differences between our domestic legal sources and sources of public international law. It will introduce you to some of the main sources of public international law and ways of locating the different materials. It is intended to be an introduction to researching this increasingly important area of law. More detailed information can be found in the texts listed in para.11.19.

The final part of this chapter looks at an important area of international law: human rights. This section introduces you to the major information sources with regard to the European Convention on Human Rights (ECHR) and the case law from the European Court of Human Rights. Many students become confused by the title into thinking that the ECHR is a piece of European Community legislation and that human rights cases are heard by the European Court of Justice. This is not the case. The ECHR is an international convention and human rights cases under the ECHR are heard by the European Court of Human Rights which is an institution of the Council of Europe.

PUBLIC INTERNATIONAL LAW

11–2 Public international law concerns relationships between states. It is a wholly distinct system of law. Public international law is very different from Scots law. It does not have a legislature. The rules of international law do not have the authority of an Act of Parliament. They are unable to bind states in the same way as an Act of the UK Parliament binds individuals in the UK. To a large extent international law is based on the goodwill of states. If a state chooses not ratify a treaty, it is not bound by that treaty. If there is no legislature, where do the rules of public international law come from? Article 38(1) of the Statute of the International Court of Justice has come to be regarded as a statement of the sources of international law. It states that the court shall apply: international conventions; international custom; general principles of law recognised by civilised nations; judicial decisions and the teaching of respected jurists.

For a discussion of the sources of international law see I. Brownlie, *Principles of Public International Law* 6th edn (Oxford: Clarendon Press, 2003.

11–3 There are now two international courts. The longer established of the two, the International Court of Justice, deals with civil matters: principally disputes between states. Unlike UK courts, it does not adopt a system of binding precedent. It does not have jurisdiction over states in the same way as national courts have jurisdiction over individuals within a state. The International Criminal Court has only existed since 2002 and hears cases about serious crimes but only those committed on the territory of, or by one of the nationals of, one of the states who agreed to the setting up of the court.

One difference in researching international law is the pre-eminence of electronic material. It is **11–4** increasingly important in all areas of law but none more so than international law. A list of online gateways to international law materials is included at para.11.29.

PRIMARY SOURCES OF INTERNATIONAL LAW

Treaties

The Vienna Convention on the Law of Treaties 1969, art.2(1)(a) defined "treaty" as "an **11–5** international agreement concluded between States in written form and governed by international law, whether embodied in a single instrument or in two or more related instruments and whatever its particular designation". Treaties are different from statutes in the UK as they do not have universal application. They only apply to states which agree to them. A treaty can be between two states (bilateral) or several states (multilateral). Some international organisations are able to make treaties with states but individuals do not have the capacity to make treaties. Treaties can also be referred to as conventions, covenants, pacts, agreements or charters. A protocol tends to refer to an agreement subsequent to a treaty which has amended the original treaty.

Treaties are divided into articles and paragraphs as opposed to Acts of Parliament which have sections. Treaties do not automatically come into force at the moment the parties come to agreement. The signing of a treaty does not bind a state to ratify it at a later date. Signature only indicates an intention to ratify. There can be a considerable period of time between the signature of a treaty and its coming into force. Individual treaties can specify different periods. It is normal for a treaty to come into force after it has been ratified by a certain number of signatories. As stated earlier, even when a treaty does come into force, it is only binding on states which ratify it.

Citation of treaties

The normal way of referring to treaties is by their title and the year of signature/adoption, *e.g.* **11–6** the Vienna Convention on the Law of Treaties 1969. Full citation details will include a reference to the relevant treaty series where the treaty appears. See para.11.7 for more information about the different treaty series. The possible citations for this treaty include:

> ➤ 1155 U.N.T.S. 331. This refers to the United Nations Treaty Series (see para.11.7) Vol.1155 and p.331.
> ➤ U.K.T.S. 58 (1980), Cmnd. 7964. This relates to the entry in the United Kingdom Treaty Series. This series forms a sub-series to the Command Papers. This means that treaties are referred to by the Treaty Series number, a Command Paper number and the date of issue (treaties are only published in this series after ratification).
> ➤ (1969) 8 I.L.M. 679. This refers to International Legal Materials (see para.11.18) 1969, Vol.8 and p.679.

Information about the citation of international legal materials is provided by the Oxford Standard for Citation of Legal Authorities (OSCOLA). The most recent version is OSCOLA 2006 and this can be found at *http://denning.law.ox.ac.uk/published/oscola.shtml*

11–7　*Collections of Treaties*

1. *The Consolidated Treaty Series* covers the period 1628–1920 and the *League of Nations Treaty Series* covers 1920–1946. The major series of modern treaties is the *United Nations Treaty Series* (U.N.T.S.) which includes material from 1946 onwards. This is a collection of treaties and international agreements which have been published by the Secretariat of the United Nations. The collection currently has over 158,000 treaties and related material which have been published in over 2,200 volumes. The United Nations Treaty Series is available as an online subscription service: *http://untreaty.un.org/English/treaty.asp* This site allows you to search the entire treaty series which has been published in printed form. You can search by: date, party, title, subject terms, registration number or a combination of these.

The site also allows you access to *Multilateral Treaties Deposited with the Secretary—General*. This publication contains information on the status of major multilateral instruments which have been deposited with the Secretary—General of the United Nations. It is updated on a weekly basis. It allows you to find out about the status of instruments as the process of signature and ratification by states takes place. The printed version is published annually.

2. *The United Kingdom Treaty Series* is the UK's national collection of treaties. It is an official series published by the Foreign & Commonwealth Office. It started in 1892 and forms a sub-series to the Command Papers. Treaties are published in this series only after ratification by the UK.

3. An excellent and widely available source of information about treaties (and other matters) is *International Legal Materials*. This publishes the texts of treaties along with annotations. See para.11.18. The text of treaties will tend to appear here much earlier than in the printed series.

4. There are many websites which allow access to a selection of treaties. A good academic treaty collection site is: *http://fletcher.tufts.edu/multilaterals.html* This site has been produced as part of a Multilaterals Project. This is an ongoing project to make the texts of multilateral treaties and conventions available. It is run by the Fletcher School of Law and Diplomacy, Tufts University, Massachusetts, USA. It contains the full text of a large selection of important treaties and is easy to use. You can access treaties chronologically (1899–present) or by subject (ranging from atmosphere and space to trade and commercial relations).

Another US based site is the frequently cited treaties and other international instruments site run by the University of Minnesota: *http://www.law.umn.edu/library/tools/pathfinders/ most-cited.html*

The Council of Europe European Treaties website allows free access to treaties and agreements of the Council of Europe: *http://conventions.coe.int/* The site is free. The official versions of the treaties are contained in the *European Treaty Series* (ETS) 1949–2003 and the *Council of Europe Treaty Series* (CETS) 2004 onwards. The Council of Europe was established by the Statute of the Council of Europe in 1949. Its aim as stated in Article 1(b) is to encourage progressive European agreement on economic, social, cultural, scientific, legal and administrative matters and to maintain and work towards the further realisation of human rights and fundamental freedoms. Its principal achievement is the European Convention on Human Rights. See paras.11.31 and 11.32.

5. There are student editions of important treaties such as Blackstone's *International Law Documents* 7th edn (Oxford: OUP, 2005). This does not contain any annotations. A widely-used text which includes both primary material and useful commentary is D.J. Harris, *Cases and Materials on International Law* 6th edn (London: Sweet & Maxwell, 2004).

6. When a treaty is incorporated into UK law it is common practice to include the text of the original treaty in a schedule to the Act or statutory instrument. However, the ease with which these can be located when you only know the name of the treaty depends on how closely the short title of the UK legislation matches the treaty title.

Aids to tracing Treaties **11–8**

> ➤ The search facilities available via the websites mentioned in para.11.7 above: the U.N.T.S., the Council of Europe European Treaties and the Multilateral project.
> ➤ Each of the paper treaty series mentioned above in para.11.7 has extensive indexes.
> ➤ Bowman and D.J. Harris, *Multilateral Treaties: Index & Current Status* (1984) and updated by cumulative supplements. This was a very useful publication but its importance has lessened in recent years with the increasing amount of information becoming accessible via the internet.

Custom

Custom has traditionally been regarded as one of the most important sources of public inter- **11–9** national law. However, its importance is lessening due to the increase in the number of treaties which are codifying custom. Custom in the international sense does not equate with custom in Scots law. In public international law there are two elements which must be present for a custom to exist: state practice and the belief that a legal obligation binds you to act in a certain way (referred to as *opinio juris et necessitatis*).

How is it possible to find evidence of custom? Brownlie states that:

"The material sources of custom are very numerous and include the following: diplomatic correspondence, policy statements, press releases, the opinions of official legal advisers, official manuals on legal questions, *e.g.* manuals of military law, executive decisions and practices, orders to naval forces, etc., comments by governments on drafts produced by the International Law Commission, state legislation, international and national judicial decisions, recitals in treaties and other international instruments, a pattern of treaties in the same form, the practice of international organs, and resolutions relating to legal questions in the United Nations General Assembly." I. Brownlie, *Principles of Public International Law* 5th edn (Oxford: Clarendon Press, 1998, p.5).

It is obviously easier to find information about some of the above than others. Sources of **11–10** information about custom include state papers such as the British & Foreign State Papers produced by the Foreign Office Library between 1812 and 1968. A compilation of British practice is the *British Digest of International Law* edited by C. Parry (this work is incomplete). The Foreign & Commonwealth Office website provides access to official documents from 1997: *http://www.fco.gov.uk/servlet/Front?pagename = OpenMarket/Xcelerate/ShowPage&c = Page &cid = 1007029395375*

The International Law Commission mentioned above exists under the auspices of the United Nations. Its role is to promote the progressive development of international law and its codification. Information about it and its activities can be found at its website: (*http://untreaty.un. org/ilc/ilcintro.htm*).

Sources of current information about state practice can be gleaned from the "Current Legal Developments" sections in *International and Comparative Law Quarterly* and the *British Year-*

book of International Law. Newspapers and online news services are another good source of information.

Cases

11–11 The International Court of Justice (ICJ) and sometimes referred to as the "world court" is situated in The Hague in the Netherlands. It was established at the same time as the United Nations in 1946. Its predecessor was called the Permanent Court of International Justice which had been established under the League of Nations.

The International Court of Justice derives its mandate from the Statute of the International Court of Justice which is annexed to the Charter of the United Nations. Article 59 of that Statute states that "the decision of the court has no binding force except between the parties and in respect of that particular case". Although there is no formal doctrine of binding precedent, previous cases are not ignored.

International Court Reports (I.C.J. Reports) (1947–)

11–12 This is the official series of law reports which has the full title of *Reports of Judgments, Advisory Opinions and Orders of the International Court of Justice.* These reports appear in both English and French. All cases brought before the court since 1946 are available on the web: *http:// www.icj.cij.org/*

Pleadings, Oral Arguments and Documents (I.C.J. Pleadings) (1947–)

11–13 This is also published by the court. The series contains the documentation for each case which is made public after the final decision has been given. These are also available on the court's website together with the judgment.

Yearbook of the International Court of Justice (I.C.J. Yearbook)

11–14 This contains information about the work of the court, its members and activities in a year.

Reports of case law of the Permanent Court of International Justice

11–15 The predecessor of the International Court of Justice was the Permanent Court of International Justice (P.C.I.J.). Between 1922 and 1946 P.C.I.J. judgments were published in Series A (Nos. 1– 24): Collection of Judgments (up to and including 1930) and Series A/B (Nos. 40–80): Judgments, Orders and Advisory Opinions (beginning in 1931). These are all available at the International Court of Justice website: *http://www.icj-cij.org/pcij/*. A selection of its case law can also be found in *World Court Reports 1922–1942*. This is a four-volume work edited by Manley O. Hudson.

11–16 The International Criminal Court (ICC) came into being when 120 States adopted the Rome Statute, the legal basis for establishing the permanent International Criminal Court. It has existed since 2002 and can hear cases of genocide, crimes against humanity and war crimes committed after July 1, 2002. The Court may only exercise jurisdiction if: the accused is a national of a State Party or a State otherwise accepting the jurisdiction of the Court; the crime took place on the territory of a State Party or a State otherwise accepting the jurisdiction of the Court; or the United Nations Security Council has referred the situation to the Prosecutor, irrespective of the nationality of the accused or the location of the crime. The court is based in the Hague, in the Netherlands. It is independent of the UN. Information about the ICC is available at its website (*http://www.icc-cpi.int/*). The Official Journal of the ICC is available at *http://www.icc-cpi.int/about/Official_Journal.html* and it includes the Statute of Rome, rules of procedure and evidence and details of the crimes. The site has a section called Legal Tools which is currently being finalised. It will contain much useful information about the workings of the court when it is complete.

International Law Reports (I.L.R.)

This series started in 1919 and was originally called the *Annual Digest of Public International* **11–17** *Law Cases*. This is the name for volumes 1–16. From Vol.17 (1950) they have been called International Law Reports. The aim of this series is to provide English-language access to judicial matters that have a bearing on international law. It covers the International Court of Justice, European Court of Human Rights, Inter-American Court of Human Rights and other international tribunals as well as national decisions from many countries which have a public international law angle. Cases can be accessed in alphabetical order, by court, by country and by subject headings. There are three volumes of consolidated indexes:

> ➤ Volume 1 contains subject indexes for Vols 1–35 and Vols 36–80.
> ➤ Volume 2 contains the following material all relating to Vols 1–80:

List of abbreviations
Consolidated Tables of Cases arranged alphabetically
Consolidated Tables of Cases arranged by jurisdiction
Key Word Index to the Table of Cases
Consolidated Table of Treaties
Index to Treaties by Name in Common Use
Index to Treaties by parties
Index to Treaties by subject

> ➤ Volume 3 contains the following material all relating to Vols 81–100:

Abbreviations
Consolidated Table of Cases arranged alphabetically
Consolidated Table of Cases arranged by jurisdiction subdivided into international and national
Consolidated Table of Treaties (in chronological order)
Consolidated Index

International Legal Materials (1962–present) 📖 and ⌁

This is a bi-monthly publication produced by the American Society of International Law. It **11–18** provides wide coverage of developments in international law. The main criterion for selection is that the documents are of substantial interest to a large number of legal scholars, practising lawyers and officials dealing with public and private international law. This is a very useful source of information. It is usually the first available source of full text information about key documents. The entries are arranged under the following headings:

> ➤ Resolutions, declarations and other documents
> ➤ Treaties and Agreements
> ➤ Judicial and similar proceedings
> ➤ Legislation
> ➤ Judicial and similar proceedings
> ➤ Briefs
> ➤ Other documents received

There is a subject index at the end of each annual volume. It is available online via *LexisNexis Butterworths* from 1962 and on *Westlaw* since 1980.

Secondary Sources of International Law

Books

11–19 Key texts include:

> *Oppenheim's International Law* edited by R. Jennings 9th edn (Harlow: Pearson, 1992)
> Brownlie, *Principles of Public International Law* 6th edn (Oxford: Clarendon Press 2003)

More introductory texts include:

> A.Boyle & C Chinkin, *The Making of International Law* (Oxford: OUP, 2007)
> M. Dixon, *Textbook on International Law* 5th edn (Oxford:OUP, 2005)
> R.M.M. Wallace, *International Law* 5th edn (London: Sweet & Maxwell, 2005)

Bibliographies include:

> *Contemporary Practice of Public International Law* edited by E.G. Schaffer and R.J. Snyder (Dobbs Ferry NY: Oceana Publications,1997)
> *Public International Law—A Current Bibliography of Books and Articles* (1975–)
> E. Beyerly, *Public International Law—A Guide to Information Sources* (London: Mansell, 1991)
> Older works could be found in *A Current Bibliography of International Law*, J.G. Merrills (London: Butterworths, 1978)

Journals

11–20 The most widely available journals are:

> *International and Comparative Law Quarterly* (I.C.L.Q.)
> *American Journal of International Law* (A.J.I.L.)
> *European Journal of International Law* (E.J.I.L.)

There are many more international law journals especially in the U.S. There are also an increasing number of journals relating to specialist areas of international law, *e.g. Journal of Air Law & Commerce.*

British Yearbook of International Law (B.Y.I.L.) (1920–present)

11–21 This contains the following material for the year under review: in-depth articles; detailed book reviews; decisions of British courts involving questions of international law; decisions on the European Convention on Human Rights; decisions of the Court of Justice of the European Communities; and UK materials on international law cited from a wide range of sources and arranged by subject within the realm of international law.

Finding journal articles

Public International Law: A Current Bibliography of Books and Articles 📖
11–22 This is published twice a year. Over 1400 journals, yearbooks and commemorative compilations are regularly evaluated for this bibliography.

Index to Legal Periodicals 📖 and ⌂ subscription indexing service
This index references legal periodicals and books which are published in Great Britain, Ireland, **11–23**
US, Canada, Australia and New Zealand. It is an American publication and the majority of
material is American. The online version goes back to 1982 and now allows access to some
journals in full text. It has good search facilities and is updated daily. Pre-1981 articles are
referenced in the bound volumes.

Index to Foreign Legal Periodicals 📖 and ⌂ subscription indexing service
This is another US based index. It covers selected international law and comparative law **11–24**
periodicals and collections of essays. The paper volumes go back to 1960 and the online version
contain material back to 1985.

HeinOnline ⌂ subscription database of legal journals
This increasingly popular database is expanding quickly and is changing its interface at the time **11–25**
of writing. The journals are image-based so that you see the original printed page.

Westlaw ⌂ subscription database
Westlaw UK Journals contains the Legal Journals Index and a number of full-text articles. The **11–26**
Legal Journals Index currently indexes over 800 legal journals from the UK and English lan-
guage European journals, see para.8.48.

Foreign Law Guide (FLAG) database ⌂ free
FLAG (*http://ials.sas.ac.uk/library/flag/flag.htm*) is an inventory of the collections of foreign, **11–27**
comparative and international law materials in UK universities and the British Library. It
describes the contents of different collections noting shelf marks and providing web links to each
of the libraries included in the database. It is not intended to indicate who holds the issues of a
particular serial but it will tell you which libraries have certain collections.

Current awareness sources 11–28

> ➤ *Bulletin of Legal Developments* ⌂ subscription
> This published fortnightly by the British Institute of International & Comparative Law:
> *http://www.biicl.org/publications/bild/*
> ➤ Foreign & Commonwealth Office website latest news section ⌂ free
> *http://www.fco.gov.uk/servlet/Front?pagename = OpenMarket/Xcelerate/*
> *ShowPage&c = Page&cid = 1007029390554*
> This site is updated throughout the day with speeches, transcripts and press releases.
> ➤ International Court of Justice—latest press releases ⌂ free
> *http://www.icj-cij.org/presscom/index.php?p1 = 6&p2 = 1*
> ➤ International Criminal Court homepage has latest news, highlights and recent updates
> sections ⌂ free
> *http://www.icc-cpi.int/home.html&l = en*
> ➤ BBC news site, world section ⌂ free
> *http://news.bbc.co.uk/1/hi/world/default.stm*
> This site also allows you access to search all BBC news on-line stories since November
> 1997.
> ➤ ITN World News ⌂ free
> *http://itn.co.uk/news/world.html*
> ➤ CNN ⌂ free
> *http://www.cnn.com/*
> ➤ *Keesing's Record of World Events* (originally known as *Keesing's Contemporary
> Archives)* 📖 and ⌂ subscription

This contains summaries of world events. The entries are short and do not contain much depth.

11–29 **Online legal gateways (all free) to international law materials:**

> *Access to Law—International Law Materials*
> *http://www.accesstolaw.com/site/default. asp?s = 33*
> This is a UK based site of links which are accompanied by useful annotations.

> *Electronic Information System for International Law*
> *http://www.eisil.org/*
> This is a US based site is produced by the American Society of International Law. It aims to provide authoritative links to primary materials, websites and research guides on the different aspects of international law. It provides useful ancillary information about the resources it contains.

> *ASIL Guide to Electronic Resources for International Law*
> *http://www.asil.org/resource/Home.htm*
> This is a US based site which has separate "chapters" for different areas of international law. It provides comments and advice on the resources it lists.

> *Foreign and Commonwealth Office Official Documents*
> *http://www.fco.gov.uk/servlet/Front?pagename = OpenMarket/Xcelerate/ShowPage*
> *&c = Page&cid = 1044520986961* This site gives links to various websites giving details of treaties covering different areas.

> *GlobalLex* http://www.nyulawglobal.org/globalex/#
> This includes research guides to many aspects of international law.

> *Intute: international law*
> *http://www.intute.ac.uk/socialsciences/cgi-bin/browse.pl?id = 120449*
> This site has links and introductory information about a host of international law information sources.

> *LAWLINKS international law materials*
> *http://www.kent.ac.uk/lawlinks/internationallaw.html*
> This is a UK based site which has gathered together an impressive array of links with brief descriptions.

> *WorldII*
> The *www.worldlii.org* site is not really a gateway to international material but is an important gateway to legal information about countries worldwide. It was launched in 2002 by the World Legal Institute. It contains 850 databases of legal information from 123 countries. In addition to the databases available there is a subject category of links under each country which gives an indication of which material are available in English.

International legal research online tutorial

11–30 This tutorial at *http://www.law.duke.edu/ilrt/* is designed to teach students research strategies and methodology for researching both print and electronic sources of international legal materials. It has been designed by two US Schools of Law.

Human Rights Law

11–31 Public international law can be divided into discreet areas such as the law of the sea, international environmental law, world trade law and international criminal law. One area of international law which is increasingly important is human rights law. The European Convention on Human Rights is an international convention and the Human Rights Act 1998 incorporated it into our national law. This means that human rights jurisprudence developed over decades in the European Court of Human Rights (set up in 1959) had to be applied in the UK from October 2000. This has had an impact on almost every area of national law and it is important to be able to locate human rights materials.

The European Convention on Human Rights (whose proper title is The Convention for the Protection of Human Rights and Fundamental Freedoms) was adopted by the Council of Europe in 1950 and entered into force in 1953. The European Court of Human Rights (ECHR) was set up in 1959. It is located in Strasbourg. Originally there was a European Commission on Human Rights (formed in 1953) whose role was to examine cases with regard to admissibility. Following Protocol No. 11 the Commission was disbanded.

Primary sources of human rights law

European Convention on Human Rights   **11–32**

> ➢ The Council of Europe European Treaties website (see para.11. 7) allows free access to the full text of the Convention, protocols and status (dates signed and ratified by the various states, date of coming into force and any reservations or declarations): *http:// conventions.coe.int/general/v3IntroConvENG.asp* Click on the *full list* option under Council of Europe conventions and the ECHR will appear as number 005 (third on the list). Alternatively you can link through to the ECHR from the Council of Europe's homepage. The link is under *activities, human rights.*
> ➢ The European Court of Human Rights website (*http://www.echr.coe.int/echr/*) also contains a link to the ECHR from its homepage, click on *basic texts.*

Case law from the European Court of Human Rights

The Council of Europe published judgments and decisions in *Publications of the European Court* **11–33** *of Human Rights.* Series A contained judgments and Series B pleadings, oral arguments and documents. From 1996 there has been a series called *Reports of Judgments and Decisions.*

The *Official Collection of Decisions of the European Commission on Human Rights* was published by the now defunct Commission and contains decisions which they made where cases were not passed on to the court.

The European Court of Human Rights website ⌁ free   **11–34**
This site (*http://www.echr.coe.int/echr/*) contains a large amount of information:

> ➢ Information about the court, and its procedures.
> ➢ The text of the Convention on Human Rights and additional protocols.
> ➢ Case law. This contains lists of recent judgments and decisions. The case law database can be searched using HUDOC. This is a portal which allows you to search the case-law of the European Court of Human Rights, the European Commission of Human Rights and the Committee of Ministers. It has a powerful search facility which allows you to search using numerous fields. Results can be sorted by relevance, date, title, respondent state or application number.
> ➢ Reports about the court.
> ➢ Pending cases.
> ➢ Press information which contains a calendar of scheduled hearings and press releases.
> ➢ Information for applicants.

European Human Rights Reports 📖 and ⚙ subscription

11–35 The leading paper source for the decisions of the European Court of Human Rights is the commercially produced *European Human Rights Reports* (E.H.R.R.) (1979–present). This covers the case law of the European Court of Human Rights and also included admissibility decisions of the European Commission on Human Rights until it was disbanded. It is also available in *Westlaw*.

Case law from courts in the UK

11–36 The sources of human rights cases before the UK courts are the same as for UK cases generally, see Chapter 4. The volume of human rights cases in the UK has now spawned law reports which solely cover human rights cases: *Human Rights Law Reports UK Cases* (H.R.L.R.).

Secondary sources of human rights law

11–37 *Books which discuss human rights law in Scotland:*

> ➤ K. Ewing and K. Dale-Risk, *Human Rights in Scotland; Text Cases and Materials*, (Edinburgh: W. Green, 2004).
> ➤ C. Ashton & V. Finch, *Human Rights and Scots Law*, (Edinburgh: W. Green, 2002).
> ➤ Murdoch, *A Guide to Human Rights in Scotland*, 2nd edn (Haywards Heath: Tottel, 2007).

Journal articles

11–38 Dedicated sources include:

> ➤ *European Human Rights Law Review* (E.H.R.L.R.) published six times a year.
> ➤ *Human Rights Law Review* (H.R.L.Rev.) published three times a year.
> ➤ *The Yearbook of the European Convention on Human Rights* provides an account of the area for a given year. Its publication is usually delayed by several years.

Finding journal articles

Westlaw ⚙subscription database

11–39 Westlaw UK Journals contains the Legal Journals Index and a number of full-text articles. The Legal Journals Index currently indexes over 800 legal journals from the UK and English language European journals, see para.8.48.

11–40 Current awareness free sites

> ➤ Ministry for Justice has responsibility for human rights
>   *http://www.justice.gov.uk/index.htm*
>   Commissioner for Human Rights. The commissioner is an independent institution within the Council of Europe, mandated to promote the awareness of and respect for human rights in forty-six Council of Europe member states.
>   *http://www.coe.int/t/commissioner/*
> ➤ *European Court of Human Rights*
>   *http://www.echr.coe.int/ECHR/EN/Header/Case-Law/HUDOC/HUDOC+database/*
>   click on recent cases.
> ➤ *Parliamentary Joint Committee on Human Rights*
>   *http://www.parliament.uk/parliamentary_committees/joint_committee_on_human_rights.cfm*
> ➤ *One Crown Office Row—Human Rights Update*
>   *http://www.1cor.com/humanrights*

This service is provided by a civil law set of barristers Chambers, One Crown Office Row, based in Temple, London. It contains over 800 reports and commentaries, dating back to 1998, on human rights cases and is updated weekly. It also contains practical guidance on the Human Rights Act and the Convention and articles on human rights issue by 1 Crown Office Row. To view most of the content you need to register. There is a weekly email alerter service.

➢ *Amnesty International*
  http://thereport.amnesty.org/eng/Homepage
➢ *Liberty*
  Liberty is a campaigning organisation also known as the National Council for Civil Liberties.
  http://www.liberty-human-rights.org.uk/index.shtml

Online gateways to human right materials 11–41

➢ *Department of Constitutional Affairs—Human Rights*
  http://www.dca.gov.uk/peoples-rights/human-rights/index.htm
➢ *ASIL Guide to Electronic Resources—Human Rights* which is published by the American Society of International Law
  http://www.asil.org/resource/humrts1.htm

12-1 This chapter examines topic based research and the legal investigation process. It covers various search strategies for the efficient gathering of relevant information. The chapter starts by providing guidance on finding the law on a given topic and then looks at literature search strategies for essays and problem questions. Legal research can involve focusing on the substantive rules such as examining the legal rules for controlling pollution or analysing how the courts have interpreted the wording of the principal pollution offence. However, legal research is not restricted to looking at legal rules in isolation. Socio-legal research examines how law operates in a variety of social spheres, e.g. whether the pollution legislation has changed attitudes and behaviour towards polluting activity. In recognition of this fact, this chapter includes a brief discussion of methods of data collection that are common to all the social sciences—questionnaires, interviews and observation studies.

Literature Search Strategies

Topic based research: Finding the law on ...

12-2 "All this stuff on cases and legislation is fine, but how do you actually find out what the law is on something?"

Finding the law on a particular topic has in some ways become much easier with the increased availability of online materials and databases where the researcher can search across large amounts of different data using sophisticated search techniques. You may already be familiar with using Google (or one of the other major online search engines) to search the internet. However, this is not to be recommended for researching a legal topic. The reasons are many:

> The search will be so wide that you will get a large number of irrelevant hits as you cannot restrict it to legal information sources.
> There is no quality control and therefore you do not know the accuracy of the information or the amount of weight that you should attach to it.
> The free sources of primary legal information (with the exception of the *Statute Law Database*) do not contain amended legislation or details of whether cases have been overruled. This means that if you search for primary materials using Google you will retrieve the original version. This is worse than useless as you then have to carry out the further step of finding out if it has been amended. This means that this method of locating information, which is extremely useful for a multitude of other purposes, is not useful for legal research because of the importance attached to identifying the current version of primary materials.
> Internet subject searches increasingly retrieve *Wikipedia* as high on the order of relevant hits. This online "encyclopaedia" may be an interesting source of recreational material but it lacks the authority and accuracy to be used for legal research.

This does not mean that the internet should not be used for legal research but it does mean that **12–3** it should be used in a different way than you use it for recreation. Instead of using general search engines you should become familiar with the various legal databases and information gateways (para.2.13). These are collections of information which can be trusted as they have been constructed by information experts and so there is a degree of quality control. Electronic databases (such as *Westlaw*) have superior search facilities which allow you to search across both primary materials (such as cases and legislation) and secondary materials (such as legal journals and legal commentary) using Boolean searching (para.2.33) However, it can often be more efficient to make information sources such as encyclopaedias (para.8.2) and reference works (para.8.10) your first stop in your topic based research. Why?

- ➤ Encyclopaedias and reference works are written by experts and are specifically designed to cover the law on a *subject by subject* basis.
- ➤ The databases provide you with a list of hits that are linked to the words in your search. However, they do not provide you with background information, the legal context or how the different pieces of information relate to one another. Sources such as the *Stair Memorial Encyclopaedia* (or other reference works) will not just identify a piece of legislation or a case, they will place it in context. This means that they will: explain its background and how it fits in to the whole area of law; discuss how it has been interpreted; offer comment on it; and consider how the law might be developed. This means that they are the ideal starting point for research by subject.
- ➤ Most encyclopaedias are updated either by appearing in looseleaf or online formats.
- ➤ Consulting an encyclopaedia or reference work as a starting point for your research means that you can use them to obtain the information necessary to construct more appropriate search terms when you move on to searching the full text databases. If you try to conduct a subject search on *Westlaw* with a broad subject term you will retrieve hundreds or even thousands of hits which it may take a long time to work through. If you use a more appropriate search term you will search far more effectively and efficiently as you will retrieve fewer and more relevant hits.

It is rather unhelpful (but nonetheless true) to say that the precise search strategy will depend on **12–4** what exactly you are trying to find. However, a suggested search strategy is to start by locating a source that will provide you with a general overview of the subject and identify relevant further reading or primary materials. Encyclopaedias and reference works are an ideal starting point for your research. See paras 8.2 and 8.10.

If you do not have access to an encyclopaedia then you could look for a book on the subject area. Advice for finding books on specific subjects is in para.8.33.

Once you have found background information about your topic it is then time to start honing in **12–5** on the particular issue.

You could do this by following leads from these sources. They may refer to other books, journal articles or primary materials in their bibliography, further reading sections or footnotes.

At this stage you should also identify if any journal articles have been written on the subject. They may be referred to in the original background reading but they may have been published since the reference work/encyclopaedia was last updated. You should therefore carry out your own search. Advice on this is given in para.8.41.

The next step will depend on the further sources identified in your initial search. This could **12–6** involve finding:

- ➤ Cases which are relevant to the subject (see para.4.69).

> ➢ Cases which have interpreted certain words in a particular way (see para.4.84).
> ➢ Bills of the UK Parliament (see para.6.5) and/or Scottish Parliament (see para.7.8) which concern a subject.
> ➢ Acts of the UK Parliament (see para.6.81) and/or Acts of the Scottish Parliament (see para.7.43) which concern a subject.
> ➢ Statutory instruments (see para.6.176) and/or Scottish statutory instruments (see para.7.113) which are relevant to a certain subject.
> ➢ Debates in the UK Parliament (see para.6.21) and/or the Scottish Parliament (see para.7.21) which have discussed a subject.
> ➢ UK (see para.8.85) and/or Scottish (see para.8.105) official publications discussing a subject.
> ➢ Scottish Law Commission or Law Commission reports on a subject (see para.8.117).
> ➢ Relevant internet sites. Look in legal information gateways (see para.2.13).

Updating a legal literature search

12–7 Once you have carried out your subject search, your attempt to find out "what the law is on ..." is not over. You must take steps to update your search. It is vitally important that you are aware of any recent developments that may have changed the law. The appropriate steps may depend on the topic but here are some suggestions of sources you should check:

> ➢ Online legal databases which are updated on a daily basis. Examples include *Westlaw*, *Lexis* and *Lawtel*.
> ➢ Websites that contain information on current legal developments in the subject area (see para.8.75).
> ➢ Looseleaf updating services/encyclopaedias. These are useful but make sure that you check the date of the most recent update.
> ➢ *Current Law* Monthly Digest/Statutes Service File. See paras 8.15 and 8.23. These are updated every month. They tend to be about six weeks behind events.
> ➢ Current editions of journals in the appropriate subject area. Weekly journals will have the most up to date information.

Literature search strategy for essays/research projects

12–8 This section covers literature strategies appropriate for essays and research projects and is summaried in diagram 12.1. Essay writing techniques are covered in para.14.9.

> ⇒ **Step 1** Start the investigation process by looking at general information about the topic and moving on to more specific material. Reading general information is not just necessary to become familiar with the topic, it is also important to enable you to put the topic into context.
>
> ⇒ **Step 2** Decide what the essay is about/what your research topic is. This is not as straightforward as it sounds. Do not trust your first impressions. Re-read the question many times to ensure that you are completely clear about exactly what you are being asked.
>
> ⇒ **Step 3** Select appropriate search terms. Do not just search using one term. You will inevitably miss lots of material. Think of broad terms, narrow terms and related terms and search under all of them. Do not forget synonyms or alternative terms. If your essay is about the regulation of agricultural pollution you could search using the following terms: environmental protection; pollution; agricultural pollution, water pollution, waste disposal, farm waste, nitrates, silage, slurry, etc.

⇒ **Step 4**   Decide on your search parameters. These will affect the range of sources which you consult.

   (a) Jurisdiction—are you just concerned with Scotland? The UK? Or is it EU-wide or indeed international?

   (b) Time period to be covered—is it an analysis of the current law or a historical study, and if the latter, which period?

   (c) How up to date does your knowledge have to be? At university you may be told that your work must be current up to a certain date (obviously a solicitor has to ensure that his knowledge is as up to date as possible).

   (d) Is the main thrust of the work to be the substantive law or is it on a more theoretical level such as socio-legal, criminological or jurisprudential?

⇒ **Step 5**   Initial search:

   At university → Lecture notes and/or recommended reading for the course will have identified for you the most relevant and up-to-date textbook.

   For a research project or post university → the Library catalogue should be consulted. Search under the relevant subject area to identify the most up to date dedicated textbook. Do remember that you are not restricted to the materials in the one library. You can use the internet to gain access to the catalogues of other university libraries and order materials through the inter-library loan scheme. Alternatively, try searching legal bookshop websites (see para.8.35). You could also try using one of the bibliographies of law books such D. Raistrick, *Lawyers Law Books* 3rd edn (Bowker Sawer: London, 1997) however this is now becoming very out of date. If you cannot find a dedicated textbook, try looking in a general reference work such as the *Stair Memorial Encyclopaedia* or Gloag & Henderson, *Introduction to the Law of Scotland* 12th edn (Edinburgh: W.Green due in 2007). General reference works will not tend to provide much detail but should provide you with an introduction to the subject. They should enable you to identify more specific information sources.

   Remember to make use of one of the best resources in a library—a librarian.

⇒ **Step 6**   Once you have located a relevant textbook, consult the appropriate sections. A textbook is likely to give you some general background information on your topic and to contain references to where more specific/detailed information is located. It should be used as a springboard to the more detailed information sources. Make full use of references listed in footnotes or in any further reading sections. These could identify relevant statutes/case law/secondary material.

   One dedicated text is never going to provide you with the complete answer. At the very least you will want to look at other people's views and interpretations of the issue. This may involve looking for alternative texts and/or journal articles (see para.8.48). You will probably need to consult primary sources such as cases or statutes to enable you to give *your* view of the law (see para.4.69 for searching for cases by subject and para.6.81 and para.7.43 for searching for statutes by subject). *Remember that any text will be out of date and you will need to update the information.*

⇒ **Step 7**   Follow up the references you have identified. See para.12.6.

   As you search through this material you may wish to alter your search terms or indeed your search parameters. If you cannot find many references, it may be that the original search term used is too narrow. You should try to broaden out your search using a more general term. If you find too many items under the search term, try a more specific term.

⇒ **Step 8** Even if no journal articles have been identified in the textbook, it will still be worth carrying out a journal search. This is because material could have been written since the text was published. Journals will be more up to date than a textbook and could help you to update your information. Search strategies for locating journal articles are covered in para.8.44.

⇒ **Step 9** Ensure that your search is as up to date as possible. You can do this by checking:

    (a) Online legal databases such as *Westlaw*, *Lawtel* or *Lexis*. They should help to locate any very recent developments.

    (b) Relevant websites. This would depend on the topic but might include: Scottish Parliament; Scottish Executive; The Scottish Official Listing; House of Commons Weekly Information Bulletin, Hansard, UK Government departments, The Stationery Office's Daily List, lobby groups, trade organisations. The previous two types of organisations would be identified by a legal information gateway's subject guide.

    (c) The current editions of relevant journals.

    (d) Newspapers and news organisations for current comment (see para.8.68).

    (e) *Current Law* Monthly Digests and Statutes Service File (paras 8.15 and 8.23). This should identify if there have been any legal developments over the last couple of months.

    (f) Updating services available for various sources. Make sure that you check the frequency with which it is updated and the date of the last update. Some updating services are only updated on a six-monthly basis.

⇒ **Step 10** When you do find relevant material you should note down the full bibliographic reference. Bibliographic references are discussed more fully in paras 13.27-13.57. This will save you a lot of time and frustration later when you come to compile your bibliography. You may wish to compile a database of your own references—a personal bibliography. Personal bibliographies are covered in para.13.63. It is important to be systematic and thorough when checking sources of information and obtaining relevant items. You will stay in control of your research if you keep a check on:

    ➤ Sources which you have already read.

    ➤ Sources which you have photocopied but not read.

    ➤ Sources still to be consulted.

    ➤ Items requested via the library on inter-library loan.

Failure to do this can result in:

    ➤ Important sources of information being overlooked.

    ➤ The same publication being covered more than once, wasting time and effort by duplicating references.

    ➤ Some vital element in a reference to a publication being missed out, requiring it to be checked.

    ➤ The discovery, when finally writing up the project, that indexes and catalogues should have been checked under a term which you now realise to be important.

Literature search strategy

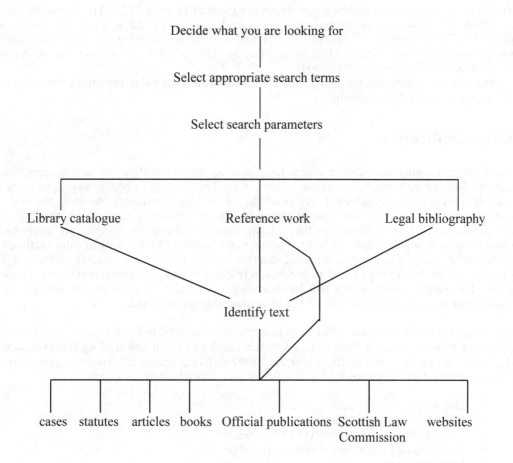

Decide what you are looking for

Select appropriate search terms

Select search parameters

Library catalogue   Reference work   Legal bibliography

Identify text

cases   statutes   articles   books   Official publications   Scottish Law   websites
                                                                Commission

Legal Journal search

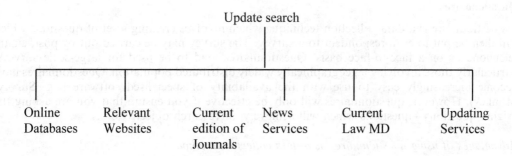

Update search

Online   Relevant   Current   News   Current   Updating
Databases   Websites   edition of   Services   Law MD   Services
                                  Journals

Diagram 12.1: Literature Search Strategy

Literature search strategy for problem questions

12–9 Techniques for answering problem questions are covered in para.14.25. The literature search approach for answering problem questions is very similar to the strategy for essays, see para.12.8. The strategy is different in that you will be limited to looking for information that is specific to the question. Your reading for an essay question will have to be more general in order to allow the topic to be put in context.

Once you have identified the area of law concerned, you will need to investigate that area and identify the current legal position.

EMPIRICAL RESEARCH

12–10 Legal research can often involve researching beyond the substantive law and gaining information about certain people or sections of the public. This is likely to be the case if you research socio-legal issues or criminology. It is a common mistake for law students to underestimate the difficulties in carrying out this type of research. This is because it tends to involve different methodologies and skills from traditional legal research. The methodologies are likely to be more familiar to social science students. This section is going to look briefly at three methods of collecting primary data: questionnaires, interviews and observation studies. Although the methods are dealt with separately, in practice, a researcher may use several methods within one piece of research. The methods will be described, an indication given of the strengths and weaknesses of each approach and details of dedicated texts provided.

12–11 In all projects where empirical research is involved it is essential to be clear about the aims and objectives of your research. Failure to do so can result in the collection of irrelevant data that does not tell you anything useful. There are many different research techniques which can be used to collect data. The choice of which to use will depend on factors such as:

> ➢ The purpose of the study.
> ➢ The type of information you want to collect.
> ➢ Accessibility of the subject(s) of the research.
> ➢ The nature of the subject(s) of the research.
> ➢ Time constraints.
> ➢ Cost.
> ➢ The level of skills you possess, e.g. if you have an aptitude for figures you may be keen to use questionnaires and statistical analysis.
> ➢ Personal preference.

Questionnaires

12–12 A questionnaire is a data collection technique which involves creating a set of questions which will then be put to each respondent to a survey. The survey may be carried out by post, email, telephone or on a face-to-face basis. Questionnaires tend to be used for large-scale surveys, particularly those involving a geographically widely distributed population. Questionnaires have become increasingly easy to use with the availability of specialised software (e.g. Survey-Monkey). However, questionnaires will only be effective if you ensure that you are asking the "right" questions—questions which will achieve your research objectives.

12–13 *Advantages of using questionnaires as a data collection method*

> ➢ Questionnaires are an efficient way of gathering information from respondents who are widely dispersed geographically or who live in inaccessible places.

➢ The cost of using questionnaires is low compared with carrying out interviews or observation studies.

➢ Questionnaires enable the researcher to gather information from a large number of people in a resource (time and cost) efficient way.

➢ The collection of standardised data which can be analysed quantitatively using software such as Excel or SPSS and presented using tables, graphs, diagrams etc.

Disadvantages of questionnaires as a data collection method   **12–14**

➢ The major disadvantage is the low level of response rates currently achievable. This is important because of the bias that can result. Bias occurs because your respondents may not be representative of your sample i.e. they may have a particular interest in the specific topic.

➢ There is no opportunity to probe beyond the answers you receive on the questionnaire.

➢ There is no opportunity to clarify an ambiguous answer.

➢ There is no opportunity to check either the accuracy or truthfulness of the answers.

➢ The researcher cannot be sure who, within an organisation, has answered the questionnaire. Has it made its way to the most appropriate person?

➢ The researcher has no control over the order in which questions are answered.

➢ The researcher has no way of ensuring that all your questions are answered.

➢ Questionnaires are unsuitable for certain groups of respondents: people with poor literacy skills or poor sight, the very old, children younger than ten and people with language difficulties.

Tip: It is essential that the questions you ask are interpreted by your respondents in the way you intend and that the data you collect will answer your research questions. One way to help ensure that this will happen is to pilot your questionnaire. Getting real responses will help you gauge if you need to change the wording (in which case the amended questionnaire should again be piloted) and analysing the data obtained should indicate whether it will achieve your research objectives.

Further reading

Texts providing an overview of questionnaires: **12–15**

J. Bell, *Doing Your Research Project* 4th edn (Buckingham: Open University Press, 2005) Ch. 8.

L. Blaxter, C. Hughes and M. Tight, *How to Research* 3rd edn (Milton Keynes: Open University Press, 2006).

M. Denscombe, *The Good Research Guide for Small-Scale Research Projects* 2nd edn (Buckingham: Open University Press, 2003) Ch. 9.

T. May, *Social Research* 3rd edn (Buckingham: Open University Press, 2001) Ch. 5.

Texts which contain more practical advice for carrying out a questionnaire exercise:

J.M. Converse and S. Presser, "Survey Questions: Handcrafting the Standardized Questionnaire", *Sage University Paper series on Quantitative Applications in the Social Sciences* (1986).

D.A. de Vaus, *Surveys in Social Research* 5th edn (London: UCL Press, 2002), Chs 7 and 8.

G. Hoinville and R. Jowell, *Survey Research Practice* (Gower: Aldershot, 1985).

C.A. Moser and G. Kalton, *Survey Methods in Social Investigation* 2nd edn (Heinemann Educational 1971), Chs 11 and 13.

A.N. Oppenheim, *Questionnaire Design, Interviewing and Attitude Measurement* (2nd end (Continuum International publishing, 1992) Chs 7 and 8.

Interviews

12–16 Interviews should not just be viewed as a chat with someone about your research. In order for the information obtained to be useful you must plan your interview and think about exactly what information you want to obtain from your interviewee.

There are four different types of interview:

(a) Structured interview: where a questionnaire checklist is completed by the interviewer, not the respondent.
(b) Semi-structured interview: questions are normally specified by the researcher but the interviewer is free to probe beyond the answers.
(c) Informal interview: the respondent is allowed to talk about an issue in any way he chooses.
(d) Group interviews: allow the researcher to focus on group values and group dynamics around the issue under investigation.

12–17 *Advantages of using interviews as a data collection method*

➢ The response rate will tend to be better than that achievable by mail questionnaires.
➢ The interviewer can ensure that the respondent understands what they are being asked by the repetition or rephrasing of questions.
➢ An interview ensures that the respondent answers the questions in the sequence intended.
➢ There is an opportunity to probe beyond an answer.
➢ The respondent has scope to talk about issues in more detail than it would be possible to write down in response to a questionnaire.
➢ Respondents who cannot write fluently are able to express their opinions.
➢ The interview situation allows data to be collected not only from the answers provided by respondents but also from how they gave their answers. This includes factors such as body language.

12–18 *Disadvantages of using interviews as a data collection method*

➢ Interviews can be very time-consuming.
➢ Interviews can be costly. Travel costs depend on the location of your interviewees.
➢ If too little structure is maintained then it becomes difficult to use the data in a comparative exercise.
➢ The possibility of bias being introduced by the interviewer. An interviewee can be influenced by the way a question is asked. This does not just involve the language used but the inflection of the voice and body language.

Tip: Prepare detailed questions. Think about possible answers that could be given by your interviewee. Think about subsidiary questions to your main questions in case your initial question does not get the information you wanted. Be aware that your interviewee is doing you a favour by allowing themselves to be interviewed and that you cannot force them to provide you with all the information that you want. Make sure that you remain objective. No matter how strongly you feel about the subject, you should not argue with your interviewee!

Further reading

Texts providing an overview of interviews: **12–19**

J. Bell, *Doing Your Research Project* 4th edn (Buckingham: Open University Press, 2005) Ch. 9.
M. Denscombe, *The Good Research Guide for Small-Scale Research Projects* 2nd edn (Buckingham: Open University Press, 2003) Ch. 10.
T. May, *Social Research* 3rd edn (Buckingham: Open University Press, 2001) Ch. 6.

Texts providing more practical information about carrying out interviews

C.A. Moser and G. Kalton, *Survey Methods in Social Investigation* 2nd edn (Heinemann Educational, 1971), Chs 12 and 13.
A.N. Oppenheim, *Questionnaire Design, Interviewing and Attitude Measurement* 2nd edn (Continuum International Publishing, 1992), Chs 5 and 6.

Observation studies

Observation not only involves watching, recording and analysing events of interest but also includes talking to people and examining relevant documents such as diaries or records. "The distinguishing feature of observation ... is that the information required is obtained directly, rather than through the reports of others; in the area of behaviour one finds out what the individual does, rather than what he says he does."

C.A. Moser and G. Kalton, *Survey Methods in Social Investigation* 2nd edn (Heinemann Educational, 1971) p.245.

Advantages of using observation studies as a data collection method   **12–20**

➢ It allows the spontaneous element of the data to be captured because you are recording behaviour as it takes place.
➢ It enables the study of those who are unable to comprehend and provide accurate answers to questions in questionnaires or interviews, e.g. young children.
➢ It is not dependent on memory. People can distort the past either intentionally or unintentionally. Observation allows the researcher to witness events.

Disadvantages of using observation studies as a data collection method   **12–21**

➢ The subjectivity of the researcher. It is the researcher's selection and interpretation of events that will emerge.
➢ The bias of the observer. It is not easy to maintain the detachment of an objective observer. The more familiar the observer becomes with the observed, the more likely that data could be omitted or misinterpreted.
➢ Observation studies tend to generate a large amount of material which can easily turn into a mass of unstructured notes.
➢ Undertaking an observation study can be very time-consuming.
➢ You may not end up measuring reality but a false environment because of people's tendency to behave differently as a result of being observed.
➢ It is only possible to observe events which have a set duration. Observation is usually not an appropriate way of studying opinions and attitudes. This disadvantage may be mitigated by combining the use of an observation study with one of the other methods of data collection.

> ➤ There are some situations where observation may not be possible, e.g. doctor/patient interviews.
> ➤ The research is very dependent on the personality of the researcher. You need to be able to communicate effectively with people and to be adaptable. You will need to be accepted by, and build up a relationship with, those you are observing.

Tip: Adopt a clear and systematic approach to data collection. You will observe a lot of information and it is important to be clear what you should note and how you should note it in a way that will be both time efficient and useful for achieving your research objectives.

Further reading

12–22 Texts providing more information about observation studies:

J. Bell, *Doing Your Research Project* 4th edn (Buckingham: Open University Press, 2005) Ch.11.

M. Denscombe, *The Good Research Guide for Small-Scale Research Projects* 2nd edn (Buckingham: Open University Press, 2003) Ch.11.

B.R. Dixon, G.D. Bouma and G.B.J. Atkinson, *A Handbook of Social Science* (New York Oxford University Press, 1987), pp.69–79.

V. Jupp, *Methods of Criminological Research* (London: Unwin Hyman, 1989).

T. May, *Social Research* 3rd edn (Buckingham: Open University Press, 2001) Ch.7.

C.A. Moser and G. Kalton, *Survey Methods in Social Investigation* 2nd edn (Heinemann Educational, 1971) Ch.10.

Conclusion on empirical research

12–23 Once you have collected your data you cannot just present it in its raw state, you have organise, analyse and interpret it. Organising your data can be repetitive and boring. However it is a most important part of the research process and you must take care to be consistent (e.g. in the way you categorise the raw data) and to pay attention to detail. If you fail to bring these qualities to the analysis you will be in danger of misreporting your data.

Initial organisation of your material will be followed by analysis. This involves examining the raw data and looking for patterns, similarities, differences, groupings and items of particular significance. The analytical techniques which you use, will depend on the type of data that you have collected. It is essential to adopt the most appropriate method of analysis.

If you have used only a small number of questionnaires you may be able to analyse them manually, however if you carried out a large scale questionnaire you will have to enter the raw data into a suitable computer package. There are now many software packages currently available for statistical analysis and the choice may depend on the level of statistical sophistication you want to achieve and also access to the software. If you are carrying out basic statistical tests a spreadsheet like Excel may be appropriate but if you wish to use more sophisticated statistics you will require to use specialist software such as SPSS. SPSS is a statistical programme specifically designed for social scientists and many of the statistical texts now incorporate its use. If you used interviews or observation studies the appropriate analytical techniques will depend on the form your data has taken. If you have used the structured or semi-structured approach your data will probably be able to be presented in numeric form. If you have used a less structured format you will have to use other analysis techniques more suitable to qualitative data. This involves the selection of relevant, illustrative or interesting material and quotations.

Chapter 13
Making Effective Use of Information

This chapter discusses the effective use of information once it has been located. It starts by **13–1** looking at how to get the most out of lectures and tutorials. These will be an integral part of your university studies and represent a very efficient way of assimilating information. The chapter then looks at time management and different reading and note-taking techniques. The chapter also provides guidance on the evaluation of documentary material and record-keeping. The chapter concludes by discussing referencing conventions for the different sources of information and the construction of a bibliography.

LECTURES

The first point is to stress the importance of attending lectures. They are a vital part of your **13–2** university studies and should not be viewed as an optional extra. Not only are they a positive learning experience, lectures are also the quickest and easiest way of obtaining information about a topic. The information given in an hour long lecture would take you far longer than one hour to find yourself in a paper or virtual library. Those who think that they can complete a course by skipping lectures and just reading a book instead will find that they have chosen the difficult way to study a subject. The most time-efficient way to study is to attend lectures and use them as a basis for your own reading. They will provide a framework and should help identify important areas for you to follow up. The information in lectures has been selected and structured by your lecturer. It has been tailored to your course and is therefore appropriate for the level you are at and also useful as guidance to the content of course assessments. Lectures also allow you to gain experience of the way legal material should be presented e.g. the way your lecturer refers to legal authority.

How to get the most out of a lecture

If you are expected to do any preparatory reading, you should ensure that you arrive at the **13–3** lecture suitably prepared. This may involve downloading and familiarising yourself with materials from your university intranet.

Make sure that you arrive on time. If you are late you will probably miss the lecturer's outline of the lecture, handouts and any important announcements. You will then find it an uphill battle to understand what is going on.

Writing down every word like an automaton is a mistake. You may end up with a record of everything that was said—but was everything important? What did the lecturer highlight? You will not know because you were too busy writing to notice. Another result of trying to write down every word will probably be completely illegible notes.

It is much better practice to take an active role in the lecturing process. This involves you thinking about what is being said and asking yourself:

Is this important?
Do I understand this? If not, make a note and check the point in the recommended reading or raise it in a tutorial.

13–4 Try to identify the structure of the lecture. At the beginning the lecturer may outline the structure of the lecture and/or at the end they may summarise the material. Alternatively, you may be provided with an outline in your course materials.

How do you know what is important? There are several clues for you to look out for:

> ➢ The emphasis given by the lecturer. They may say directly that something is important or use terms such as "a leading case".
> ➢ The time spent on a topic. If something is only mentioned briefly it is probably a minor point.

It is very tempting to write down everything, especially at the beginning of your university career. You may feel that you want to do this and gradually build up your confidence in your own note-taking abilities before you move to a more active participation in the lecture.

It is very important that you can easily read your own notes. Several suggestions to aid this:

> ➢ Develop your own shortened versions of words, *e.g.* do not write out House of Lords each time it is mentioned—put HL.
> ➢ Mark out cases and statutes in some way, such as underlining.
> ➢ Do not write in a continuous prose with no breaks. Do not cram everything in together in an attempt to save paper. It will be incredibly difficult to read at a later stage. Try and break up the text with headings. Separate out different points—either by numbering or by leaving a line between them. It will be much easier to use the notes if they are easy to read and you can identify the main points.

Note-taking is covered in more detail in para.13.15.

Soon after the lecture you should re-read your notes to check that you understand what you have written and that you can read your writing or make sense of any shortened versions of words you have used. Do this quickly while the contents of the lecture are still fresh in your mind. If you have typed your notes, you should also make sure that you back them up regularly.

Follow up the lecture by reading any materials recommended by the lecturer. Do not try to read everything—you will not have time. Select the most important materials. Your selection should be based on the emphasis accorded by the lecturer and whether the material is highlighted in your course materials.

13–5 Uses to be made of lecture material

> ➢ Your lectures should initially be your principal source of information—they are designed to introduce you to the subject area and to provide a structure and overview for you to flesh out.
> ➢ Do not regard your lecture notes as all you will need to pass exams. Lecture notes are just one source of material. Your work for a course should include lecture notes but will also include notes from your own reading and interpretation from primary and secondary sources. You are expected to follow up a lecture by reading key materials mentioned by the lecturer. If cases are discussed in a lecture, you should read the case report for yourself. This will not only help your understanding of the topic but it will build up into a bank of notes useful for revision purposes.
> ➢ Your lectures will be more up to date than textbooks. Lectures can include developments which have taken place up to the previous day whereas textbooks are likely to be several months out of date by the time they are published. Do remember that your lecture notes will go out of date quickly. You cannot dig up your old lecture notes years later and assume that they will still apply. The basic underlying principles may still

apply but even these can change over time. You must be able to update the information yourself.

➤ Note-taking is a subjective process. Copying out someone else's notes is no substitute for attending the lecture yourself. If you lend your lecture notes to someone, make sure that you keep a copy in case the borrower never returns the notes.

➤ Lectures are not just useful for the content. You should also pay attention to how the lecturer has structured the material and how they have used legal authority such as cases and statutes. This should help you in structuring your essays and using authority in legal argument.

Further reading 13–6

H.L. MacQueen, *Studying Scots Law* 3rd edn (Haywards Heath: Tottel, 2006) pp.129-133.
L. Marshall and F. Rowland, *A Guide to Learning Independently* 3rd edn (Melbourne: Longman, 2001) Ch. 10.

TUTORIALS

How to get the most out of a tutorial 13–7

Tutorial sessions involve small groups of students having a discussion with the tutor about a topic which has previously been covered in lectures. Tutorials are viewed as a crucial part of the learning process. It is therefore important that you attend all of your scheduled tutorials. If you miss a lecture you can copy someone's notes. Tutorials are much less easy to miss. People will tend to take fewer notes than in a lecture and it will be difficult to find out exactly what was discussed.

The more effort that you put into a tutorial, the more you will get out of it. You will usually be given a tutorial exercise to prepare. Make sure that you have carried out the work expected. If you attend having done no preparation you will not understand the discussion and will probably not be able to take part.

At the tutorial you should be ready to participate in the discussion by asking questions, listening to other people's contributions and responding to issues raised. You should make notes of anything that you consider helpful or if the tutor stresses a particular point. Otherwise you should concentrate on participating and not writing. The best practice is to spend a short time after the tutorial writing up salient points. Do not leave too much of a time-gap between the tutorial and writing up notes as your memory will inevitably let you down.

Uses to be made of tutorials 13–8

Use tutorials as an opportunity to raise questions about anything that you have not understood in the lectures. If you are unsure of what is expected from you in a piece of coursework or in the exam, the tutorial is the place to raise it with the tutor.

Tutorial sessions are where you will develop problem-solving skills which will be essential to cope with exam questions and the practice of law generally. Lectures will tend to cover the content of the law in a given area. In tutorials you will apply that law to problem scenarios. The application of the law to factual situations is a fundamental skill for lawyers. Exam questions may be discursive essays or they will consist of problem questions. Working through problem scenarios in tutorials is excellent preparation for the eventual exam at the end of the course.

Tutorials will tend to be the setting for receiving feedback on your assessments. This will give you the chance to see both your strengths and where you are going wrong.

Tutorials also give you the opportunity to improve your oral communication skills. At first it may be nerve-wracking, but the more you speak in the small tutorial setting the more confident you will become speaking generally. This will help you when you come to give presentations.

Tutorials are an important point of contact, not only with the tutor but also with your fellow students. It is always useful to share ideas. It can also be very reassuring to find out that everyone else is finding it as difficult as you are.

13–9 Further reading

H.L. MacQueen, *Studying Scots Law* 3rd edn (Haywards Heath: Tottel, 2006) pp.133-136.
L. Marshall and F. Rowland, *A Guide to Learning Independently* 3rd edn (Melbourne: Longman, 2001) Ch. 11.

TIME MANAGEMENT

13–10 Your success at university depends on YOU. You are in control of your own destiny. One of the most productive things that you can do is to organise yourself and your time at an early stage in your university career. You will be studying several different subjects at the same time and you will also have different activities to undertake such as attending lectures, preparing for tutorials, writing assessments and revising for exams. You will find that the level of activity will not be even and you will have to plan for periods when you there are many different and competing demands on your time e.g. when deadlines for different pieces of coursework coincide.

Time management skills are increasingly important in a world where the majority of students are employed in part-time work. Financial constraints often mean that time that would ideally be spent in the library is instead spent behind a shop counter or bar. It is vital to maintain a balance in your life that does not work to the detriment of your studies.

There is no "correct" way of managing your studies. It is up to you to find ways that suit you and your lifestyle. This section contains some suggestions to help you manage your time effectively.

> ➤ Make sure you are familiar with your university timetable and know when and where your classes are. Most universities number the weeks of terms/ semesters and use this as a way of referring to events/ deadlines. Make sure you know the system your university adopts and mark the numbers into a diary. Failure to do this can result in you missing a compulsory class or a deadline for an assessment.
> ➤ Establish a routine and organise yourself into a regular study schedule.
> ➤ Try to be flexible about where you can work. Make use of "spare" bits of time such as bus journeys. Make the most of breaks between classes and work in the library.
> ➤ Develop a system for filing your notes. When you start revising for an exam you do not want to be faced with a large file of disorganised notes.
> ➤ Make sure that you have a system of backing up your notes regularly—save them onto a USB or a CD. Do not rely on the hard drive of a PC as you will lose everything if it fails or it is stolen. Backing up material can seem like overkill but it only takes minutes and can save you an awful lot of hassle if things go wrong.
> ➤ Be aware of deadlines. Think ahead and plan your work. Timetables, diaries or planners can be useful aids. Being able to work to deadlines is not only important at university but is a skill which is vital for every kind of job.
> ➤ In addition to timetabling "external" deadlines you may find it helpful to set your own target dates for achieving things. Choose dates which are well ahead of any external deadline (such as a submission date for an assessment) but which are also realistic. Organising yourself to your own target dates allows you to build in some leeway for yourself to allow for the unexpected.

> ➤ Do not put off doing something because you think it is difficult. The sooner you get started, the better your work will be. You will probably find that it is not as difficult as you thought. It will certainly not become any easier by leaving it to the last minute.
> ➤ Do not leave coursework until just before the deadline for submission. A problem with your PC or a broken printer can prove disastrous.
> ➤ It can be helpful to make lists of specific goals and cross off each one as you achieve them. Review your list regularly. Prioritise your work depending on its urgency and its importance.
> ➤ You will find tasks easier to tackle if you break them up into small parts. It is much less daunting to start a small task than to face the whole task at once.
> ➤ It is far more productive to work in short bursts than to work through a whole day and into the night. Taking breaks refreshes the mind.
> ➤ It is also helpful to build variety into your studying—do not spend an entire evening on one task.
> ➤ Finally, do not sit on your own and worry about work. Make use of your lecturers and tutors. Ask for help or additional explanation. You should also make use of your fellow students. Talking and bouncing ideas off each other can be very productive. Even a good moan can be beneficial!

Further reading

Further reading on time management can be found in: **13–11**

S. Drew and R. Bingham, *The Student Skills Guide* 2nd edn (Aldershot: Gower, 2004).
A. Northedge, *The Good Study Guide* (Milton Keynes: Open University Press, 2005) Ch. 2.

EFFECTIVE READING TECHNIQUES

Before you start reading a book or article make sure you are clear about your reasons for **13–12** reading it. Reasons for reading a book/article include:

> ➤ The factual content;
> ➤ To gain an insight into the author's interpretation of the law/events;
> ➤ To look at the author's style of writing;
> ➤ To find out which sources the author has used.

The following are suggestions to help you read effectively:

> ⇒ Do not feel compelled to read a book from cover to cover. Use the contents page and the index to identify chapters or shorter sections of the text which are relevant. If this does not help, start by reading the introduction and the concluding chapter.
> ⇒ Critically assess what you are reading. As you read you should be thinking what your opinion is about the text.

> ➤ Is it easy to understand the author's arguments?
> ➤ Are the arguments backed up by authority?
> ➤ Are the arguments consistent?
> ➤ Do you agree with the arguments?
> ➤ If yes, why?
> ➤ If no, why not?

13–13 Make notes as you read. This will help you to retain the essential points. It is also one way of keeping your mind active while you read. If you read without taking any notes you will forget a lot of the material. You may even end up having to re-read it. This is duplication of effort and a waste of your time.

One way of making notes is to mark your book by highlighting or underlining sections. This focuses your attention on the text and you will have a permanent reminder of your first thoughts as you read the text. It goes without saying that you should only do this if the material belongs to you. Do not do this to a library book.

Notes made while reading should not be a shorthand copy of the text. As you read you should try to identify relevant information by asking yourself "What exactly is this about?", "What do I need to remember?". Your notes should be clear and concise. It is essential that you can understand your own notes. This is not as simple as it sounds. It is easy to become familiar with a text, grow tired of making full notes and to end up with almost cryptic notes. When you come to read over your notes several months later, they will not make sense.

Make sure you write down sufficient details about the material you read (see paras 13.27-13.57 on referencing conventions regarding appropriate details for various sources). In addition, it is advisable to note down the library reference. These precautions enable you to reference the material in a piece of coursework or find it again with a minimum of difficulty. It is very frustrating to find that you have a really good quotation which you want to include in an essay and yet you have no idea where you found it. It is even more frustrating to find that you have finally finished an essay and yet you have not noted down bibliographic details. You then have to spend time rechecking the details.

13–14 Further reading

L. Marshall and F. Rowland, *A Guide to Learning Independently* 3rd edn (Melbourne: Longman, 2001) Ch. 9.
A. Northedge, *The Good Study Guide* (Milton Keynes: Open University Press, 2005) Ch. 5.
K. Williams, *Study Skills* (Macmillan, 1989) Ch. 1.

NOTE-TAKING

13–15 When you are taking notes do not merely copy out passages verbatim. Try to think about the material and put it into your own words. If you do use the actual words of the source, make this clear by putting them in quotation marks. This will help avoid unwitting plagiarism (see para.14.6).

There are various styles that you can use to take notes. There is no "right" way to take notes. Use whichever style suits you:

13–16 Précis

!Example

There are five formal sources of Scots law. The most important of the sources is legislation. The second most important is case law. The institutional writers were very important but their influence has diminished. Custom and equity are the other recognised formal sources of Scots law.

Prose may be appropriate where you want to abstract important details of key ideas. The disadvantage of using continuous prose is that it is rarely easy to scan. Breaking the text up by using paragraphs helps to make it easier to read.

Headings and sub-headings   **13–17**

Formal sources of Scots law

- ➢ Legislation
- ➢ Case law
- ➢ Institutional Writers
- ➢ Custom
- ➢ Equity

Numbered sections   **13–18**

1. Formal sources of Scots law
   1.1 Legislation
   1.2 Case law
   1.3 Institutional Writers
   1.4 Custom
   1.5 Equity

Annotated diagrams   **13–19**

Colour code   **13–20**

Using different colours for, e.g. case names and details of cases, titles of statutes, etc.

Annotated photocopied material   **13–21**

Marking up a photocopy with your own comments. If you use this method be careful not to fall into the trap of photocopying and filing efficiently but failing to actually read the material.

Direct entry into a PC   **13–22**

This can make it easier to manipulate the material using cut and paste functions. However, it does not remove the question of how you should arrange the material.

13–23 Card index system

You can put notes of specific items on to a small card index which can then be stored alphabetically. Many people use this method for notes made from cases. It should enable you to find the relevant case note easily. It has the added benefit of forcing you to make your notes concise as they have to fit on to the card.

EVALUATION OF DOCUMENTARY SOURCES ONCE THEY ARE LOCATED

13–24 Once you have located information, you need to evaluate it. Information sources can be divided into primary and secondary sources. Primary sources include sources which represent the law such as legislation and cases. Data collected by the researcher, e.g. through the use of questionnaires, is also regarded as primary data. Secondary data is material collected and analysed by someone else. Secondary sources include books, articles, Government statistics, White and Green Papers, etc.

The fact that a document has been compiled by someone else can affect a researcher's use of the document. An example is the crime statistics published by the Government. They can be criticised for failing to reveal the true extent of crime. Reasons for the number of reported crimes being an underestimation of the real extent of crime include:

> ➢ A large amount of crime is not reported to official authorities for a variety of reasons
> ➢ Official statistics reflect the activities of the authorities, *e.g.* if the authorities decide to concentrate on breath testing drivers the number of reported crimes of drink-driving will increase.

Given this weakness, the official statistics could be used as a piece of evidence about the extent of crime rather than being regarded as definitive. Other pieces of evidence could also be used.

As a general rule, no matter what type of document you are reading, you should not accept it at face value. You should be alert to any possible bias or distortion that it may contain. The distortion need not be deliberate but could be due to the way the information is collected, categorised and interpreted. Even if you do detect bias that does not render the whole document worthless. The important point is that you are aware of the bias and take account of it. The document may still contain some useful information but requires cautious examination.

13–25 As you read a document you should consider various questions. The relevancy of the questions will depend on the nature of the document under consideration but here are some suggestions:

1. Who is the author? What are their qualifications for writing on the subject? Are they well respected? What else have they written on the subject? Anything? Are they legally qualified? If they are an academic, which university are they from? What is its reputation? If the subject matter is practical, has the author qualified as a lawyer or are they "just" an academic who might fail to identify practical issues?
2. What is the date of the publication? You need to ensure that you are reading the most up-to-date information possible. If there is more than one edition, check that you have the latest edition. You will need to be aware of whether the law has changed since the document was produced.
3. Which jurisdiction(s) is the work purporting to cover? Is it referring to Scots law or UK law or another jurisdiction? Is it an area that is UK-wide or is that jurisdiction different from Scotland in any key respect?
4. Why was it produced? Has any funding been obtained? If so, from whom? The preface or introduction may contain details of the purpose/objective of the work. Bear in mind

that this will be the publicly declared purpose, whereas the real purpose may be very different.

5. Is any bias declared? e.g. membership of a particular political party or pressure group?
6. How was the research carried out? If the document presents results of research, how much information is given about the research process and the methodologies employed? Can the methodology be justified? Has the methodology been used appropriately? Has it been used according to convention, *i.e.* followed current guide-lines. Is it an established methodology? Is it experimental? Further relevant questions would depend on the methodology employed but might include: Is there a copy of the questionnaire, details of sample size or mention of the response rate? Are the results produced in a way which allows the reader to assess their validity, *e.g.* if percentages are used, is there sufficient information to allow the reader to convert them to real numbers?
7. How well has the document been researched? Footnotes/references will provide an indication.
8. What are its underlying assumptions?
9. How is the argument presented? How well supported and convincing is its argument?
10. Are any conclusions which have been reached based on the evidence presented?
11. What does the document not say? Are there any omissions?
12. How does the document relate to other works? Does it follow on from previous work? Is it part of a trend? Has it disagreed with all previous work? How does it relate to later works? Has anyone taken the research further? Have they confirmed this work or have they contradicted it?
13. What do other sources have to say about it? Has it received critical reviews? If it has, who has been criticising it—experts in the field or competitors?

RECORD-KEEPING

Make sure that you write down sufficient details to enable you to locate the reference again and **13–26** to use it in a bibliography. For the specific details required for the different types of sources of information, see paras 13.27-13.57.

It is important to be systematic and thorough when checking sources of information and obtaining relevant items. A check on the sources already consulted, those still to be read and a list of items requested via the library on inter-library loan will enable you to remain in control and organised about the progress of your research.

BIBLIOGRAPHIC REFERENCING CONVENTIONS

A bibliography is a list of books, journal articles, reports, theses or any other secondary sources **13–27** of information consulted during the preparation of a piece of research. Primary sources of information (such as cases and statutes) are not included in a bibliography. They should be listed in separate tables of cases/statutes, if appropriate.
A bibliography is used to:

➢ Acknowledge the sources which have been consulted.
➢ Enable readers of the research to access the material.

References in a bibliography have to convey certain details which give enough information so that others can locate the materials. The information should be accurate, complete and presented in a consistent style. An excellent guide for correct referencing details is the Oxford Standard for Citation of Legal Authorities (OSCOLA). The most recent version is OSCOLA 2006 and this can be found at *http://denning.law.ox.ac.uk/published/oscola.shtml*. However, you will find that styles do vary over different publications. This is principally due to different publishers adopting different house styles. While there is no one agreed version of referencing legal authorities, OSCOLA is generally accepted however, this does not include many of the distinctively Scottish materials.

A guide to the more common bibliographic references is given below. Please note that elsewhere in this book the conventions itemised below have not been adhered to because of the need to conform to the publisher's house style.

13–28 When referring to a source you should always reference the source you actually used. If you did not use the primary source but instead e.g. looked at a case in a casebook or an excerpt of an article in a collection of shortened versions (sometimes called 'readers') then you should acknowledge this. This means referring to it e.g. J. F. DiMento 'Can Social Science Explain Organisational Non-compliance with Environmental Law?' (1989) 45 (1) *Journal of Social Issues* 109-132 in B. M. Hutter *A Reader in Environmental Law* (Oxford: OUP, 1999) 218.

Cases

13–29 Case name *in italics*; citation (See para.3.22 for more details about citations).

If you are referring to a particular judgment you should refer to the name of the judge, the page number and corresponding letter in the margin (if included in the series of law reports) e.g.

McNulty v Marshalls Food Group Ltd, 1999 S.C. 195, *per* Lord Macfadyen, p.206F.

If you are using a media neutral citation to refer to a post 2005 case in Scotland (post 2001 in England) you should refer to the paragraph number e.g.

Dow v West of Scotland Shipbreaking Company Limited [2007] CSOH 71 [24]

Note: if a case is published in a printed format and also available electronically, you should reference the printed source for the case.

Legislation

13–30 *Acts of the Scottish Parliament (pre–1707) – referred to as Scots Acts*

The correct citation of Scots Acts is by the short title or by the calendar year and chapter number or by the volume, page and chapter number of the *Record edition*. The Acts did not originally have short titles but all surviving Scots Acts were given short titles by Sch.2 of The Statute Law Revision (Scotland) Act 1964. An example from Sch.2 is the Act formerly known by "For pwnishment of personis that contempnandlie remanis rebellis and at the horne". It acquired the short title The Registration Act 1579.

Prior to 1964 Scots Acts were cited by calendar year and chapter number in the Glendook edition or by the volume and page number of the *Record edition*. This is still the case for Scots Acts which have been repealed.

13–31 *Acts of the UK Parliament*

Modern statutes. The normal citation is the short title with no comma before the date e.g. Marriage (Scotland) Act 1977

A complete citation would also include the chapter number e.g. Marriage (Scotland) Act 1977 c 15.

Older statutes. It is preferable to include the appropriate regnal year and chapter number. In the example below the information in parentheses indicates that the Act was given Royal Assent in the 20th year of the reign of George II. It was the 43rd Act given the Royal Assent in that Parliament, hence it is called "chapter 43".

Heritable Jurisdictions (Scotland) Act 1746 (20 Geo 2 c.43)

If you are referring to a particular part of an Act, you should include the following details:

> ➢ If you are referring to a section: Protection of Animals (Scotland) Act 1993 s 1.
> ➢ If you are referring to a subsection: Scotland Act 1998 s 57(2).
> ➢ If you are referring to a paragraph in a subsection: Law Reform (Miscellaneous Provisions) (Scotland) Act 1980 s 22(1)(d).

Local and Personal Acts. Local and Personal Acts are cited in the same way as Public General Acts, except that, in order to differentiate them, the chapter number is printed differently.
The chapter numbers of Local Acts appear in lower case roman numerals, e.g. Peterhead Harbours Order Confirmation Act 1992 c xii.
The chapter numbers of Personal Acts appear in italicised arabic figures e.g. John Francis Dare and Gillian Loder Dare (Marriage Enabling) Act 1982 *c 1*

Statutory Instruments   **13–32**

Title, date, and number (if available) or, alternatively, by year and running number *e.g.*

Control of Pollution (Silage, Slurry and Agricultural Fuel Oil) Regulations 1991/324
or
SI 1991/324 (alternatively SI 1991 No. 324).

The statutory instruments themselves frequently stipulate the citation by which they should be referred e.g. regulation 1 of the above regulations states "These Regulations may be cited as the Control of Pollution (Silage, Slurry and Agricultural Fuel Oil) Regulations 1991."

Acts of the Scottish Parliament (1999–)   **13.33**

Short title with no comma before the date e.g. Aquaculture and Fisheries (Scotland) Act 2007

A complete citation would also include the asp number e.g. Aquaculture and Fisheries (Scotland) Act 2007 asp 12

Private Bills enacted by the Scottish Parliament become Acts of the Scottish Parliament and are cited in the same way as Public General Acts e.g. Stirling-Alloa-Kincardine Railway and Linked Improvements Act 2004 asp 10.

Scottish Statutory Instruments (1999–)   **13–34**

Name, date, and number e.g.

The Number of Inner House Judges (Variation) Order 2007 SSI 2007/258
or

SSI 2007/258 (alternatively SSI 2007 No 258).

The instruments themselves frequently stipulate the citation by which they should be referred e.g. art.1 of the above order states "This Order may be cited as the Number of Inner House Judges (Variation) Order 2007."

Books

13–35 Author, surname and initials, *title in italics* followed by the publication information in parentheses (edition if other than the first edition, publisher, place of publication, date of publication) e.g.

DM Walker, *The Scottish Legal System* (8th edn, W. Green: Edinburgh 2001)

If a book has three or more authors you should include the first named author and then put "*et al*" meaning "and the others" e.g.

C Ashton. *et al.*, *Fundamentals of Scots Law* (W. Green: Edinburgh 2003)

13–36 *Chapters in books*

Author, 'title of chapter' in inverted commas, in author/editor of main work, title of main work, followed by the publication information in parentheses (edition if other than the first edition, publisher, place of publication date of publication). The page numbers for the contribution are unnecessary.

WG Carson 'Symbolic and Instrumental Dimensions of early Factory legislation: A Case Study in the Social Origins of Criminal Law' in R Hood (ed), *Crime, Criminology and Public Policy* (Heinemann, London 1974)

The Laws of Scotland: Stair Memorial Encyclopaedia

13–37 The style of reference to the Stair Memorial Encyclopaedia depends on whether the material is from one of the original volumes or a reissue.
   Material in a title in one of the original volumes should be styled: *The Laws of Scotland: Stair Memorial Encyclopaedia*, vol 6, paras 896-922
   Material in a title that has been reissued should be styled: *The Laws of Scotland: Stair Memorial Encyclopaedia* Criminal Procedure Re-issue, para 183.
   Note that there is no need to cite the date of publication given that this encyclopaedia is updated on an ongoing basis.

Journal articles

13–38 Author, 'title of the article' in inverted commas followed by the publication date and volume number, title of the journal and the page number marking the first page of the article e.g.

V Aubert, 'Some Social Functions of Legislation' (1966) 10 Acta Sociologica 97

Points to note:

> If the publication date identifies the volume, the year reference should not be in brackets unless it is an English journal in which case it should appear in square brackets e.g.
> DM Walker 'The Importance of Stair's Work for the Modern Lawyer'1981 JR 161;

C Boch 'The Enforcement of the Environmental Assessment Directive in the National Courts: A Breach in the "Dyke"'[1997] JEL 129.

➢ Normal practice is to abbreviate journal titles but if you are referring to a lesser known or foreign journal you should provide its full title.

➢ If you are referring to a particular page within the article you should put a comma between the first page of the article and the particular page number. If you are referring to a paragraph number as opposed to a page number it should appear in square brackets.

Electronic journal articles   **13–39**

If an article is published in a printed format and also available electronically, you should reference the printed source for the article.

Some journals are only published electronically in which case they should be referenced as above but with the following additional details: the website address within angled brackets and most recent date of access e.g.

M Apistola and A R Lodder 'Law Firms and IT: Towards Optimal Knowledge Management' [2005] 2 & 3 JILT
< http://www2.warwick.ac.uk/fac/soc/law/elj/jilt/2005_2-3/apistola-lodder/ > accessed 7 April 2007

Law Commission materials   **13–40**

Scottish Law Commission

Scottish Law Commission Reports should be referenced by title followed by the following details in parenthesis (number, any Scottish Executive or House of Commons paper numbers as appropriate and the year) e.g.

Report on Variation and Termination of Trusts (Scot Law Com No. 206, SE/2007/42, 2007)

The reference for Scottish Law Commission Discussion Papers should include the DP number which indicates that it is a discussion paper as opposed to a final report e.g.

Discussion Paper on Personal Injury Actions: Limitation and Prescribed Claims (Scot Law Com DP No 132, 2006)

English Law Commission

Murder, Manslaughter and Infanticide (Law Com No 304, 2006)

UK Government publications

UK Parliament Bills

Each Bill is given a number. However, if the Bill is reprinted it will be given a new number. The **13–41** number of a Bill has no connection with the chapter number that will be allocated when it becomes an Act.

The elements of the citation of a Bill are: the initials of the House (e.g. HC or HL, the session of Parliament (e.g. 2006–07) and the Bill number which will be in square brackets if it is being considered by the House of Commons.

Example of a Bill being considered by the House of Commons: Rating (Empty Properties) Bill HC 2006-07 [102].

Example of a Bill being considered by the House of Lords: Forced Marriage (Civil Protection) Bill HL 2006-07 70 (this is the Bill as reprinted following amendments, the Bill was originally introduced as the Forced Marriage (Civil Protection) Bill HL 2006-07 3).

Command Papers

13–42 Name of author/department/institution/body, 'title of report' in inverted commas followed by the (Command number and date) in parenthesis e.g.

The Scottish Office, 'Scotland's Parliament' (Cm 3658, 1997).

Note that how the reference to Command papers is styled depends on the year of publication. See para.8.79 for details. From 1986 the appropriate abbreviation is Cm.

Hansard

13–43 You should include the following details in a reference: Hansard, the appropriate abbreviation for the House, full details of the date and column number e.g.

Hansard HC 17 June 1974, Col 134

Scottish Parliament materials

13–44 More information about referencing material from the Scottish Parliament can be found in A Guide to Recommended Citations for Scottish Parliament Publications, FS3-12, 19 October 2005 which is available on the Scottish Parliament website.

The reference styles below should be used for both electronic and print versions of the various documents.

Bills

13–45 Bills should be referenced by Scottish Parliament (SP) Bill number, title, [printing], session, (year) e.g.

SP Bill 75 Rights of Relatives to Damages (Mesothelioma) (Scotland) Bill [as introduced] Session 2 (2006).

SP Bill 58A Edinburgh Airport Rail Link Bill [as amended at Consideration stage] Session 2 (2007).

SP Bill 59-ML2 Christmas Day and New Year's Day Trading (Scotland) Bill [Marshalled List of Amendments selected for Stage 3] Session 2 (2007).

Unlike UK Parliament Bills, Scottish Parliament Bills keep the original numbering. Subsequent revisions are indicated as follows:

SP Bill 1	Bill as introduced
SP Bill 1A	Bill as amended at Stage 2

Accompanying documentation and lists of amendments are given references which are linked to the citation of the Bill.

SP Bill 1- PM	Policy memorandum
SP Bill 1-EN	Explanatory notes and other accompanying documents
SP Bill 1-ML	Marshalled list of amendments to the Bill as introduced—if there are several marshalled lists of amendments then they are numbered SP Bill 1-ML1, SP Bill 1-ML2 etc
SP Bill 1A-ML	Marshalled list of amendments to the Bill as amended at Stage 2
SP Bill 1A-EN	Supplementary explanatory notes for the Bill as amended at Stage 2
SP Bill 1A-FM	Supplementary financial memorandum for the Bill as amended at Stage 2
SP Bill 1-G	Groupings of amendments—if there are several groupings then they are numbered SP Bill 1-G1, SP Bill 1-G2 etc
SP Bill 1-DPM	Delegated powers memorandum
SP Bill 1B	Bill as passed

Official Report

The reference for the Official Report for meetings of the Parliament should include SP OR **13–46** followed by full details of the date and column numbers e.g. SP OR 29 March 2007, col 33710-33712.

The reference for the Official Report for Committee meetings should include SP OR followed by the appropriate committee abbreviation, the date and column numbers e.g. SP OR ERD 24 April 2006, col 3061-3104.

The reference for the Official Report for written answers should include SP WA followed by the date and parliamentary question number e.g. SP WA 28 March 2007, S2W-32485.

Committee abbreviations

Below is a list of all Scottish Parliament committees since 1999. **13–47**

Committee Name	Abbreviation
Ad Hoc Standards	AHS
Audit	AU
Baird Trust Reorganisation Bill	BAIRD
Commissioner for Children and Young People (Scotland) Bill	CC
Communities	COM
Edinburgh Tram (Line One) Bill	ED1
Edinburgh Tram (Line Two) Bill	ED2
Education	ED
Education, Culture and Sport	ED
Enterprise and Culture	EC
Enterprise and Lifelong Learning	EL
Environment and Rural Development	ERD
Equal Opportunities	EO
European	EU

European and External Relations	EU
Finance	FI
Health	HC
Health and Community Care	HE
Justice and Home Affairs	JH
Justice 1	J1
Justice 2	J2
Local Government	LG
Local Government and Transport	LGT
National Galleries of Scotland Bill	NG
Procedures	PR
Public Petitions	PE
Robin Rigg Offshore Wind Farm (Navigation and Fishing)(Scotland) Bill	RR
Rural Affairs	RA
Rural Development	RD
Salmon and Freshwater Fisheries (Consolidation) (Scotland) Bill	SF
Scottish Parliamentary Standards Commissioner Bill	SC
Social Inclusion, Housing and Voluntary Sector	HS
Social Justice	SJ
Standards	ST
Standards and Public Appointments	ST
Stirling-Alloa-Kincardine Railway and Linked Improvements Bill	SAK
Subordinate Legislation	SL
Transport and the Environment	TE
Waverley Railway (Scotland) Bill	WAV

Minutes of Committees

13–48 Minutes of Committees should be referenced as follows: SP M followed by the appropriate committee abbreviation and the date e.g. SP M SL 29 November 2005.

Minutes of Proceedings

13–49 Minutes of Proceedings should be referenced as follows: SP MOP, volume, number, session and date e.g.

SP MOP vol 4 no 41 Session 2, 14 December 2006.

Petitions

13–50 Petitions are referenced according to their PE number e.g. PE975.

Scottish Parliament papers

These should be referenced as follows: author/committee/body, report number, year, title (SPP **13–51** number) in parenthesis e.g. Environment and Rural Development Committee 1st Report, 2006, Stage 1 Report on the Animal Health and Welfare (Scotland) Bill (SPP 502).

Scottish Parliament Information Centre (SPICe) publications

These should be referenced as follows: title, series in abbreviated form, number, date. The **13–52** abbreviations for the various series are below:

Series name	Abbreviation
Fact Sheet	FS
IPRN Briefing	IPRN
Research Note (until 31 December 2001)	RN
Research Paper (until 31 December 2001)	RP
SPICe Briefing	SB
Subject Map. Comparative Series	SM CS
Subject Map. Devolved Area Series	SM DA
Subject Map. Scottish Parliament Series	SM SP

Examples include:

Sustainable Development – Scrutiny of Legislation, SB 06/75, 16 October 2006
Allotments, RN 00/102, 23 November 2000
The Water Industry, SM DA21, 21 December 1999

Scottish Executive papers

Scottish Executive papers are given a running number as they are published within a calendar **13–53** year: e.g. SE 2006/19.

Conference proceedings

The style of reference will depend on whether the conference proceedings have been published. **13–54** If this is the case the following details should be included:

Author(s), 'title' (of specific paper), conference title, publisher; place of publication, date, paper number of specific paper, if given.

A Murray 'The Nature of Law' Proceedings of the Conference on Legal Things, Research Association, Dundee 2006, Paper 3.

If the conference proceedings are only available at a conference or directly from the author they should be referenced by author, title, conference title and date.
  If the conference proceedings are only available online the reference should include the additional details of the web address and date of access.

Theses

13–55 Author, 'title' in inverted commas, followed by the remaining information in parentheses (degree or award, university or other institution, year).

AD Smith, 'Some Comparative Aspects of Specific Implement in Scots Law' (PhD thesis, Edinburgh University 1989).

Newspaper articles

13–56 Author/editorial/anon as appropriate, 'title of article' in inverted commas, name of *newspaper in italics,* followed by the publication details in parenthesis (city of publication, the full date), page number.

I Bell , 'Springtime in Quangopolis' *The Scotsman* (Edinburgh, 17th March 1999) 19.

If the article is from a newspaper's web site and there is no page number, the reference should include the website address and date of access e.g.

W Tinning 'Hotel smoking area has legal Lord fuming' *The Herald* (Glasgow 6 April 2007) < http://www.theherald.co.uk/news/news/display.var.1313196.0.0.php > accessed 6 April 2007.

Online and CD Rom materials

13–57 See paras 2.52-2.54.

REFERENCING SYSTEMS

13–58 There are three referencing systems which you can use to link statements in the text to bibliographic details of documents which support these statements. The choice of which system may be determined by your institution or it may be up to you. The important point is that you use one system **consistently**.
   The systems are:

Running notes

13–59 With running notes, numerals in the text, [in brackets] or [superscript], refer to notes numbered in the order they occur which contain references and sometimes other information. Multiple citations of the same document receive separate numbers. Details of the documents referred to (e.g. page references) should be given in the notes. This system can be used to incorporate explanatory footnotes as well as bibliographic references and is widely used in U.K. legal journals. Running notes can be listed at the foot of the page where reference is made to them (footnotes), or in numerical sequence at the end of the chapter or the work (endnotes).
   In the list of references/bibliography the works cited are listed in numerical order.
   If more than one reference is made to a document when running notes are used, it is possible to avoid a full reciting of the document by using the following terms:

Ibid (*Ibidem*—the same) can be used if successive references are made to the same document. Each use of "ibid" should be followed by the page number.

Op.Cit. (*Opere citato*—in the work previously cited) where the document has been cited at an earlier point, but not immediately before this reference. The author's name and page number are required. The original citation should contain full bibliographic information.

Loc.Cit. (*Loco citato*—in the place cited). This is similar to *op.cit.* but is more specific, as it refers to the same part of the work which has already been cited.

!Example

Recent research [1] has shown that ... however a respected author [2] has disagreed. After much debate the findings of the original work [3] have now been accepted.

[Excerpt from list of references:]

1. Wallace W. *New Law Book* Edinburgh: W. Green, 2006
2. Bruce R. *Even Newer Law Book* Edinburgh: W. Green, 2007
3. Wallace W. *New Law Book* Edinburgh W. Green, 2006

The numeric system

Documents are numbered in the order in which they are first referred to in the text. At each **13–60** point in the text at which a reference is required, its number is inserted — [in brackets], or in superscript. Subsequent citations of a particular document receive the same number as the first citation. If details of a particular document, e.g. page number are required they should be given after the reference number.

In the list of references/bibliography the works cited are listed in numerical order.

This system produces a list of references which is easy to prepare and easy to look up whilst reading the text, but it is not in any useful order as a bibliography. BS 4821:1990 (withdrawn) recommends that this system be coupled with a separate bibliography in alphabetical order of author.

!Example

Recent research [1] has shown that ... however a respected author [2] has disagreed. After much debate the findings of the original work [1] have now been accepted.

[Excerpt from list of references:]

1. Wallace W. *New Law Book* Edinburgh: W. Green, 2006
2. Bruce R. *Even Newer Law Book* Edinburgh: W. Green, 2007

The name and date system (also known as the "Harvard System")

The author's name and date of publication are inserted in brackets at each point in the text **13–61** where reference to the particular document is required. If the author's name occurs naturally in the text, the date only should be in brackets. If reference is made to different works by the same author in the same year, distinguish them by small case letters after the year.

The works cited would be listed alphabetically by author in the references/bibliography. The date is given after the name and not repeated at the end of the reference. If there are several works by the same author, they should be listed in chronological order.

!Example

Recent research (Wallace 2006) has shown that ... however a respected author (Bruce 2007) has disagreed. After much debate the findings of the original work (Wallace 2006) have now been accepted.

[Excerpt from list of references:]

1. Bruce R. (2007) *Even Newer Law Book* Edinburgh: W. Green.
2. Wallace W. (2006) *New Law Book* Edinburgh: W. Green.

Additional reading

13–62 David P. Bosworth, *Citing your references: a guide for authors of journal articles and students writing theses or dissertations* (Underhill Press, Thirsk, 1992).
D. French, *How to Cite Legal Authorities* (Blackstone Press, London, 1996).

Further information is also available in the following British Standards: British Recommendations for References to Published Materials (BS 1629: 1989). Recommendations for Citing and Referencing Published Material (BS 5605: 1990). British Standard Recommendations for Citation of Unpublished Documents (BS 6371: 1983).

CONSTRUCTING YOUR OWN BIBLIOGRAPHY

13–63 The purpose of recording all the references that you have found is so that you can find the material in the future and incorporate them into a bibliography, e.g. for a piece of coursework. There will tend to be a time gap between collecting the references and making use of the information. In order that you can find the information when you need to use it, you may want to construct your own bibliography as a place of safe-keeping for all these references. This will also enable you to build up your own research base and will help with other work undertaken in the future.

There are different ways of constructing your own bibliography:

➤ A manual record card system maintained in alphabetical order of the author's surname.
➤ A database in electronic form. This can be achieved by constructing a table in Word or by using a spreadsheet such as Excel. There are also a number of specialist database software packages such as Access.
➤ In either case you should include full bibliographic details. You may also want to include a keyword system describing the contents of the item. A third section for supplementary information may also be useful. This could include your comments on the work.
➤ There are bibliographic software products to which your university may provide access. These allow you to record and store references and generate bibliographies. Examples include Endnote and Reference Manager.

Chapter 14
How to Use Your Research to Produce High Quality Work

This chapter provides practical advice on using your research to produce work of a high **14–1** standard. It starts by providing guidance on the appropriate use of authority, use of quotations and how to avoid plagiarism. The chapter then looks at preparing university assessments and in particular essays, problem questions and oral presentations. Construction of research projects is also discussed. The chapter concludes with discussion of how to evaluate your own research followed by guidance on revision strategies for exams and exam technique.

APPROPRIATE USE OF AUTHORITY

If you are making points or arguments you must back them up with supporting authority. In **14–2** this case authority means reasons/evidence/justification. If you are talking about legal issues, you must refer to the relevant legal authority. Legal authority means a case, legislation or other authority, such as a statement by one of the Institutional Writers. The best way of developing the technique of using authority is to look at how it has been used by others: judges in their opinions; legal writers in their legal texts; lecturers in their lecture notes.

A statement such as "Distances mentioned in Acts of Parliament should be measured in a **14–3** straight line" is unsubstantiated assertion. You have produced no evidence to back up your statement. At the other end of the scale, a full reference could consist of the following "Section 8 of The Interpretation Act 1978 states that distances referred to in Acts of Parliament 'shall, unless the contrary intention appears, be measured in a straight line on a horizontal plane'". This version has quoted words from the relevant statute in order to make the position absolutely clear. You may wish to quote from the actual words of the statute if you feel that they would make your point more clearly. However, you should never need to write out the *entire* statutory provision. An acceptable level of reference to authority would be "Unless specifically stated otherwise, references to distance in Acts of Parliament should be measured in a straight line, (Interpretation Act 1978, s.8)".

When using cases as authority it will rarely be sufficient to refer simply to the correct citation of **14–4** the authority:

!Example

"The offence of causing pollution contained in s. 85(1) of the Water Resources Act 1991 should be regarded as a strict liability offence—*Alphacell v Woodward* [1972] A.C. 824."

The narration of excessive factual detail about a case is not appropriate:

!Example

"The offence of causing pollution contained in s.85(1) of the Water Resources Act 1991 should be regarded as a strict liability offence—*Alphacell v Woodward* [1972] A.C. 824. This case concerned a company who had premises on the banks of the River Irwell. They treated manilla fibres as part of the process of manufacturing paper. The fibres had to be boiled and the water in which they were boiled became seriously polluted. This water was drained into two settling tanks on the edge of the river. One settling tank was higher than the other and the overflow from the higher tank went into the lower. In a shed nearby, there were two pumps which ensured that there was no overflow from the lower tank. If the pumps failed the liquid went straight into the river. This happened one day in November 1969. The court found Alphacell guilty."

The best practice is to mention what is relevant about the authority to illustrate your point. This will probably be a summary of the *ratio decidendi* of a case either in your own words or as a quotation.

!Example

"The offence of causing pollution contained in s. 85(1) of the Water Resources Act 1991 should be regarded as a strict liability offence, *Alphacell v Woodward* [1972] A.C. 824. This House of Lords case examined the concept of causation and decided that the word "cause" should be given a common sense meaning. Negligence, knowledge and intention were all regarded as irrelevant. The important factor was that an active operation had resulted in polluting matter entering a river."

QUOTATIONS

14–5 If you want to repeat the exact words used in one of your sources of information you must use quotation marks. Everything between quotation marks, including punctuation, should be exactly as in the original text. If you add something you should put it in square brackets. If you omit something you should mark this by adding an ellipsis (...). The quote should be referenced and, in addition, the page from which it was taken should be included in the reference.

!Example

"In homicide, it is not an offence to kill whether intentionally or recklessly, by omission, unless one is under a duty to act ... In the pollution cases the courts have attempted to make a similar distinction."

N. Padfield, "Clean Water and Muddy Causation: Is Causation a Question of Law or Fact, or Just a Way of Allocating Blame", Crim L.R. [1995] 683 at p.690.

PLAGIARISM

14–6 The Oxford English Dictionary defines plagiarism as "The action or practice of taking someone else's work, idea, etc., and passing it off as one's own; literary theft". Expressing ideas from someone else's work in your own words and acknowledging the source is known as paraphrasing. This is acceptable practice. Expressing someone else's ideas and presenting them as your own is plagiarism. Plagiarism also includes copying out chunks of (or an entire) article, section of a book or another student's essay and submitting it as your own. Plagiarism is not an acceptable academic practice. If you do this your work will be penalised and you may well be awarded no marks at all and/or face disciplinary action.

University study is all about exploring the literature and being influenced by new and different ideas. However, there is a fine dividing line between plagiarism and taking advantage of the many academic influences to which you will be exposed. In order to avoid plagiarism:

> ➤ Make sure that you acknowledge the sources which you have used.
> ➤ If you want to paraphrase make sure that you refer to it as, *e.g.* X's view of Y is ...
> ➤ If you want to use the exact words, use a quotation.

UNIVERSITY ASSESSMENTS

Different types of assessment are used throughout a law degree. These include: essays, problem **14–7** questions, oral presentations, group work and exams. Assessment of a law course is not simply a memory test. You will be required to display more than a knowledge of the law in a particular area. You will have to apply legal rules and principles to particular situations. You will have to display analytical and critical skills and to present and communicate an argument in a clear and logical manner.

A key part of any assessment is the feedback you receive. Keep a copy of your assessment as it is unlikely that it will be returned to you. You will probably receive a feedback sheet containing comments. If, having read the comments, you do not understand where you went wrong—go and see the person who marked it. It is very important that you find out how to improve your work so that you can ensure that you will perform better in the future. It is never pleasant to receive criticism but it is in your best interests to take it on board and learn from it.

General points for all types of assessments

14–8

> ➤ Make sure that you understand what is expected of you. You should read the assessment criteria to be adopted. They will usually be contained in your course materials.
> ➤ Ensure that you answer the question set.
> ➤ Do not include unsubstantiated personal opinion.
> ➤ Always back up your arguments with authority.
> ➤ It is better practice to reference the person who originated the idea than the people who have written about it subsequently.
> ➤ Do not include substantive points in footnotes to get round the word limit.
> ➤ Your work should be intelligible at first reading. It is important to ensure that your meaning is clearly communicated to the reader.
> ➤ Make sure that your grammar and spelling are accurate. If necessary make use of the spell-check facility, a thesaurus or a dictionary.

ESSAY WRITING TECHNIQUES

Essays are one of the ways in which students are required to express themselves and present **14–9** information in a written form. Essays are likely to be part of the assessment you encounter at university either as coursework or as part of an exam. This section is designed to help you enhance your essay writing skills.

Compliance with requirements

Your course materials will contain information about the university's assessment criteria for the **14–10** essay. Make sure that you familiarise yourself with these. If you do not understand what any of the criteria means then you should ask your tutor.

Make sure that you are aware of any special requirements, such as word limits or format stipulations. Word limits can be useful guides as well as being a requirement. If you are having difficulty finding enough material and are woefully short of the word limit, you may be searching under the wrong terms or you may have misunderstood the question. If you have written far in excess of the word limit, you have included extraneous material. You should re-read it and remove material that does not directly relate to the question.

Understanding the question

14–11   Examine the wording of the question and decide what you are being asked to do. This is more easily said than done. One way to help focus your thoughts is to underline key words in the question. You should be aware that essay titles are always carefully chosen. The basic topic will tend to be broad, but one or two key words in the title will narrow the essay's scope.

Example essay title — *The threat to the environment can only be reduced by strengthening the existing legal controls. Discuss.*

It is a common mistake for students to read a title like this and to conclude that they are being asked to write as much as they know on "the environment" or "strengthening the existing legal controls". These factors are relevant but they are not the major focus of the question. The title is asking you to identify the most probable ways of reducing the threat to the environment and then to assess whether strengthening existing legal controls is more effective than any of the other options.

14–12   The title determines what is going to be relevant to the essay. Your answer must address the central question. Everything you write should be relevant to answering the specific question asked. You will not gain any marks for irrelevant material—no matter how accurate. The inclusion of irrelevant material will detract from your answer. If you ensure that you understand the question then you should be able to identify what is relevant from the material you have researched. If you are unsure of what is relevant you need to take a step back and reconsider the question and clarify your understanding of your research.

14–13   **Key Words in Questions**

Analyse:	Break up ... into component parts and examine each part.
Compare:	Look for similarities and differences between ...
Contrast:	Bring out the differences between ...
Criticise:	Present and evaluate evidence before reaching a judgement about ...
Define:	Set out the precise meaning of ...
Describe:	A detailed account of ...
Discuss:	Explain the meaning of ... and examine the reasons for and against ...
Evaluate:	What is the value/worth of ...
Explain:	Make ... plain and understandable and account for it.
Identify:	Establish the nature of ...
Illustrate:	Make clear by giving examples.
Interpret:	Use your judgement to make clear the meaning of ...
Justify:	Use arguments to make a case for ...
Review:	Make a survey of ... and examine it critically.
State:	Present in brief, clear, concise form.
Summarise:	Give the key points of ...

This is based on a table by S. Drew and R. Bingham, *The Student Skills Guide* (Aldershot: Gower, 1997) p.57.

Collecting relevant material   **14–14**

Once you have decided what the question is asking, you should start your literature search. See para.12.8.

Planning the essay   **14–15**

Examine all the material you have gathered and select the main points which you want to include in your essay. Do not be tempted to try to use all of the material which you have gathered. It may not all be relevant or possible to include due to word limit constraints. You should always keep the essay title uppermost in your mind. You must discard irrelevant material, no matter how interesting it may be.

Construct an essay plan outlining the basic structure of the essay. Essays tend to conform to a basic framework which consists of three parts: introduction, discussion and conclusion.

Introduction

In your introduction you essentially set out how you are going to tackle the essay. You might **14–16** include:

> ➤ How to interpret any ambiguous terms in the title (*e.g.* what you understand by "the threat to the environment").
> ➤ Any assumptions you are going to make rather than argue in detail.
> ➤ The criteria you are going to use to reach your conclusions (*e.g.* "the environment is so important that I shall assume that anything which has an unknown effect must be assumed to have a bad effect").
> ➤ How you are going to structure your essay.

It is often a good idea to write your introduction after you have completed the rest of the essay. This will ensure that your introduction matches what you have actually done.

Discussion

This is the main portion of the essay. Each paragraph should deal with a single point. Each main **14–17** point should be considered, developed and justified by relevant authority.

Do not include unsubstantiated opinion. Avoid phrases such as "it is obvious that ..." Common sense is not authority. Authority should be either a case, a piece of legislation or a secondary source such as a journal article or commentary from an encyclopaedia.

You should not present only one side of an argument. You should show the reader that you have taken account of any apparently conflicting evidence. An outline of a discussion might be Smith's theory of X is well-founded because of (a), (b), (c). However, it can also be said that (d), (e), (f) apply. Consequently ...

Conclusion

Your conclusion should bring your whole argument together into a set of points that you want **14–18** the reader to retain. It should be based on your arguments already made in the essay and should not include any new material. Do not confuse "conclusion" with "summary". You do need to summarise all your arguments.

Bibliography

It is important to include a bibliography. Failure to do so will result in marks being deducted. **14–19** See paras 13.27-13.57 for guidance on bibliographic references.

Writing the essay

14–20 Write a draft of the essay which conforms to your essay plan and includes all your ideas. Do not expect to hand in the first draft. You should use that as a basis and hone your ideas from it. If possible, leave it alone for a couple of days and do something else. Return to the draft with a fresh mind and review what you have written.

Do not just put down everything you know and presume that the marker will extract the relevant/correct sections. YOU should identify the relevant/correct items and should leave out the irrelevant. The inclusion of extraneous material detracts from the appropriate material you have presented.

You should aim to present a clear and concise discussion of the topic. Try to use simple straightforward language. Use short sentences. Avoid using words you do not understand. Employing complicated language will not give a favourable impression if it is obvious that the writer does not understand its meaning. If you are in doubt about the meaning of a word, check a dictionary or a thesaurus.

You should always include a bibliography at the end of your essay. This should include references to all the materials you have used in preparation of the piece of work. Lecture notes and primary sources such as cases and legislation should not be included. Neither should you refer to online databases such as *Westlaw* or *LexisNexis*. This would be the equivalent of referring to a law library!

14–21 Before submitting your essay you should:

> ➢ Re-read the essay to ensure that you have answered the question set.
> ➢ Check spelling and punctuation. If in doubt about spelling make use of a dictionary or word processor spell-check facility which is set to UK English.
> ➢ Check that all your references to authority are accurate and spelt correctly.
> ➢ Ensure that your writing is legible or that you use a font which is clear.
> ➢ See also para.14.54: "Evaluation of your own Research".

14–22 The thought of the whole process of writing an essay can be daunting. You may find it easier if you break it down into smaller tasks, *e.g.*:

1. Analyse the title and decide what exactly you are being asked to do.
2. Consider possible approaches.
3. Collect relevant material.
4. Decide on an appropriate structure.
5. Write the discussion section.
6. Write the conclusion.
7. Write the introduction.

Receiving feedback

14–23 One of the most valuable parts of the essay writing process is receiving feedback from whoever marked it. You should make use of any comments to help you improve your assignments in the future.

Make sure you do not make any of these common mistakes:

> ➢ Regurgitation of lecture notes/books.
> ➢ Failure to address the question asked.
> ➢ The inclusion of material without linking it into the essay question.
> ➢ Failure to back up arguments with legal authority.

> ➢ The inclusion of too much description and too little analysis.
> ➢ Use of colloquial terms.
> ➢ Using words inappropriately.
> ➢ Inclusion of unsubstantiated personal opinion.
> ➢ Failure to communicate ideas clearly.
> ➢ Poor use of English language.

Further reading   **14–24**

E. Finch & S. Fafinski, *Legal Skills* (Oxford: OUP, 2007) Chs 10 and 11.
B. Greetham, *How to Write Better Essays* (Basingstoke: Palgrave McMillan, 2001).
J. Holland & J. Webb, *Learning Legal Rules* 6th edn (Oxford: OUP, 2006) pp.93-96.
R. Huxley-Binns, L. Riley, C. Turner, *Unlocking Legal Learning* (Hodder: Arnold Abingdon 2005) Ch.7.
H.L. MacQueen, *Studying Scots Law* 3rd edn (Haywards Heath: Tottel, 2006) pp.179-186.
A. Northedge, *The Good Study Guide* (Milton Keynes: Open University Press, 2005) Chs 10 and 11.
S.I. Strong, *How to Write Law Essays* (Oxford: OUP, 2006).

TECHNIQUES FOR TACKLING PROBLEM QUESTIONS

The problem question format is used frequently in tutorial exercises, coursework and exams. A **14–25** problem question will provide a set of facts. You will be expected to identify and apply the relevant law to these facts. You will then usually be asked to come to some form of conclusion. This will depend on the question but may involve advising one or more of the parties as to the legal remedies available to them. This section is designed to help you enhance your problem solving skills.

Problem questions are popular forms of assessment at university because problem solving is one of the essential skills for a lawyer. Being presented with a set of facts and asked to advise on their legal implications is an everyday activity of the practising lawyer.

Problem questions are different from essays in that they are far more specific than essay **14–26** questions. You are not provided with a general topic area for discussion, instead there are particular questions to address. When you construct your answer to a problem question you should not include a long introduction. There is no need to start with a general discussion of the area of law. You should go straight into dealing with the specific issues raised by the question.

Read the question carefully to ensure that you understand it. Problem questions are often quite detailed. Make sure that you have not misread any details. This is particularly easy to do under exam conditions. Never write out the question. This is a waste of time and if you are required to keep to a word limit it will waste words. As part of your preparation underline key words to help focus your thoughts.

At university, problem questions will tend to be centred around one area of law which is familiar **14–27** to you. After you leave university you will be faced with problems which do not neatly fit into one subject which you have just studied and which may include elements which are completely new to you.

Even though university questions will tend to concentrate on one area of law that does not mean that they contain just one issue. They may contain several different issues. Do not read the questions through quickly and leap to the conclusion that the problem centres on a single issue. You should also be aware that the answer to a problem question is never "yes" or "no". If you think the answer is very straightforward, re-read the question because you have probably missed something.

Identify the problem by looking at the legal issues which are raised by the facts.

Identify the *relevant* information which you have and the *relevant* information which you do *not* have. In problem questions, as in real life, the complete factual picture is often missing some key details. If facts are missing say so. It may be appropriate to say if X then ... if Y then ... (and back up your points with authority).

When you have detected the legal issues you should then begin your literature search to find the current law on the subject. See para.12.8.

14–28 Writing your answer

1. Think out a logical structure. The structure will depend on the nature of the problem. In the case of delictual problems the approach might be:

    ➢ Is there a duty of care owed?
    ➢ Has that duty been breached?
    ➢ Did the breach cause loss?
    ➢ Is the loss quantifiable?
    ➢ Are there any defences open to the defender?

2. Keep your answer relevant to the question. Credit will be given for the appropriate *application* of the relevant law to the factual scenario. Do not be tempted to include long descriptive passages. Do not write a general introduction about the particular area of law.
3. Never just provide an answer to the question—you must justify your position and back up your arguments by reference to authority (see paras 14.2–14.4).
4. You have to apply the law as you find it. If you personally disagree with it or find it unfair, that is irrelevant to answering the question. Personal opinion should not be included.
5. Make sure that you do what has been asked of you. If you are asked to advise X, make sure that you advise X. This does not mean ignoring arguments against X's position. You should take into account any counter-arguments against your adopted position.
6. Do not spend ages agonising over the conclusion to the problem. There is indeed unlikely to be one correct answer. If you feel that there is no one answer to the problem, discuss the possible alternatives. At university level the conclusion that you reach is not *that* important. You will receive credit for the presentation of cogent arguments, backed up by authority. In real life the conclusion is, of course, very important.

Summary of the approach to problem questions
Examine the available facts
⇓
Identify the legal issue(s) raised by the facts
⇓
Identify the *material* facts
⇓
Be aware of the omission of any material facts. Locate missing facts (if possible).
⇓
Carry out a literature search to find the current legal position
⇓
Apply the relevant law to the factual scenario
⇓
Advise client on available options/remedies. In practise this will involve matching the client's need, desires and resources to possible courses of action (legal and non-legal).

Further reading 14–29

E. Finch & S. Fafinski, *Legal Skills* (Oxford: OUP, 2007) Ch.12.
R. Huxley-Binns, L. Riley, C. Turner, *Unlocking Legal Learning* (Hodder Arnold Abingdon, 2005) Ch.8.
A.T.H. Smith, Glanville Williams, *Learning the Law* 13th edn (London: Sweet & Maxwell, 2006) Ch.8.

ORAL PRESENTATIONS

This section concerns oral presentations which are increasingly used as a form of assessment at 14–30 university. You may be asked to give a presentation either as an individual or as part of a group.

Initial preparation

Make sure that you know:

> ➢ *When* the presentation will take place;
> ➢ *How* long the presentation is to last;
> ➢ *Where* the presentation is to take place;
> ➢ *Who* your audience will be;
> ➢ *What* your audience is expecting from you.

Construction of a presentation

Careful planning is the key to a successful presentation. Once you have identified the infor- 14–31 mation you will need and collected that information, you should:

> ➢ Establish the main points you want to make;
> ➢ Ensure that you have material to support these points (support could be in the form of e.g. a case, a statutory provision, an example, statistics or a quotation);
> ➢ Put your main points and supporting material into a clear and logical order.

The structure of the presentation should conform to the essay model: introduction, discussion of the main points and conclusion.

The beginning and end of the presentation require special attention. At the beginning of the talk 14–32 you want to attract your audience's attention. Ways of making an initial impact include: a controversial statement, a question, a quotation or a joke. You should also always include a clear outline of your presentation.

In a situation that everyone finds nerve-wracking, do what you feel happy doing. If you are good at telling jokes (and they are appropriate to the subject) then by all means include some. If you shrink in horror at telling a joke in such a setting then the best advice is not to include any.

At the end of the presentation you want to ensure that your audience goes away with a firm understanding of the message of your presentation. You should always provide a brief summary of your main points. Ways of ending your presentation include a recommendation, a challenge or a quotation.

Notes

14–33 No matter how good your memory, you will find that you will need some form of notes to guide you through the presentation. Notes help ensure that you do not omit anything from your talk. Some people write/type out everything they are going to say, others use small cards which contain only the main points of the talk. There is no right or wrong method, it is up to you to choose whichever approach makes you feel comfortable.

If you are inexperienced at giving presentations you may feel happier writing out the full text. If you do this:

> ➢ Use large writing or typeface;
> ➢ Use double line spacing;
> ➢ Use only one side of a piece of paper;
> ➢ Number the pages (just in case you drop them).

Delivery of the presentation

14–34 Make sure that you are familiar with your talk. Practice speaking it out loud, ideally in the room where you are to give the presentation. This will help you to judge the length of the talk. This should also prevent you from becoming too nervous on the day of the presentation.

Organise any visual aids that you are to use. Visual aids help to break up the talk and can help maintain the attention of the audience. Use visual aids that you feel happy operating. If you know that you get nervous and your hands shake do not use a laser pointer. The appearance of a shaky point on a screen will probably gain you the sympathy of your audience but will detract from the message that you are trying to get across. Make sure that you know how to operate any visual aid. When you are nervous it may not be very clear how to start a PowerPoint presentation. A few moments familiarising yourself with any equipment will be time well spent.

Examples of visual aids are:

> ➢ PowerPoint slides
> ➢ Black/white boards
> ➢ Flip charts
> ➢ Physical objects
> ➢ Handouts
> ➢ A lap top computer for internet access

If you are going to produce a handout or copies of PowerPoint slides do not include every word of your talk. Your audience will just sit and read it and will not pay any attention to you. A handout should summarise the main points of your talk. Try and make it as attractive as possible. Pay attention to design and layout. The more eye-catching the handout, the more positive an impression will be created.

If you use PowerPoint make sure that the slides are not too crowded. Short summaries or bullet points should be used. Do not include large sections of prose. This only results in a loss of visual impact as key sections disappear in the middle of the detail. The font should be large enough to be read from the back of the room.

14–35 Do not read your presentation out word for word. It is important to maintain eye contact with your audience. Try and look at your script, memorise the next few words and then look at members of the audience while you are speaking. They will be very bored if you merely read out material in a monotone! Try and vary the tone of your voice. Put some feeling into your presentation. This will make it much more interesting for your audience. You can achieve this by practising your presentation. The more times you practise it, the easier it will be to build in these features.

Be aware of your body language. Good posture shows the audience that you are relaxed and confident. Do not fold your arms or stand with your hands behind your back. Try to avoid waving your arms around—it is very distracting for the audience.

The pace at which you speak is very important. Remember that your audience does not know what you are going to say and will need time to listen and digest your words. At the start of the talk, make a conscious effort to slow down your speech pattern. Do not talk too quickly or you will lose your audience.

Make sure that you speak loud enough so that the people at the back of the room can hear you.

Make sure that you keep to time by putting your watch on the table or somewhere you can see it easily. You should try and work out beforehand which section you could cut if you run out of time. It is also useful to have some extra material if you end up with too much time.

Questions

Waiting for questions can be daunting. The more prepared you are, the easier it will be to **14–36** answer any questions. If someone asks a question which you do not understand, say so. Ask them to clarify exactly what they mean.

You can give yourself an extra few seconds to think of and structure an answer by repeating the question. You can say that this is so that everyone can hear the question.

If someone asks you something that you do not know it is better to be upfront and admit that you do not know. It may be something outside the ambit of your talk that the questioner knows about. You could always try asking the questioner what they think.

Nerves

Everybody is nervous before making a presentation. There is no way of avoiding nerves alto- **14–37** gether but here are some hints to help you control your nerves:

- ➢ Be well prepared and practice your talk out loud;
- ➢ Remember that you may be only too aware of your nerves but your audience will probably not notice that you are nervous;
- ➢ You should be confident that you will know more about the topic than your audience;
- ➢ If you drop your notes or lose your place, pause, get yourself organised and take a deep breath. You may feel that the whole process took an hour but the audience will not perceive the delay as anything but minimal;
- ➢ If you get short of breath during the presentation, pause and take a deep breath. Then continue ...

Further reading   14–38

S. Drew and R. Bingham, *The Student Skills Guide* 2nd edn (Alershot: Gower, 2004).
A. Northedge, *The Good Study Guide* (Milton Keynes: Open University Press, 2005) Ch.7.

RESEARCH PROJECTS

Presentation of research can take many forms: 14–39

⇒ *Abstract*
An abstract is a concise overview of the research highlighting any important findings. Abstracts could be viewed as advertisements for your work. You might send an abstract to a conference

organiser or journal editor hoping to get your paper/article accepted. Abstracts also form part of written research, see para.14.43 below.

⇒ *Poster*
A poster is a more detailed form of abstract but is shorter than a full paper, usually about six to eight sheets of A4. It is presented as a wall chart, literally a poster. Posters are generally used to present preliminary results and are displayed at conferences. In a conference there will be set sessions in the programme in which delegates can inspect the posters. During this period the researcher has to "man" their poster and answer any questions. This can be a very useful exercise in that it enables you to receive advice as well as to advertise your work.

⇒ *Report/paper/dissertation*
Presentation of research in written form is the principal method of communication and will be dealt with paras 14.40–14.52.

⇒ *Conference paper/oral presentation*
This is equivalent to giving a short lecture on your research. The normal length would be around 20–30 minutes and you would be expected to deal with questions from the audience. See paras 14.30–14.38 on oral presentations.

Structure of written forms of research presentation

14–40 The exact structure of the research report/paper/dissertation may vary and indeed may be subject to requirements by various institutions. The following sections represent the conventional form of presenting research:

Title page

14–41 This page should include the title of your work, your name, institution, date and, if the work is being submitted for a particular qualification, you should include the relevant details. The title should be concise and provide an accurate impression of the nature of your work.

Acknowledgements

14–42 It is usual to include any acknowledgements and thanks after the title page. You should bear in mind any assurances of confidentiality which you have given and make sure that these are not breached.

Abstract

14–43 An abstract is usually required in all presentations of academic research. It should be regarded as independent of the research and should not be referred to in the text. The purpose of the abstract is to provide a brief and concise overview of the research and to highlight any important findings.

Contents

14–44 This should include a list of chapter headings and page numbers along with details of any appendices.

Chapter 1 — Introduction

14–45 This should include:

- ➢ Aims
- ➢ Objectives
- ➢ Research questions/hypotheses which have been investigated
- ➢ Proposed methodology in general terms
- ➢ Indication of why the research topic was chosen
- ➢ The scope of the work

Chapter 2 — Literature review **14–46**

This should contain a review of previous work on the topic. It should not be a descriptive account of every work published on the topic. You should display skills of critical analysis by commenting on previous works, selecting only relevant material and organising its presentation in an appropriate way.

Chapter 3 — Methodology **14–47**

This should include a discussion of the methodology(ies) adopted and a justification of your choice. Another important element of this chapter is to discuss any limitations in the methods employed. The research instruments which were used should be included in an appendix, e.g. the questionnaire or interview schedule or descriptions of various statistical tests.

Chapter 4 — Presentation of results/findings **14–48**

Presentation of results should be accurate and clear. Detailed comment and interpretation should be left until the following chapter.

Chapter 5 — Discussion **14–49**

This is the key section of the work. It should start by mentioning your research questions/hypotheses as outlined in your first chapter. You should then make use of the results/findings from your fourth chapter to back up your lines of argument. You should then tie in these lines of argument with your research questions/hypotheses. You should also refer to how your research relates to the previous works in the area discussed in your chapter two. Any limitations in the research design should be included along with suggestions of alternative approaches.

Chapter 6 — Summary and conclusions **14–50**

This should involve bringing all your arguments together and drawing conclusions. You should only include conclusions which can justifiably be drawn from your results/findings. You should not introduce new material in this concluding chapter. You should indicate that you are aware of any limitations of the work and steps that you have taken to minimise these. It is a good idea to mention whether your work has implications for further research in the area.

Bibliography **14–51**

This should include all the sources which you have consulted during your research. See paras 13.27–13.57 for details about bibliographic references.

Appendices **14–52**

As stated above this should include copies of the research instruments which were used, e.g. the questionnaire or interview schedule or descriptions of various statistical tests.

14–53 Further reading

J. Bell, *Doing Your Research Project* 4th edn (Buckingham: Open University Press, 2005).

L. Blaxter, C. Hughes and M. Tight, *How to Research* 3rd edn (Milton Keynes: Open University Press, 2006).

S. Cottrel, *The Study Skills Handbook* 2nd edn (Basingstoke: Palgrave McMillan, 2003) Ch. 9.

M.B. Davies, *Doing a Successful Research Project* (Basingstoke: Palgrave McMillan, 2007).

R. Huxley-Binns, L. Riley, C. Turner, *Unlocking Legal Learning* (Hodder Arnold Abingdon, 2005) Ch. 9.

M.Salter & J. Mason, *Writing Law Dissertations: An Introduction to the Conduct of Legal Research* (Harlow: Pearson Longman, 2007).

J.A. Sharp and K.Howard, *The Management of a Student Research Project* 3rd edn (The Open University/Gower, 2002).

EVALUATION OF YOUR OWN RESEARCH

14–54 When you write up your research (be it an essay or research project) be prepared to work through several drafts. One draft will not be sufficient for many reasons: your ideas will evolve; you may need to bring the work more up to date, or you may need to either lengthen or shorten it. In order to facilitate revisions, you should insert a header or footer which includes the number of draft and the date. If you are handwriting you should leave extra room for alterations and only write on one side of a page.

Before submission of a piece of work you should put it to one side and forget about it for a period of time. You should then read it again with fresh eyes. This should enable you to pick up any errors which you might have missed previously because you were too close to the work. This requires you to have produced your draft well in advance of any submission deadline. If you find this difficult see para.13.10 "Time Management".

14–55 When revising your work check for the following:

1. Have you answered the question/addressed your research questions?
2. Does it have a logical structure?
3. Is your meaning clear?
4. Are your arguments backed up with authority?
5. Are the most important points sufficiently emphasised?
6. Are there any faults in the logic?
7. Has it taken into account any conflicting arguments?
8. Are the conclusions justified?
9. Does it read well?
10. Are its style, vocabulary, abbreviations, and illustrations appropriate?
11. Is the spelling accurate? Most word processing software will include a spell-check facility. You should, however, ensure that you adopt the British spelling options and do not slip into American-English spelling. A dictionary and a thesaurus can also be useful.
12. Grammar—is your meaning clear or clouded by clumsy grammatical constructions? Short simple sentences are preferable. It is particularly important to check your use of tenses. It is very easy to slip from one tense to another, especially when you are writing over a period of time. Most software now has a grammar check facility. However, it is generally not as useful as the spell-check facility.
13. Are your references accurately presented?

An additional way of reviewing your work is to persuade a colleague to read your work and to comment on it. Even if they do not belong to the same discipline, they will be able to identify linguistic and stylistic flaws.

Additional reading   14–56

J. Bell, *Doing Your Research Project* 4th edn (Buckingham: Open University Press, 2005) Ch.12.
L. Blaxter, C. Hughes and M. Tight, *How to Research* 3rd edn (Milton Keynes: Open University Press, 2006).
T.R. Black, *Evaluating Social Science Research: An Introduction* (Thousand Oaks: Sage, 1993).

REVISION STRATEGY FOR EXAMS

There is no one technique that will suit everyone. The following section contains suggestions. You should experiment and pick the way that suits you.

Make sure that you are aware of what is expected of you   14–57

Ways of doing this are:

> ➤ Make sure that you know the syllabus of the course and which topics are examinable.
> ➤ Obtain copies of past examination papers. They are useful for guidance but do not be tempted to use them to question spot. This is a very dangerous strategy. If you concentrate only on a few areas and they fail to come up in the exam, you may fail. You cannot presume that the exam set for you will always be in the same format. Courses change over time and you should obtain up-to-date information from your tutor. You should also remember that the law changes and issues relevant in the past may no longer exist. The best way to make use of past papers is to work through them attempting to answer the questions. It can be beneficial to do this with another student. This means that you can pull resources and discuss the answers. If you feel that you are struggling, go and see your tutor and ask the tutor to work through the answer with you.
> ➤ If you have any doubts about what is expected of you, ask your lecturer/tutor.

Make sure that you have all the information you need   14–58

Organise your notes. Far in advance of the exam date you should ensure that you have a full set of lecture notes and handouts for the subject. Organising this in advance gives you time to catch up on any notes that you have missed. You will find people more willing to lend notes at some distance from the exam.

Ideally you should have been reading around the lectures and preparing for tutorials throughout the term. When it comes to revising you should have sufficient notes. You should not need to look up textbooks at this stage. It is too late. You should concentrate on the material you already have. The only time you should consult books is to clarify any points that remain unclear.

Use the feedback received from any tutorial exercise or assessment. Build your tutor's comments into your revision materials.

The process of revising   14–59

> ➤ Do not sit and look at a thick file of notes. If you do that you will find yourself putting off the evil hour when you have to start revising. All sorts of jobs around the house will

suddenly appear far more appealing than sitting and opening this awful file. The way around this is to start by consulting the syllabus for the course. You will find that it can be broken down into several topics or parts. Pick the topic you are most interested in and start with that.

➤ Try to get a grasp of the major topics. Then move on to the less important points.
➤ Once you have identified, e.g. six topics, gather together all your material on the topics. This may include lecture notes, tutorial preparation and notes, independent reading (could include case notes, notes from statutes, notes from journal articles or texts). Read the material for one topic. Go through it and identify the key points and make revision notes for the topic. These should contain the essential points from all your materials. These notes should not be very long (four to five sides of A4) and should consist of lists with various headings, categories and sub-categories. You should then try to learn these lists.
➤ Some people like to make notes from notes until they end up with bullet points of vital issues. Others may prefer just to read over and over their original notes. Others prefer to dictate revision notes and to listen to them over and over again.
➤ Almost all exams aim to test, not just for knowledge of facts, but for understanding and the ability to use them. When revising ask:

⇒ What are the key points?
⇒ What is the authority/evidence/argument for each proposition?
⇒ Is there any counter evidence?

➤ Test yourself by doing brief outline answers to questions from old examination papers.
➤ Build periods of free time into any revision schedule. You need to maintain a balance between work and normal life.
➤ Do not sit up all night the night before an exam. You will end up being exhausted and jaded in the exam. It is far better to organise your revision timetable so that the evening before an exam you can relax. You will then perform much better the next day.
➤ Do not worry because you do not "know everything". No one ever does. Constantly remind yourself of what you do know rather than worrying about what you do not know.
➤ Finally, make sure that you know the correct *date, time and location* of the exam.

14–60 EXAM TECHNIQUE

➤ Arrive in good time for the exam.
➤ Remember to conform to any university requirements such as bringing your matriculation card for identification purposes.
➤ Read any instructions *carefully*. Make sure that you know how many questions you are required to answer and if any questions are compulsory. Always answer the required number of questions even if your last answer(s) are short and scrappy. The few marks you gain may be vital for your final result. Never leave a question blank. Make sure that you answer all parts of a question.
➤ Read quickly through the whole paper to get an idea of the content of the questions. Re-read the paper *slowly and carefully* and decide what each question is actually asking. Underline "key words" which indicate the kind of answer you should give. Then select the questions that you intend to answer.
➤ Before writing anything, decide on the order you will tackle the questions. Choose the question that seems "easiest" first and work through to the "hardest". By answering the first question well you will be better able to tackle the more difficult ones. Do not be

phased by people who sit down and immediately start to write. You are better advised to sit and take stock, rather than ploughing straight in and realising later that you have misread/misinterpreted the question.

➢ Make notes for each question, jotting down ideas. Try to make these brief notes for all questions before you start writing. This gets you thinking about other questions even when you are writing your first question. In jotting down some ideas, questions that appeared impossible to answer may become clearer. More ideas about other questions will come to you as you are answering the first one.

➢ Allocate your time properly. If each question bears an equal number of marks, spend an equal amount of time on each question. If the marks are different for different questions spend an appropriate proportion of your time on each question. If you use up your time-limit on a question you will already have gained most of the marks that you are going to get. Another five or ten minutes writing is unlikely to get you many more marks. The same time spent concentrating on the key issues in a new question will earn you more marks. Remember that the first few marks in each question are the easiest ones to get.

➢ Do not write out the question—this just wastes valuable time.

➢ Answer the question set, not the one which you would like to have answered. No credit will be given for irrelevant material, no matter how accurate it may be. For each question, sort out the main points, weeding out irrelevancies. Do not attempt to write down everything you know about the topic; expect to have to go into depth on only part of what you know.

➢ Remember to back up your arguments with authority. You will not be required to remember full reference details e.g. the full citation of a case. Ideally you should put down the names of the parties, e.g. *Smith v Bloggs* but in exam conditions it is easy to forget the precise name of a case. As a minimum you should try to write down sufficient details to show the examiner that you have identified the correct case. If you cannot remember the names of either of the parties, you should put down some detail about the case that identifies it, e.g. the case about the XXX. In a hand-written exam you should underline case names. When referring to a case do not include a descriptive account of the facts of the case. The part of the case that you should use is the ratio decidendi. Writing down lots of facts will not gain you any extra marks—it will merely waste precious exam time and detracts from the cogency of your answer.

➢ If you miscalculate the time badly, finish the question in note-form. This is better than nothing and may pick up a few valuable marks.

➢ Re-read everything at the end to check for errors and inaccuracies.

Open Book Exams

It would appear to be a student's dream come true to be allowed to take statutory material into **14–61** the exam. But the author has certainly found open book exams to be more difficult than unseen exams. It can be reassuring to have a volume of statutes sitting on your desk but if you are not familiar with the material you can waste large chunks of the exam time just trying to find the relevant provisions. Learn to find your way round the statute.

Never copy out statutory provisions. This just shows the examiner that you are able to copy from one document to another. You should be trying to display understanding and analytical skills.

What NOT to do in an exam
14–62

➢ Get the time/date wrong!

➢ Fail to answer the question asked.

> ➢ Fail to use authority to back up your arguments.
> ➢ Include lots of description (e.g. narration of facts of cases) instead of critical analysis.
> ➢ Fail to stick to a plan about time.
> ➢ Fail to write enough, e.g. a question worth 25 marks is not going to be answered sufficiently in six or seven lines.
> ➢ Make jokes and/or frivolous comments. This is not appropriate.
> ➢ Fail to express yourself clearly.
> ➢ Messy handwriting. You will be under pressure in an exam but do try to write legibly.
> ➢ Use abbreviated text language e.g. gr8. This is not appropriate for academic work.

14–63 Further reading

S. Cottrell, *The Exam Skills Handbook* (Basingstoke: Palgrave McMillan, 2007).

E. Finch & S. Fafinski, *Legal Skills* (Oxford: OUP, 2007) Ch. 13.

R. Huxley-Binns, L. Riley, C. Turner, *Unlocking Legal Learning* (Hodder Arnold Abingdon, 2005) Chs 11 and 12.

H.L. MacQueen, *Studying Scots Law* 3rd edn (Haywards Heath: Tottel 2006) pp.186-196.

H. McVea and P. Cumper, *Exam Skills for Law Students* 2nd edn (Oxford: OUP, 2006).

Appendix I
Summary of Search Strategies for Finding Legal Information with Paragraph Numbers for Easy Reference

CASES

Finding cases by name only—citation unknown

The best method of locating a case when you only know the parties' names is to use one of the online legal databases (*Westlaw* 4.49 or *LexisNexis Butterworths* 4.50) unless you are looking for an older case.

A paper-based alternative is the Current Law Case Citator (4.52).

Other alternatives include:

4.55 Current Legal Information
4.56 Justcite
4.57 The Laws of Scotland: Stair Memorial Encyclopaedia
4.59 Tables of cases in relevant textbooks
4.60 Indexes in the law reports

If the case is recent the following could be used:

4.21 Scottish Courts Website
4.22 BAILII.

Indexes that are helpful for locating older cases (4.64-4.67): The Index to *Morison's Dictionary*, Scots Digest, The Faculty Digest and The Digest.

Finding cases by subject

Encyclopaedia (8.2-8.9), reference works (8.10) or textbooks (8.29) are ideal starting points for research by subject. They can also be useful to narrow search terms before moving on to search online databases.

4.74 Westlaw
4.75 LexisNexis Butterworths
4.19 Justis UK and Irish Primary Case Law/Specialist Case Law
4.40 Justcite
4.78 Current Legal Information
4.79 Current Law Yearbooks
4.80 Subject indexes in various series of law reports

Finding cases on words or phrases

4.85 Judicial dictionaries
4.86 Current Law Yearbooks
4.87 Subject indexes of law reports
4.88 Halsbury's Laws of England
4.89 The Law Reports Index
4.90 Westlaw
4.91 LexisNexis Butterworths

Finding cases interpreting legislation

The easiest method of locating this information is using *Westlaw* (4.92) or *LexisNexis Butter-worths* (4.95) with Current Law Legislation Citators representing the best paper-based alternative (4.96).
    Other alternatives are:

4.98 Current Legal Information
4.99 Law reports indexes
4.100 Using tables of statutes to locate discussion of relevant cases in textbooks

Current status of a case (i.e. whether the case has been considered by the court on a subsequent occasion)

4.113 Westlaw
4.116 LexisNexis Butterworths
4.40 Justcite
4.118 Current Law Case Citators
4.120 Current Legal Information
4.121 The Law Reports Index

Finding out about very recent cases

The quickest way of locating very recent judgments is to access the website of the court concerned: The website of the Scottish courts (para.4.21), Scottish Land Court (para.4.25), House of Lords (para.4.23) and the Judicial Committee of the Privy Council (para.4.24). *BAILII* (para.4.22) is useful as it enables you to search for very recent cases from several different courts at the same time.

4.127 The WLR Daily
4.129 Westlaw UK
4.26 Casetrack
4.30 Lawtel

Finding cases from other courts and tribunals

4.135 The Court of the Lord Lyon, the Scottish Land Court, Lands Valuation Appeal Court and the Lands Tribunal for Scotland
4.137 Decisions of the Social Security Commissioner
4.143 Other Tribunal decisions

Many tribunal decisions are available via the BAILII (4.22)

Putting cases into context

Understanding the relevance of a very recent case

UK LEGISLATION

Finding out which stage a UK Parliament Bill has reached

Finding out about parliamentary debates on a UK Parliament Bill

Finding UK statutes by subject

Current status of a UK statute—Is It in Force Yet?

6.97 Current Law Legislation Citators and Current Law Statutes
6.98 Current Legal Information
6.99 Statute Law Database
6.100 LexisNexis Butterworths
6.101 Journals
6.102 The Stationery Office Daily, Weekly or Monthly Lists

Current status of a UK statute—finding amendments and repeals

Westlaw (6.103) is currently the best source of finding this information (until the Statute Law Database (6.104) is fully updated) as it contains the up-to-date fully consolidated versions of legislation affecting Scotland.

Other alternatives are:

6.105 The best paper-based source — Current Law Legislation Citator
6.107 Lawtel
6.108 Halsbury's Statutes
6.109 LexisNexis Butterworths
6.110 Chronological Table of the Statutes

Sources of Local and Personal Acts

6.123 Current Law Statutes
6.124 OPSI
6.125 Statute Law Database
6.126 Library collections of Local and Personal Acts

Finding a statutory instrument when only the title is known

6.162 Westlaw
6.163 Lawtel
6.164 Current law Yearbooks and Monthly Digests
6.165 Current Law Statutory Instrument Citator
6.166 Current Legal Information
6.167 The Laws of Scotland: Stair Memorial Encyclopaedia
6.169 Subject specialist encyclopaedias and collections of legislation
6.170 Justis UK Statutory Instruments
6.171 The Statute Law Database
6.172 OPSI
6.173 BAILII

Finding statutory instruments by subject

6.176 The Laws of Scotland: Stair Memorial Encyclopaedia
6.178 Specialist looseleaf encyclopaedias and collections of legislation
6.179 Westlaw
6.180 Lawtel
6.181 Current Law Yearbooks and Monthly Digests
6.182 Justis UK Statutory Instruments
6.183 The Statute Law Database
6.184 OPSI
6.185 BAILII

Current status of statutory instruments—finding amendment and repeals

6.188 Westlaw
6.189 Lawtel
6.190 Current Law Statutory Instrument Citator

Finding statutory instruments made under an enabling Act

6.193 Westlaw
6.194 Lawtel
6.195 The Current Law Statute Citators
6.196 Current Legal Information

SCOTTISH PARLIAMENT LEGISLATION

Finding out which stage a current Scottish Parliament Bill has reached

7.10 Scottish Parliament website
7.11 The Business Bulletin
7.12 Lawtel
7.13 Current Law Monthly Digest
7.14 Scottish Official Daily, Weekly and Monthly Listing
7.15 Journals
7.16 Newspapers

Finding out about debates on a Bill in the Scottish Parliament

7.21 The Scottish Parliament Official Report
7.25 Explanatory Notes
7.26 Current Law Statutes
7.27 Passage of the Bill series
7.28 The Business Bulletin

Finding Acts of the Scottish Parliament by subject

7.43 Major textbooks/reference works/encyclopaedias
7.44 Westlaw and LexisNexis Butterworths
7.45 Statute Law Database
7.46 OPSI
7.47 BAILII
7.48 Justis UK Statutes
7.49 Current Law Yearbooks and Monthly Digests

Current status of an Act of the Scottish Parliament —Is It in Force Yet?

7.50 The Act itself
7.51 and 6.93 Westlaw
7.52 LexisNexis Butterworths
7.53 Is It in Force?
7.56 Lawtel
7.57 and 6.97 Current Law Legislation Citators
7.58 Current Legal Information
7.59 Statute Law Database
7.60 Journals

JOURNAL ARTICLES

Search strategies for finding articles in journals on a particular subject

8.48 The best source for tracing articles UK legal journals since 1986 is Westlaw UK which includes the Legal Journals Index
8.53 Current Legal Information
8.54 LexisNexis Butterworths
8.55 Lawtel
8.56 Blackwell Synergy
8.57 HeinOnline
8.58 Index to Legal Periodicals
8.59 Index to Foreign Legal Periodicals
8.60 Current Law Index
8.61 Current Law Yearbooks

Finding journal articles or case notes about a case

Westlaw (4.104) is the best way of tracing this information as it contains the Legal Journals Index within its *Journals* section.

4.106 LexisNexis Butterworths
4.107 Current Legal Information
4.108 HeinOnline
4.109 Current Law Yearbooks
4.110 Journals
4.111 Lawtel
4.112 Justcite

Finding whether any articles have been written about an Act

6.112 Westlaw is the best way of tracing this information as it contains the Legal Journals Index
6.113 Current Legal Information
6.114 LexisNexis Butterworths
6.115 HeinOnline
6.116 Current Law Yearbooks and the latest Monthly Digest
6.117 Journals
6.118 Lawtel

Finding "non-law" journal articles

8.62 Periodical Index Online
8.63 Zetoc
8.64 British Humanities Index
8.65 Applied Social Sciences Index and Abstracts (ASSIA)
8.66 Social Sciences Citation Index/Arts & Humanities Citation Index
8.67 CSA Sociological Abstracts Database

BOOKS

Finding legal books

8.33 Textbooks, general reference works and encyclopaedias
8.33 Library catalogue(s) using a keyword search
8.34 The Advocates Library catalogue
8.35 Websites of legal booksellers and publishers
8.36 Legal bibliographies
8.36 The Stair Society

OFFICIAL PUBLICATIONS

Aids to tracing official UK publications

8.85 The Stationery Office (TSO)
8.86 Collections of parliamentary publications
8.87 The United Kingdom Official Publications Database (UKOP)
8.88 British Official Publications Current Awareness Service (BOPCAS)
8.89 LRDI Grey Paper Index
8.90 Lawtel
8.91 Parlianet
8.92 British Official Publications Collaborative Reader Information Service (BOPRIS)

Aids to tracing official Scottish publications

8.105 Scottish Parliament website
8.107 Scottish Parliament and Statutory Publications
8.113 Scottish Official Listings
8.85 The Stationery Office Daily List
8.111 Scottish Executive website
8.112 The Scottish Executive Publications List
8.115 and 8.87 UKOP

EC LAW

Finding EC legislation on a subject

The best search option is *Eur-lex* (10.23 and 10.18)

10.24 Justis Celex
10.24 LexisNexis Butterworths
10.24 Westlaw
10.25 European Communities Legislation: Current Status
10.26 The EU's General Report on the Activities of the European Union
10.27 Looseleaf encyclopaedias and texts
10.28 European Current Law Yearbooks

Current status of EC legislation

The best search option is *Eur-lex* (10.29 and 10.18)

10.30 Justis Celex
10.30 LexisNexis Butterworths
10.30 Westlaw
10.31 and 10.20 European Communities Legislation: Current Status.

Tracing if a Directive has been implemented in national law

10.32 N-Lex
10.33 Westlaw
10.34 EC Legislation Implementator
10.35 Current Law Monthly Digest

Finding EC cases

The information source which is the best for speed of access to recent materials and range of information is the European Court of Justice website (10.47).

10.48 and 10.44 *Eur-lex*
10.48 LexisNexis Butterworths
10.48 Westlaw

Finding journal articles about EC law

10.62 Westlaw
10.63 Current Legal Information
10.64 European Commission Library catalogue (ECLAS)
10.65 European integration current contents
10.66 European Current Law

Appendix II
Law Library Exercise

This library exercise is designed to test your knowledge and ensure that you know your way around the primary materials in a law library. The answers are online in the student section of W.Green's website.

1. What do the following legal abbreviations stand for:
   S.C.C.R.
   For. Cas. & Op.
   Reg.Maj.
2. Which colliery was involved in *Lockhart v National Coal Board* 1981 SLT 161?
3. What is the chapter number of the Welfare Reform Act 2007?
4. What official activity was the applicant unhappy about in *Kopp v Switzerland* (1999) 27 E.H.R.R. 91?
5. Give the asp number and the date of royal assent of the Bankruptcy and Diligence etc. (Scotland) Act 2007.
6. Which product was manufactured by the process at the centre of *Alphacell v Woodward* 1972 AC 824?
7. (a) What is the citation of the Water Environment (Controlled Activities) (Scotland) Regulations 2005?
   (b) When were the regulations made?
   (c) Under which enabling authority were they made?
8. *Muirhead & Turnbull v Dickson* (1905) 7 F. 686
   (a) Which musical instrument is this case about?
   (b) Who is the first judge to give his judgement?
9. What kind of pollution is mentioned in *Commission v Germany* [1991] E.C.R. I-2607?
10. What is the Hansard reference for the substantive debates in the House of Commons and House of Lords on the Slaughter of Animals (Scotland) Act 1980 (c.13)?
11. What is the name of the original song in *ZYX Music GmbH v King and Others* [1995] 3 All E.R. 1?
12. What is the title of the statutory instrument with the following citation: 1993 No. 1733?
13. With what drinks is *Georg von Deetzen v Hauptzollamt Oldenburg* [1994] 2 C.M.L.R. 487 concerned?
14. *Rodden (George Fisher) v HMA* 1995 SLT 185
    Has this case ever been disapproved by a court? If yes, state the name and citation of the case(s).
15. In *Lindsay v Fairfoull* (1633) Mor. 2031 before whom had Lindsay & Scott obtained decreet?
16. What animal is mentioned in the long title of the Law Reform (Miscellaneous Provisions) (Scotland) Act 1985?
17. Which legislation is mentioned in *Berrisford v Woodard Schools (Midland Division Ltd)* [1991] I.R.L.R. 247?

Appendix III
Electronic Resource Exercise

This exercise is designed to ensure that you are familiar with key legal electronic sources. The answers are online in the student section of W.Green's website.

1. How many Bills are currently in progress in the Scottish Parliament?
2. Name the most recent judgment by the Privy Council in a devolution case.
3. How many official Scottish sites are listed in LAWLINKS?
4. Who is the chairman of the Scottish Law Commission?
5. What do the following abbreviations stand for:
   S.C.
   E.L.& P.D.
   W. Va. L. Rev.
6. Name the most recent publication produced by the Scottish Executive.
7. When did the Scottish Parliament (Elections etc.) Order 2007 come into force?
8. How many cases have cited s.24 Marriage (Scotland) Act 1977?
9. How many new sheriffs were appointed on 29th September 2006?
10. Name a journal article that has been written about *Gibson v Orr*?
11. Where would you find an online version of the Unlawful Jurisdictions Act 1584 and what is its introductory text?
12. When was the debate on Stage 3 of the Bill that became the Dog Fouling (Scotland) Act 2003?
13. What is the most recent research briefing produced by SPICe?
14. How many fatal accident inquiry opinions are currently available on the Scottish courts website?
15. How many articles have been written about the Damages (Scotland) Act 1976?
16. Who was the Advocate General in C-321/03 *Dyson Ltd v Registrar of Trade Marks*?
17. What is the name of this piece of legislation: OJ 1982 L213/8?
18. What is the title of the statutory instrument with the following citation: 1987 No.1132?
19. State the *Hansard* references for the debates on the second reading of the Serious Organised Crime and Police Act 2005 in the House of Commons and House of Lords.
20. What is the asp number of Salmon and Freshwater Fisheries (Consolidation) (Scotland) Act 2003?

Index